COLDITZ

The Full Story

P. R. Reid

Zenith Press

First published in 1984 by Macmillan London Ltd. This edition published in 2015 by Zenith Press, an imprint of Quarto Publishing Group USA Inc., 400 First Avenue North, Suite 400, Minneapolis, MN 55401 USA

Zenith Press titles are also available at discounts in bulk quantity for industrial or sales-promotional use. For details write to Special Sales Manager at Quarto Publishing Group USA Inc., 400 First Avenue North, Suite 400, Minneapolis, MN 55401 USA.

To find out more about our books, visit us online at www.zenithpress.com.

ISBN: 978-0-7603-4651-8

Library of Congress Cataloging-in-Publication Data

Reid, P. R. (Patrick Robert), 1910–1990.
Colditz : the full story / P. R. Reid.
pages cm.
Originally published: Colditz : the full story / P.R. Reid. London :
Macmillan London Ltd., 1984.
Includes bibliographical references and index.
ISBN 978-0-7603-4651-8 (sc)
1. Schloss Colditz (Colditz, Germany) 2. World War, 1939–1945—Prisoners and prisons, German. 3. World War, 1939–1945—Prisoners and prisons, British. 4. World War, 1939–1945—Personal narratives, British. I. Title.
D805.G3R355 2015
940.54'72430943212—dc23
2014032078

Acquisitions Editor: Erik Gilg
Project Manager: Madeleine Vasaly
Art Director: James Kegley
Cover: Kent Jenson
Layout: Diana Boger

Printed in the United States

10 9 8 7 6 5 4 3 2 1

To the men of Colditz who tried but did not succeed, yet generously helped those few who did; to all prisoners of tyranny, wherever in the world they may be cruelly confined; and to the young people of the world that they may be vigilant in the pursuit of Freedom and guard it with tenacity and courage.

Contents

Acknowledgments

FIRST OF ALL I would like to thank my principal collaborators in this book—ex-Colditz men Peter Allan, Jędrzej Giertych, Kenneth Lockwood, "Mike" Moran, Dominic Bruce and, latterly, Ted Beets. From the beginning we formed a loose committee, meeting every month to survey progress. There were over sixty books concerning Colditz in our bibliography, several in French, German, Dutch or Polish, all of which had to be perused and annotated. There were interviews to be carried out in France, Switzerland, Germany, Belgium, Holland and the United States, as well as the United Kingdom.

Each one of the books listed in the Bibliography at the end of this work has helped me in one way or another to formulate the study and ease the burden of research, and I am indebted to their authors and publishers and thank them. Certain books have never been far from my desk: *Colditz: The German Story*, *Les Indomptables*, *Colditz Recaptured*, *Padre in Colditz*, and my own two books, *The Colditz Story* and *The Latter Days*. More so than any of these, I have, however, had the benefit of the use of the Rev. Ellison Platt's own day-by-day, handwritten diary, penned at Colditz throughout the war. It is an enormous volume. I thank Mrs. Ellison Platt very much for so generously giving me the use of this diary. I have employed it in preference to Margaret Duggan's edited work, *Padre in Colditz*, yet wish to thank her too for the help her book gave me as a quick reference to particular dates or events. Likewise, I have had the benefit of a translation from the original German diary written by Reinhold Eggers. I have preferred to use this rather than his book, *Colditz: The German Story*, wherever possible, as the latter is an edited version in English. For the original translation from the German diary I am indebted to Michael Booker, who possesses the finest collection of Colditz memorabilia in existence. He has also provided me with plans and illustrations. For some illustrations I am also indebted to John Watton, the Colditz artist.

The following associations have been most forthcoming with their assistance: the International Red Cross, Geneva (particularly Françoise Perret and Tibor Boleman); the Polish Red Cross (Anna Sydlowska); the Association of Czechoslovak Legionaries (Major Gst. M. F. Kaspar C. de G.); the Royal College of Heralds; the French ex-Colditz Association (Pierre Mairesse Lebrun, Edouard Duquet, "Fredo" Guigues and the writer Albert Maloire); RAF Historical Research (Alan W. Cooper); the Public Records Office; the *Times*; the *Illustrated London News*.

Many individuals have been most generous with their time and expertise. I mention but a few: Professor M. R. D. Foot, David Ray, Jozef H. Hlebowicz, Zdzisław Kępa, P. R. Charlier, Brian Degas, Jack Pringle, Professor R. V. Jones, T. P. Huguenan, Joan Worth and Sylvia Gilpin, who typed the manuscript so well. Further Polish helpers living in England are: Josef Tucki, Antoni Karpf, Jerzy Stein and Jerzy Ponewczynski. From America I have had access to photos, prints and the privately printed autobiography of Elizabeth Schunemann Boveroux, who was born in Colditz Castle. I am indebted to the Boveroux family for their kind gesture. I must also mention Colin Burgess, who has allowed me the use of material from a book forthcoming in Australia, *Diggers of Colditz*.

In conclusion I acknowledge gratefully the many constructive criticisms and perceptive suggestions of my wife, Nicandra, emanating from our over-the-dinner-table talk in the evenings, and the care with which she nourished the toilers in the "Ops" room for months as the paperwork mounted on her dining-room table.

P. R. Reid
London, June 1984

1

Yesterday's Shadows

Autumn 1939

THE STORY OF Colditz Castle in the Second World War begins on the narrow peninsula of Hel. Hel is little more than a very long sandbank on the Baltic coast of the Polish Corridor, directly north of Gdynia.

The story also begins in the person of Lieutenant Jędrzej Giertych, a reserve officer of the Polish Navy—very tall, robust, with a strong, handsome face, brown hair, aged thirty-six, married with four small children.

The day was Thursday, 24 August 1939. Russia and Germany had signed a pact of friendship the day before. The pact could only mean one thing for Poland. She would be attacked very soon, by one or the other, or by both.

Jędrzej was roused from his bed at his home in Warsaw at 7 a.m. by a repeated ringing of the doorbell. A policeman was there. He saluted, handing Jędrzej a paper which stated that he was called up for service, that he was to arrange his private affairs in the next two hours, then to proceed by all speed to the railway station, take the train for Gdynia and report to the naval dockyard at Oksywie. He arrived that evening.

Jędrzej did not see his wife or children again for six years. The youngest child was only two months old.

He was marooned at naval headquarters for two days before being assigned a post. In the meantime, on the Polish political front, general mobilization was delayed at the request of the Western Allies "so as not to increase international tension." The blindness, culpable and cowardly, of those Allies today seems incredible. When mobilization came it was already too late. Hitler had seized the initiative.

Jędrzej was assigned to the Detachment of Fishing Cutters, centered round the commandeered local tourist passenger ship called *Gdynia*, acting as a "mother" ship. The captain was Lieutenant-Commander Yougan. Together they hoisted the flag of the Polish Fighting Navy on the *Gdynia*. Jędrzej was allotted a cabin. He unpacked his portmanteau, taking from it first of all a framed picture, blessed in church, of Our Lady of Swarzewo. Swarzewo is a coastal village containing a shrine dedicated to the Blessed Virgin, which is venerated by the Polish fishermen of the Baltic Sea.

The cutters arrived on Thursday, 31 August, with their owners and crews, the fishermen, in twos and threes and in larger clutches. They mustered soon between seventy and eighty and were immediately divided into groups of six boats. Jędrzej became the proud commander of such a group. On the next day each existing cutter crew would be augmented by two or three army reservists. He would be the officer in charge of about thirty-five men. That night he went to his bunk very late. There had been much to do.

At 4 a.m. he was awakened by the sound of planes overhead, followed at once by the scream of dive bombers. German stukas, in number, were bombing the naval installations all around him. This was the opening bombardment of the Second World War.

The *Gdynia* was anchored in the naval harbor. The early morning aerial bombardment continued at intervals. Naval shells began to fall on the city. Jędrzej went ashore and managed to collect his reservists—eighty of them—from the naval barracks. These were transported to the *Gdynia* temporarily before being allocated to their cutters. At this point, at about 2 p.m., the *Gdynia* received orders to move out of port into the Bay of Puck. The naval airport at Puck had been one of the main targets of the morning aerial bombardment.

He studied the coastal marine charts on the bridge. The town of Puck was at the head of the bay, where, from the mainland, the peninsula of Hel formed a hook, turning sharply from north to south-east, continuing almost in a straight line like a needle, at some points only 200 meters wide. Along this needle lay three fishing villages, Chatupy, Kuznica and Jastarnia, the last with a little harbor, facing south-west into the bay and out towards the mainland.

Jędrzej, in the last cutter, followed the *Gdynia* and the lines of little ships out of the port. In the afternoon the aerial bombardment of *Gdynia* grew to massive proportions. The whole skyline darkened to a livid mauve as Jędrzej watched, and the thunder of explosions vibrated in the marrow of his spine. Black erupting clouds split open with the lightning strokes of detonation. Whirlwinds twisted the fountains of building ash into gaping red mouths, spewing rubble and debris, the vomit of destruction. The devastation inflicted by Hitler's onslaught was spread over many Polish cities and military targets on that first day of the war.

The *Gdynia* was now anchored in shallow water in the bay, about nine miles from the city whose name she bore. Jędrzej reported on board. The eighty reservists were to stay on the ship that night, along with the civilian ship's crew. The ship's total crew would be 120.

Dusk had fallen when Lieutenant-Commander Yougan ordered Jędrzej to lead a convoy of the cutters to the shallows around Jastarnia, which was about three miles distant, to disperse and anchor them amongst the sandbanks, and take himself and the fishermen crews off to rest in the port and village for the night. This task completed late into the night, Jędrzej wrapped his overcoat around him, lay down on the cobbles of the jetty and, with his head leaning against a bollard, went sound asleep.

He was awakened, once again, by the sound of planes. They were soon overhead—large formations of heavy bombers and dive bombers from the direction of Königsberg, heading for the Polish mainland. Out of one formation, suddenly, a group of planes divided. Stukas again. One after the other they turned, seemed to drop—then with accelerating, calculated fury, they descended on the *Gdynia*. The ship seemed to break up like matchwood—into several pieces. She sank within ten minutes. Men were hurled into the sea in large numbers. Then the stukas came again. They machine-gunned the men in the water and dropped anti-personnel bombs as they dived. Some managed, though wounded, to reach the shore, only to die later. Some were dragged from the water by helpers from the land. They also died later. Yougan survived, because he too had been called ashore.

The ship's secret instruction papers went down with the *Gdynia*. Jędrzej does not know to this day what purpose the "Cutter Detachment" was scheduled to fulfil. His holy picture of the Virgin of Swarzewo went down with all his other belongings, save a briefcase that he had taken ashore with him.

On Sunday, 3 September, the Detachment was disbanded and the survivors were transformed into a "Yougan Company" of naval marines, soon reinforced by crews of other sunken ships.

Over the radio they heard of the declaration of war by Great Britain and France.

The village of Hel at the head of the peninsula had contained a mainly German population up to 1914; though originally Dutch, they had become German. Between the wars the population became predominantly Polish, and the village grew and became a naval establishment with a naval basin and a commercial port. Polish submarines, as well as surface craft, were based on Hel. It was well defended with artillery, naval guns and anti-aircraft guns.

The peninsula was now invested by the Germans. A German land force advanced from Puck but was halted at the narrowest part between Chalupy and Kuznica, where the front could only take one company of men at a time, facing an enemy company.

Hel, with a garrison of some 3,000 men, was subjected to a most devastating attack. The two German battleships, *Schleswig-Holstein* and *Schliesen*, bombarded systematically and incessantly. German aerial bombardment, too, was without respite. The next danger for the defenders was a German landing. Jędrzej was incorporated into a company, which was given the task of organizing the defense against such a danger. They fortified the beach at the most likely place, near Jastarnia, where there was a good depth of water close inshore.

The German land force advanced slowly. The *Schleswig-Holstein* and the destroyer *Leberecht Maas* were damaged by Polish artillery, and a German minesweeper was sunk. The German landing did not materialize. But the pressure never relaxed.

A month after the commencement of hostilities, the peninsula of Hel remained the last remnant of Poland's territory still unconquered; Rear-Admiral Unrug was its commander. In the early hours of 2 October, with his artillery silenced for lack of ammunition, he decided to surrender in order to avoid civilian losses in the peninsula's fishing villages, which the Germans were about to storm. The whole of Poland was already in German or Soviet hands, with the exception of a Polish Army composed of several battered, numerically reduced divisions still on the move in the neighborhood of Lublin. This Army fought, on 6 October, a last battle against the combined Germans and Russians near the small town of Kock. It was destroyed in this battle, except for a detachment of cavalry under the command of Major Hubal, which survived in the Polish forests until the spring of 1940, when it was destroyed by the Germans and its commander killed.

The decision to surrender the peninsula of Hel was, for Unrug, a painful one; but the continuation of resistance by this isolated redoubt no longer served a useful purpose. Jędrzej, learning of the impending surrender, asked and was granted leave to escape. Five officers and men joined him; a stout rowing boat was purchased, and at nightfall it was launched into heavy seas off the beach at Jastarnia. Men waded breast-high in the surf to help it over the breakers. They rowed a long way into the night in the direction of Sweden. High seas breaking over sandbanks in shallow waters were their undoing. The boat was overturned by a freak wave. They all swam for their lives, reaching the main shore safely.

The next morning Jędrzej went to the seashore to see if anything had been washed up. They had loaded the boat with heavily packed suitcases. He had only taken his briefcase. It was the only thing washed up.

Jędrzej reports that some men succeeded in reaching Sweden in motor launches from Hel. He declined a generous offer of concealment by a local fisherman, and eventually went into captivity, a prisoner of war.

First of all, he was incarcerated in the *Oflag* at Nienburg near Bremen. At the beginning of November 1939 he was moved by train to an unknown destination, and in the middle of the night he, with others, was able to escape from the train. He traveled by another train to Berlin, was arrested there, and spent two weeks in the central Gestapo prison at Alexandraplatz. His briefcase was now in the Gestapo's possession. Later in November, he was handed over to the military authorities. They had the courtesy to inform him that he would shortly be incarcerated in a prison called *Oflag* IVC, situated in a town called Colditz.

On 31 October 1938, the German *Oberkommando der Wehrmacht*—which can be translated as the Overall Command of the Defense Power of Germany—had commandeered Colditz Castle. It was given the military title of *Oflag* IVC. *Oflag* is an abbreviation of *Offizierlager* meaning "Officers' place of detention." The Roman numerals and the letters denoted districts.

The *Oberkommando der Wehrmacht* (OKW) had laid plans, in advance of 1939, for a special camp, known as a *Sonderlager*, for enemy officers, prisoners of war, who for some reason merited strict treatment and a more careful watch than was kept on others. Among them were to be those who escaped but were recaught and suspected of intending to escape again.

Colditz Castle was designated to be this camp.

At first, however, as no "special" prisoners were yet picked out, the German military authorities did not consider it wise to keep such an expensive establishment empty and began to use it as a transit camp for Polish officers.

Jędrzej Giertych was escorted to Colditz in November 1939. A German cavalry captain (*Rittmeister*), accompanied by a dozen soldiers, awaited him at the station. He told Jędrzej that Colditz was a place from which it was not possible to escape: "Do not try to escape from here; *Sie beissen hier auf Granit* [here you will bite into granite]." He was led to the Castle in a curious way: all the soldiers had bayonets on their rifles, which they pointed into him. He walked in the middle of the street and the soldiers marched awkwardly, their rifles forming a star around him. Two sergeants marched beside the soldiers on the roadway. The captain walked on the pavement. This strange procession attracted the attention of passers-by, who stopped and gaped. An elderly man looked out at him from a window, laughed and pointed with his finger to his forehead. He thought the spectacle crazy.

When Jędrzej entered the Castle, he was immediately locked in a "solitary" cell near the gate. (Later this cell was abolished, but a whole corridor of cells was built nearby.) He spent two weeks there, in bad conditions, in great cold, on a bed of boards with a couple of blankets but without even a straw mattress. For furniture there was a stool, a washing bowl and a stove with a basket of coal. He was not allowed matches. The stove always went out at night. He saw, through a little window, that the camp was full of Polish officers, several hundreds of them. He had no contact with them. Food was brought to him by a Polish orderly underguard from the main prison kitchen. He was not allowed to talk to him. Sometimes he received notes hidden in the food. In one of these he was asked if it were true that he murdered a German when escaping from a prison camp, and had been condemned to death and was awaiting execution. For the first week he was really completely alone. Food and washing water were brought to him in silence. Removal of the toilet bucket was done in silence. Dirty water was poured through a hole in the ground.

During the second week, a Lieutenant Priem became a regular visitor to his cell. He sat on the stool and conducted long conversations with Jędrzej, who sat on the edge of his bed. He said that Jędrzej was, in reality, the first inmate of Colditz Castle as it was designated to be—a *Sonderlager* or special camp. All the prisoners of war milling around in the courtyard were in temporary occupation. Priem visited sometimes two or three times a day. He would not discuss the situation on the war fronts, nor did he allow the prisoner any newspapers. But history, yes—he would discuss European history at length, candidly, without prejudice; and he was unearthing the history of Colditz and its Castle.

So Jędrzej learned that about the middle of the sixth century the region was invaded by Slavs, the Sorben tribe, who came from Serbia, Dalmatia and Croatia. The Sorben were good farmers. They gave the region a new look: cut-down forests, dried-up marshes and built villages. The Serbian influence was evident in the names of the villages all ending in "tz"—Podelwitz, Meuselwitz, Raschitz, Zollwitz, Terpitzsch, Zeitlitz, Colditz (early spelling Koldyeze). Colditz in Serbian means "Dark Forest."

Colditz town probably began to be built in the year 892 by a Christian settlement. In 928 the German King Henry I won the battle of Gana, beating the Dalemincier (Dalmatians), a sub-tribe or sect of the Sorben, and the whole area became a German province. Eventually the town came under the rule of Count

Wiprecht von Groitsch, who in 1080 began the building of a castle on a great rock promontory overlooking the River Mulde.

On one occasion Priem recounted the story of the first Colditz escaper. He said that in 1294, the Castle of Colditz was a garrison for the troops of the Emperor of the Holy Roman Empire, Adolph, Count of Nassau. In that year, war broke out between the emperor and the two sons of the Margrave of Meissen, Albert II. Albert's wife Margaretha had been given the Castle as her dowry in 1257; her two sons (whose names were Frederick and Dietzmann) were almost certainly born there, and probably lived in the Castle from birth. Although the Castle returned to the possession of the then emperor, Rudolph, in 1282, the two boys remained there, holding it with their troops until March 1289 when, presumably under duress, they relinquished it to Rudolph at Erfurt. But in 1294 they were at war with the new emperor, Adolph. In due course they forcibly took possession of the towns surrounding Colditz, such as Rochlitz, Grimma, Leisnig and Borna. The Castle and its garrison, however, remained true to the emperor, resisted attack and became a rallying point and refuge for his supporters.

Count Philip of Nassau, a nephew of the emperor, was defeated in a battle at Luckau in 1294. He was captured in flight, sent first to Leipzig, then imprisoned in Rochlitz. One night, due to the laxity of the guards, he was able to escape. He made his way successfully to Colditz Castle, some fifteen miles away, where he was welcomed with open arms by the defenders.

"Count Philip was therefore," Priem said, "the first historically recorded escaper of Colditz; albeit that he escaped into Colditz rather than out of it! This kind of escape," he added wryly, "is the only kind that will be permitted during the present hostilities!"

During the fifteenth century the town and Castle became the property of the electors of Saxony. In 1430 the Castle was fired by Hussites and razed to the ground. It was rebuilt many years later, in the form of forward and rear castles, each consisting of several buildings. Priem discovered there had been another great fire in 1504—only a few buildings of the front castle survived. The town likewise was almost destroyed. Rebuilding began in 1506.

Electors ruled in succession until the inheritance passed in 1553 to Duke August. August was especially attracted by the position of the Castle and the hunting grounds around; he showed a marked preference for Colditz and continued the beautifying of it in 1554. His wife was a Danish princess, and their coat of arms remains today over the main gateway. Also in this year (1554) the laying-out of the park began, the elector encircling an area with planks between the Castle and Hainberg. Colditz Castle now became a favored residence of the

Saxon princes, and was occupied for much of the year by the princes and others of noble rank.

In 1586, Christian I, August's son, who was also fond of Colditz Castle, built a pleasure garden with pavilions. In 1589 a wall was begun around the park beneath the Castle, but in 1590 and 1591, by buying several properties in Zschadrass, Zollwitz, Terpitzsch and Colditz, the area was increased to 125 acres and became known as the *Tiergarten* (zoological gardens). A wall was built all around it, which exists to this day.

In 1591, Christian I, now the elector, came to Colditz for the last time. He became ill on a stag hunt near Ebersback, was brought back to the Castle, and from there to Dresden, where he died. In 1603 his widow, the Duchess Sophie of Brandenburg, together with the court and government officials, moved into the Castle and remained there until 1622.

Plague devastated Colditz at times over two centuries. In 1521 there were more than 800 deaths; in 1607–1608, 428 people died; in 1637 there were 350 victims and in 1680, it claimed the lives of 125 citizens.

Jędrzej, though closely confined, had seen enough of the Castle to appreciate its points as a fortress. Most fortresses had secret passages, escape routes out of the Castle for use during sieges. He questioned Priem: "What sieges has this Castle undergone?" Priem came back with the surprising answer that from the end of the Thirty Years War (when it was occupied successively by troops of the emperor and of King Gustav Adolf of Sweden) in 1648, and more particularly since 1694, the Castle had seen little fighting and no sieges. "It became," he explained, "the home of retirement for royal widows and dowagers. It was not even fortified, relying simply on its massive gates to keep unwelcome intruders out."

"But surely," argued Jędrzej, "its strategic position commanding the river and the bridge at Colditz would have made it a natural strongpoint to guard and hold?"

"No," said Priem. "Duke Friedrich August ['the Strong'], who was elector from 1694–1733, built many other castles for the defense of Saxony, and so reduced the strategic importance of Colditz."

"So the Castle, being undefended and peaceable, never had to withstand sieges or bombardments?"

"Indeed," Priem said. "Invading armies would know it was occupied or owned by dowagers and pass by."

But Priem had overlooked a point which became apparent as the nineteenth century unfolded.

In 1800 the Castle became a poorhouse for the Leipzig district, with part of it set aside for use as a priory, and still, throughout the ensuing Napoleonic era, it remained aloof from the military activity taking place all around. Colditz was right in the path of advancing and retreating armies, and with remorseless regularity the town found itself supporting billeted troops. From time to time it even became a battlefield itself, as in March 1813 when French soldiers seized the bridge over the Mulde. In May of that year, after its defeat at Lutzen, the whole Prussian Army retreated through Colditz, Marshal Blücher setting up a temporary headquarters in the market place. The pursuing French troops were headed by Napoleon himself, and a few days later, after the Prussians had pulled out, he in turn stayed in the town, in Nicolaigate.

From the end of the Thirty Years War until the Battle of Waterloo in 1815, the town of Colditz paid the price of its position on a strategic high road, suffering poverty, starvation, pillage, press-gangs, rape and disease. It is ironic that the Castle, intact and unblemished throughout those years, had been built by Count Wiprecht "in order to protect the town."

In 1829 Colditz Castle was converted to an asylum and the criminals were moved to a prison in Zwickau. Until 1924 the Castle remained a mental, insane and psychiatric institution—a sanctuary for the most unfortunate of people. It also became the home of a family for several generations.

How this ambivalent role came about is revealed by the following extract from the memoirs of Mrs. Elizabeth (Elsa) Schunemann Boveroux of San Francisco.

> My great grandfather Voppel was a member of the household of the King of Saxony. He expected his son to follow in his military career, but Grandpappa had other ideas. He wanted to study medicine, be a doctor, being especially interested in the mentally sick, who were confined and often kept in chains. His idea was to give them freedom to develop and gain confidence, directing them to follow their individual trends, and allowing them to work and play in the open. The King became interested and furthered these ideals. Eventually Grandpappa studied and finally graduated from the University of Jena.

So Colditz Castle became an asylum. At the time Dr. Voppel was probably about twenty-nine. He was married in the Castle chapel and his twelve children were christened there, including Mrs. Elizabeth Schunemann Boveroux's mother, and later were confirmed there in the Lutheran faith. There too Elizabeth's mother was married and Elizabeth herself christened.

Dr. Voppel had his offices on the ground floor in the old Castle (POW section), and there was a life-sized oil painting of him in his office which disappeared in Hitler's day. His private apartments were on the first floor—drawing-room and living-rooms—reached by a circular stone staircase. These rooms were occupied by the British POW contingent in the Second World War from November 1940. Elizabeth often played there and Grandma's work-table and comfortable chair stood in the deep, raised alcove of a window in her living-room, overlooking the park (*Tiergarten*).

In those days there was usually a family gathering after the noon-day nap, in the courtyard if the weather was pleasant, in a secluded section to the left of the private entrance. A vivid description of her grandmother and daily life in the Castle at that time, written by Elizabeth, is given in her private memoirs.

Elizabeth's mother, Margret Voppel, went to school in Dresden, where she was taught to play the piano by Clara Schumann, wife of the composer. Her father, Max Schunemann, the youngest son of a wealthy Hamburg shipping merchant, voyaged as far as San Francisco at the age of nineteen, fell in love with the place and became an American citizen. Max returned to Germany to visit his father, who by then had retired to a villa beneath the walls of Colditz, and there he met Margret at a social gathering in the Castle. They were married in the chapel in 1873. Elizabeth says that the wedding festivities were gay and memorable—over 300 guests were entertained.

Elizabeth spent her first five years in the Castle. In March 1879 she and her mother left Colditz to voyage across the Atlantic from Le Havre (Hamburg and Bremen were closed because of the plague), then across America by the Union (Western) Pacific railroad, which brought them to San Francisco. Max, who had travelled ahead of them, was waiting to greet them at the Oakland Mole; he had disliked Bismarck's regime in Germany and had decided to emigrate for good.

This unusual interlude of domesticity, combined with the fulfilment of that laudable human and Christian motivation—love of one's neighbors—which was manifest in the care of the mentally sick, lasted for more than fifty years. For Jędrzej, the philosopher and historian, it contained a lesson of hope which did not fail to support him in those first black days and nights in his solitary cell. Castles are linked historically in the mind with war, siege, imprisonment and cruelty. Here was an exception. Castles, after all, are mute accomplices. Man can make good use of his accomplice as well as bad.

There is no evidence that Colditz Castle became a prisoner-of-war camp in the 1914–1918 war, although the rumor was put about in 1940, probably by the German command, that it had been so used and had been found to be escape-proof. Indeed there were large numbers of psychiatric patients in the Castle during the First World War, of whom 912 are recorded as having died of malnutrition. Three wards were converted to a tuberculosis sanatorium, only to revert to psychiatric wards after the war. After the disastrous German inflation (1922–1923), shortage of funds forced the closure of the asylum in 1924. For two years the Castle stood empty; then in 1926 it became a remand home.

For the history of the period 1921–1938 one has to rely on a book published by the communist-controlled Colditz town council in 1965. (Colditz became part of the DDR after the war.) From this we learn that as soon as Hitler came to power in 1933, the Castle was turned into a Nazi concentration camp, where members of the Communist party were incarcerated, ostensibly in "protective custody." By May there were already 600 prisoners, many of whom were tortured. From 1935 to 1937 the Castle was a camp for Nazi brownshirts, and in 1938 it became an asylum once more.

Jędrzej was curious about the cell in which he found himself, but Priem closed up like a clam whenever he broached the subject of the immediate pre-war incumbents of the cell. Eventually, through the Polish orderly and a few more surreptitious notes, he discovered to his severe discomfiture that he was almost certainly in a condemned cell where previous prisoners had been held before being tortured.

Paul Priem was born in about 1893 in the region of Bromberg-Schneidemühl, which is now part of Poland but was then part of the German Reich of Kaiser Wilhelm II. It carried a mixed population of Germans and Poles. He had fought right through the First World War, and afterwards he had continued to fight as a volunteer in the *Grenzschutz* (frontier guards) to keep his home territory part of Germany instead of being incorporated in the new Poland. A Polish insurrection started on 27 December 1918 in Pznania, or Provinz Posen as it was called by the Prussians, to whom it had belonged from the end of the Napoleonic Wars until December 1918. The Polish insurgents seized power in almost the whole of the province, fighting victoriously against a powerful German Army and its *Grenzschutz,* in which Priem served. The victorious Poles were confirmed in their victory and were treated as part of the Western Allies when Marshal Foch negotiated at Trier on 16 February 1919 the renewal (with new terms) of the 11 November Armistice.

Priem was the son of a German schoolteacher, and was himself a schoolteacher, in fact a headmaster, from Briesen, a town in this disputed territory. It was therefore little wonder that he was a belligerent (though never fanatical) supporter of Hitler, who had won back this land for Germany in 1939. Jędrzej found that despite this background, Priem felt no dislike for the Poles. In fact, he showed a grudging respect and sympathy for them.

Jędrzej asked permission of Priem to go to Mass in the chapel with the other Polish prisoners. This was refused at first, but then the order was reversed. On the next Sunday, when all the other prisoners were inside the chapel, he was conducted by Priem through the empty courtyard—empty save for one Polish officer, whom Jędrzej recognized. He was a very left-wing socialist, in fact, a communist, also an atheist: a member of the City Council of Warsaw, of which Jędrzej was also a member. They exchanged salutes in silence. The atheist was embarrassed.

What an arresting momentary picture of allegory and symbolism that untoward meeting evokes! The cobbled courtyard, the high gray walls—punctuated with barred windows—mounting to the sky; the muted sound of the chapel organ, and men's voices intoning the opening "*Introibo ad altare dei . . .*" the two men, brought together by the bonds of prison, confront each other. The loyal Polish Christian patriot and the communist pro-Russian, atheistic Pole stand with the German victor between them, click their heels and salute. . . . Jędrzej was escorted up to the balcony of the Chapel, where he remained alone, save for his escort Priem, throughout the service.

One evening, just as Jędrzej was wrapping his blankets around him on the hard board bed, Priem came to him: "Get up and dress. You are leaving Colditz in ten minutes."

A car was waiting. Priem and two sergeants composed the escort. They set off for a railway station some distance from Colditz; thence took a train to Leipzig, and then to Munich, travelling all night. On this long journey they had a compartment to themselves. Priem became very much at ease, and talked freely of the political situation without rancor. He gave Jędrzej a copy of the newspaper, the *Völkischer Beobachter*. He recounted the story of the sinking of the great Polish liner, the *Pilsudski*, in the North Sea, and expressed his regret, asking Jędrzej if he had known anyone on it.

"Yes," Jędrzej said, "I knew the captain."

"I am so very sorry," Priem said. "He went down with his ship—a true sailor."

Russia and Finland were at war, Jędrzej learned. The Finns were giving the Russians a good thrashing, which pleased Jędrzej enormously. Priem noticed this. "We can share our feelings on this subject," he said. "This will make it easier for us to deal with Russia in due course."

Jędrzej did not react.

From Munich, where they changed trains in the morning, they travelled on to Murnau in the Bavarian Alps. There, it transpired, was a large *Oflag* for Polish officers. Again, Jędrzej was at once placed in solitary confinement. There he spent a month.

Priem, besides being friendly, had expressed condolences in a roundabout way for Jędrzej's situation: being a prisoner—in solitary confinement—having lost the war—and having lost his country—his independence gone. At this stage, Jędrzej had brought him up sharply: "The war is not finished. Neither is Poland lost. It will be restored. The war will be won by the Allies—including Poland."

Priem had not pressed the point again, respecting his views. So they never quarrelled.

For far too long the Allies had prevaricated, hoping that the bogeyman would just go away. Only at this point, with the Polish nation subjugated, with men like Jędrzej enduring the devastation of their country, did the Western leaders begin to face the harsh reality of war, forced before their reluctant gaze.

2

Poland Leads the Way

1940

JĘDRZEJ GIERTYCH WAS BORN in 1903 in Sosnowiec in central Poland. He was educated at home by a private tutor and he had two nannies in turn—one French, one German—so that from his earliest childhood he spoke these two languages. During 1913 and 1914 when Jędrzej was ten years old, he attended a private boarding secondary school in Kielce, his mother's native town in Poland, at that time under Russian rule. There he was taught in Polish, which was allowed after the revolution of 1905, but he had to learn Russian as a subject. When war broke out he could no longer attend school in Kielce, because it was in the war zone. Instead he went to a German school, a Lutheran cathedral college, at Tallinn, in Estonia, where his father was deputy manager of the largest shipyard in the Russian empire. The school was closed by the Russians after a year and Jędrzej found himself finally in the Russian "Real Gymnasium," being educated in Russian.

In 1917 the family moved to the then capital of Russia, Petrograd, the old St. Petersburg and the present Leningrad.* Jędrzej attended a school run by the Polish School Society, whose organization exists to this day in some countries, including England. However, soon after the Treaty of Brest-Litovsk in 1918 his parents decided it was time to escape from revolutionary Russia.

During the First World War the Polish nation was divided into two camps, opposed to each other as violently as in a civil war. The great majority of the Polish nation was on the Allied side. Overwhelmingly, this was the Polish right wing, patriotic, traditionalist, religious (Roman Catholic), conservative in social outlook. They believed that the most dangerous enemy of Poland was Prussia,

* Now restored to St. Petersburg since 1991.

and thence the whole German nation. The leader of this majority was Roman Damowski. The minority of the Polish nation, predominantly socialist and opposed to the church and to religion, was on the side of Germany and Austria, and was sympathetic to the Russian revolutionaries. Jędrzej was, from his earliest childhood, on the side of the right wing and, from the beginning of the war, on the Allied side. Later in life he became a personal follower and disciple of Damowski, who admitted him into his closest circle of collaborators. Damowski was later the Polish negotiator and signatory to the Versailles Treaty.

In 1918 the Giertych family returned to Poland, then under German and Austrian occupation. Jędrzej went back to school in Kielce. On 30 October 1918 a substantial part of Poland, around the city of Cracow, liberated itself from Austrian rule. The next day the regions around Kielce, Lublin and Cieszyn followed suit. Troops of schoolboys were the main forces which secured Polish authority in the liberated territories (adults were mostly conscripts in the Austrian Army on the Italian front). Jędrzej was in such a force in Kielce. He was fifteen years old and served for the first time under arms. On 31 October 1918, twelve days before the end of the First World War, he stood as sentry in Kielce, with a very old Austrian rifle and bayonet on his shoulder and with only one cartridge up the barrel. This was his total participation in the First World War. A few weeks later he returned to school.

His family finally settled in Warsaw in 1919, where Jędrzej attended the Mazowiecka school, with an interval for military service. In July 1920, an appeal was made to Polish civilians for volunteers to increase Polish military effectiveness against the invading army of Bolshevik Russia. Jędrzej volunteered immediately. He found himself in the 201st Infantry Regiment which was formed at the beginning of July in Warsaw. The regiment had one week of training and in the middle of July went to the front. A month later Jędrzej took part in the great battle of Warsaw, or of the Vistula, also called "the miracle of the Vistula," in which the Russian Army was crushingly beaten. The Poles thus won not only the campaign but the war. Jędrzej's company was led in this battle by a cadet. On the decisive day of the battle, 15 August, the Feast of Our Lady, his company and his battalion went over the river Ukra, an important tributary of the Vistula. They waded through the water breast-high, holding their rifles and ammunition over their heads. The Russians occupying the other bank fled, but opened up from a distance with machine-guns. Jędrzej was wounded a few minutes after having reached the bank of the river. He spent the rest of the campaign in hospital. He was demobilized in October 1920 and returned to school. He was seventeen years old.

Throughout his formative years he was greatly influenced by a secret Polish movement—the Polish Boy Scouts! It came into the open only in 1917. The movement was strongly Catholic and anti-Marxist. Jędrzej published his first book in 1929 as a leader of this movement, called *We the New Generation*. The book was a collection of his talks to the scouts on morals, patriotism, spartanism and Catholicism. Later editions contained an introduction by the then primate of Poland, Cardinal Archbishop Hlond. The book is still in circulation today. He left the scout movement in 1930 after disagreements with its new leaders over political issues.

Jędrzej performed his national service in the Navy; in 1935 he was gazetted as a sub-lieutenant of the Polish Naval Reserve. He had already become a journalist after six years in the Polish Ministry of Foreign Affairs. He also became a member of the central committee of the Nationalist Party, the largest party in Poland, which was persecuted by the socialist Pilsudski dictatorship. He was elected a member of the city council of Warsaw, but did not try to become a member of parliament because his party boycotted the elections of 1935 and after.

One day during his month's confinement at Murnau, Jędrzej was conducted to the *Abwehr* officer. He relates what transpired:

> This officer was called Doctor Falke and was an elderly Lieutenant and member of the Abwehr, the German Military Intelligence. Another German officer whose name I do not know was also present.
>
> Doctor Falke told me that he had something to say to me. He told me that if I tried another escape I would be shot. "*Erschossen*."
>
> I answered: "You mean that I may be hit by the bullet of a guard? Yes, of course, I realize that this is a risk which has eventually to be taken when trying to escape."
>
> "*Nein, Sie werden füsiliert* [No, you will be executed]."
>
> "I am not in a position to do anything," I retorted, "except accept this as the existing situation. But how can this be reconciled with the text of the Geneva Convention?"
>
> "What convention?"
>
> "The convention about prisoners of war."
>
> "Do you know Latin? If you do, you should realize that the word convention comes from the word *convenire*. And for *convenire*, two parties are necessary. The Geneva Convention has ceased to be applied to you because Poland has ceased to exist. It has been extinguished by

way of debellatio, an accepted concept of international law. You are now a subject of the Reich who for security reasons has been placed in internment for the duration of the war. It is only an act of benevolence and also a matter of convenience that you have all been put under a regime which is essentially an application of principles similar to those of the Geneva Convention, but with some exceptions. One of these exceptions is that you are not permitted under the penalty of death to try to escape. And remember: whatever privileges you enjoy, the privilege of being treated as an officer and so on, are not your right, but only a favor which was given but may be withdrawn."

I replied that a debellatio of Poland had not taken place because the invasion and conquest of Poland had started a world war and this war was still in progress, which meant that neither had the Polish resistance ceased nor had the collapse of Poland been tacitly recognized by the community of nations. Besides, I was sufficiently well informed to know that the Polish government had settled in Paris; that a new Polish Army was being organized in France and a part of the Polish Navy, of which I was an officer, had reached Great Britain and continued to fight. Poland still legally existed and we were her subjects; not subjects of the Reich. What I was now told was a violation of international law.

"Poland has ceased to exist and will never rise again," answered Doctor Falke.

"*Deus mirabilis, fortuna variabilis*," I replied. "These are well-known words which were said by a prominent Pole three hundred years ago on the occasion of a similar Polish defeat. They were proved right at that time and at other times. And they will prove to be right again."

The two Germans whispered something among themselves—and then Doctor Falke said: "With your attitude you cannot hope for an improvement in your condition."

The conversation was finished and I was sent back to my cell.

That conversation explained clearly to me that it was not the intention of the German Army to apply the Geneva Convention towards us, Polish prisoners. This is certainly true. And I cannot deny that I left Doctor Falke's office indignant and angry.

A short time after he arrived in Murnau, three other Polish officers were brought to the camp and placed in the solitary cells beside him. They were Captain Majewski, the chief of staff of the Polish Navy, who had signed, at dawn on 2 October 1939, the surrender of the peninsula of Hel, having been sent by Rear-Admiral Unrug to confirm in writing the arrangements agreed by telephone; Colonel Mozdyniewicz, commander of the Polish 17th Infantry Division, who, in the September campaign, undertook a local counter-offensive against the German Army and obtained a local victory, inflicting severe losses on the Germans and causing some large German units to retreat in disorder for several days; and Lieutenant Paweł Jasiński.

Majewski and Mozdyniewicz were sent to the "solitary" because of their unwelcome patriotic influence in their earlier *Oflag*, Jasiński because of an escape. Originally they could not communicate with each other, but later on they were allowed to meet sometimes in one cell (for the first time on Christmas Eve 1939) and to subscribe for one copy of the German newspaper *Völkischer Beobachter*, which they read in turn. In January 1940, two more prisoners were brought in and placed in the two other cells. Both were from the local *Oflag* of Murnau. One of them was General Tadeusz Piskor, who in the 1920s and early 1930s had been chief of staff of the Polish Army and who, during the September campaign, had been commander of one of the Polish armies, the Lublin Army. The second was Major Władysław Steblik, before the war deputy military attaché at the Polish embassy in Berlin and, during the campaign, the operations officer of the Cracow Army. (After the war he became well known as the writer of a scholarly book on the history of the Cracow Army in the September campaign.) So now they were six in this solitary confinement block attached to the Murnau *Oflag*. They all went later to Colditz.

But they were there as six only for twenty-four hours. The next day, after the arrival of Piskor and Steblik, all six were moved by train to Srebrna Góra in the Sudeten mountains in Middle Silesia. They travelled there via Vienna, through the Czechoslovak province of Moravia nad Wroclaw. Jędrzej considered the possibility of escaping on the way, then trying to go by train to neutral Italy, but he rejected the idea as the temperatures were well below freezing and the snow very deep. There was no chance of success. In Srebrna Góra they were joined early in January by Admiral Unrug.

The Germans had organized an "isolation" camp, smaller than Colditz but larger than the six cells in Murnau, at an ancient fort on top of a mountain not far from the small town, called Srebrna Góra in Polish, Silberberg in German. The town belonged to Poland in the Middle Ages, was later in the possession of Bohemia and Austria, and came, in the eighteenth century, under Prussian rule. The population was Germanized. Srebrna Góra was beyond the Polish-German linguistic border and was German-speaking. It was situated in a separate mountain-chain called Gory Sowie, or Eulengebirge, which means "Mountains of the Owls." During the Seven Years War (1756–1763), the Prussian king, Frederick the Great, had built three forts on mountain tops, dominating the passage from Silesia to Moravia. One of these forts, Fort Spitzberg, became the mini-Colditz. It was a very unpleasant place, and had served previously as a mountain shelter for the Hitler Youth. Several underground bunkers had recently been adapted as sleeping quarters. They resembled cellars and were very wet. In the vaulted ceilings, there were stalactites already ten centimeters long.

When Jędrzej's group arrived, there were already seven Polish prisoners there. They had come the previous day and were all unsuccessful escapers. Their number increased every few days, especially when spring began. More and more escapers were hauled in. Several of them, Jędrzej included, tried to escape from Fort Spitzberg, but no one ever succeeded.

There was room for ninety prisoners and this number was soon reached. In April 1940 the Germans set up a similar camp at the nearby Fort Hohenstein and twenty prisoners, amongst them Jędrzej, were moved from Fort Spitzberg to Fort Hohenstein.

Towards the end of May 1940, ten officers were able to escape from there. They climbed through a hole made in the wall of a room that had been barred off from the prison and descended on a rope made from cotton sleeping-bags into the shallow moat. The remaining ten officers covered the escape successfully. It was discovered twenty-four hours later at the morning *Appell* or roll-call. The German commander of their *Oflag* was later tried by court-martial, because fifty percent of the inmates of Fort Hohenstein had escaped!

The escapers travelled in three separate groups. They had no civilian clothes so they went on foot, sleeping in forests during the day and walking, guided by the stars, at night. They intended to reach neutral Hungary. One group of three succeeded. Another group was caught after three days. Jędrzej's group (the other members were Michal Niczko and Zdzisław Ficek) marched for twelve nights and reached the environs of the town of Olomouc in Czechoslovakia, halfway to Hungary. They were caught there and brought back to Srebrna Góra and the Fort of Hohenstein. The German *Kommandant* informed them of the fall of Paris and the approaching end of the war. They spent their time in solitary confinement, instead of being shot as they had expected, until the seven of them who had been recaptured were transferred once more to Fort Spitzberg. Soon afterwards, more prisoners were brought to Fort Hohenstein. When the maximum of fifty was reached (forty-nine Poles and one French airman) at

Fort Hohenstein, and ninety at Fort Spitzberg, the whole Srebrna Góra contingent, including Admiral Unrug and General Piskor, was transferred to Colditz, which officially became the "special" camp for escapers and other unwelcome prisoners. This was on 1 November 1940. Initially there were only these Poles and the Frenchman.

Three RAF officers arrived on 5 November and six British Army officers on 7 November, followed later by some more French. So the Castle became an international camp for selected "special" prisoners.

On his arrival Jędrzej was greeted like an old friend by Priem, now promoted to *Hauptmann* (captain).

During the period from October 1939 to October 1940 when Colditz had been a transit camp, Poles were not the only incumbents. They left for other destinations in the early summer of 1940. A large number of Belgian officers, prisoners of war, were held there during the summer, replacing the Poles. According to Hauptmann Eggers, who was an *Oberleutnant* (lieutenant) at Colditz in 1939–1940, the Belgians were released on a "general parole" to return to their country.

On 1 November 1940, the German command at Colditz Castle consisted of the camp commandant (*Herr Kommandant*), Oberstleutnant (Lieutenant-Colonel) Schmidt. His second-in-command was Major Menz. The adjutant was Hauptmann Kunze. The principal camp officer, responsible for the administration and discipline of the POWs, was Hauptmann Priem. His assistant was Eggers.

Eggers says that at the beginning the German staff were quite naive about "security." He states: "When I arrived at the Castle I found many meters of good rope hanging in the bell tower, quite openly." There were two security officers, Hauptmann Hans Lange and Hauptmann Lossell. The camp doctor was Hauptmann Dr. Rahm, who bore the familiar title of *der Arzt*, meaning "the doctor," and also (for the prisoners) a more familiar ribald title of *der Tierarzt*, meaning "the horse-doctor" or "vet." The staff paymaster was Rittmeister Heinze.

When the Polish contingent of 140 arrived on 1 November 1940, the camp was empty. The Castle, besides being called a *Sonderlager* ("special camp"), was also labelled *Lager mit besonderer Bewachung* ("camp with special surveillance").

The *Kommandant*, Oberstleutnant Schmidt, addressed the Polish contingent at the first *Appell* upon their arrival. Part of his speech was as follows:

> According to dispositions set out in the Geneva Convention for the treatment of prisoners of war, the *Oberkommando der Wehrmacht* has

> instituted this Special Prisoner-of-War Camp, *Oflag* IVC Colditz into which you Poles have been admitted as an exceptional case. Poland no longer exists and it is only due to the magnanimity of our Führer that you are benefiting temporarily from the privileges such as will be accorded to prisoners of war of the other belligerent powers who will be held in this camp. You should be grateful to Adolf Hitler who, by his decision, has favored you. You, who in 1939 by your stupid obstinacy were responsible for starting this war.

The three RAF officers who arrived on 5 November were Flying Officers Howard D. Wardle, Keith Milne and Donald Middleton. Wardle, or Hank as he was called, was a Canadian who had joined the RAF shortly before the war. He was dropping propaganda leaflets over Germany in April 1940 when his bomber was shot down. He parachuted and landed in trees. He was one of the earliest British POWs of the war. He had escaped from the *Schloss* camp of Spangenburg, about twenty miles from Kassel, by climbing a high barricade on the way to a gymnasium just outside the camp precincts. The other two, also Canadians, had escaped dressed as painters, complete with buckets of whitewash and a long ladder, which they carried between them. They had waited for a suitable moment when there appeared to be a particularly dumb Jerry on guard at the gate, marched up briskly, shouted the only words they knew in German and filed out. Having passed the gate, they continued jauntily until they were half-way down the hill on which the *Schloss* reposed. They then jettisoned ladder and buckets and made a bolt for the woods.

These escapes were in August 1940 and were probably the first of the war from regular camps. None of the three travelled very far before recapture and it was, alas, only a matter of hours before they were back behind the bars. They suffered badly at the hands of their captors, being severely kicked and battered with rifle-butts.

The three RAF officers had arrived in Colditz at night and had seen no one. They were told that sentences awaited them and that they would probably be shot. On the first morning at dawn they had been marched out to some woods in a deep valley flanking one side of the Castle and halted beside a high granite wall. They had then been told to exercise themselves for half an hour! The Germans took a sadistic pleasure in putting the complete wind up the three of them. By the time they had reached the high wall in the early half-light, they had given up hope of ever seeing another sunrise. This joke over, the Jerries took them back to their rooms.

The next six British arrived on 7 November. Their journey from Laufen, *Oflag* VIIC, had lasted three days. The party of six consisted of Captains Rupert Barry of the 52nd Light Infantry, Kenneth Lockwood of the Queen's Royal Regiment, Harry Elliott of the Irish Guards, and Dick Howe MC of the Royal Tank Regiment, with 2nd Lieutenant "Peter" Allan of the Cameron Highlanders, and myself, a captain in the Royal Army Service Corps. We had all been recaptured after escaping via a tunnel at Laufen (described in my book *The Colditz Story*).

There was little or no chance of escape on the train journey. Moreover, we had no escape material or reserve food (except potatoes!). The guards were watchful; we were always accompanied to the lavatory. We travelled sometimes in second class, sometimes in third, at all hours of the day and night. There were many changes and long waits, usually in the military waiting-rooms of stations. Passers-by eyed us curiously but without great animosity. Those who made closer contact by speaking with our guards were concerned at our carrying potatoes with us. After three months of starvation diet, followed by many weeks of bread and water, we were taking no risks and would have fought for those cold scraggy balls of starch with desperation!

We arrived at the small town of Colditz early one afternoon. This was my impression:

> Almost upon leaving the station we saw looming above us our future prison; beautiful, serene, majestic; and yet forbidding enough to make our hearts sink into our boots. It towered above us, dominating the whole village. It was the fairy castle of childhood's story-books. What ogres there might live within! I thought of dungeons and of all the stories I had ever heard of prisoners in chains pining away their lives, of rats and tortures, of unspeakable cruelties and abominations.
>
> In such a castle, through the centuries, everything had happened and anything might happen again. To friendly peasants and tradespeople in the houses nestling beneath its shadows it may have signified protection and home, but to enemies from a distant country such a castle struck a note of doom and was a sight to make the bravest quail. . . .
>
> It was built on the top of a high cliff promontory that jutted out over a river. The outside walls were on an average seven feet thick, and the inner courtyard of the Castle was about two hundred and fifty feet above the river-level. The Castle rooms in which we were to live were about another fifty feet above the courtyard.

The river (the Mulde) is a tributary of the Elbe, into which it flows forty miles to the north. Colditz itself is situated in the middle of the triangle formed by the three great cities of Leipzig, Dresden and Chemnitz; in 1940 it was therefore in the heart of the German Reich and 400 miles from any frontier not directly controlled by the Nazis—a daunting prospect.

I continued in *The Colditz Story*:

> We marched slowly up the steep and narrow cobbled streets from the station towards the Castle, eventually approaching it from the rear, that is to say, from the mainland out of which the promontory protruded. Entering the main arched gateway, we crossed a causeway astride what had once been a deep, wide moat and passed under a second cavernous archway whose oaken doors swung open and closed ominously behind us with the clanging of heavy iron bars in true medieval fashion. We were then in a courtyard about forty-five yards square, with some grass lawn and flower-beds, and surrounded on all four sides with buildings six stories high. This was the *Kommandantur* or garrison area. We were escorted farther; through a third cavernous archway with formidable doors, up an inclined cobbled coach way for about fifty yards, then turning sharp right, through a fourth and last archway with its normal complement of heavy oak and iron work into the "Sanctum Sanctorum," the inner courtyard. This was a cobbled space about thirty yards by forty yards, surrounded on its four sides by buildings whose roof ridges must have been ninety feet above the cobbles. Little sun could ever penetrate here! It was an unspeakably grisly place, made none the less so by the pallid faces which we noticed peering at us through bars. There was not a sound in the courtyard. It was as if we were entering some ghostly ruin. Footsteps echoed and the German words of command seemed distorted out of reality. I had reached the stage of commending my soul to the Almighty when the faces behind the bars suddenly took on life; eyes shone, teeth flashed from behind unkempt beards and words passed backwards into the inner depths:
>
> "*Anglicy! Anglicy!*"
>
> Heads crowded each other out behind tiny barred windows, and in less time than it took us to walk thirty yards there was a cheering mob at every window; not only at the small ones which we had first seen and which we were to come to know so well, but from every other window

that we could see there were jostling heads, laughing and cheering. Welcome was written on every face. We breathed again as we realized we were among friends. They were Polish officers. . . .

Later that evening we made our first acquaintance with the Poles. There were hushed voices on the staircase, then four of them appeared beyond the grill. They unlocked the door [into our attic room] with ease and advanced to greet us. We were the first English they had seen in the war, and the warmth of their welcome, coupled with their natural dignity of bearing, was touching. . . .

They brought food and some beer. Two of the four could speak English and the remainder French. They all spoke German. The meeting soon became noisy and there was much laughter, which the Poles love. Suddenly there was a warning signal from a Pole on the look-out by the stairs, and in less than no time they were all distributed under beds in the corners of our two rooms, where suppressed laughter continued up to the instant of the entry of a German officer with his *Gefreiter* [corporal].

The attic door, and others below, had, of course, been locked by the Poles, so that there was nothing to cause suspicion other than our laughter, which the Germans had overheard and had come to investigate. The officer was shocked that we, reviled prisoners, whose right to live depended on a word from him, should find occasion to laugh. It was like laughing in church, and he implied as much to us. He noticed we had shifted all the bunks to make more floor space and promptly made the *Gefreiter* move them back again into orderly rows. The Poles moved with the beds. No sooner had they departed than the Poles, like truant schoolboys, reappeared, laughing louder than ever at the joke. They called the corporal "*la Fouine*," the French for a marten, which has also a figurative meaning, namely "a wily person" whose propensities have been translated into English as "ferreting." The merriment continued for a while, then they departed as they had come, leaving us to marvel at the facility with which they manipulated locks. In order to visit us they had unlocked no fewer than five doors with a couple of instruments that looked like a pair of button hooks. Such was our introduction to Colditz, which was to be our prison house for several years.

The Polish contingent constituted a unique cross-sectional representation of their nation. Their most senior officer was General Piskor. Then there was

Admiral Unrug, who though older was junior to General Piskor. His sailors were very thin on the ground in Colditz—not more than half a dozen. So Piskor's Army contingent made the running. Unrug nevertheless acted as SPO,* probably because he understood German perfectly.

Tadeusz Piskor was born in 1889 in central Poland. A member of the Polish Socialist Party, he fought with the Polish Legion on the side of Austria from 1914 to 1917, and rose to command the Lublin Army in the September campaign of 1939. Having been forced to capitulate, he was made prisoner. In *Oflag* VIIA at Murnau he was the senior prisoner. There is extant a photograph of him standing at attention with his hands held rigidly to his sides, in response to the offer of the German camp commander, a general, to shake his hand. Piskor's was a gesture of defiance. For this affront to a German general and for his patriotic leadership of the prisoners in Murnau camp he was sent, in January 1940, to Silberberg, and from there to Colditz.

Piskor was short and rather plump and not of military bearing. He was essentially tolerant and kind, although his small mustache gave him an expression which rather belied that kindness. The impression was that of severity coupled with energetic intolerance.

Piskor brought along with him to Colditz many well-known Polish officers, among them Colonel Mozdyniewicz, who was secretly the chief of the Polish Resistance movement within the German prison camps, in touch with the Home Front from Colditz. He used microfilms from the end of 1941 onwards. There were also Colonel Bronisław Kowalczewski, Lieutenant-Colonel Eugeniusz Szubert, Major Walerian Klimowicz and Major Władysław Steblik; then 2nd Lieutenant Jan Niestrzęba, 2nd Lieutenant Zygmunt Mikusiński, Pilot-Officer Zdzisław Dębowski and 2nd Lieutenant Jerzy Klukowski, who had composed one of the escape parties from Silberberg. Three others who were close friends and who were to be persistent escapers were 2nd Lieutenants Pawel Zieliński, Stanisław Bartoszewicz and Feliks Maj.

When three newly arrived British padres were being "deloused" on 3 December, prior to being let loose in the prison, they met three more Poles in the delousing shed who had arrived the same day after recapture from an escape. The chief of them was Lieutenant Wacław Gassowski, a Polish Air Force pilot and athlete of international renown. Also there was his friend Lieutenant Wacław Gorecki, another Air Force pilot.

---

* Senior Polish Officer

Jozef Unrug's father, a Pole, served in the Prussian Army and became a general. Jozef's mother was a countess of Saxony, Isidora von Bunau. However, both Jozef (born in 1884) and his brother were brought up and educated as Polish patriots—an offense for which their father was prematurely retired (dismissed) from the Prussian Army by Bismarck.

It is worth noting that during the period when Poland was partitioned by its three powerful neighbors (Prussia, Russia and Austria) in the years 1795–1918, and especially when no Polish Army existed (1831–1917), it was a principle of Polish patriotism to encourage young Poles to serve in the armed forces of the partitioning powers (also in the armed forces of France and some other countries) in order to acquire the necessary military skills which might one day be needed in the service of resurrected Poland.

Jozef Unrug was born in that part of Poland which was under Prussian rule. He enrolled therefore into the German Navy. In 1914 he was a German lieutenant-commander and in command of a German submarine. After the outbreak of the First World War the German naval authorities apparently did not trust him as a Pole, and withdrew him from this command. They named him instead commander of a school of submarine training for naval other ranks. When the war ended and he became free from his obligations to the German Navy, he offered his services immediately to Poland and entered the Polish Navy.

Poland, after having recovered by the Treaty of Versailles a small sector of her ancient Baltic coast, lost since the partitions of Poland, undertook immediately to build a large port at Gdynia and to create a Navy. Originally that Navy was composed only of a few small ships, but slowly it became bigger, obtaining a number of modern destroyers, submarines, minesweepers and also one large minelayer. Apart from the Navy in the Baltic, Poland had also a Naval River Flotilla on the river Pripet, a tributary of the Dnieper, which played an important role in the Polish-Soviet war of 1919–1920.

These two units, the Baltic fleet and the River Flotilla, formed the Polish Navy, under the administration of the Naval Office in Warsaw. In 1939, the head of the Naval Office was Rear-Admiral Swirski, the commander of the River Flotilla was Captain Zajaczkowski, and the commander of the Navy in the Baltic was Rear-Admiral Unrug. He commanded that fleet from 1925. He was to a great extent the educator of the Polish Navy and creator of its *esprit de corps*.

A few days before the outbreak of war three large destroyers were sent to Great Britain. The battle lasted nineteen days on the mainland against an overwhelmingly powerful German attack. On 19 September—the last heights of Kępa Oksywska, north of Gdynia, were taken by storm by the Germans and the commander of the Polish defenders, Colonel Dabek, committed suicide rather than give himself up.

Unrug became a prisoner of war. The Germans were insolent enough to offer him a return to the German Navy, which he treated with disdain and anger. In consequence, at the beginning of 1940, he was placed in the "special" camp of Srebrna Góra in the Sudeten mountains. The Germans considered Unrug a traitor to the German nation not only because he was a former German officer, but because they considered him to be a German baron, descendant of an old German family, the Barons von Unruh; then of course his father had been a Prussian general and his mother a German countess. They tried hard to convert and exploit him during the time he was in Colditz, but the admiral rebuffed them. He always demanded a Polish/German interpreter to be present at meetings with them and spoke exclusively in Polish. When asked once by a German general why he did not speak in German (which he spoke fluently) he replied: "The language which I use officially is exclusively Polish."

Unrug became recognized as the father of the Polish Navy—a strict disciplinarian and a capable instructor. His outstandingly courageous defense of the besieged peninsula of Hel throughout September 1939 has earned him his place in history.

3

The Challenge

Christmas 1940 to Early Spring 1941

TIME PASSED MORE QUICKLY for the British, making new friends in the new surroundings. The Germans, after a week or so, gave us permanent quarters; a dormitory with two-tier bunks, a washroom, a kitchen and a day-room in a wing of the Castle separated from the Poles. The rooms were severely white-washed and every window was heavily barred. The courtyard was the exercise area. At first the British exercised at different hours to the Poles but the Germans eventually gave up trying to keep us apart. To do so would have meant a sentry at every courtyard door, and there were half a dozen of these. Moreover, the Castle was a maze of staircases and intercommunicating doors, and the latter merely provided lock-picking practice for the Poles. Prisoners were so often found in each other's quarters that the Germans would have had to put the whole camp into "solitary" to carry out their intentions, so they gave it up as a bad job.

A trickle of new arrivals increased the British contingent, until by Christmas we numbered seventeen officers, seven other ranks and one civilian, Howard Gee (he had been captured returning as a volunteer in the defense of Finland). French and Belgian officers appeared. All the newcomers were offenders, mostly escapers, and it was impressed upon them that the Castle was the "bad boys' camp," the *Straflager*, the *Sonderlager*. At the same time, they also began to appreciate its impregnability from the escape point of view. This was to be the German fortress from which there was no escape and it certainly looked for a long time as if it would live up to that reputation. The garrison manning the camp outnumbered the prisoners; the Castle was floodlit at night from every angle despite the black-out, and, notwithstanding the sheer drop of 100 feet or so on the outside from barred windows, sentries surrounded the camp within a palisade of barbed wire. The enemy seemed to have everything in his favor. Escape would be a formidable proposition indeed.

The eight British newcomers who arrived before Christmas were: two Anglican Army chaplains, Padres Heard (Dean of Peterhouse College, Cambridge) and Hobling; one Methodist chaplain, Padre Ellison Platt; Lieutenant-Colonel Guy German of the Royal Leicestershire Regiment; Lieutenants Peter Storie-Pugh of the Queen's Own Royal West Kent Regiment, Teddy Barton of the Royal Army Service Corps, Tommy Elliot of the Royal Northumberland Fusiliers, and Geoffrey Wardle of the Royal Navy. Lieutenant-Colonel Guy Johnson German, a territorial army officer educated at Rugby School, was the Senior British Officer in Colditz for a long time. He was familiarly called "the SBO." A handsome, young-looking colonel (he was thirty-eight in 1940), he was broad-shouldered, tall, well built, with bright blue eyes. His nature was very down to earth and good-tempered, but he was quick in decision. This quality probably accounted for the fact that in spite of his size he played scrum-half for Oxford University, playing at Twickenham against Cambridge in 1923. He brooked no nonsense and was feared by the Germans.

His father had founded the firm of estate agents known as John German and Sons. Guy had studied farming seriously as well as country estate and property management. Much of his peace-time activity was that of farming consultancy. His firm provided an advisory service to farmers and landowners up and down the country. Along with several others, I started a course in agriculture under his direction and tuition which continued for a year. Guy had taken part in the Norwegian campaign, sailing from Rosyth in HMS *Devonshire* under Captain Mansfield on 17 April 1940. He fought a rearguard action at Tetten. His battalion was saved, returning to Glasgow on HMS *Rodney* in May, but he himself was captured on 23 April. Imprisoned at Spangenburg, he publicly burnt all the copies of an issue of a German magazine for POWs—as "dangerous propaganda." That sent him to Colditz.

A remarkable *rencontre* had taken place when Padre Platt stood with others before the gate into the prisoners' courtyard on his arrival at the Castle. A German officer approached out of the darkness. It was Eggers.

"Good evening, my English friends!"

The POW group (six of them) came to attention and saluted. Eggers waved their stiff approach aside.

"You must be tired after so long a day. . . . You will sleep well tonight. . . . Oh, by the way, which is the Methodist chaplain?"

Padre Platt stepped forward. Eggers with an engaging smile said:

"A very personal friend of mine is a Methodist minister. He stayed in my home when he studied in Germany. Do you happen to know Rev. Connell?"

Dick Connell and Jock Platt had been at college together and played on the same football team. There was an immediate friendly exchange of experiences between the German and the Englishman. Platt confirms that it softened the hard edges of the Castle's walls as he passed through "the needle's eye" of the gate into the penumbra of the courtyard.

Padre Joseph Ellison Platt was born in 1900 and educated at a local grammar school in Winsford, a small town in Cheshire. His father was a Methodist preacher. When Jock was about twenty-five, he entered Hartley College, Manchester, to train for the Methodist ministry. Here he met Dick Connell. On 29 May 1940 Platt found himself at the 10th Casualty Clearing Station in Kzombeke, a Belgian village, in the no-man's-land between the advancing Germans and Dunkirk only a short distance away.

Nine hundred wounded men lay head to foot in the village church. The doctors were working round the clock and Platt found himself performing the task of anesthetist. He was taken prisoner with the rest of them. He found himself eventually at *Oflag* IXA—at Spangenburg. He was accused of having brought into the camp from *Stalag* IXA "a housebreaking instrument—a jimmy—for escape purposes." Actually it was a piece of wire he used for propping up the lid of his battered suitcase. This was enough to send him to Colditz! Well built, of medium height, he possessed stern features, carried a mustache and wore hornrimmed spectacles. Though only forty years old, his hair was already graying and he was regarded as an "elder."

Over Christmas the Poles entertained the British with a marionette show of Snow White and the Seven Dwarfs. They had received a few food parcels from their homes in Poland. The British were overwhelmed by their hospitality. We only had German prison rations until on Boxing Day fifteen Red Cross parcels arrived! The excitement had to be seen to be believed. They were bulk parcels; that is to say they were not addressed individually, nor did each parcel contain an assortment of food. There were parcels of tinned meat, of tea, of cocoa, and so on. Apart from a bulk consignment which reached Laufen the previous August, these were the first parcels of food from England and we British felt a surge of gratitude for this gift, without which our New Year would have been a pathetic affair. We were also able to return, at least to a limited extent, the hospitality of the Poles. We had to ration severely for we could not count on a regular supply, and we made this first consignment, together with thirteen parcels which arrived early in January (which we could have eaten in a few days) last for two months.

Padre Platt's unpublished diary, written at the time, describes the end of 1940 in Colditz:

> *New Year's Day 1941*
> The New Year's party was a roaring success. An extension of lights until 12.30 a.m. made a real new year's scene possible. Our hosts (the Poles) were in great form. A special allowance of beer had already "lighted up" one or two of the younger officers. Song and laughter greeted us as we were conducted to the central table as guests of honor. It was a perfect Beggars' Opera, for we were the most ragged and out-at-elbows people in the room.

A few days later he noted his impressions of life in the Castle:

> *Saturday 11 January*
> If this is a *Strafe* [punishment] camp—as it is—my chief regret is that I was not strafed from the first date of capture. During my period of detention in Germany I have had nothing that is better and much that is worse than *Oflag* IVC.
>
> The ways in which IVC is superior to any of the other camps in which I have been detained are, in order of importance:
>
> (a) The British community itself! We are few in number, but apart from the chaplains who are three quite ordinary fellows, the fighting officers are of the best British type. They would not have been in this camp [were they not] of bolder spirit and larger initiative than their fellows in other camps. An escaper is always in danger of being shot like a rabbit, and I think the German authorities—who would be proud enough of any of their officers who had made an escape—honor these fellows for their daring and their refusal to be nice comfortable prisoners who give no trouble.
>
> In all other officers' camps that I know, certain elite sets have segregated themselves and have lived in indigent, but pompous, isolation. . . . There is no hint of that in this camp. We are seventeen officers in number. No two are alike except in good comradeship. Some of England's number one group of public schools are represented; while some of the RAF officers would make no wider claim than an intense willingness to serve their country. My present judgement is that there are none who regard

themselves as being of different clay from the rest. Regulars, Territorials, Emergency Reserve, etc., take each other for what they are worth; and it seems to me that their worth as men and soldiers is pretty high.

(b) We have been mercifully preserved from the presence of that arch-tormentor of prisoners of war, the organizing genius. . . .

(c) The Poles and the French are excellent fellows. They are all of the difficult-prisoner type. But difficult prisoners make interesting prison companions. There is always something going on—planning escapes, or putting plans in process of execution; swapping war stories. So, though monotony is almost inescapable in these conditions, it is by no means as prevalent as in non-difficult-prisoner camps.

(d) The final reason, and a very cogent one, is the attitude of the *Lager* authorities. By and large, they are the best type of German officers I have met since the 10th CCS [Casualty Clearing Station] was overhauled by their front-line troops. To maintain discipline, they do not resort to a weak man's refuge—petty tyranny—but treat us, after they have taken every precaution to prevent escapes, as gentlemen who know the meaning of honor and possess a gentleman's dignity.

Lieutenant-Colonel Schmidt, the *Kommandant*, and Major Menz, the second-in-command (who went to school in Eastbourne in his boyhood), strike me as being desirous of doing nothing that even an enemy prisoner could regard as unfair. When either of them comes into the *Hof* [courtyard] or our quarters, and one of the accompanying German officers gives the command "*Achtung*," they scarcely wait for us to make the initial effort to rise before waving us back to whatever pursuits we were following. Needless to say, we are more meticulous in their presence about military etiquette than would otherwise be the case.

Apart from the Red Cross parcels, there was little respite from the dreary food provided for us by the Germans. Padre Platt's diary reveals one ruse for relieving the monotony:

Monday 27 January

Dick Howe is receiving extensive Californian sympathy mail these days. He wrote to Ginger Rogers' Hollywood address in July, at a time when letters could not be sent to England. Miss Rogers herself has not replied, but her publicity agent made front page news of the letter in the Los Angeles *Observer*.

A largish number of aspirant stars saw the notice, and at once wrote to Dick furnishing details about their height, weight, figure, color of eyes and hair (monotonously blue and blonde) and stating their fixed preference for this, that, and the other. "Please don't think me fast or husband-seeking because of this letter. I am a career woman (age 17) and have told Mum and Dad a score of times that I shall never, never marry"—and so they all end! In nine letters out of ten a pretty photograph of the "career woman" is enclosed, showing her in a devastatingly attractive bathing costume, or in trousers and silk shirt. We hope for lots more. Their entertainment value is high indeed.

However, from a practical point of view the whole thing is a wet squib! The original letter was one of many written by officers to people they thought might be good for a monthly food and tobacco parcel. Of course the ulterior motive was not openly avowed in the letter but there were some who received letters who thought at once of a parcel. Dick drew a blank. Letters, yes, parcels nary-a-one! Still, the letters are of unspeakable value; they give our forcing-house of humor a much appreciated zest.

At the end of February 1941, 200 French officers arrived under the leadership of General Le Bleu, who hated all things *Boche*. One of them, General Le Brigant, in his book *Les Indomptables* describes their arrival (my translation):

> Carrying their personal possessions, surrounded by armed guards with bayonets fixed, the future guests of the *Schloss* cross the town and the stone bridge over the Mulde river, painfully climb the steep narrow alleyways, and arrive at last at a postern gate situated between two deep moats. The papers handed over by the accompanying guards are carefully examined. A telephone call is made to obtain permission to open the main entrance doors. . . . A German officer approaches, a cloak over his shoulders. He welcomes the new recruits with an artificially friendly smile. He says "Welcome to the Escaping Academy! But from here there is no escaping!"
>
> A face appears behind the bars of a high-up window. A voice calls out "Are you prisoners? So am I. But what's the time? We no longer know anything in this place!" Threatened by a guard, the face vanishes. A *Feldwebel* turns an enormous key in the massive oak, iron-bound door which gives access to the interior of the *Schloss*. . . .
>
> The newcomers are ready to sleep after their heavy day, but an urgent voice from the other side of the door tells them to look out at midnight.

> Sharp on midnight (when the change of guard was taking place) strings appear outside the window to which, item by item, they tie their contraband. Compasses, German money, maps, and a few items of civilian clothing. They are pulled up to the next floor. The new arrivals begin to feel a little less despairing.

Not all the new French officers were escapers by any means, but about a hundred of them were. Among the remainder were a number of French Jewish officers who were separated from the rest by the Germans and given their own quarters on the top floor of the Castle.

The *Kommandant* of Colditz carried sole responsibility for the inmates of Colditz. Oberstleutnant Schmidt had been carefully selected by the OKW because of the peculiar nature of the post: the safe-keeping of rebellious, intransigent, *Deutschfeindlich* prisoners. (*Deutschfeindlich*—meaning "enemy of Germany"—was an annotation appended along with a red seal to the records of a majority of the prisoners in Colditz.) He was empowered to use whatever means he considered necessary to ensure control over the prisoners.

Under the terms of the Geneva Convention, the detaining power is permitted to create "special" camps for the control of "escapers" and "offenders" provided the principles of the Convention are not contravened. In practice, this involved more roll-calls, more searches, more sentries, less exercise space, less privacy, less privileges, no parole.

Schmidt was an officer of the old school. Despite his rigid outlook and approach to his job, he retained the concept of chivalry in which he had been brought up. He tolerated no slackness in his staff and dealt severely with offenders. He ensured that so much was *verboten* in the prison regulations that he found little difficulty in discovering misdemeanors when he wished to. He accepted the right of officer POWs to attempt to escape and he did his best to comply with the rules of the Geneva Convention. But orders from Berlin often overruled its terms, and it was these OKW orders which he had to obey.

While with one hand he was capable of ordering the confiscation of all Penguin books (the objection was to certain advertisements in the notice pages), he tried to help the small British contingent, which from November onwards found itself without any "reading" in the English language. Guy German made a spirited approach and the *Kommandant* reacted by involving the German Red Cross in an endeavor to find some reading material in English within the fastnesses of the German Reich. His appeal found its response and a large boxful of heterogeneous English literature found its way to the British quarters, after careful scrutiny and censorship by the *Kommandant*'s staff employed for that purpose.

Amongst the diverse literature that turned up, from English translations of Goethe and Nietzsche to speeches by Hitler, an inconspicuous little book received the Colditz censor's "*Geprüft*" stamp. It was *Stratosphere and Rocket Flight (Astronautics)* by Charles G. Philp, published in 1935. The book attracted me at once (as well as being a civil engineer, I was also a visionary). Philp's book should never have passed the German censor. Chapter 13 was headed "Man achieves his First Rocket Flight." It gave graphic details of an ascent by a man in a rocket early in November 1933 up to six miles high, and his safe descent by parachute. The experiment took place on the Island of Rugen. Chapter 14 was headed "The Rocket in Warfare." The OKW bought up all the patents and the accompanying technical know-how on the spot. At this point the story must be left in abeyance because nothing further happened until 1943.

Guy German placed me in charge of escape operations. He relied upon me to tell him only the barest essentials; in this way he could keep aloof from these operations and so be in a stronger position vis-à-vis the Germans. Guy nevertheless was keen to participate in any escape attempt into which he could be fitted.

I began reconnoitering the possibilities of escape from the Castle:

> As at Laufen we concentrated on parts of the Castle not used by ourselves . . . we were learning from the Poles their art of lockpicking. . . . I was next attracted by the drains. . . . Inside the canteen [so called, though it was nothing more than a shop; in German it was labeled *Kantine*], where we bought our razor-blades and suchlike, in front of the counter on the buyers' side was a manhole cover. I had not far to seek for assistance in opening up this manhole, for Kenneth [Lockwood] had already provided the solution. Some weeks before he had had himself appointed assistant manager and accountant of the canteen!
>
> Kenneth was a London Stock Exchange man and the idea of keeping even the meager canteen accounts evidently made him feel a little nearer home. He had been educated at Whitgift School and was by nature a tidy person, meticulous in his ways and in his speech. . . . [He relentlessly inflicted demoralizing propaganda on the German *Feldwebel* in charge.] Within a few months he had broken down the morale of the *Feldwebel* to such an extent that the latter was preaching sedition to his colleagues and had to be removed.

> The table which Kenneth and the *Feldwebel* used for writing was situated under the only window in the room, at some distance from the counter. While a few people stood at the counter, and Kenneth distracted the German's attention with some accounting matter at the table, it was comparatively simple to tackle the manhole cover. . . . [It] came away after some persuasion.
>
> Sure enough, there were tunnels leading in two directions, one connecting with the tunnel already noticed from the yard, and the other leading out under the window beside which Kenneth and the German worked. A second reconnaissance in more detail showed this latter to be about eighteen yards long and built on a curve. Under the window it was blocked up with large hewn stones and mortar. Outside the shop window and at the level of the canteen floor was a grass lawn, which also abutted the German section of the Castle. At the outer edge of this lawn was a stone balustrade, and then a thirty foot drop over a retaining wall to the level of the roadway which led down to the valley in which our football ground was situated. Maybe the tunnel led out to this wall. We had to find out.

Padre Platt made a diary entry at this time as follows:

> It will be necessary to cut through the foundations when they are reached; and in the meantime to dispose of the rubble, etc. The line they are following passes right under the canteen, and will eventually come out beneath the eastern ramparts. It will occupy about three months, working two or three hours a night after lights out. Having to work in darkness increases the difficulties, and the necessity for silence, lest a night sentry should become suspicious, adds to the other complications. At present there are two watchers who use a system of signals to indicate when the sentry on his beat is near enough to hear unusual sounds.

In her edition of Padre Platt's diary, Margaret Duggan took up the point that this diary entry was surprising in the light of its contents which when subjected to censorship could have compromised the escape attempt. (Platt had told Eggers that he kept a diary and Eggers' initial response had been that it must be confiscated and would be destroyed. Platt, however, managed to reach an understanding with Eggers that, provided that he handed his diary over for censorship, it would be returned to him after scrutiny and this arrangement was adhered to on both sides.) I too have examined this censor's *"Geprüft"* stamp and think that it may well be forged. However, unless this page was inserted at a much later date, there was a grave risk that the censor might, without notice, demand to reread it with earlier pages. Furthermore I have examined the stamps on other pages carrying "classified" information, and I regret to say that these stamps appear to be quite genuine.

To return to *The Colditz Story*:

> A few days later we had made out of an iron bedpiece a key which opened the canteen door. Working at night as before we would open our staircase entrance door and cross about ten yards of the courtyard to the canteen door. This opened, we would enter and lock it behind us. We then had to climb a high wooden partition in order to enter the canteen proper, as the door in this partition had a German-type Yale lock which foiled us. The partition separated the canteen from the camp office; a room in which all the haggling took place between our Commanding Officer and the German Camp *Kommandant* on his periodic visits. The partition was surmounted with the aid of a couple of sheets used as ropes. . . .
>
> My . . . idea was to make a vertical shaft which would bring the tunnel up to the grass. I would construct a trap-door which would be covered with grass and yet would open when required, thus repeating my Laufen idea of having the escape tunnel intact for further use. Escapes involved such an immense amount of labor, sometimes only to serve in the escape of one or two men, that it was always worthwhile attempting to leave the escape exit ready for further use. In this case the intention was that the whole British contingent would escape!
>
> Once out on the grass patch we could creep along under the Castle walls in the dark; descend the retaining wall with sheets; then continue past the guards' sleeping-quarters to the last defense—the twelve-foot wall of the Castle park surmounted for much of its length with barbed wire. This obstacle would not be difficult provided there was complete concealment, which was possible at night and provided there was plenty of time to deal with the barbed wire. We had to pass in full view of a sentry at one point. He was only forty yards away, but as there were Germans who frequently passed the same point, this was not a serious difficulty.
>
> I constructed out of bed-boards and stolen screws a trap which looked like a small table with collapsible legs—collapsible so as to enter the tunnel. . . .
>
> Before all this happened, our plans were temporarily upset. Two Polish officers [the two Air Force officers Lieutenants Gassowski and Gorecki]

> got into the canteen one night when we were not working and tried to cut the bars outside the window. . . . Cutting bars cannot be done silently. They did not take the precaution of having their own stooges [look-outs] either to distract the attention of the nearby sentry or to give warning of his approach. Throughout our work on the tunnel we had a signalling system from our rooms above which gave warning of this sentry's approach. He was normally out of sight from where our tunnel exit was to be, but he only had to extend his beat a few yards in order to come into view.
>
> The Poles were caught red-handed and within a few days a huge flood-light was installed in such a position as to light up the whole lawn and all the prison windows opening on to it.
>
> This was a good example of what was bound to happen in a camp holding officers bent on escape. We had already asked the Poles for liaison on escape projects so that we would not tread on each other's toes all the time, and now Colonel German called a meeting with their Senior Officers, at which an agreement was reached. The Senior Polish Officer was in a difficult position because he frankly could not control his officers; he knew that they might attempt to escape without telling him or anybody else. However, after this meeting the liaison improved, and when we offered some Poles places in our tunnel escape, mutual confidence was established. . . .
>
> We had to come to an arrangement with the French Senior Officer over escape projects similar to that agreed with the Poles, but unfortunately the French liaison system was also found wanting—at the expense of our tunnel—before a workable understanding was reached.

Before the arrival of General Le Brigant, the French Senior Officer was Colonel de Warren. He had refused to allow a pro-Pétain poster to be hung in his camp office entitled "*Français, n'oubliez pas Oran*"—anti-British propaganda. De Warren had said, "*Messieurs,* our officers form their own opinions of their own accord." He was packed off to Colditz the next day.

Le Brigant arrived with his German-speaking interpreter Lieutenant André Jung from Gros Born, Westphalenhof (*Oflag* IID). He had been the Senior French Officer there. Being a no-nonsense Breton and pugnacious at that, he had made an enemy of the German officer in command of his prison block by his alleged "subversive reflections." André Jung, from Lorraine, was also deemed "criminal" because he had refused to append his signature to a document of allegiance to Germany as a citizen of Lorraine.

On 24 February, two French officers, Alain Le Ray and André Tournon arrived. They had escaped from *Oflag* IID at Jastrow, not far from the Baltic Coast and east of Stettin. They had crossed the Rhine at Mainz but were retaken at Bingerbruck, some 600 miles away, on 24 January after five days of freedom. Their escape took place in the depths of a Baltic winter; in fact they had dug a snow grave and hidden in it.

On 18 March, two French lieutenants, Paillie and Cazamayou, were caught tunnelling in the clock tower. They made too much noise. Eggers states in his diary that Hauptmann Lange, the German security officer at the time, thereupon had all doors at different floor levels which led into the tower walled up. The consequences were serious for the Germans. The French constructed a secret entrance to the tower under the roof of the Castle, and thenceforth were able to descend the tower and recommence their tunnel at the bottom in undisturbed privacy.

The British tunnel in the canteen was making good progress. On Saturday night, 22 March, Dick Howe, Rupert Barry and I were working in the tunnel. Geoffrey Wardle and Peter Storie-Pugh were keeping a look-out through the canteen windows in the courtyard and on to the lawn.

The Germans had been having a party. The sounds of their revelry could be heard everywhere. In fact, they were keeping our orderlies, who slept nearby, awake. Solly Goldman, a Jew from Whitechapel, had arrived in Colditz as Colonel German's batman. With the other orderlies he had a place reserved in the tunnel for the second "go." He possessed a redoubtable Cockney wit and an unquenchable bubbling temperament which expressed itself in explosive laughter whenever the opportunity arose. When Guy German had been interviewed by the *Kommandant* on his arrival, Goldman was beside him and became so voluble at the interrogation that he was mistaken by the *Kommandant* for our new Senior British Officer.

Tonight Goldman wanted to go to sleep. So he lifted the black-out curtain, opened the nearest window and started barracking a nearby sentry. Shots rang out and Goldman withdrew his head smartly. Very soon a posse of Goons (as the British called the German guards) entered the courtyard heading for the British quarters: Hauptmann Priem and the German Regimental Sergeant-Major, Oberstabsfeldwebel Gephard, the corporal known as the *Fouine* (ferret) and half a dozen soldiers. They burst into the quarters shouting "*Aufstehen!*," waking everyone and prodding men out of bed. They discovered four officers missing. They lost their heads. They had expected and intended to have fun at the prisoners' expense. The new turn of events shook them.

Eventually Priem sent out orders for the dogs to be summoned. He then announced that "Hauptmann Howe" (pronouncing it "Hover" in German fashion) had been seen escaping and had been shot. He observed the reaction to this announcement, and probably deduced from the merriment that an actual escape had not taken place. In any event, his face showed marked relief.

Gephard now appeared following in the trail of the Alsatian dogs and dogmen. This part of the proceedings, the *Schnüffelhunde* (POW slang for the dogs) in action, interested everybody tremendously. But notwithstanding the dogmen's encouraging "*Such! Such! Such!*" and their gentle thrusting of the dogs' noses into bedding and clothing, the dogs appeared to have little idea of what was required. When they produced nothing, Priem sent out orders for the whole camp to be paraded. It was about 2 a.m. by then. Suddenly, "Stooge" Wardle, who was the look-out in the canteen shouted "They're heading this way." He had scarcely time to jump down into the tunnel, and I to pull the manhole cover over, before the Jerries were in. They searched the canteen and tried hard to lift the manhole cover, but were unable to do so as I was hanging on to it for dear life from underneath, fingers wedged in a protruding lip of the cover. They departed.

As soon as Wardle noticed that a "General *Appell*" had been called, I told Rupert and Dick in the tunnel with me to start at once building a false wall halfway up the tunnel, behind which we put the store of food and other escape paraphernalia such as rucksacks, maps, compasses and civilian clothing which were normally kept hidden there.

The Poles and French chanted a dirge as they stood and shivered in the yard. It was the first midnight *Appell* since the British arrived.

By 3:45 a.m. the *Schloss* had been searched from end to end without success. The other nationalities were dismissed from the *Hof*, and the British were ordered to bed; Colonel German had to appear for a few minutes in the *Evidenzzimmer* (the evidence, or conference, room) to answer questions; always the same answer: "*Ich weiss nicht.*"

Rupert and Dick quietly continued their work and in a few hours had constructed a forbidding-looking false wall with stones from the original wall which had been demolished, jointed with clay from under the lawn and coated with dust wherever the joints showed.

By 5 a.m. all was quiet again. We departed as we had come and went to bed wondering how the Germans would react to our reappearance at morning *Appell*. They had apparently been put to a great deal of trouble. While the Jerries had had the whole camp on parade, they had carried out an individual identity check. Every officer paraded in front of a table where he was identified against his photograph and duly registered as present. We were recorded as having escaped, and messages, flashed to the OKW, brought into action all over the country a network of precautions for the recapture of prisoners.

At the morning *Appell*, when all were found present, confusion reigned once more. We refused to explain our disappearance and were remanded for sentence for causing a disturbance and being absent from *Appell*. The OKW orders had to be countermanded and the *Kommandant* had a rap over the knuckles for the incident.

The Goons were upset and watchful. They again visited the canteen, and although they managed to remove the manhole cover and descend to the tunnel, they found nothing unusual. Kenneth, who was in the background of the shop at the time, trying to appear occupied with his accounts, breathed an audible sigh of relief.

A mock funeral was held to commemorate the death of Dick Howe: the cortège, led by crucifix and candlebearers; a coffin consisting of a dormitory locker, draped with a blanket chalked in the colors of the Union Jack carried by four tall men; Chopin's Funeral March provided by two accordionists; a solemn procession, medals on a cushion, wreathbearers, moving with slow measured tread; a tearful, skirted (kilted) widow draped in black, supported by two Polish officers—close relatives of the deceased; a banner with a strange device—a skull and crossbones; all passed before the astonished gaze of Hauptmann Priem, who took it in good humor until a funeral oration given *ad lib* by a Frenchman, and not anticipated by the cortège, showered such insults at the German Reich and its representatives in Colditz that Priem called out the guard and put a stop to it. Later Colonel German was called and formally presented with a note by Priem. It turned out to be a note of condolences for the demise of Dick! A nice turn—calculated to weaken the *entente cordiale*! Not satisfied with that, Priem announced by interpreter at the next morning's *Appell*, "In future, no funerals shall take place without twelve hours' notice being given."

The saving of the tunnel produced a wave of enthusiasm. There was little more work to be done now. The British contingent—all of whom, except for the three padres, were scheduled to escape—began feverishly preparing their personal kit. Polish officers, participants also in the escape, came to and fro. For days the conversation had been concerned only with food, money, maps, and frontiers.

"Solitary confinement" is translated into the *Wehrmacht* regulations as *Stubenarrest*. The Geneva Convention specifies that POW officers should be treated in the "same way as German officers would be treated for an offense.

Stubenarrest was solitary confinement for not more than thirty days in a room with the bare essentials of comfort—mattress, table, chair, bucket and water jug—on standard rations and with books, writing material and cigarettes allowed. There were about half a dozen solitary-confinement cells in the Castle precinct; they were about four yards square and each had one small, heavily barred window. There were so many offenders in Colditz that the cells nearly always housed two or three POWs instead of one—and there was a waiting list. We, the canteen tunnellers, were awarded seven days *Stubenarrest* for "being absent from . . . quarters and for attempting to tunnel out of the camp from the church." The Germans had actually discovered tools and the beginnings of a tunnel in the chapel. It is not known who the tunnellers in this instance were.

A further incident towards the end of March 1941 provoked an incipient discord within the international community. Two Frenchmen decided to attempt the same escape tried by the two Polish officers, through the window of the canteen immediately above where our tunnel was already debouching. André Boucheron and Jacques Charvet made too much noise trying to cut the window bars. A sentry overheard, approached the window, saw shadows within and raised the alarm. To add insult to injury, whilst the two Frenchmen regained their quarters without demur, the Germans, convinced that the British or the Poles, whose quarters were near the canteen, must be the culprits, obliged them to spend most of the night on parade in the freezing temperature of the courtyard while the French snored their heads off under warm blankets. The next day, or very soon thereafter, the Germans posted a sentry permanently on a beat that included the grass lawn by the canteen window! He passed the window at one-minute intervals, day and night. He often stood over the exit of the British tunnel.

On 27 March, twenty-seven Polish officers were ordered without notice to pack and parade for transfer to another camp. Rumor had it that they were going to Fort Spitzberg. The most pertinent common factor among those who were leaving was that they were all determined escapers. Jędrzej Giertych was one of them. Padre Platt was told by the Polish kitchen officer that it was considered amongst their contingent that such an accurate discriminatory selection of men could not have been achieved without the aid of a "stool-pigeon" (an informer). (It transpired later that the Polish kitchen officer was the stool-pigeon!) This was the first information of any substance that the British received of such a likelihood. The Poles would naturally be very circumspect in telling their Allies that they were virtually certain they were infiltrated by a spy.

4

Restless Captives

Spring 1941

ON 9 APRIL, AS IF TO SIGNAL the opening of the "escaping season," the British contingent was summoned to the courtyard to have fingerprints and identity photographs taken by a Berlin Gestapo expert. A preposterous number of smudged prints and grimacing photos resulted. This occurrence lends credence to the statement made by General Le Brigant in his book that the Gestapo under the personal direction of Himmler demanded and obtained some rights of surveillance and control vis-à-vis the OKW over the Colditz prisoners. He says Colditz was officially declared a *Sonderlager* for this purpose.

On 12 April at *Appell*, the French Senior Officer notified the absence of a French officer. In order to identify him, the Germans had to check the identity cards of the whole contingent—a long, arduous process as the photos of the French were all nearly a year old, and beards and mustaches had come and gone. Alain Le Ray was identified as missing. Priem suspected he might be hidden up in the Castle. He brought in the *Schnüffelhunde*, but to no avail. Priem had a nasty time from his superiors—in the form of a *dicke Zigarre* (translated as a "rocket") from the *Kommandant*, followed by searching if futile enquiries from *Abwehrstelle* Four of the OKW Dresden. Then Berlin intervened with further questions. Priem was in disgrace. More barbed wire appeared on roofs and chimneys; more searchlights, stronger arcs.

Le Ray had escaped; the first out of Colditz!

Harry Elliott, who had taken on duties as adjutant of the British contingent, exchanged language lessons with Le Ray. They had become friends. Thus, when the whole contingent was infuriated by the action of Boucheron and Charvet, I took the matter to Colonel German, who deputed Harry to open the case with the French. He started by explaining the situation to Le Ray. Le Ray was already planning his own lone escape in secret. The situation was delicate. Many would-be escapers were "loners," always on the look out for a propitious moment anywhere in the camp, ready to take a split-second opportunity. Most escapers were unwilling to share their ideas or plans with anyone else until sometimes at the very last minute. They were generally teamed up in twos, threes or fours. Each one kept the scheme secret. Secrecy was considered essential to success; secrecy from the Germans, secrecy from rivals who might steal a promising plan and secrecy from a possible stool-pigeon.

The Polish contingent posed a further problem in that, being the first prisoners in Colditz, they reckoned that every new scheme that came to light was theirs, arguing that they had thought of it before the other nationalities arrived! So they claimed priority.

No nationality was blameless. After all, the British had informed nobody of their canteen tunnel. The British also, unwittingly, had caused the discovery of the chapel hole, for which no recognizable team would accept responsibility. After Le Ray's own escape, though he was blameless, the question was again highlighted.

After Harry's earlier discussions with Le Ray and with several other officers besides, diplomacy gained the day and a meeting of Senior Officers initiated an escape committee which drew up a code of cardinal principles and a minimum of rules by which everybody was expected to abide. Individual escapes were permissible so long as the Senior Officer of the contingent was informed. In practice, and as soon as officers appointed to take charge of escape matters established trust and confidence in each other, there arose a continuous liaison between them.

Le Ray's escape was a tonic for us all. Serving as a lieutenant in the Alpine troops division, he had commanded a company in the winter of 1939–1940 and had been wounded and taken prisoner. He was a handsome, black-haired, debonair young man, and a great athlete. He gave his own account of his escape in his book *Première à Colditz*:

> The Germans in Colditz, respecting the Geneva Convention, let us out in the castle grounds from time to time to walk around in a wooded park

surrounded on three sides by a fence of barbed wire and on one side by a wall. But it was such a nuisance to get ready for the park walk—assembling in the courtyard, being counted and recounted—that many of the prisoners could not be bothered to go.

Apart from the wired-off section reserved for prisoners, the park was not particularly well guarded. On the other hand, the castle guards could survey the whole area including the path down to it.

For the walk, our guards counted us twice, inside and then outside the inner courtyard before we marched. Then again after arrival in the park, and the same on the way back. This was done although the walk down took us only fifteen minutes. In spite of these precautions, I felt that this was a weak spot in the castle's defenses and made my plans accordingly.

On the walk back from the park on Good Friday, 11 April, Le Ray dived out of the line of prisoners and hid in the cellar of a house. The path curved at that point and he had relied on the accompanying guards not being able to observe all the prisoners at once. His absence went unnoticed at the count on re-entering the courtyard because two of his colleagues staged a fight. Le Ray made his way back down to the park and managed to climb the wall surrounding the Castle grounds by using the adjoining barbed-wire fence as a ladder. After travelling by train to Nuremberg he assaulted a German civilian and stole his money and his coat.

From now on, my voyage became a pleasure trip. I went through Stuttgart—Tuttlingen—Singen. On the evening of the Easter Monday, I was only ten kilometers from the Swiss frontier, near Schaffhausen. During the Monday night, I made my way through woodland paths to Gottmadingen, the last station before the frontier and customs-control, where I waited hidden in the bushes. A train passed at about 11:00 p.m. and the locomotive stopped five meters in front of me for the train to be searched. When the doors were shut again, I crept up to the engine, and when the engine driver gave the whistle signal to start, I sprang up onto the front of the locomotive between its headlights, where I hid. The driver opened the throttle and the train roared through the fresh air of the spring night. Five minutes later we passed the red lights of the enemy guard post; on under the bridge, and then into Switzerland. I had reconquered for myself the right to freedom.

Meanwhile, on that same Easter Monday, 14 April, the Polish Lieutenant Just was returned to Colditz after a week's absence and after the first escape attempt from outside the perimeters of Colditz. Two Polish officers, Bednarski and Just, had been escorted on 5 April to a hospital at Königswartha, about thirty miles north-east of Dresden, for the treatment of some alleged ailments. They escaped from the hospital. Just was recaught but made another attempt by leaping from a train. This time he was injured so badly that he gave up. Bednarski reached Cracow in Poland but was eventually also recaught and returned to Colditz.

There were six new arrivals on 16 April: three RAF officers, Flying Officers Don Thom, "Erroll" Flynn and Don Donaldson, Army Lieutenant John Hyde-Thompson and two Fleet Air Arm lieutenants, Alan Cheetham and John Davies. They all arrived from underground incarceration in the old fortress of Thorn in Poland where they had been sent from Spangenburg as a reprisal for the alleged crowded and insanitary conditions of imprisonment of German officers at Fort Henry, Ontario, Canada.

From Thorn, Thom, Donaldson and Flynn had escaped and, dressed as German air mechanics, had tried unsuccessfully to steal an enemy plane. Hyde-Thompson had also escaped from Thorn and was eight days at liberty before recapture. The two Fleet Air Arm officers had discovered an old escape-tunnel working which they followed only to emerge facing the muzzle of a machine-gun.

On Sunday evening, 26 April, after some high-spirited singing around the piano, Peter Storie-Pugh started halloaing from a dormitory window after lights-out. He was brought to his senses by a bullet which splintered the glass above his head and sent him ducking for cover. This would duly be made a serious cause of complaint by the SBO. In reality Peter was, of course, goading the German sentry.

On 10 May, a rare opportunity presented itself. Some French troop prisoners who were held somewhere in the town arrived at the Castle in a German lorry to collect some straw palliasses (the standard prison mattresses). There was no time to lose. Peter Allan—who was small and light and spoke German fluently—was stuffed into one of our own palliasses. With some difficulty I persuaded one of the Frenchmen to carry this bundle down the stairs and load it on the lorry. Then we watched the lorry drive out of the Castle. It looked as if a successful escape was in the making.

More French escapers arrived in May, in particular fifteen officers from a party of twenty-four who had broken out from a tunnel in the prison of Hoyerswerde on 29 March. Eight of the twenty-four succeeded in reaching France. One, though recaptured, for some reason never came to Colditz. Amongst the newcomers were Colonel Damidaux and Lieutenants Duquet, Gérard, Groquet, Jung, Lamidieu, Warisse and Besson-Guyard (these last two escaped successfully later).

Around this time, two Polish lieutenants, Mietek Chmiel and "Miki" Surmanowicz, were caught by the Germans in a locked-up attic in the *Saalhaus*. This was a wing of the Castle containing the theater which housed the Senior Officers (POWs). The two Poles were promptly placed in solitary confinement.

Miki was the most daredevil Polish officer at Colditz among a bunch of daredevils. He was a weedy-looking young man, though with a fanatical ardor glowing in his eyes. He was a great friend of mine, and he taught me all I ever knew about lock-picking, at which he was an expert. It was Miki who had been one of the first visitors up in the loft on arrival of the British at Colditz. The manufacture of magnetic compasses was also a pastime of his.

He now occupied a cell which had a small window, high up in the wall, opening on to the courtyard. Meitek Chmiel occupied the cell next door. On 12 May I received a message from him saying that he and Chmiel were going to escape that night and would I please join them! I declined, mainly because I had the canteen tunnel on my hands. However, I passed on his invitation to a few of the most hare-brained in the British company, but it was politely refused by all. Flight-Lieutenant George Skelton, a South African, who had arrived the day before and had gone straight into cells, was also offered by Miki the chance of deliverance from his cell to immediate freedom that very night. But he too thought the idea crazy.

No one believed Miki could ghost his way out of his heavily barred and padlocked cell, open Chmiel's cell and then unlock the main door of the "solitary" cell corridor which opened on to the courtyard. Having accomplished this feat he was inside the prison camp, the same as everyone else!

In *The Colditz Story* I described what happened next:

> He left the invitation open, giving a rendezvous in the courtyard outside the solitary confinement cells at 11 p.m. that night.
>
> I was at my window watching as 11 p.m. struck, and on the minute I saw the door of the cells open slowly. All was dark and I could only faintly distinguish the two figures as they crept out. Then something dropped from a window high up in the Polish quarters. It was a rope made of sheets with a load strapped at the bottom—their escape kit, clothes and rucksacks. Next I saw the figures climb the rope one after the other to a ledge forty feet above the ground. What they were about to do was impossible, but they had achieved the impossible once already. I could no longer believe my eyes. The ledge they were on jutted four inches out from the sheer face of the wall of the building. They both held the rope, which was still suspended

> from the window above them. My heart pounded against my ribs as I saw them high above me with their backs against the wall moving along the ledge inch by inch a distance of ten yards before reaching the safety of a gutter on the eaves of the German guardhouse [roof].
>
> Once there, they were comparatively safe and out of sight if the courtyard lights were turned on. I then saw them climb up the roof to a skylight through which they disappeared, pulling the long rope of sheets, which was let loose by Polish confederates, after them.
>
> Their next move, I knew, was to descend from a small window at the outer end of the attic of the German guardhouse. The drop was about one hundred and twenty feet, continuing down the face of the cliff upon which the Castle was built.

At 5.30 a.m. the bells rang for an *Appell* and the whole camp paraded in the yard for an hour while the Germans established the number of POWs missing. The Poles had evidently been discovered. Midnight *Appells* were no longer a curiosity but the 5.30 a.m. variety was a new and unwelcome one until everyone discovered what had happened.

The next morning the two Poles were back in their cells. They had made one small but fatal mistake. Miki wore plimsolls for the climb, but Chmiel, with Miki's agreement, preferred to wear mountaineering boots. As they both descended the long drop from the guardhouse, the boots made too much noise against the wall and awoke the German duty officer sleeping in the guardhouse. He opened the window to see the rope dangling beside him and a body a few yards below him only a hundred feet from the ground. He drew his revolver and shouted "*Hände hoch!*" ("Hands up!") several times to no avail, then called out the guard. The two Poles apparently laughed so much when they heard his order that they very nearly let go of the rope.

I spent a month in Miki's cell later on without being able to discover how he had opened the door! The secret has since been revealed, however. The cell door was fixed to the outside of the cell. There were two hinges on one side. A heavy metal bar was fixed to the door and was padlocked to the wall on the opposite side to the hinges. The door overlapped the wall at the top and on both sides and at the bottom fitted close to the passage floor. On the inside the bottom of the door was concealed by a wooden strip.

Miki had some tools and keys smuggled into his cell. With the tools he removed the wooden strip and levered the hinge side of the door upwards so that the door came off the vertical hinge posts attached to the wall. He replaced the wooden strip on the inside of the cell. He then went out into the corridor, unlocked Chmiel's padlock, let him out, and locked up both cells, having put his door back on the hinges.

After this episode the Germans placed a sentry in the courtyard. He remained all night with the lights full on, which was to prove a nuisance for later escape attempts.

The escaping season was indeed getting under way. On 14 May, four new British diehards arrived: Lieutenant-Commander Stevenson RN, Squadron-Leader Brian Paddon and Flying Officer "Bricky" Forbes of the RAF, and Lieutenant Airey Neave RA. A fifth arrival was a Belgian major whose reason for transfer to Colditz was more bizarre than usual. The document relating the charge under which he was transferred reads as follows:

Oflag VIIb Punishment Eichstadt 12.3.41

Kmdtr.

Camp Order No. 341

I punish POW Major Flébus with ten days' confinement because on 2.3.41 he captured a cat, not belonging to him, and on 4.3.41 did share in the unnatural consumption of the same.

2) I punish POW Lt. Louis Marlière with fourteen days' confinement because he killed a cat, not belonging to him, in a way cruel to animals, cooked the same, and together with Major Flébus consumed it in an unnatural way, although the menu for P.O.W.s [*sic*] is excellently prepared and abundantly apportioned.

Signed Feurheerd, *Oberleutnant* and *Kommandant*

The Germans opened another room on 22 May to serve as a dormitory for the new British arrivals, who came in twos and threes. Several officers of field rank added their dignity to the company, and the first evidence of their presence was (a) a wish to organize everything, and (b) to separate the sheep from the goats by making the new dormitory not a new arrivals' room, but a room for subalterns.

A search was sprung by the Germans at 2 p.m. that day. Teddy Barton had been careless enough to have seventy *Reichsmarks* in his pocket, and Stevenson and Paddon lost some in the same way. Other officers were not a little angry. *Reichsmarks* were difficult to come by, and that officers should carry them on their persons instead of depositing them in one of the two safe hideouts was considered unpardonable. Much of the tunnelling kit and a quantity of escape clothes were found and confiscated. The searchers had a fair day.

The only source of consolation was Peter Allan's escape. It was twelve days since he had got away, and with reasonable luck he should have crossed the frontier. The British were pretty certain he had made it, otherwise the news of his recapture would have been publicized with immense satisfaction.

Eggers reported that a further escape was made by rope from a solitary-confinement cell on 14 May by the Polish Lieutenant Just. He was aided in this by Lieutenant John Hyde-Thompson MC, of the Durham Light Infantry. Just was recaught near Basel while trying to swim the Rhine. The Germans had concealed barbed wire under the surface of the river and Just got himself enmeshed.

I was thinking again about the canteen tunnel, which had been in the doldrums for some time. I was reluctant to try lengthening it because that would only increase our chances of being discovered. At this stage of wondering what on earth to do with it, the civilian Howard Gee, an excellent German-speaker, told me of his success in corrupting one of the German sentries, who had been smuggling eggs and coffee for the prisoners. Howard soon persuaded him that on a given day and after a predetermined signal he should "look the other way" for ten minutes while on sentry duty. His reward was to be 500 *Reichsmarks*—100 as an advance and 400 dropped out of a convenient window one hour after the ten-minute interval.

The first escape party was to consist of twelve officers, two of them Poles, and we decided on 29 May, after the evening *Appell* (about 9 p.m.), as the best time. That evening we all wore under our Army uniforms the "civilian" clothing we had been preparing for months: Army overcoats altered and dyed; trousers and slouch caps made from gray German blankets; knitted pullovers and ties; dyed khaki shirts, and so on. In addition we all had maps and home-made compasses.

After the *Appell* the twelve escapers and a look-out slipped into the canteen. After an hour the bribed sentry was reported to be at his post and I gave the signal for him to start looking the other way. Working frenziedly at the far end of the tunnel I cut round the collapsible tray I had inserted above the vertical shaft, and then heaved it upwards, muddy water streaming on to my face. The windows of the *Kommandantur* (the German quarters) loomed above me. The whole area was brilliantly lit by a floodlight only ten yards away. I climbed out on to the grass and Rupert Barry, immediately behind me, started to follow. My shadow was cast on the wall of the *Kommandantur*, and at that moment I noticed a second shadow beside my own. It held a revolver. I yelled to Rupert to get back as a voice behind me shouted, "*Hände hoch! Hände hoch!*" I turned to face a German officer levelling his pistol at me.

The Germans were hopping with excitement, and they eventually located the start of the tunnel in the canteen. One after the other the would-be escapers emerged from the manhole, and there was uproar when Colonel German himself, who was a member of that first escape party, appeared at the tunnel entrance. It was a big night indeed for the Germans.

The next day the usual inquiry took place. Special attention was paid to Kenneth Lockwood, of course, as canteen assistant. He was made to sit in front of a table on which reposed the official key of the canteen. Two German officers asked him "How did you get into the canteen?"

Kenneth replied, "Have you ever read *Alice in Wonderland*?"

This was duly interpreted. "No," they said. "Why?"

"Because Alice got through small doors and keyholes by eating something to make her smaller."

The interpreter had difficulty in getting this over, but suddenly they broke into roars of laughter and Kenneth was allowed to go.

Padre Platt's diary of the day of the escape includes the following passage:

> In the middle of the morning the "bribed guard," who is already in possession of Rm 100 and will receive the remainder once they are out, came up to our quarters to change the time of the getaway from 9:30 p.m. to 9:50. He affected to be nervous and stood behind a bookcase, sheltering from the eyes of another guard accompanying some workmen. But from my vantage point I saw an exchange of glances as he entered the room, and the workmen's guard became intensely absorbed in the rain outside the window.
>
> I went into the dormitory to Pat who was just ready to take his pack to the tunnel and said "Pat, the Germans know!" and told him what I had observed and what I was sure it meant.
>
> "Oh, go away," he said angrily. "You're trying to put the wind up us. Anyway, we've got to see it through now!"

Padre Platt's account must have been written down after the events and their consequences had taken place. If he wrote them before or during the episode, he would be guilty of endangering its success. His written material could be picked up and read at any time by German security, in which event the escape would be compromised.

Eggers' version of the story (in his book *Colditz: The German Story*) ends: "And the guard? He kept his 100 Marks; he got extra leave, promotion and the War Service Cross. It was worth it: our first big success and due solely to the loyalty of one of our men."

Peter Allan was brought back to Colditz on 31 May—a Saturday. He went straight to cells. He was limping. He had been absent for twenty-three days and everyone thought he had made the "home-run." It was a sad day and some bitter comments went the rounds when details of his story filtered through the grapevine channels. Peter had extricated himself from his palliasse after being dumped "somewhere in Colditz." He found himself on the ground floor of a deserted house in the town. He opened the window, climbed out into a small garden and from there to a road.

Peter reached Stuttgart and then Vienna. There he went into a park and fell asleep on a bench. When he awoke in the morning he found his legs paralyzed with cramp. He crawled to the nearest house and was taken to hospital, where his resistance broke down.

There was a heatwave during the last days of May and early June. The courtyard every day was strewn with shining, sweaty bodies in various stages of redness, rawness and suntan. The British orderlies decided to stage a mutiny and refused to serve their officers (it was taken for granted in the Geneva Convention of 1929 that officers were entitled to servants). Lieutenant-Commander Stevenson RN had become Senior Officer while the colonel was in cells. It was a pretty difficult task to get the orderlies in any kind of shape. Rooms were dirty, insolence was frequent, two of them regularly talked for our benefit about revolution and parasites. Stevenson stepped into the arena and if, by methods honored by long usage in the Navy, he made matters worse instead of better, the fault is not his entirely! Having drawn up a list of times and duties he called the orderlies together, and addressed them as though speaking from the bridge with the authority of the Admiralty behind him. But the orderlies declared they would take orders from no one but the Germans. With his bluff called in that fashion, there was just nothing more to be done. He had no power to punish disobedience other than by appealing to German authority, and the orderlies made a pretty shrewd guess that he would do no such thing.

Only three orderlies continued to do anything at all (Goldman was sick and in hospital). The job was far too big for three, so officers shared out the work of laying and clearing tables, sweeping floors, and so on. Padre Platt continues:

> Among the officers there has at no time been any lack of discipline. Colonel German has no more immediate authority over officers than over the

orderlies; but, there is an intelligent appreciation of the position, as well as an affection for the Colonel himself. He is precisely the right type of Senior Officer for a P.O.W. camp. There is not one British Officer who does not trust his administration.

An immediate consequence of Stevenson's effort to deal with the wretched orderly position came this afternoon. The orderlies as from noon are quartered on the other side of the *Hof* with the French and Polish orderlies. That will at least excuse us from suffering their insolence, and from their monopolization of the WCs and wash bowls. As from today instead of sharing food with us as hitherto they will draw separate rations and receive Red Cross parcels and other communal parcels on a strictly numerical basis.

The three, MacKenzie, Smith and Wallace, who have declared themselves ready to continue work will come over to these quarters at specified times. The others, led by Wilkins, Doherty and Munn, are forbidden to enter the officers' quarters at any time. The *Kommandant* has been officially requested to return the malcontents to a *Stalag*, and to bring other British soldiers to replace them.

On 31 May a second Frenchman, Lieutenant René Collin, escaped. He was never recaptured.

On 1 June, Eggers was promoted to *Hauptmann*. From that time he was mostly occupied as a camp officer in the *Schützenhaus*, which housed about 150 Russian officers, or at least officers of Russian origin, culled from the Allied armies and enemies of the Bolsheviks. The *Schützenhaus* ("shooting gallery") was a building with a paddock and range situated about half a mile from the Castle near the river. It was hired by the OKW in 1940 and was easily transformed into a detention camp. The White Russians had been captured while serving as officers, either in the Polish, Yugoslavian or French forces. They or their fathers had left Russia in 1920–1921 after fighting unsuccessfully against the Bolsheviks. They were not unruly and many even asked to be allowed to fight with the German Army in Russia. The OKW initially refused this request, but during the last days of 1941 the decision was reversed and Eggers escorted them to special camps at Zietenhorst and Wutzetz in Mecklenburg.

Morale among the prisoners was a matter of great importance, and one to which the Germans might be expected to give some attention. There had been a large influx of French and Belgians recently, necessitating a change-over of quarters between them and the Poles. In turn the Belgians were separated from the French. In addition a first contingent of ten Jewish French officers, picked from other prisons, had arrived in April and had been allotted separate quarters, which were immediately dubbed the Ghetto. Alain Le Ray considered that the German intention behind this was to subdue "escapist" morale by introducing diverting and conflicting elements into the community of POWs. They would seek to exploit any counter-assimilation of new elements by the creation of suspicion and distrust amongst the POW community.

Pierre Mairesse Lebrun (whose adventures I recount in Chapter 5) states that the French Jewish officers were transferred to Colditz as hostages. Certainly the French banker, Eli de Rothschild, who was among them, would be considered one. Few were escapers, and they were collected together from various camps. By now in mid-June they numbered about sixty officers. Many were doctors, French-born.

There was a morale-booster on 22 June, when the news broke of the declaration of war between Germany and Russia. The Germans had apparently started their invasion on 20 June. Polish officers claimed they had heard the news at 7 a.m. over the radio. The atmosphere was electric all day. Padre Platt records what happened:

> All day the atmosphere was charged as though heralding an electric storm. The outlet came immediately after *Lichts aus* [lights out] when, from the other side of the *Hof*. . . a carolling voice breathed on to the still, confined air the strains of the "Volga Boatmen." I grinned, as did scores of others—it was a good joke. Within a trice a score of voices wailed the lugubrious "Yoho heave-ho" and within another second not a score but a few hundred songsters leaned from the windows and joined in a dolorous crescendo which reverberated on the age-old walls.
>
> The guards on duty are of a new detachment. They are not yet *au fait* with the drill of an officers' camp, and perhaps on such a day a Russian song made them feel hot under the collar. One of the two pulled himself to his full height and in the interval between the singing of patriotic songs of first one nation then another, he told everyone in plain Deutsch to get to bed. In response to this a couple of hundred and more voices rose and fell in lively imitation of an air raid siren.
>
> Then the storm broke! The whistle of falling bombs, the roar of dive bombers (what lungs some of these fellows have!), and as a soft background, heard only at intervals, the song of the Russian river-folk. For twenty minutes it was a perfectly hideous pandemonium in which

everyone shared! Then someone, with the idea of adding realism to the show, bomb-whistled loudly and from a great height sent a beer bottle crashing on the sets below. It was followed by a second in which the beer had been well shaken, and the crash was appropriately louder. Cries of protest went up from almost every window, and no more were dropped, but the *Hof* was gay with newspaper-folded gliders which shot gracefully across the fifteen or twenty paces to the other side, and then petered out on the ground like falling stars.

Most of us were uneasy about the bottles. They were capable of the worst interpretation; but I am persuaded they were not meant to intimidate the guards, and did not drop near them. One of the Germans, however, went to the guardhouse to seek advice and help. An *Unteroffizier* returned with him, and after examining the smashed glass shouted something that was lost in the infernal din of battle songs, war-machine noises, and screams as of terrified women.

Three officers and several NCOs next arrived, and Priem, after looking at the mess of the broken bottles, called for what was presumably silence, though his voice was lost in the hideous noise. He tried again, with no better result. Then the order to shoot was given and, quick on the draw as the guards were, we were out of the windows and crouching on the floor a good deal quicker. Rifles cracked and bullets ricocheted, spattering the walls and splintering window panes. Silence! It was as still as a grave. Yes, P.O.W.s, more than most men, know the respect due to active fire-arms.

Appell was called, and we all trooped down to the *Hof* and fell in. Instead of being harangued as we expected, Major Menz, the second-in-command, called upon the Senior Officer of each nationality to line up before him. Then he said, "Throwing bottles at sentries is not gentlemanly behavior. In future you should not expect to be treated as gentlemen."

He did not address us, the rank and file, but dismissed the parade forthwith. Once back in our quarters the Colonel addressed us and, the typhoon being spent, no one was sorry when ordered to his bunk. The net results so far today are: radios disconnected, no newspapers delivered, all exercise cancelled.

Some time about noon, Micky Surmanowicz, who has just finished his punishment for breaking out of the cells and scaling the vertical wall of the guardhouse, rather than have the whole camp strafed vicariously, confessed to Priem (through Admiral Unrug) that he had dropped the two beer bottles. Courtyard gossip had it that the real culprits have failed to come forward and Micky has done so *pro bono public*. Courtyard gossip, however, is worth little. He is now back in solitary.

The *Kommandant* had intimated that serious consequences would ensue for all unless the bottle-throwing culprit owned up. He would be court-martialled in July.

On 25 June I was in a group of POWs marching down to the park when an attractive German girl passed by, going up the ramp towards the courtyard. The prisoners whistled their admiration, for she was a veritable bronze-haired Rhine Maiden, smartly dressed and handsome—a fitting consort for a Germanic deity.

As she swept by, her stylish wristwatch fell from her arm to the feet of Squadron-Leader Paddon. The Rhine Maiden did not notice, but Paddon, ever the gentleman, picked it up and shouted: "Hey, Miss, you've lost your watch."

The girl had already passed out of sight, so Paddon signed to the nearest guard and called out "*Das Fräulein hat ihre Uhr verloren.*" The guard took the watch and, running back up the ramp, shouted to a sentry in the courtyard to stop the girl. As he made to do so, the sentry suddenly noticed something wrong. A moment's scrutiny was enough. By the time our guard arrived panting with the watch, the Rhine Maiden was exposed. Her fine hat and abundant wig were off, revealing beneath the bald head of Lieutenant Boulé, who unhappily neither spoke nor understood German. He was a reserve officer, about forty-five years old, whose baldness and fresh complexion may have been the inspiration behind his disguise.

Loudspeakers in the prisoners' dayrooms were switched on from the guardhouse in the afternoons. POWs were regaled with concert music, news bulletins and propaganda. Lord Haw-Haw's nightly talks in English were treated with contempt. Another entertaining form of propaganda was known as a *Sondermeldung* (special report). The program would suddenly be interrupted. With a crackling sound, extra power would be switched on. A fanfare of trumpets would herald an important announcement. A Liszt prelude would hold the expectant audience for some bars, followed by a tattoo of drums. Then the announcer's voice would report in sonorous tones the latest victory on land, sea or air. Most commonly in 1941 *Sondermeldungs* concerned Allied shipping sunk by German U-boats. A brass band would then strike up the war song "*Wir fahren gegen Engeland*." To the further accompaniment of falling bombs, thunder of artillery and crackle of machine guns, the interlude would culminate with a fanfare heralding victory.

The intention was to demoralize the enemy. In Colditz windows everywhere would fly open. Musical instruments, the louder the better, would emerge and a cacophony of sound would fill the courtyard, reverberating down into the streets of the town. Knowledgeable prisoners calculated that the Germans had sunk the Allied merchant fleets more than once.

Gradually the loudspeakers were silenced one by one: not because of the broadcasts, but because their insides were of use to the escaping fraternity.

5

Tameless and Proud

Early Summer 1941

LIEUTENANT PIERRE MAIRESSE LEBRUN, a handsome French cavalry officer, had succeeded in escaping from Colditz once before, on 9 June. On one of the park outings, a very small Belgian officer, Sous-Lieutenant Verkest, had been hidden during the outgoing "numbering off" parades. He had simply clamped his legs around a colleague's thighs while two others supported him by the elbows. The man in the middle wrapped his coat and some blankets round the Belgian and then nonchalantly unfolded a German newspaper. During the recreation period, Lebrun, aided by a series of diversions, climbed into the rafters of an open-sided pavilion in the middle of the park. He was not missed at the return counts because Verkest of course stood in for him. Nor did the dogs, sent in after each park visit, get wind of him.

As arranged, a bugle blown from a Castle window signaled the "all clear." Lebrun descended, wearing a smart gray suit made from special pajamas sent to him in the winter, and climbed out of the park. He walked to the station at Gross Bothen, six miles from Colditz, to catch a train to Leipzig. At the ticket office he offered a 100-mark note. To his horror the clerk pointed out that it was invalid, dating from 1924 in the time of President Ebert. He found himself in the station-master's office, suspected first of being an English spy and then of being an escaper from Colditz. Pursuing the second idea, the station-master left Lebrun alone in his office while he went off to telephone. Lebrun promptly climbed out of the window. Unfortunately he dropped at the feet of a woman who at once shrieked with terror. In moments he was recaptured.

On Wednesday afternoon, 2 July, prisoners in the Castle heard volleys of shots from the direction of the park. Mairesse Lebrun was trying to escape again.

He had got twenty-one days' cells for his park attempt. His disappointment after yet another failure is easy to understand, having for brief moments held all the trump cards in his hands. It was galling to have succeeded in getting out of the fortress and to have failed later for such a banal reason as an out-of-date bank note, a note that had been hidden in a nut-shell inside a jar of jam for many months, after arriving in a next-of-kin food parcel. During his time in cells he had many dismal thoughts and moments of despondency, but refused to allow himself to become dismayed by his bad luck. He swore that he would not be a prisoner for more than a year, so there was no time to waste before getting a new escape plan under way. Yet it seemed impossible to expect to get out of that accursed fortress once again. Even in a camp full of experienced escapers he was now very much a marked man.

For prisoners in cells the exercise period each day was from 12:30 p.m. to 2:30 p.m. An officer, a *Feldwebel* and three armed guards kept the prisoners company in the barbed-wire enclosure in the park. With Lebrun was a comrade, Lieutenant Odry, who was also in cells following an escape attempt. For the first hour, Lebrun exercised and for the remaining hour lay in the sun. Each day he ran at least 800 yards. He knew already, with a fresh plan in his head, that his legs and lungs would need to be in good shape. He had now decided to make his break during an exercise period. He could see no other solution than to leave from under the very noses of the guards, and at the risk of being shot. He was planning to jump the park fence, and he needed to clear it at one go. He discussed the plan with his companion. Odry, though he felt it tantamount to committing suicide, knew that Lebrun's mind was made up. He agreed to help.

The escape clothes were simple. Running shorts, a short-sleeved shirt that he had carefully kept for such an occasion (it was the one he was wearing when first taken prisoner and was something like a Nazi shirt), a leather sleeveless jacket, socks and plimsolls with rubber soles. He had wrapped a razor, soap, a little sugar and chocolate in a silk cravat. A rather tight belt kept the bundle in place inside the jacket.

By 25 June he was ready. His comrades smuggled thirty *Reichsmarks* into his cell; they also sent him nourishing food every day—after all, he needed to be fit. For five exercise periods he was ready to go, but each time the circumstances were not quite right. These false starts put an enormous strain on his nerves—he was too tense before each of them even to eat.

On 2 July the sky was overcast. He told Odry as soon as they arrived in the park that, whatever happened, he was going to have a go that day. They would walk round and round for an hour to reassure the guards. As they walked they chose the exact spot for the leap over the wire, which was eight feet high. They marked the spot with a pebble. At last Lebrun warned Odry that the next circuit of the park would be the last. When they arrived at the pebble, Lebrun placed a foot in Odry's clasped hands; a strong heave and he was over the wire, landing in a dive rather awkwardly on the other side. Then he sprinted in a zig-zag for the wall of the Castle grounds, fifty yards away, as a sentry started shouting. The three sentries fired and the bullets hit the wall in front of him. He knew that he now had to get over while the sentries were reloading. He leaped, pulled himself on to the top of the wall and jumped down on the other side.

He ran for the nearby wood, and as he made his way through it he crossed a river twice, hoping in that way to throw the dogs off his scent. By the time he reached the edge of the wood, a siren was warning of an escaped prisoner, so it was now vital that he should not be seen by a farmworker. He decided to hide in a cornfield, slowly walking in backwards, lifting up the flattened stalks as he went. It was 2:30 p.m. He would have to wait until darkness fell at 10:30 p.m.

For three nights and two days it rained continuously, so being dressed in shorts it was better not to be seen by anyone. He travelled at night, following the River Mulde to the south-west, until on the morning of 5 July the sun started to shine again. As soon as his clothes were dry he walked into the town of Zwickau and stole a bicycle. He was still only fifty miles from Colditz, but now he looked like a German cyclist on tour. Eventually he reached Switzerland and freedom, nearly 400 miles away.

"If I succeed, I would be grateful if you would arrange for my personal possessions to be sent to the following address. . . . May God help me!" That message was on a label tied to a suitcase Pierre had left in his cell and which contained the few things that he treasured. With them was a piece of sausage, heavily peppered to put off the dogs who would certainly be taken to sniff his parcel and then sent on his heels. The *Kommandant* of the camp complied with the request, and some months later a box arrived for Pierre which contained the few souvenirs of his stay in Colditz. He was deeply grateful for this gesture from those he refers to as "True Soldiers."

Born in 1912, Lebrun's childhood was dominated by the Great War—for years afterwards it seemed the only topic of conversation. So, although his family had little military tradition, he joined the cavalry. Armored tanks had replaced many horses at the Saumur Cavalry School, from which he passed out in 1936, but horsemanship was the ruling passion of every young officer. Pierre was the youngest of his class, yet he outshone his brother aspirants in almost every sport he indulged in and he loved many forms: from polo to tennis, from dressage to Alpinism, from horse trials to swimming. He was a natural sportsman and Saumur in those days was made for such men. In fact, Saumur had altered very little from the gilded days before the First World War. From 1935 until the outbreak of the Second War, Pierre's reputation as a polo player and a showjumper grew to international proportions. His life became a continual grand tour of polo tournaments and *concours hippiques*. He was poised to compete in the Olympic horse trials of 1940 with his own personally trained horse. This was an outstanding achievement for a young career Army officer. In fact, Pierre admits that when war was declared he was more concerned at first with the dashing of all his personal hopes and ambitions than with the fears and tragedy of France once more at war.

His independent nature had already led him in peacetime to opt for any individual operation that came his way. As soon as war was declared he volunteered for and organized independent missions which he himself named the "*Corps Francs*." These were small bodies of troops, self-contained and sent forward into enemy areas as probes with various tasks to perform from pure reconnaissance to active sabotage or silencing of enemy positions. In fact he was originating the "commandos." He was also making sure for himself that he had an independent role to play, fighting his own war, unhampered by the irksome and ponderous inefficiency of commands emanating from above him. He thus evaded the possible consequences of what might have been branded as indiscipline.

Within weeks of the German attack on France in May 1940, Lebrun had won the Croix de Guerre and the Légion d'Honneur. On 14 June—the day the Germans entered Paris—he received orders to hold Châtel sur Moselle to the bitter end, a sacrificial mission to stop the Germans crossing the Moselle. He was in the extraordinary situation now of facing the Germans attacking from the west while he had the Maginot Line behind him to the east. There was little liaison and scant information after a month of fighting. He knew the war was going badly, but little did he know how badly. He thought perhaps the French were fighting another battle like that of the Marne. He did not even know that Paris had already fallen. He knew nothing of Dunkirk. He did not know that an armistice was demanded on 17 June. He had his orders so he fought on. On 22 June he finally decided to surrender. France officially capitulated on that day. His ammunition was finished. He had lost half of his men. The German commander, in fact, in accepting his surrender, accorded him and his survivors full military honors.

Pierre was taken for the night to a church in the village of Maurville not far from Châtel where, the next day, he found himself in dire trouble. One day accorded military honors—the next in a field with the other French officers facing four German machine-guns, about to be shot. The reason: during the night a German sentry had had his throat cut. Moreover his ears had been cut off. This was enough to convince the Germans that an African soldier was responsible (a unit of North African French black troops had fought with Pierre). Pierre and his brother officers were deemed responsible for the correct behavior of their troops and of course for any dereliction thereof. Summary justice and retribution for the murder was demanded.

One of the younger French officers, Lieutenant Mehu, was standing beside Pierre when a German command car drove into the field; out stepped several German officers to supervise the execution. Suddenly, Mehu exclaimed, *"Je connais bien cet officier là!"* Hurriedly he told Lebrun that the officer he had recognized had been his opposite number in Berlin when he was in the French Ministry of Foreign Affairs, some time before the outbreak of war. Mehu broke ranks in front of the machine-guns, approached the German officer and saluted. There was immediate recognition on a friendly note, and the execution was called off.

Pierre and his whole contingent were transported to a temporary POW camp at Lunéville where they were held for a few days. Pierre admits, as do so many others who found themselves in a similar situation, that this was the time he should have chosen to escape. He was still in France. Escape was comparatively easy. He was held back by rumors of a cessation of hostilities and early liberation. He felt he had a duty to stand by his junior officers and his troops in the same predicament.

At Lunéville the separation of regular Army officers from the rest took place. Instead of being liberated and sent home (there had been rumors of a ceasefire) he was transported into Germany and ended up at Warburg prison, arriving on 5 August 1940, a few weeks after his capture. The camp consisted of a few huts on a treeless plain near the small village of Dössel, and was surrounded by the regulation double barbed-wire fences. Watch towers every 200 yards were manned by armed guards, with foot patrols between each of these points. Only an ancient feudal castle relieved the dreariness of the landscape.

On 11 October he and a colleague escaped, having cut through thirty-five strands of wire. Hiding up in a wood three days later, they were surprised by German soldiers on exercise; Lebrun got away but his colleague, still recovering from wounds, was recaptured. After many adventures Lebrun came to the frontier at the Swiss enclave on the German side of the Rhine, opposite Basle. Knowing that he must be patient until nightfall, he decided to hide in a wood 300 yards away. As he crossed a field towards it a boy who was looking after some cows called out "*Bonsoir, monsieur.*" Lebrun paid no attention. But he had already been careless. He had been seen surveying the sentries from the top of a hill. Less than an hour after reaching the wood, a patrol on the look-out for him caught sight of him, and fired as he tried to sprint for the frontier. He was recaptured and handed over to the Gestapo. A Gestapo officer who spoke fluent French interrogated him. Lebrun had nothing to tell him except about meeting the boy whose "*Bonsoir*" had puzzled him. At that the interrogator exclaimed "*Mon pauvre vieux*, you were in Switzerland!"

Soon he was returned to Warburg. His friends had gone. The French had been moved and replaced by Poles. None of his possessions remained. After five days in cells Lebrun was sent to Münster, *Oflag* VID, where he was given a noisy welcome. At that time, out of 3,000 prisoners in the camp, he was the only escaper. Everyone asked for information. Escaping was the constant topic of conversation, but although many had all sorts of plans, very few risked putting them to the test. Lebrun decided to have another go. The Dutch frontier was only forty miles away. He passed through the main gate easily with a group of workmen from whom he had previously stolen, item by item, the necessary clothing. But he got no further.

On 3 December 1940, without any explanation, Lebrun was removed from *Oflag* VID and transferred to Colditz.

Sixty-eight Dutch officers arrived in Colditz on 24 July. The population of the camp was now approaching 500 officers and other ranks. There were 140 Poles, fifty British and about 250 French.

At this time, Eggers, as has been mentioned in the previous chapter, had security responsibility for the *Schützenhaus*, the lower prison in Colditz town. It was not heavily guarded like the Castle and it housed a number of French officers and men of White Russian origin who had been syphoned off, like the Jews, from other camps.

The White Russians were mostly members of the Russian Orthodox faith and were allowed the special concession of receiving the Orthodox bishop of Dresden and his choir for services at a few important religious festivals during the year. The 17/18 July was one such occasion. When the bishop and his mixed choir of men and women departed, the French White Russian Lieutenant Tatischeff was missing at the evening roll-call. It transpired that a lady of the choir, Miss

Hoffman, had succumbed to his amorous advances and had helped him to escape. He successfully reached France. She was apprehended and imprisoned.

The escaping season was now in full flood; hardly a day passed without an incident. On 26 July, Lieutenant Lados and Captain Harry Elliott made an unsuccessful attempt to hide on the way back from the park. On 28 July, the French Lieutenants Perrin and Thibaud, having cut bars in the window of an air shaft in the *Saalhaus*, descended three stories by rope and posing as German workmen with regulation yellow armbands walked out of the Castle through the gate to the park. Having let them pass, the duty sentry at the last gate had second thoughts. Although he had no pass checklist at this post and the display of brass discs was not required there, he reported the matter, and soldiers on bicycles caught up with the escapers on the way to Leisnig railway station.

On 31 July, the British at night broke through a wall into a lavatory closet on the German side. Eight of a party of twelve, dressed as civilians, passed through the hole. They had to find their own way out of the *Kommandantur* and then out of the Castle grounds. After forty minutes, the men climbing through at five-minute intervals, our stooges at the window had still not spotted any of them exiting from the *Kommandantur*. I advised the remaining four to stay put. It was just as well. The Germans knew all about our hole, and the eight had been allowed to creep down a long corridor outside the *Abort* (lavatory) before being quietly apprehended.

Such a failure was demoralizing in itself (not that I had ever had much confidence in the venture), and no doubt the Germans had deliberately played the whole thing out to demoralize us as much as possible. To make matters worse, each of the eight had been caught in his full escaping kit—a waste of months of effort by the prisoners and a valuable prize for the Germans.

At this period of captivity, escape equipment had become organized. Although every officer had not yet been equipped with identity papers, each had a home-made compass of one kind or another, a set of maps painfully traced over and over again from originals, and each was given some German money. Every officer possessed his private escape kit, which he had ample time to devise during the long hours of enforced idleness. It was surprising what could be produced in the way of civilian clothing by dyeing and altering, by cutting up blankets, and by imaginative sewing and knitting. Officers had their specialties and turned out articles in quantity.

I, for instance, concentrated on the manufacture of "gor blimey" caps and rucksacks. My particular brand of cap, cut out of any suitably colored blanket, having a peak stiffened with a piece of leather or other water-resisting stiffener and lined with a portion of colored handkerchief and a soft-leather head-band, looked quite professional. My rucksacks were not always waterproof; they were made from dark-colored or dyed, tough Army material, with broad trouser-braces adapted as straps, and the flaps and corners neatly edged with leather strips cut from boot tongues. They would pass in Germany as workmen's rucksacks.

Dyeing with "ersatz" coffee or purple pencil-lead became a fine art. The blue Royal Air Force uniform was readily adaptable and with skilful tailoring could become a passable civilian suit. Of course, real civilian clothing was what every officer ultimately aimed at possessing. I described in *The Colditz Story* one of the ways we tried to obtain it.

> During one of the very rare visits of a German civilian dentist to supplement the work of the French Army dentist, he was accompanied by two leech-like sentries, who kept so close to him that he hardly had room to wield his forceps. The dentist's torture chamber (I had blunted all the drills trying to make keys) was approached through a number of small rooms and had two doors, one of which was supposed to be permanently locked but which was opened on nefarious occasions with the aid of a universal key. On the back of this door was a coat-hook, and on the hook the German dentist hung his Homburg hat and a fine fur-collared tweed overcoat.
>
> This was "big game." Dick Howe, with another British officer, "Scorgie" Price, and a French officer named Jacques Prot were soon hot on the trail.
>
> Dick arranged to pay an officer's dentist's bill. The dentist was paid in *Lagergeld* [camp money] and Dick sought out an officer with a heavy bill—it came to a hundred marks. He collected the whole sum in one-mark notes. This would give him plenty of time. He arranged a signal with the other two. The operative word was "Right." When Dick said "Right" loudly, Price was to open the locked door and remove the coat and hat.
>
> Dick went to the dentist's room and insisted on interrupting the dentist's work to pay his brother-officer's bill. He drew him over to a table; the two sentries dutifully followed; and Dick started to count out laboriously his *Lagergeld*.
>
> "*Eins, zwei, drei* . . ." he started and carried on to *zehn*, at which point he looked up to see if he had the full attention of the dentist and the guards. "Not quite," he thought, and he carried on painfully, "*elf, zwölf*. . . ." By the time he reached *zwanzig* he had all their eyes riveted on the slowly rising pile of notes, so he said "Right." As he continued he sensed nothing had happened. At *dreissig* he repeated "Right" a little louder. Again nothing

happened. At *vierzig* he filled his lungs and shouted "Right" again. Still nothing happened. Doggedly he continued, holding the attention of all three, as his reserves of *Lagergeld* dwindled. As *fünfzig, sechzig, siebzig* passed his "Rights" crescendoed, to the amusement of his three spectators. Nothing happened. An operatic bass would have been proud of Dick's final rendering at *achtzig, neunzig,* and *hundert.* The scheme had failed, and the only persons laughing were the Germans at Dick's, by this time, comic act.

The dentist, still guffawing, collected all the notes together and before Dick's crestfallen gaze, started recounting them. As he reached *zehn* he shouted "R-r-reight," and Dick, to his own utter astonishment, felt, rather than heard, the door open behind them, and sensed an arm appearing around it. Before the dentist had reached *zwanzig* the door had closed again. Dick continued the pantomime and eventually, after assuring himself that the coat and hat had really disappeared, he retired from the scene with apologies—a shaken man.

The concealment of such contraband was a perennial problem. The common hiding-places and those at various times (often found out by the Germans) were: behind false-backed cupboards, in trap-door hides, under floorboards and sewn into mattresses and overcoat-linings. Small items were often sealed in cigarette tins, weighted and dropped into lavatory cisterns or concealed in stores of food. There were myriad possibilities.

The escape attempts continued. On 2 August, Lieutenant Lados, in the cells from his previous attempt, escaped by a rope made from torn strips of blanket. He had filed through a bar on his window. He reached the Swiss border but was recaught, utterly exhausted. Then on 4 August, two British, Don Thom and "Bertie" Boustead, attired as young German Hitler Youths in sports gear, attempted a get-away in the park. Their Hitler salutes were so bad that they were stopped and hauled over the coals by a German sergeant. Unable to reply effectively to his questions in German, their game was up. Eggers states that their disguise, shorts and vests with a swastika on the chest, were first class.

6

Sixty-Eight Dutchmen

Summer 1941

ON 16 AUGUST, A SATURDAY, a major upheaval took place. Two Dutch officers had been missing from *Appells* the day before. The Dutch did nothing by halves! Five of their officers were now missing at a *Sonderappell* (special roll-call) soon after the park walk. The Germans could not believe their eyes or their arithmetic. It is time to explain the presence of these Dutchmen.

They were nearly all Netherlands East Indies Army officers. At the outbreak of war, they had sailed home with their troops to Holland in order to help the mother country. When Holland was occupied, the German High Command offered an amnesty to all those Dutch officers who would sign a certain document.

The capitulation of Holland had taken place on 15 May 1940. The Queen of the Netherlands, together with the other members of the Royal family and the ministries of the Government, had already landed in England. Meanwhile the Dutch armed forces were regarded as prisoners of war by the German High Command. By the end of May, General Christiansen, commanding the German forces, received a letter from Hitler indicating the terms upon which the Dutch armed forces were to be released. For conscripts there was no problem; they were released unconditionally. For the regular forces it was another matter. A document, or "Declaration" as it was called, was to be signed by all career officers of the regular armed forces of Holland. It read:

> I hereby declare on my word of honor that during this war, or as long as the Netherlands is in a state of war with the German Reich, I shall not take part in any way, either directly or indirectly, in the fight against Germany. I

shall not take any form of action, either positive or negative, which would endanger the Reich in any possible way.

The reason why a small group of sixty-eight officers—later called the Colditz group—did not sign was, briefly, that to sign the Declaration was in conflict with the oath of allegiance to the Queen, taken by all officers. This made it impossible to sign a conflicting declaration on their honor to the Germans. After all, the Queen and her ministers had gone to England to continue the fight against the Germans and the Dutch colonies (not yet occupied) were still part of the Queen's realm.

On 14 July 1940, 2,000 officers and 12,400 other ranks signed the declaration at various centers in the country and were later sent home. Seventy-three officers, including three generals, three Dutch Home Army officers and twelve officer cadets, refused to sign and were sent to a POW camp, Juliusberg at Soest in Westphalia. Later the generals were sent to another camp to join General Winkelman (the Dutch commander-in-chief) and two other generals. The Queen was reportedly most upset when she heard that practically the entire Dutch officer corps had signed the declaration (though many later joined the Resistance).

The three Dutch officers of the Home Army who refused their signatures were Captains H. J. van der Hoog and N. Hogerland, and Lieutenant J. J. L. Baron van Lynden. They arrived in Colditz included in the "sixty-eight." Van der Hoog, of noble bearing, stood tall and erect and walked the yard alone with a military step. A long black cloak gathered over his shoulders like a toga earned him the title of Julius Caesar. Baron van Lynden, also tall but rather bowed, had been an *aide-de-camp* to Queen Wilhelmina and had become in the war an adjutant of General Winkelman. Two other naval adjutants were Captain H. W. Romswinckel and Lieutenant D. J. van Doorninck.

Three others were Lieutenant-Colonel T. Rooseboom, chief of Dutch home intelligence, whose orders for the detention before the war of certain Dutch Nazis were afterwards betrayed by the Dutch Nazi Party to the Germans; Captain J. D. Schepers, a military lawyer who had remained free until the Germans discovered that he had been responsible for shipping to England 800 German prisoners of war: parachutists, aviation personnel and advance shock troops, just a few hours before the advancing German Army could rescue them; and the third, Lieutenant J. S. M. Eras, a reservist, detained for the same reason.

After many vicissitudes, including unending wordy battles with the Germans and numerous escape attempts, the "sixty-eight" finally ended up lock, stock and barrel in Colditz. (Two Netherlands East Indies Army officers,

Captain H. Trebels and Lieutenant F. van der Veen, had escaped successfully earlier and were not in the sixty-eight.) Since they all spoke German fluently, were as obstinate as mules and as brave as lions, heartily despised the Germans and showed it, they presented special difficulties as prisoners!

Their Senior Officer was Major Engles. They were always impeccably turned out on parade and maintained a high standard of discipline among themselves. From the beginning, close relations were maintained between the British and Dutch and, though at the start this did not involve revealing the full details of respective plans, it soon developed into a close co-operation, which was headed on the Dutch side by their escape officer, Captain van den Heuvel.

The Dutch were not very long at Colditz before van den Heuvel warned me of an impending attempt. "Vandy," as he was inevitably called, was a tall, big-chested man with a round face, florid complexion and an almost permanent broad grin. His mouth was large enough in repose, but when he smiled it was from ear to ear. He had hidden depths of pride and a terrific temper, revealed on rare occasions. He spoke English well, but with a droll Dutch accent.

The Germans could never tell if anything was going on among the Dutch. Their behavior was always the same—perfect discipline, quiet in their manner, naturally and easily dropping into and out of a conversation whenever they wished. They did not make themselves conspicuous. Hence their success in springing surprises. Only then would they approach the bounds of familiarity, with the broadest of grins among themselves, occasionally shared with the British. They rejoiced in the park exercise ground as a field for escape maneuvers, and profited by it more than anyone else. Within weeks of their arrival at Colditz, they achieved some break-outs.

Van den Heuvel, as escape officer, had decided to give up all attempts himself, merely organizing and assisting in escapes for others. He was indispensable and many successful escapes were attributable to his tireless efforts.

While taking a stroll in the park one day he had noticed a concrete manhole top, flush with the ground and closed off by a wooden lid, three feet square. The lid had hinges on one side and a few small air holes. Having summoned a few others, who seated themselves around the lid and kept up an animated conversation, he lifted the top a few inches. It was a well—fairly deep, too.

The next time the Dutch went for a walk they sat right on top of the well while Vandy carefully lowered a stone on a string through one of the holes. The cavity proved to be about ten feet deep with five feet of water. So many POWs had looked at this well cover, walked across it and probably sat on it. Nobody had realized the tremendous possibilities it offered.

Captain A. L. C. Dufour and Lieutenant J. G. Smit, officers of the Netherlands East Indies Army, would be the first to have a go at it. Lieutenant E. H. Larive (who later described the escapes in *The Man Who Came in from Colditz*) primed them for hours on "musts" and "must nots" for the journey to Switzerland. He drew them a detailed map of the Swiss border region of Singen.

On Wednesday afternoon, 13 August 1941, the Dutch assembled for the park exercise parade. British officers had been temporarily deprived of this privilege and as usual tried to get out in borrowed uniforms, but two were recognized by the guards when counted and were sent back. This proved to be a lucky coincidence.

An hour after their arrival in the park the plan was set in motion. The Dutch formed a great circle around the well and were throwing a football across to each other. Gradually they moved in closer. When the circle was so small that they touched each others' elbows and had effectively screened the well, Dufour and Smit moved into the middle. The sentries along the fence were being watched and at a suitable moment a signal was given. Dufour lifted the lid and they quickly slipped in, closing the lid above them. The ball game went on and gradually the circle was enlarged again until the groups broke up. Nothing had been noticed.

The trickiest part, however, had yet to come.

A whistle sounded indicating that the time was up and the prisoners formed up near the gate for counting before being marched off. "*Donnerwetter*—two short!" The Germans searched the grounds, but as expected, overlooked the well, flush with the ground. Why not? The prisoners had overlooked it for a long time. Someone suggested that the numbers were quite correct, as the guard commander had sent two Englishmen back before leaving the Castle.

Although they had counted the prisoners on arrival at the park and should have realized two were missing, the remark seemed to have its effect in casting doubts. The prisoners were marched back forthwith. On arrival at the camp, however, they were not allowed inside. At the outer gate they were recounted seven times by three different Germans who disagreed as to whether there were two short or not.

The only answer was an *Appell* for all those who had not been out in the park. The Germans still could not make up their minds. The park parade was marched in and there was another *Appell*, this time the whole camp together. The answer foxed them completely—all present! The German officers present deliberated for five minutes and then gave up. The parade was dismissed.

They had slipped up on one point.

The Dutch group always stood in rows of five when fallen in, which made counting easy. The Germans merely counted the rows and so many times five plus an odd man or two gave the correct number. From the front, side and back the Dutch formed neat, straight lines. The Germans were so used to this that they had stopped looking from the side; if they had done so that day they would have noticed that the lines were not quite straight. To conceal the gaps caused by two absentees, two rows of four had to shift position slightly, thereby disturbing the "dressing" of the line. As customary, the Germans had only counted the rows—the officer from the front, the sergeant from the back. Correct!

During evening *Appell* the same positions were adopted. The duty officer counted them from the front, made his calculations and said, "*Stimmt*"—correct! The sergeant completed his check-up and reported two rows of four! "*Unmöglich*," said the duty officer—impossible. He had personally counted them and found everything in order.

The next morning the same officer counted the Dutch very carefully, checking row by row. "Correct!" he told his subordinate. "You see!"

After roll-call the Dutch thanked two Poles who had taken the places of Dufour and Smit.

The Polish roll-call, however, had not disclosed any absentees either. They had their own method.

They had two corner rooms in their wing which were interconnected by a little sliding panel window in the wall, making it possible to move from a bed in one room to a bed in the other room faster than a person could walk from one room to the other. During the *Appell*, four Poles were reported sick in bed. A German orderly was sent up to check; as soon as he had seen the two Poles in the first room, the latter shot like rabbits through the hole in the wall into the next room and tucked themselves nicely away under the blankets where they were counted again.

"Four sick in bed," reported the German orderly.

This ruse was kept up for twenty-four hours. Lieutenants Flanti Steinmetz and Larive himself would make an actual attempt at breaking out through the well on 16 August while three others, Lieutenants Douw van der Krap, van Lynden and "Bear" Kruimink (all Royal Netherlands Navy), would hide inside the Castle for an indefinite period before actually attempting another form of get-away at a suitable moment. The Germans would be looking for five escapers when only Steinmetz and Larive had escaped. By the time the search activities for five absentees had ceased, the concealed three would at least be free from the pressure of a hunt. A camouflaged hole in the wall of the Dutch quarters led to a concealed space between two rooms. Ten days later, unfortunately, the Germans made a very thorough search of their quarters and discovered the three missing men.

An additional distraction in the exercise park was added to the original scheme, to draw attention away from the well. After arrival in the park, Lieutenant G. Dames settled himself under a tree near the barbed wire, in between two guards, and, leaning backwards, was seen to be quietly reading a book. At a given signal, he began cautiously cutting a hole in the wire behind his back.

While the Dutch circle gradually closed in on the well, another officer started to pull playfully at the barbed wire in another section of the fence until he had infuriated the nearest guard. The latter's angry shouts drew the attention of all the other guards. When he was just about ready to shoot, the circle closed in and Steinmetz and Larive dropped into the well.

At this moment, Dames, having completed his little hole, quietly pretended to creep through. As expected, he was seen practically the moment he tried. Raising his hands in surrender, he and others in the park shouted at the top of their voices: "Run, run!"

The two escapers in the well took off their shoes, socks, pants and underwear, which they hung around their necks, and, descending a ladder of rungs, went right down into the water. To conceal this presence further they had a dark gray blanket which they spread out above their heads, holding it up in the corners with their hands. The camouflage might work.

In a matter of minutes the Germans would start their escape-alarm system, if the search of the park proved fruitless. The two would remain in the well until it grew dark at 10 p.m. It was 3 p.m. now. The ruse whereby Dames made a hole in the wire, and the shouts of "Run, run!", had the desired effect. The Germans only made a cursory search of the park after the count had revealed two were missing. After a couple of hours, when it became unlikely they would look in the well, the two Dutchmen crept out of the water and remained on the rungs inside the well; it was at least dry there and, by pressing their backs against the wall, they could rest their aching arms. Time crawled by for the two men and splitting headaches gradually numbed their brains, while their lungs heaved laboriously in the effort to breathe. Larive suddenly realized what the matter was—lack of oxygen—they were slowly suffocating. He dragged himself up the steps, lifted the lid an inch and inserted a pocket-knife to keep it ajar. With lips touching the lid they sucked in the life-bringing air.

At 10 p.m. it was pitch dark. They nipped out, climbed over the barbed-wire fence and scaled the twelve-foot wall via a tree. They reached Leisnig at daybreak, in time for the first train.

Steinmetz, who spoke the better German, bought tickets to Dresden. Aware of the fact that all railway stations in the neighborhood would have been alerted to look out for suspicious characters, they dreaded this moment. Incredibly enough, nothing happened. They did not waste any time in Dresden and went straight on to Ulm.

Once in the train they asked the conductor for the best route to Ulm and he advised them to change at Markt-Redwitz instead of travelling via Regensburg as they had intended to do. The connections at Ulm would be better he said. The journey was quiet and peaceful. They had money enough to travel in comfort all the way to Singen. They enjoyed the scenery like tourists. The only scare they had was the appearance from time to time of the military police patrols. Fortunately, however, they seemed to confine their activities to checking military personnel.

At midnight they arrived in Nuremberg and discovered to their dismay that the train for Ulm did not leave until 6 a.m. They eventually found what they were looking for—just off the main street, completely in the dark, a church. In the garden were a number of benches, most of which were occupied by courting couples. As it might look strange for two men to sit in a garden in the dark, they had to pretend to be lovers as well.

At 6 a.m. they caught their train and arrived in Singen an hour before dusk. After handing in their tickets they left the station and turned left, right and left again, crossed the single line, turned left and came to a road running parallel to the double track. Larive could not miss. He was sure and confident as if it were his home town. He had learned something about Singen in the past.

Maybe he was overconfident. They suffered many vicissitudes during that afternoon: they were spotted and suspected by guards, they had to run for it, they were shot at and the frontier alarm was raised. They were near Gottmadingen. Hiding in a wood they observed great activity at a nearby guardhouse. The sky was heavily overcast and dusk was falling quickly now—a few minutes later it even started to rain. Good, the harder the better; it would make the night pitch black and the guards less observant. A group of soldiers on bicycles left the guardhouse and rode off towards the village. Every quarter of a mile one got off and took up guard duty on the road, which they had to cross to reach the Swiss border. That was not so good, but it was an advantage to know they were there. Suddenly they heard rifle shots behind them and the barking of dogs. The hunt was on! Not having the scent, the Germans were probably trying to raise the escapers by firing their rifles in the hope that the dogs would pick up the scent or sound of running feet.

After a quarter of an hour the hunters seemed to have moved on and only the pitter-patter of rain dripping from the leaves could be heard.

At about 10 p.m. Larive and Steinmetz left the wood. Utter darkness reigned all around, making it impossible to see more than a few yards ahead. With the aid of their phosphorus-dialed compass, they struck south, creeping forward on elbows and stomachs, yard by yard, repeatedly stopping to listen. Gradually they approached the road and moved even more stealthily when they could distinguish the outline of trees.

Before crossing the road they took off their shoes and then slithered across, still on their stomachs. They were not taking any more chances and they kept up their reptile-like progress for the next hundred yards before putting on shoes to proceed on foot. It was about 2 a.m. now. It had taken them four hours to cover 600 yards!

Carefully picking their way between the crops they slowly moved on, as if walking on thin ice, constantly stopping to listen for any signs of danger. On a southerly course they hit a road running due south. That would be the road from Gottmadingen to Switzerland. Then they noticed a signpost; Steinmetz climbed up the pole to distinguish the letters. "God! *Deutsches Zollamt*—German Customs!" he exclaimed and dropped down like a dead duck. If there were to be a sentry anywhere it would be here! Away they went again, as fast as they could.

According to Larive's calculations they should have crossed the border by now, but . . . had they? They were becoming extremely tired; they had been on their way for two and a half days now, without sleep and with only a couple of bars of chocolate to eat, while constantly on the alert or on the move. They were soaked through and the chill had numbed them. They leaned against the wall of a barn. They were now liable to do stupid things. Suddenly the stinging white beam of a strong torch flashed on them, making it impossible to see what was behind it. They could hear only the slushing sound of heavy boots in the mud—coming closer.

They stood as if riveted to the spot, rigid with fright and pinned to the wall by that beam. Three feet in front of them the invisible man stopped and played the beam from left to right and from top to bottom. Then they heard what they feared to hear most of all—German! "*Wer sind Sie? Was machen Sie hier?* Who are you? What are you doing here?" Then he spoke again: "*Sie sind in der Schweiz. Sie müssen mit mir kommen!* You are in Switzerland. You'll have to come with me."

In the village further down, called Ramsen, the police took particulars and when they heard that they were Dutch asked whether they knew Trebels and van der Veen. These two had crossed the border at the same spot and were actually taken into custody by the same Swiss guard.

The Swiss had no knowledge, however, of Dufour and Smit.

Back in Colditz the park was now so suspect as an avenue of escape that all walks were cancelled for some time. During the search in the Dutch quarters after the five were found missing, the Germans discovered a map "with detailed instructions how to get from Tuttlingen in south-west Germany to the Swiss frontier and over it."

There is a long story behind this map. After the Dutch capitulation, Larive had found himself in the naval barracks at Amsterdam, where officially the Dutchmen were prisoners of war, though they were free to move where and when they liked. When the time came on 15 July 1940 to sign the Declaration, Larive refused, and was joined by only one of his colleagues from the barracks, Lieutenant Steinmetz. They were taken to *Oflag* VIA in Soest. From Soest Larive escaped. He reached the Swiss frontier near Singen, where he was trapped, and taken to the area headquarters of the Gestapo. He was escorted into a room. Behind a desk was a big, bull-like man in a dressing-gown. In the corner a young man was typing. Larive told them he was an officer of the Merchant Navy, called into active service last year in the Far East. He was now on his way back to the Far East.

The "bull" quite believed his story and became rather friendly in the end. He told Larive that he had been chief cook in a Dutch hotel a few years before the war. Larive described the last part of his journey. The "bull" remarked that the only clever thing Larive had done was getting off the train at Singen—all the rest was damned stupid.

"Why?" asked Larive.

"You must have known that Singen was the last station where anyone could get on or off the train without showing an identity card."

"No, that was just a guess."

"Having managed to get that far it was stupid to take a train instead of walking across the border," he said.

"Well, the reason is that I didn't know how to get through the defense line."

"Defense line!" the "bull" exploded. "Defense line against whom? Surely not against those damned Swiss? What a crazy idea. There are no defenses at all; we haven't got a single man to guard the border! You could have walked straight across."

From a drawer he produced a staff map and Larive had to point out the route he had taken.

"You fool," he said. "Look." He indicated the spot where Larive had unknowingly walked past a part of the Swiss border jutting into Germany, at a distance of only about 300 yards. He asked Larive whether he remembered a certain house at the edge of a wood and the road leading past that house into the wood—the sharp bend further down? Well, a quarter of a mile beyond that bend Larive should have turned left off the main road and followed a path. After a few hundred yards, he would have been in Switzerland—just as easily as that.

Larive asked him for some more information on various points. Naturally he would not manage to escape for the second time and besides, the war would be over by Christmas; it was not worth the risk of being shot for such a short term of imprisonment. Larive asked questions about everything which would be of any interest to an escaper, and he learned a lot.

Within a year, five of his friends as well as himself escaped into Switzerland, making use of this information, and crossing the border as indicated by the "bull."

In November 1940, Larive was moved to *Oflag* VIIIC in Juliusburg, near Breslau. The new camp was small and rather peculiar. It consisted of part of a nunnery-cum-orphanage and was called Amalienstift. Two-thirds of the main building had been requisitioned for a POW camp, while the remaining part was still occupied by nuns and orphans. There were about 450 Belgian prisoners and four Dutch officers, the latter having been sent there direct from Holland. Among them were Trebels and van der Veen, and it was from Juliusburg that they made their escape, crossing safely into Switzerland by means of Larive's information about Singen.

Also at *Oflag* VIIIC was van den Heuvel. The Germans soon realized that he was the leading personality in the escape organization and they tried to get rid of him. A sentry was posted in his cell with orders to shoot him at his first suspicious move—so van den Heuvel remained most of the time in his bunk. When the Germans could not eliminate him this way, they withdrew the sentry from the cell and tried another way.

Van den Heuvel took his daily exercise by walking up and down along the barbed-wire fence. Their intention was to take him out for his airing during a meal hour when the other prisoners would be inside the building. The sentry accompanying him outside would remain out of the way and van den Heuvel would then be shot close to the wire from one of the machine-gun towers, allegedly trying to escape. One of the *Oflag* censors, however, a German who had lived most of his life in Belgium and had often passed the Dutch useful information in return for chocolate, coffee and other items, warned them in time against the plot. The next day several Dutchmen remained outside the building, unobtrusively reading newspapers and chatting on the steps. Half an hour before van den Heuvel was due to be "aired," the guards in the machine-gun towers were relieved by soldiers who were recognized as Nazis, belonging to the SS, although it was not the usual time for guard-changing. Van den Heuvel had been warned.

He stayed close to the wall. It was a disappointed security officer who saw van den Heuvel stroll into his cell again afterwards.

Machiel van den Heuvel was born in 1900 in Haarlenmonermeer in the Netherlands. He must have spent some of his youth in the Netherlands East Indies for at the age of twenty-two he attended the military school in the Netherlands East Indies, only returning in 1924, posted to the Royal Military Academy at Brede in Holland. From 1939 to 1940 he was chief of staff of a Dutch Army unit with the rank of captain.

Towards the end of July 1941 the Dutch were given two days notice of a move. Their destination was Colditz.

Four days after the escape of Steinmetz and Larive, a Polish Lieutenant Kroner from Colditz escaped while hospitalized at Königswartha on 20 August. Much later it was known through the underground that he had reached Poland successfully. Gall-bladder trouble seemed to be the easiest of all diseases to fake. Kroner was having terrible pains that summer, it seemed. The *Tierarzt* was suspicious but finally conceded that the symptoms were genuine. His fury at the escape of two previous "patients," Lieutenants Just and Bednarski, in April, had died down by August. Kroner's condition gradually improved at Königswartha. So did his escape preparations and, in due course, he changed his blue-and-white hospital garb for civilian clothes and disappeared under the comparatively unguarded wire all round the hospital.

Padre Platt reported at this time symptoms of a different kind at the *Schützenhaus.*

> Fifty-four Yugoslavian officers and troops are quartered at the *Schützenhaus*, the building in which the baronial militia of the *Schloss* were housed in the days of ancient splendour. (This is also where the Polish orderlies live.) The news of their arrival here, about a fortnight ago, reached us by underground; but today an open intimation of their presence came by way of a letter to the Colonel. It was from the Yugoslavian senior officer, Oberstleutnant Serg M. Altuhov, asking if the British officers could relieve their necessity in the matter of food. For four months—the letter said—they have existed solely on German rations and are in greatly reduced physical condition.
>
> A mess meeting was called, and after Major Cleeve—acting for the Colonel—had read the letter, he said that the Colonel thought a gift of twenty parcels out of the fifty we have in the store would be welcome.

Someone moved thirty, and finally the whole fifty were unanimously voted to them. A further vote called for gifts of cigarettes and tobacco and any such private stores as could be spared. . . .

There is one fly in the ointment which has greatly agitated several members of our mess, viz. that the *Schützenhaus* is reported to be a center of collaboration. The French officers here have this information. There are no British at the *Schützenhaus* and, before the Yugos came, it was solely a French camp.

Seven new orderlies arrived last night from a camp in Sudetenland. They say they have been working eleven hours a day in the coal mines. They have eaten us out of house and harbour this morning and almost as thoroughly denuded our wardrobes. Three of them were entirely without underclothes and socks.

7

A Bolt from the Blue

Late Summer 1941

ON 28 AUGUST, LIEUTENANT Airey Neave tried out his German uniform on the Germans. He was to pose as a *Gefreiter* (corporal). After many experiments in dyeing he had achieved an approximation to the field-gray color of the German uniform; a pair of RAF trousers, and a uniform tunic altered by a Polish tailor, were transformed in this way. Barter obtained a pair of jackboots from a Polish orderly. German insignia were manufactured out of painted cardboard. A bayonet and scabbard were carved for him out of wood by Lieutenant R. T. R. "Scarlet" O'Hara. This was hung from a cardboard "leather" belt with a tinfoil buckle. For a cap he had to use a modified ski-cap suitably dyed. This disguise was to be used in twilight—anything brighter would expose it for what it was.

There remained the question of maps, a compass and money. He traced in Indian ink the neighborhood of the Swiss frontier from a map made available and hid it carefully in a crevice in a wooden partition of the lavatory. A Dutch officer made him a rough identity card for a foreign worker in Germany. He still had a small compass, now sewn into the lining of his converted tunic.

Kenneth Lockwood handed him a cigar-shaped container about two and a half inches long, containing money. He explained that, to avoid its capture, if Airey did not get out of the camp, he must carry it in the container inside his rectum. If the container and money were not found, he was to return them to him. Airey's experiments with the container caused some hilarity.

He attended evening *Appell* on the 28th with a British Army greatcoat over his *Gefreiter* uniform. After the order to dismiss, a colleague removed his coat and he smartly pulled his German cap on. He then marched towards the main door. There he spoke nervously to a German *Unteroffizier* (NCO): "I have a message to the *Kommandant* from Hauptmann Priem." The German took from him the brass disc which acted as a pass (obtained by bribery from an elderly house painter) and let him through.

He headed for the bicycle racks, planning to cycle to freedom. Before he got there, there were yells and after a chase he found himself surrounded by shouting Germans, most of them pointing rifles at him. The *Unteroffizier* himself screamed at him: "This is an insult to the German Army. You will be shot!" Then officers with revolvers drawn came running out of the *Kommandantur* until Neave was surrounded by at least thirty excited men. Eventually the *Kommandant* himself emerged. "What impertinence," he said in lofty tones. "Take him away to the cells."

Next morning a soldier brought him ersatz coffee in his cell. He told Airey that he was to be court-martialed and shot. At 10 a.m. an under-officer came and ordered him to the *Kommandant*'s quarters where he stood awkwardly in a long, panelled gallery, closely examined by all the officers of the camp. Their reactions ranged from ridicule to extreme anger as they surveyed his pathetic uniform. The *Kommandant* appeared. He was polite but mocking.

"Stand to attention and salute German fashion," he said. Airey saluted. "A German soldier wouldn't salute like that. Do it again!" German officers around him laughed obsequiously. The *Kommandant* smiled in superior fashion and returned to his office in silence.

From time to time police officers from Colditz and soldiers were brought in to inspect him. There was a chorus of "*Heil Hitler!*" as they stamped down the gallery. At length the tension relaxed and turned to comic relief. A photographer from the town arrived. Slowly he assembled a large Victorian camera on a tripod at the end of the gallery, and photographed him from different angles. Airey stood there, humiliated. He felt he had reduced escaping to a farce, a music-hall turn. It seemed hours before the comedy was over. Then his German uniform was taken away to be placed in the *Kommandant*'s escape museum and he was conducted back to the British quarters. There were no more threats of shooting for wearing an enemy uniform. He would do time in the cells when there was room in the town jail.

That evening Hauptmann Priem made an announcement to the assembled prisoners, which was translated into many languages: "Gefreiter Neave is to be sent to the Russian front." The roar of laughter which greeted this sally was friendly but it was not music to his ears.

By way of inquest on this failed escape, Eggers states in his diary that the number of the missing disc, no. 26, had been posted up in the guardhouse. The under-officer at the door looked at the number on the German *Gefreiter*'s disc and raised the alarm. Perhaps I, as escape officer, should have had the foresight to arrange that a digit on the disc was suitably altered before Airey used it.

Sunday, 31 August, was the birthday of the Queen of the Netherlands. The Dutch officers were keen to hold a celebration service. When making arrangements for it earlier in the week, Padre Platt found himself responsible for prayers in Afrikaans (he had worked for two years in South Africa just before the war). He composed a special prayer and submitted it, in accordance with the requirements of camp orders, to be *Geprüft* (censored). It was returned with all the references to the Royal Household deleted. Earlier, an order forbidding Padre Hobling to conduct British camp worship had been issued. This was because he had recited a prayer for the Queen of the Netherlands including a supplication that her enemies should be driven from her lands. Padre Heard had then been appointed Church of England chaplain for *Oflag* IVC. The singing of the national anthem in chapel was now also expressly forbidden.

The service for the Dutch Queen's birthday was attended by everybody who could squeeze into the chapel. There were RCs of five nations, non-conformists and Anglicans of three nations—peoples of six nationalities including the Jews. There were titled noblemen of France, Holland and Poland, and every military rank from general to private. The chapel was crammed, even to the servants' gallery which is right up under the ceiling of the chapel, like "the gods" in a theater.

The service had to be over by 11 a.m. to allow for the ceremonial opening of an International Sports Competition. At a fanfare of trumpets, the representative companies, in national costume and bearing national flags, marched out in order: Poles, French, Belgians, Dutch and British. They stood in double file before the President of Sports, the Polish Colonel Szubert, who had with him as patrons of the contest General Le Bleu, General Piskor and Admiral Unrug. Colonel Szubert delivered the introductory oration in Polish, and called upon interpreters to redeliver the greeting in French and English. There was much clapping of hands and cheering as the national Sports Presidents stepped forward to notify their countries' entries in the events.

The first game, Poles v. French, at volleyball, began. Though set out and conducted in Olympic fashion, all the contests were games played with a ball: volleyball, handball, football. But to increase the number of events, teams of different strengths played the same game; for instance, football was seven-a-side, nine-a-side and eleven-a-side. The play was fast and furious all day.

The British position in sports at close of play was: four events lost. On Monday evening the sports were in full swing when Priem stepped through the needle's eye (i.e. the main gate) and ordered the courtyard to be cleared for fire-fighting practice. The main doors swung open to admit a horse-drawn fire-engine. While the fire-brigade was engaged in winding up the fire-escape ladders and running out hosepipes, a second man-drawn engine crawled in. The second brigade got to work winding up their ladders and paying out the hose. All this, occupying about twenty minutes, was done to the accompaniment of cheers, catcalls and dive-bomber screams from the POWs at the windows.

The ladders, set in the middle of the *Hof*, were mounted by firemen swaying like birds in treetops. The main hose was passed through the camp kitchen window to connect with a water hydrant. To the surprise of everyone, Colonel German, Major Anderson and Squadron-Leader Paddon were discovered there. They had been prospecting in the kitchen area for a possible way of escape. They were led away for interrogation.

Hundreds of gallons of water spewed in torrents from two of the five points that were hoseless; shouts and jeers from the prisoners. Once in action, the hoses were turned on the jeering figures wedged in the open windows. Men were drenched, beds were soaked and windows were smashed. It was a tremendous diversion. The honors were felt to be about even, discounting Priem's bag of one colonel and a brace of majors.

It was also quite a relief from the tension created by the dead seriousness with which the sports contests were being fought. The French and the Poles in particular were coming to regard these sporting events as matters of national honor, something that allies in a prison camp could not afford to countenance without risk of feuds arising. When the proposal for the competition had first been mooted, it was accepted as something to enjoy and laugh about. The British in particular refused to take the contests seriously.

Meanwhile two other incidents diverted us. Early in September a new French officer arrived. He was recognized by several French officers as an undesirable. He was not admitted to the French officers' mess, nor allowed to sleep in either of their dormitories. His bed was carried out into the corridor. The *Kommandant* wisely arranged his *exeat* while most of the POWs were eating their midday meal, but a belligerent handful left their tables to boo him out of the yard. Before disappearing, he turned, sprang to attention and, smiling, gave the French salute. This infuriated the onlookers. He was lucky to be out of reach. It was assumed by the other nationalities that he was either a stool-pigeon or a collaborator.

A Dutch officer was married on 11 September by proxy. He wrote out an application and posted it to Dutch Army headquarters stating his wish to marry a Miss So-and-So on 11 September at 11 a.m. He received a notice saying the necessary arrangements were in hand and he could consider himself married at that date and hour!

On Sunday, 21 September, a ceremonial closing of the International Sports Competition was timed for 10:30 a.m. but was delayed by a German man-hunt for two missing Dutch officers. The park had been reopened for the Olympics a few days before. As there was no evidence of a break-out, the Germans presumed the missing men were hiding in the Castle. This ruse had been used before. But comprehensive search produced no result. The security officer was left without the slightest idea how the two officers had disappeared. At 11 a.m. the quest was abandoned, and the Sports Committee fussily set the stage for the award of diplomas. A fanfare sounded at 11.25 and the Poles and French companies marched out in resplendent style in double file before the President and patrons. The Dutch were five minutes late and the Belgians and British were ten. Under Sportführer "Bertie" Boustead's brilliant leadership, the British officers' teams had lost every event.

The two missing Dutch officers were Major C. Giebel and 2nd Lieutenant O. Drijber, both of the Royal Netherlands Indies Army. They had escaped from the park manhole on 19 September; their absence was not discovered till the 21st. From Larive's earlier account of his escape, it appears certain that there was no bolt on the manhole cover for the first two Dutch escape attempts. Before the third attempt, that of Giebel and Drijber, a large bolt and nut must have been installed. This is supported by Eggers' statement in his diary that "these two officers were concealed there by means of a wonderful invention of Captain van den Heuvel."

Vandy had arranged Bible-reading classes, led by the bearded naval lieutenant van Doorninck, to take place over the manhole cover. During these sessions the nut and bolt were carefully measured. A pair of large spanners was manufactured from iron bedparts. When the escapers were ready to go, the spanners were used to unscrew the bolt. Then the men disappeared into the manhole, taking the bolt with them. Vandy had another bolt and nut made similar in every respect to the originals. These were applied and fastened. Upon examination by a German, nothing untoward would be noticeable. However, the substitute bolt was made from a glass tube and the nut parts were made of wood. The escapers had only to prise up the manhole cover sharply to break the glass. They would then replace the real nut and bolt suitably, clear away the broken glass and make off.

Dufour and Smit had been caught on the Swiss border and on their return to Colditz were placed in solitary confinement. Nonetheless they were able to transmit to Vandy some more very useful details about leaving the Castle from the park and also about the latest dangers in the Swiss frontier crossing at Gottmadingen. This information was passed on to Giebel and Drijber.

Their exit from the Castle presented some unusual aspects. They were ready to leave on Friday, 19 September. In Giebel's own words:

> Drijber and I joined the others of the walk party in front of the closed doors at the gateway. We were, however, quite amazed to see that this time the walk party numbered more than twice its usual number. Instead of about eighty there were now some two hundred. When the doors were opened, we pushed our way through to the outer courtyard where our thirty German guards were waiting for us. We became quite a throng when we tried to line up for the roll-call.
>
> But things went wrong. Was it only accidental that Captain Priem was on the spot? Confronted with two hundred park-walkers instead of the usual eighty, he at once understood that something was brooding. But he knew how to handle the situation. With an ironic smile he addressed the POW crowd, apologizing that apparently it had not become known in time, that on this Friday the walk in the park had been cancelled. He regretted that we had not been warned earlier and suggested that we should forthwith retire behind the walls of our inner courtyard.
>
> We could do nothing but obey. Back in our quarters we learned that our escape committee had urged some of our fellow prisoners to take part in the walk that Friday because they might be needed for camouflage purposes. But it had been overdone a little bit. The committee had underestimated everybody's desire to be helpful.

On the following day, Saturday the 20th, an important football match was to be played between Polish and Dutch teams in the park. Giebel and Drijber decided to try again, but their first obstacle was an order issued by Priem forbidding the Dutch to go on the park walk. The *Feldwebel* in charge accordingly would not allow the Dutch supporters to accompany their team to the park. The Dutch players protested at once. They declared that they could not play without supporters. But the *Feldwebel* was unmoved. "It's all the same to me," he said, "whether you play or not." Then one of the Poles had a brainwave. He told the *Feldwebel* that he was interfering with the *Kommandant*'s wishes, which were that we should play the Olympic Games among ourselves. The *Feldwebel* relented and the prisoners paraded for the count. Two small Poles were secreted in the manner used to cover the absence of Pierre Mairesse Lebrun.

Once in the park the game began. Giebel continues:

> The Dutch supporters seemed to be not content with the place where they were standing, which was muddy, so we moved forward a few feet across the touchline in the direction of the manhole. When a few minutes later we moved forward again, the players objected and said we were spoiling their game and should keep off the field. But that did not stop us from moving, step by step, nearer to the manhole.

The nut proved to be very difficult to unscrew, and only ten minutes of the game were left when the manhole was at last opened. The two escapers jumped in.

The faking of the count on the park walk was accomplished successfully. Vandy however wanted to give his escapers as long a start as possible on their pursuers so he had manufactured two dummies. He had obtained a sack of ceiling plaster by bribing a workman. A Dutch sculptor carved a couple of life-size busts, which were then cleverly painted. Each had two iron hoops fixed underneath the pedestal part of the bust, which was shaped to rest on a man's arm. A shirt collar and tie were fitted round the neck and finally a long Dutch overcoat was draped over the bust's shoulders. When not in action, the dummy hung suspended under the forearm of the bearer, hidden in the folds of the overcoat—as if the bearer were carrying an overcoat over his arm. At action stations, the bearer unfolded the overcoat, an Army cap was placed on the dummy's head, now upright, and the dummy was held shoulder high by a broomstick thrust upwards through a hole in the bust's neck. This was held in position by the bearer with his arm concealed at elbow height in the flowing mantle of the overcoat. A pair of top boots was placed neatly under the coat in the position of "attention" by an assistant.

The two busts worked perfectly, concealing the absence of Giebel and Drijber until Vandy allowed the escape to be blown on Sunday morning. They had successfully covered six *Appells* and given the escapers about thirty-six hours' start. Indeed Giebel and Drijber crossed the frontier into Switzerland on 23 September. They were held in safe custody in Schaffhausen for five days before going on to Berne and then Geneva. They made use of their time to compose an intricately coded letter detailing their route and experiences, which arrived safely in Colditz—and helped later escapes. They also put together a chessboard and pieces, containing German banknotes and maps and files. The contraband was wrapped in a copy of a Dutch newspaper *Vry Nederland*, printed in London. This special edition contained the text of a message that Queen Wilhelmina had delivered a few weeks before over the BBC radio to her people in occupied Holland in a Dutch program entitled "Radio Orange." Chessboard and newspaper arrived safely in Colditz. Major Engles assembled the whole Dutch contingent and in a solemn, moving reunion read out the Dutch Queen's message.

It is appropriate to wind up the story of the well at this juncture. Some weeks after the disappearance of Giebel and Drijber, 24 November to be precise, a keen-eyed sentry observed two men entering the manhole during recreation in the park. Lieutenants Geoffrey Wardle RN and Jerzy Wojciechowski were discovered inside. Eggers recorded:

> I felt that this must really be the Dutch escape route and wondered what bargaining had been struck to induce them to lend this "open Sesame" to the British and Poles. We had looked at that cover so many times. It had a great bolt on the top, which we controlled, again and again. We had looked inside regularly. Perhaps it would have been better had we left the cover off altogether.

So it was only after this attempt that the manhole cover was effectively sealed by concreting a number of bars across it.

As for the "bargain" that Eggers had the intuition to reflect upon, the Poles had given Vandy much assistance in covering up on roll-calls. They deserved a break! But what had the British done? Stooge Wardle (that is Geoffrey, not Hank, Wardle) thinks in retrospect that the Dutch thought the escape route was "blown," and so let the British and Poles have a go. I do not remember this escape. I was probably doing "solitary."

On 21 September, an order came through from the OKW stating that all German officers had to be saluted when on duty by POWs of whatever rank. The Geneva Convention, however, stated the following in Article 18: "Officer prisoners of war are required to salute only those officers of the detaining power who are of equal or superior rank."

There had been a long history of controversy over saluting starting back in January. The *Kommandant* had decided to visit the prisoners' quarters. It was 9 January and still extremely cold. The sun did not get over the roofs into the prisoners' yard until a good 10 a.m. in the shorter days of winter, but even then many were glad to be living in a stone building and not a wooden barracks, which is always damp and cold. There weren't many people walking in the yard that morning. Eggers went in to the yard with the *Kommandant* and called out "*Achtung!*" The circulation of officers stopped for a moment. That was the drill. Everyone looked towards Guy German for a second. He saluted, the circle moved round again.

From there they went up the circular staircase in the south-east corner. On the first floor were the Polish officers. "*Achtung!*" Eggers shouted. Most of the officers were lying on their beds reading, smoking, thinking. They all got up slowly, unwillingly, all except Lieutenant Siefert, who stayed on his bed. Eggers took his name.

On the evening parade Eggers read out the *Kommandant*'s sentence of five days' arrest for failing to acknowledge a superior officer. This punishment was normal for officers in the German Army, and military prisoners were all subject to the German *Militärstrafgesetzbuch* (corresponding to Queen's Regulations). The sentence was read out also to the French, Belgian and British companies in their own language. It was all very formal. The prisoners were unimpressed by this disciplinary action—sometimes it was warmer in the cells!

So five days' arrest meant nothing to any Pole, and when Eggers dismissed the parade, his compatriots rushed to their comrade, shook his hand, embraced him, and then, gathering round, threw him again and again into the air, catching him as he fell, as the Poles like to do with those they approve of.

Eggers argued with their adjutant, Captain Jan Lados: "If you want us to treat you correctly under the Geneva Convention, you must behave correctly too." The adjutant destroyed Eggers' argument: "You Germans don't apply the Geneva Convention to us. You say Poland as a country no longer exists. You don't even allow us a Protecting Power to look after our interests as prisoners. The Swiss visit the British every three months. The French have their Scapini Committee to look after them, and they have a Government you recognize, even though it's Pétain. The Dutch are looked after by the Swedish Government. But we, the Poles, are no one's children."

The Poles had thought it all out, and were going to make a thing of it. A week later, the same incident occurred again. Again Siefert got *Arrest*. The third time it happened he got a court-martial in Leipzig. He was allowed a local lawyer, a man from the town who had been a prisoner of war in England during the First World War. He claimed to have been well treated, and was always willing to do something in return for this.

In due course the prosecution at Leipzig demanded a heavy penalty. Here was a Pole, a member of an undisciplined and savage race, so they said, deliberately insulting a superior officer. An example must be made. The defense was that the prisoner did not understand the meaning of the word *Achtung!* He got a year's imprisonment and appealed. Generaloberst (Colonel-General) von Beck, commanding the German Reserve Army, allowed the appeal and Lieutenant Siefert returned to Colditz a free man. Tremendous enthusiasm among all the prisoners in the camp! Further, the Polish Senior Officer, Admiral Unrug, protested against the insults to the Polish people uttered in court. The *Kommandant* tried in vain to get the appeal verdict upset. His failure made things worse, for the result was that saluting practically died out in Colditz, as between the Germans and prisoners, until our famous doctor tried to revive the practice a year later. The only occasion when the Germans were saluted was on roll-call. At the most, on other occasions, officers would stand up slowly when German officers entered quarters or reluctantly take their hands out of their pockets or their pipes out of their mouths when Germans spoke to them. German officers went into POW quarters only of necessity and they tried to speak, as far as possible, only to the Senior Officers of the different companies, and through their official interpreters. But over this matter, there is no doubt they had lost face.

The court decision in 1941 made things more difficult for them. Not only was it a rebuff for the *Kommandant*, who had previously given orders that offenders in the matter of saluting were to be reported and punished, but it brought out differences of opinion among the four German officers who, as *Lageroffiziere* (camp officers) were in constant contact with the prisoners, taking daily parades, attending searches, sorting out innumerable requests, inspecting quarters.

Unfortunately, as Eggers has explained, there were two standards among the four camp officers. Eggers was then LO3 (*Lageroffizier* 3). Hauptmann Paul Priem LO1 was a lively character, fond of battle, fond of life, very much a joker, fond of the bottle, too, and the only one who the British agreed had a sense of humor. Sometimes he would refer to us as "the etceteras": he would give out notices on parade as applying to the French, the Belgians, the Dutch, the Poles "*und so weiter*" ("and so on"). The British once put on a variety show in the theater performed by the *und so weiter* group. Priem did not worry much about discipline in the strict military sense. Having been a schoolmaster like Eggers, he thought he knew how to handle the "bad boys'" camp.

LO2 was a cavalry captain, Rittmeister Aurich (until March 1941). He would blow up, going blue in the face at the least provocation, as the prisoners very soon discovered. He suffered from mortally high blood pressure. He was all in favor of violence against his charges.

As for Eggers, LO3, he was not for peace at any price, but felt he was in the position that he knew so well, that of a teacher dealing with a lot of naughty boys. He knew that the first aim of unruly schoolboys is to make the person in charge angry, whatever the consequences, and Eggers also knew that if he lost his temper, he had lost the day and possibly the years to come as well. He said to the British Senior Officer once, "I will never allow you gentlemen the honor of getting me rattled. Correct behavior under the Convention or under our own disciplinary code is my line. Anything your officers do to offend, I shall report the fact. What happens then is not my affair." Eggers was severely provoked for four years on end by the hotheads among hundreds of officers of all nationalities, ages, ranks and backgrounds. In his experience, it was not easy to put up with active insolence, but dumb insolence was even harder to bear.

LO4, Hauptmann Hans Püpcke, was of much the same opinion as Eggers but the four were not a harmonious team.

After the OKW order of 21 September, the German doctor, Hauptmann Doktor Rahm, a Bavarian, decided to take up the cudgels over saluting. He insisted on his salute, or tried to. He insisted that Poland no longer existed. He insisted on a salute not only from officers of equal and lower ranks but even from General Piskor himself. This was too much even for the *Kommandant.* He refused to back the *Tierarzt,* who nevertheless persisted in his campaign throughout the autumn and winter until matters came to a head in January 1942.

On 25 September, almost a score of French officers who were born before or at the turn of the century left *Oflag* IVC to be repatriated. A number had already left on 4 August. They stood in their ranks of five, after *Appell* was dismissed, for a farewell speech from Colonel Marq who was their *Vertrauensmann* (spokesman). At the close of the proceedings, Hauptmann Priem stepped forward with a hand extended to Colonel Marq, and thanked him and them for their *Mitarbeit*—"collaboration"! There was much speculation as to the significance of that!

The only "Royal leader" pictures which the Germans would allow on the walls of the French quarters were photographs of Marshal Pétain. The French contingent was divided in itself. There were many more Pétainists than just those who left Colditz in August and September. Most of those who left at that time were probably repatriated on compassionate grounds as *les pères de grandes familles*—heads of large families who had to support their families. The rest would be *collaborateurs* who squared their consciences either by a genuine preference for the Germans as compared with the British (the old enemy) or by a cynical appraisal of the war situation.

Others of the French community were diehards—natural rebels—who preferred the atmosphere of Colditz to that of any other camp. Curiously, most of the French would admit to this—whatever their allegiance. The diehards revelled in being *Deutschfeindlich* and—typically French too—some *collaborateurs* preferred in principle to attempt to reach France by escaping rather than by repatriation for the purpose of "working for the economy of the German Reich."

This was an expression which formed part of a rigmarole relayed in French to the French and Belgian contingents at irregular intervals on *Appell.* The announcement asked for volunteers—particularly engineers, chemists or men with other technical skills—who would be lucratively employed if their skills could be fitted into "the economy of the German Reich." They were invited to state their names and professions.

There was no response for some time. Then, one day, to the horror of all assembled, a young French officer *aspirant* Paul Durant, stepped from the ranks, announcing that he wished to work for the Germans. The German interpreter beamed and translated this to the German officer taking the parade. Then he accosted the young Frenchman: "So you really wish to work for the German Reich?"

"Yes," replied Durant loudly, "I would prefer to work for a hundred Germans than for one Frenchman."

There were gasps and muttered oaths from all who could understand French.

"All right! What is your name?" from the German.

"My name is Paul Durant. I wish to make it clearly understood that I would prefer to work for a hundred Germans than for one Frenchman."

"Excellent! And what is your profession?"

"Undertaker!"

Durant was led away to the cells at once amidst the loudest laughter that the cobbled yard had echoed probably in its whole history. Even the Germans—those who could understand the French word *croque-mort*—had to join in the uncontrollable outburst.

8

The Incorrigibles

Autumn and Winter 1941

WITH AUTUMN DRAWING IN, some POWs were getting desperate. There were two incidents within a month when the sentries opened fire on POWs attempting to escape. The first was on 7 October when the French Lieutenant Desjobert climbed over a fence on the return walk from the park. Sentries opened fire and he was cornered without being hit. A second similar attempt over the park wall on 8 November, by two Belgian lieutenants, Marcel Leroy and André Lejeune, had repercussions within the Castle. The Belgians had climbed the wire in the park and were sprinting up the steep hill towards the wall when sentries opened fire. As the sentries stood in a circle they came close to hitting one another. Soon the sentries around the Castle walls joined in, and the British prisoners started trying to distract them by shouting abuse at them from their windows. In no time much of the shooting was directed at them and bullets were striking the Castle wall. Eventually Peter Storie-Pugh hung a Union Jack, left over from the Christmas festivities, out of one of the windows—this maddened the Germans and the shooting grew frenzied. Meanwhile the Belgians, having been unable to climb the wall at that point, stood with their hands up, still under fire.

The French had known that an escape attempt was on. To attract the attention of the guards they had crowded the windows, shouting, blowing trumpets and singing their favorite refrain, which originated in the First World War: *"Où sont les Allemands? / Ils sont tombés dans la merde, / Où on les enfonce—jusqu'aux oreilles."* * Shots were fired at their windows. A dummy wearing a tin hat was placed between the iron bars, and became the object of accurate fire.

---

* "Where are the Gemans? / They've fallen in shit, / Where we drive them in—up to the ears."

When the Germans conducted an inquiry, five of the sentries swore that they were actually fired on from the Castle! And two of them swore on their *Diensteid* (service oath) that they had seen the smoke from the shots! Eggers ventured a reconstruction of the action: "Presumably you could crack two bedboards together and blow out a concentration of smoke or tooth powder from a paper bag or football bladder. The five were absolutely certain that they were firing in self-defense. Thank God they killed no one." At the same inquiry, a German officer concluded, "I regret that no one was hit. I will instruct the sentries to shoot more accurately in future. There is obviously nothing served in trying to establish a Franco/German tolerance."

Five days later the French Senior Officer received the following letter from Schmidt:

> In reply to your letter addressed to me about the incident on the 8 Nov. 1941. During an escape attempt by two Belgian officers on the way to the park, there were what appeared to be shots from the French quarters, which later turned out to be artificially created, complete with smoke. At the same time, paper darts were thrown at the guards, and a steel helmet appeared at a window. It was very clear that the purpose of the demonstration was to distract the attention of the guards. Under the circumstances it was justifiable to open fire. I do not approve of the words used by a German officer, "It's a pity no one was wounded," and this I have told him.

Michal (Miki) Surmanowicz had been escorted to Leipzig on 18 July to attend his court-martial for the bottle-throwing incident. A defense fund, officers contributing five *Lagermarks* each, was raised to secure the services of the local Colditz lawyer who was later to act for Lieutenant Siefert over his refusal to salute.

The official notice was given out at morning *Appell* on 10 October that Surmanowicz had been given a four-year prison sentence. The only comforting aspect was that the war might not last the sentence out.

Admiral Unrug was indeed so incensed by what he considered the treachery of the *Kommandant* that he resigned the post of Senior Polish Officer. The *Kommandant* had assured the admiral that upon the culprit confessing his action the court would be lenient. Instead a fierce sentence of four years had been imposed. General Piskor took over the office of SPO; he ranked senior to the admiral anyway.

Meanwhile, four French lieutenants, Navelet, Odry, Charvet and Lévy, were conducted to the hospital at Elsterhorst attached to *Oflag* IVD. Pierre Odry, who had helped Mairesse Lebrun to escape, had already tried a get-away. Nevertheless the *Tierarzt* had been convinced by their symptoms that they needed hospital treatment. *Oflag* IVD was a French POW camp and the hospital was strictly guarded. The four found no exit available.

On 14 October they set out under guard on their return journey to Colditz. They had to march three miles and it was already nightfall. The first part of this journey was over open country, then continued for a mile or so through the woods. They were, of course, under guard, but being hospital cases the guards presumably thought there would be no question of their being fit enough to escape.

At a given signal, while still in the woods, all four ran in different directions, and all four succeeded in getting clear away. Of the four, Charvet got to Kassel where he took a ticket to Aachen, but unfortunately changed there on to the wrong train and came back to Düsseldorf. Here by merest chance he met up with another of the four, Lévy, and the two travelled together back to Aachen and spent the night there in a wood. On the morning of the 18th they took a tram into the town, but unfortunately were caught. They said they were French other ranks and so were sent to the *Stalag* at Arnoldsweiler where they stayed for three weeks. During this time they told differing stories as to their identities, but in the end they let it be known as certain that they came from Oschatz in east Germany. On their way back there, Charvet jumped out of the train, but was seen and retaken at Helmstett. He then admitted that he was an officer prisoner and came from Colditz. He returned to Colditz without any further trouble, and when he got back there he found that Lévy had already been brought back as well.

Navelet and Odry eventually arrived safely home in France. This was Navelet's first attempt. For Pierre, it was his fourth.

At this time the *Kommandant* requisitioned about half a dozen cells in the town jail for use by POWs on "solitary" sentences. The queue had become so long for the seven odd cells in the *Schloss* that even placing two or three together in a cell, making nonsense of course of the term "solitary," necessitated a long period of waiting between being served a sentence and actually carrying it out. The SBO was allowed to inspect the new accommodation. He approved it and Storie-Pugh (caught prospecting for an escape) was the first Britisher to have the privilege of using the accommodation.

On 25 October Mr. Giles Romilly arrived in Colditz by car under the guard of two German officers. A nephew of Winston Churchill, not by blood but by the marriage of his father, General Romilly, to the sister of Churchill's wife, he was captured at Narvik in the abortive Norwegian campaign. He was a journalist and was acting as correspondent for the *Daily Express* at the time. He was a short, dark-haired young man with a boyish face and light-blue eyes. Padre Platt described him: "There is a restless look in his eyes and a droop of discontent at the corners of his mouth—indeed he is by no means a complacent young man." The reason given for his transfer to Colditz was that he attempted an escape in female dress from an internment camp at Tost in Czechoslovakia. But this did not satisfy anyone. Colditz was a military special camp. Could this action carry an implication of the term "hostage"?

On consultation with the SBO, a complaint was submitted to the *Kommandant* next day asking for clarification of Romilly's position, as a civilian, in a military prison. In the meantime a German order was issued giving Romilly private sleeping accommodation in a cell, where he was to be locked in every night at 10 p.m. with a guard outside (and the usual spy-hole) until reveille time every morning when he would be allowed out. Romilly refused to obey the order to retire to his cell. So on Tuesday night a German squad led by Eggers appeared in the British quarters to remove him. Dressed in an RAF uniform he was not identified. The squad left and at 10:30 p.m. a general *Appell* was called. The British contingent was surrounded by guards with rifles at the ready—until Romilly was finally identified and removed to his cell with a posse of guards around him.

Eggers recounts the following about Romilly's advent: "He ranked as a *Prominenter*—a social prize (so our OKW considered) of some standing—maybe useful as a hostage. For us in Colditz he was just another security headache. Our instructions . . . came from the very highest source." According to Eggers the orders came from Hitler. Furthermore he says that a German agent in Switzerland had reported that a rescue attempt was being organized by the Allies to free Romilly. This latter story has no traceable foundation in fact and may have been planted to keep security personnel on their toes. But the order concerning his imprisonment almost certainly did come from Hitler or Himmler. It specified that the *Kommandant* and security officer would answer for Romilly's security with their heads, and that his security was to be assured by any and every exceptional measure they cared to take. These were the measures taken:

1. Romilly's code name was to be "Emil."
2. All members of the *Kommandantur* and guard companies were to familiarize themselves with Emil's appearance. (Photos were posted up in the guardroom, the *Kommandantur*, the office, etc.)
3. Anyone finding this man outside the prisoners' yard would take him at once to the *Kommandantur*.

4. The *Rollkommando* [roving search party] was to search him out every hour and note in a book where he was at that time.
5. By day he might move around the Castle where he wished.
6. No park walk. At every walk a special check to be made that Romilly was not with the group.
7. He was to be locked in his own room immediately after evening parades. A spy-hole to be put in the door, and a guard outside and the light burning all night (later just a blue light). The bed to be visible from the spy-hole.
8. His presence to be checked at night at irregular intervals.

For some months Giles reacted stubbornly to these special measures, especially the disturbance of his sleep. He used to fling his boots against the door and put paper over the spy-hole, but in the end he accepted these inconveniences. He spoke good German and certainly played his part in undermining the morale of the guards, with whom he could converse easily at his door at any time of the evening and night.

Romilly's escape as a female was from a place called the Wulzburg. It was a castle in Bavaria where there were hundreds of civilian internees. But Romilly was kept separate most of the time. When recaught he did his time at Eichstatt then went to Tost, near Breslau, in Silesia. From there he came to Colditz. A month after his arrival, 28 November, he tried to make an escape by disguising himself as an orderly. He was helping to load a cart when Priem, tipped off by the guards that he had disappeared, approached the loading team and accosted him, saying, "You should leave this work for men of lower breed!"

The first snow of that winter fell on 3 November and the first pangs of hunger began to be felt by the German command in Colditz. The OKW cut the rations for all officers of the home Army. The weekly ration of meat, for instance, was cut from 800 to 400 grams. We cheered ourselves up with the first, and possibly the best, revue produced by the British contingent. Called "Ballet Nonsense," it had its stage premiere on 15 November. Here is Padre Platt's description of the opening number:

> . . . five strapping fellows of muscular hairy limbs were dressed in ballet skirts of crinkled paper, and each with a blazing red brassiere on a brawny bear-like chest. Three of the five wore mustaches! The curtain lifted on kneeling figures, bare backs to the audience, and arms engaged in sinuous

graceful movement. A crashing swell from the band brought them to their feet dancing, and face to face with the now rocking audience. Pat Reid was the prima ballerina.

In the same month, the first British escape committee was formed. I had asked the SBO if something could be organized and Guy German gave me the go-ahead. The SBO himself was only to participate as chairman for the most important decision-making. For escaping purposes, he felt that the less he knew the better. So, by an election held in the day-room, Captain Dick Howe, Squadron-Leader Malcolm McColm and Lieutenant Airey Neave were appointed to help me in running the escape organization of the British contingent. Captain Kenneth Lockwood was appointed to concentrate on "hides" because serious losses had been incurred in searches due to a great deal of laxity as well as inefficiency on the part of individuals in concealing contraband.

This was of course an expression of our frustration at the lack of success in escaping. Padre Platt, in his diary entry for 6 December, claimed to find two more:

> For the past few weeks life has been Novemberish, flat and barren. Officers have drawn up their stools to the chess board and a new departure, a high-stake poker school, is flourishing. Teddy Barton was winning Rm1700 the other day. I suppose there is a thrill in winning £113, and something the reverse of monotony in losing it; but neither excitement contributes much to communal life beyond the opportunity to rag one another.
>
> Two of our number, on several nights since the "Ballet Nonsense" revue have sat up after all the others were abed discussing Plato's acquiescence in the homosexualism of his disciples. At one of these late-adolescent discussions they foresaw themselves as founders of a Platonic cult. Actually homosexualism has advanced little since March; it is still in the coarse humour stage.
>
> The answer to foregoing is the fact that the true life of IVC is in a state of hibernation, i.e. the escape season is virtually closed.

The French Lieutenant Michel Girot, the youngest French officer in Colditz, made his first attempt to escape on 25 November. He tried to pass through the main gate dressed as an orderly bearing a faked-up message. He had not gone far before he was recaptured. This attempt has been registered by Eggers together with the date. Girot did not know then the road he had embarked on, which ended with his fifth escape by tunnel from the infirmary in Lübeck on 27 April 1944.

The news of the Japanese attack on Pearl Harbor came on 8 December. The declaration of war by Britain against Finland, Hungary and Romania and the declaration of war by the USA and Britain on Japan were reported within hours. Then on 11 December came the news that Germany and Italy had declared war on the USA and, finally, news of the catastrophic sinking of the two British battleships *Prince of Wales* and *Repulse* by the Japanese on the 10th.

Two weeks before Christmas the Germans had a field day. That day the party for the park was rather large and more than usually unruly, particularly when being counted before the march back. The NCOs were suspicious and checked very carefully. The officer in charge, Priem, suddenly spotted the reason. He confronted the Dutch section of the parade. "All from here to the right, move to the right. All from here to the left, move to the left."

That left one file standing, plus an extra man to the right, in a file of his own. Why hadn't he moved? This Dutch officer was a dummy! After that the Germans counted again and there were two missing. They then put the dogs into the exercise area and under an untidy heap of leaves, the dogs unearthed Lieutenants Kruimink and Douw van der Krap. The leaves were sewn meticulously on to a sheet, forming a good camouflage over a shallow hollow formed by improving a natural dip in the ground surface.

What had happened over the counting was that two dummies were being employed. As soon as the first dummy was exposed, there was no point in risking the second.

Only four days later, on 16 December, two German officers presented themselves at the yard gate. The guard let them out and saluted. They marched off left downhill towards the next archway. The guard was slow. He locked the door and then thought of the passes. Orders were to demand all passes at all gates from all military personnel. He didn't want to leave his post. Still, he was suspicious and ran after the officers and asked for their *Ausweise*. "That's all right, we're coming straight back," was the answer, in good German. But not good enough. The guard was called out and stopped Lieutenant Baron D. W. van Lynden and Captain Steenhouwer.

As if these escapes were not sufficient to belie Padre Platt's diary entry about the escape close season setting in, the French had a real go with three officers on 17 December.

That day leave postings for the German garrison went up. Half of the officers had the 22nd to the 28th, but Eggers' leave was again over the New Year. He had been in Colditz for just over twelve months now and had indeed something to look back on. The *Kommandant*, sixty-nine years old, was on a month's sick leave. His deputy, Oberstleutnant von Kirchbach, was an officer with whom the staff all got on very well. He had lost an arm in the First War and was no stickler for discipline. The garrison soldiers were looking forward to their Christmas party that night.

Sure enough, for dinner the quartermaster officer did them proud, even though belts were tightening. After the meal, a show was put on by the troops. The guard company provided music and song, and a series of sketches poking fun at the officers or "dragging them through the cocoa" as the Germans say.

The proceedings were suddenly interrupted by a phone call which put "a hair in their soup" just as it was being served.

Eggers tells the story:

> The guard NCO hurried in—"Three French officers have just escaped from the dentist's."
>
> "Man all telephones. Mousetrap's the word," and we called up the local alarm network. . . .
>
> That evening, a party of seven were sent down to the town dentist, five P.O.W.s and two guards, because up in the *Schloss* the French officer dentist hadn't the material for more than simple fillings. The patients all came out of our dentist's house together after treatment. Their guard came last. It was very foggy and it was raining too that evening. Three of the party just bolted down the street; Lieuts. Durand-Hornus, de Frondeville and Prot. There was nothing the guard could do about it. He couldn't run three ways at once. He daren't fire blindly into the fog. We could do nothing more either once we had warned everyone. So back we went to our Christmas festivities, but the soup was cold and the spirit of the feast was much watered down. The three in due course got right back to France.

Eggers has claimed that it was only after this escape that the German dentist came up to the Castle to attend his victims. This is incorrect. Prot was the third man in the affair of the dentist's hat and coat, which had been stolen while the latter was working in the Castle dentistry. Indeed Prot actually used the hat and coat in his escape just before Christmas. The fact is that such dental work as the French and German dentists could do in the Castle was very limited and the more serious cases had to progress to the town operating theater.

The escape was Jacques Durand-Hornus' third attempt, Guy de Frondeville's first and Jacques Prot's second. Prot was another Frenchman whose puckishness was irrepressible and whose quick-wittedness won him freedom and later glory.

The two friends, Prot and de Frondeville, separated for safety at Leipzig. Prot, tall, dark, well-built, aged about twenty-six, went through Cologne to Aachen. As he neared the frontier he saw to his horror that his false papers were not at all like those in current use. The frontier station was heavily patrolled and guarded. He closely followed the crowd, mostly Belgian passengers, towards the barrier. He was at his wit's end. Then the light dawned! He grabbed a suitcase out of the hand of an astonished fellow-passenger and took to his heels, through the barrier and away. The psychology behind his move was inspired. For the passenger created a tremendous uproar, attracting everybody's attention for a few minutes—then, as soon as the Germans were fully aware of what had happened, they couldn't care less. An escaping French officer might have been something, but a thief running away with a Belgian's suitcase did not raise the slightest interest. Nine days out from Colditz, Prot arrived in Paris, to the surprise and joy of his family, on Christmas Eve 1941.

He reached Tunis via the French Free Zone in 1942, and joined the 67th Artillery Regiment (Algerian). From Paris he returned the suitcase to the owner, whose address he found inside, and from Tunis he sent to the German dentist a large consignment of real coffee with apologies for the removal of his hat and coat. He fought through the Tunisian campaign to Cassino, where during the first offensive (Mount Belvedere) on 29 January 1944 he gave his life for France.

Winter came in real earnest as the year 1941 ended: heavy falls of snow; ten degrees of frost; snowballing and a slide down the middle of the courtyard.

New Year's Eve was a day of small interest until Hauptmann Püpcke announced that the yard would be open until the time of *Lichts aus* at 1:30 a.m. and that the New Year's morning roll-call would be at 10 a.m. instead of 9 a.m.

The evening was about to close after the "Auld Lang Syne" followed by the national anthem, when the Dutch officers, led by Major Engles, who bore a symbolic broom-at-the-masthead recalling Admiral Tromp's boast in 1666 that he would sweep the British Navy from the sea, swept in and round our day-room, hands to shoulders, in a chanting human chain. On their heels came a bellowing Belgian chain, followed again by a shorter international one. National anthems were sung, and the British had to sing theirs again.

Two hundred POWs linked hands to shoulders then danced out over the snow in the courtyard, on a tour of all the quarters of the *Schloss*. After running up and down thousands of steps on spiral staircases, through low, narrow passages and rooms filled with tobacco smoke and black-out fug, the human chain of sweating bodies ended up in the yard and the snow again.

Dr. Eggers, who had just entered the main gate, handled the situation at this point with admirable tact. The different nationalities were all now in national groups, some standing silent while one or other group sang fiercely of home, love and liberty. Many were expecting that Eggers would stop them singing and drive them indoors. Had he done so he would have had to call out the guard and to have thrust officers indoors under threat of gun-fire—a bad beginning for the New Year. Instead he paced about until each nation had had its turn, and then stepped forward and said, "Now you have had your songs, it is time to go to your quarters," and everyone went without incident or ill-feeling.

By the end of 1941, Eggers recorded the following escape figures:

	British	**French**	**Belgian**	**Polish**	**Dutch**
Number of tries to get away	25	30	6	19	14
Caught inside camp	23	6	6	10	8
Caught outside camp	2	14	0	8	2
Home runs	0	10	0	1	4

On 2 January 1942, Padre Platt made the following cryptic entry in his diary:

Three weeks ago I introduced Dick to an entry I made in December. He thought there was some mistake and said how hesitant he would be to make such an entry but our conversation gave direction to his observation.

I have waited these three weeks with considerable anxiety; if he failed to observe, and decided against my judgement, my plan to short-circuit the miserable business (a carefully thought-out plan, too) would fall to the ground. However, to my intense relief, he came to me this morning boiling with indignation, having proved the matter against his own wish and will.

He has real influence with a more or less central person in the wretched affair, and is prepared and willing to use it to the utmost. I cannot begin my personal contacts until Dick wins his round.

This was followed by another entry on 5 January:

Dick engaged his man in earnest conversation today. He was frightfully ashamed of his conduct and promised to cut it out. At tea time he asked to

> see me and made a frank but shame-faced confession. Now the stage is set, and I must attempt as difficult a task as has yet come my way.
>
> Some of those to whom I propose to speak will deny all knowledge of anything of the kind; while one, I imagine, will tell me to mind my own business. But this happens to be my business; I half wish it were not! The thing I must avoid is direct accusation. At least in the initial stages. I think I will begin by enquiring confidentially of each of the persons concerned if they have observed any homosexual tendencies. What they think of such perversion and of the perverts. The answers will no doubt reveal with what deliberateness or otherwise such indulgences have been embraced.

A severely curtailed version of Padre Platt's diary, edited by Margaret Duggan, was published in 1978. The original written manuscript of the diary was kindly lent to me by the padre's widow in 1983. The above entries and that of 6 December 1941, all of which I have checked against the original, caused a great fluttering in the dovecot of Colditz POWs and Colditz fans. As Dick Howe was named as collaborating with Padre Platt in the latter's aim of excising the cancer, Commander "Mike" Moran, the Colditz ex-POWs organization voluntary secretary, wrote to Dick in 1979 asking for his views on Padre Platt's pronouncements. In his answer Dick regretted that "perversion should be used to pervert the truth." He was adamant that throughout his three years as escape officer his stooges, who were watching the movements of the Germans twenty-four hours a day in several parts of the Castle, would have noticed any midnight liaisons and reported them to him. He continued:

> As for daylight liaisons, I would think it would be easier to have a homosexual relationship in a tube train. Ironically, the only two people who could have had an undisturbed relationship were Padre Platt and Padre Hobling, who were the only two people who had a room to themselves, which was known as the "Priests' Hole." The rest of us had to suffer the discomfort of something like twenty to a room with not a place in the castle where one could go for a bit of peace and quiet, not even the loo, which if you remember only had half doors. . . .
>
> I can recall as if it were yesterday Don Donaldson saying to Platt in his wise-cracking Canadian way that the only thing Platt could write about was Padre Hobling; as you may recall Platt hardly ever ventured outside the Priests' Hole or the British common-room. Platt used to reply to Don Donaldson that he knew more than most people thought, but then we all

knew Platt to be the leading bullshitter in the camp and Don always told him so—I was more polite! Platt could have kept some pages to himself, but I doubt it, and I have some sympathy for anyone trying to edit what I regarded as rubbish and not very interesting at that.

I would hardly regard Pat Reid's opinion as worth much as he was only there for about a third of the life of Colditz as a POW camp. [He means as a *Sonderlager*. My "opinion" related to an overall approval of the book *Padre in Colditz* and I admit to no knowledge of homosexuality while I was in Colditz] . . .

I must re-study my old mates to see which ones he is thinking about as I can only think of one individual who had those tendencies but, poor chap, there was nowhere with any privacy to practice them.

Of course there were individuals who found the frustration almost unbearable and I am surprised the slime pedlars have not picked up the incident of the fellow who cut off his penis as he reckoned he would not have any further use for it. To my certain knowledge, there were more cases of self-inflicted wounds due to sexual repression than homosexuality, which I would say was non-existent or so rare as to have missed the attention of my all-embracing stooging system. . . . Come to think of it, Micky Burn and I could have had a good time when we were locked in the radio cabin for two hours at a time.

9

A Voice in Every Wind

Winter 1941–1942

IT WAS TIME THE BRITISH had a break. They had had no successes to record during the whole of 1941. So it was exhilarating for the camp to learn on morning *Appell* on 7 January that two British officers and two Dutch officers were missing. Eggers describes it thus:

> We ran another of our special searches from 10 a.m. to 2 in the afternoon of that day, keeping over 500 prisoners in the cold of the yard while we did it. The uproar was so loud, unceasing and so threatening, that the *Kreisleiter* [District Organizer, Nazi Party] phoned from the town to ask what was up. He said the townspeople were getting upset! We found nothing. . . .
>
> By then the OKW was getting worried. They began to ask about the "spoil" from an obvious tunnel which we had been reporting off and on for weeks. They bombarded us with questions and advice. One night they rang up, "Is Romilly there? Is Emil there?" We sent [an] NCO to his cell. "Yes, he's there. No, there's not somebody in his place. No, it's not a dummy. We've been in and woken him up."

Now follows a most significant report by Eggers:

> A few days later I found our Emil trotting round the yard. I hadn't seen Romilly taking exercise like this before.
>
> "What does this mean?" I asked jokingly. "In training?"
>
> "Aha!" he replied, "when it's my turn to make the trip I must be fit."

> "Well," I thought, "that's a smart reaction. If Romilly has it in mind to be away too, the exit must be from inside the Castle and not down in the park. Romilly never leaves the Castle yard."

Eggers accordingly determined to make a thorough search of every conceivable place where an exit could have been made. But meanwhile the four escapers were travelling quickly away from Colditz. How had they got out of the Castle?

The story began when I was doing a period in "solitary" in the autumn of 1941. All I could see from my cell window was the wall of a section of the *Saalhaus* or theater-block, and staring blankly at it one day I suddenly realized the potential significance of its structure. I was an engineer, given to visualizing the skeletons of buildings, and what I had so suddenly understood was that the theater's wooden stage extended over a part of the Castle, sealed off from the prisoners, which led by a corridor to the top of the German guardhouse immediately outside the courtyard.

As soon as I was released from my cell, I examined the stage. I found I could crawl underneath by removing some wooden steps, and so inspect that part of the floor over the scaled room. It was just straw and rubble lying on a lath-and-plaster ceiling. Later, with Hank Wardle's help, I cut through this ceiling and descended by sheet-rope to the room below. It was empty. I picked the lock on the door, made a quick reconnaissance down the corridor, relocked, and began work. This involved the installation, in the hole we had made, of a wooden frame and false ceiling. It fitted snugly and after laborious work over many days we eventually made it virtually undetectable to anyone looking up at the ceiling of the sealed room.

On a further reconnoiter along the German corridor I unlocked another door to find myself in the attic over the German guardhouse. From here a spiral staircase led down to the guards' quarters. My plan was simple enough. The escapers would sortie in two pairs, dressed as German officers, on successive evenings immediately after a change of guard stationed at the front entrance to the guardhouse. Thus the new sentry would not know which officers, if any, might have entered the guardhouse in the previous two hours.

I had already chosen Airey Neave and Lieutenant John Hyde-Thompson as the first escapers, provided they could produce first-class imitations of Gennan officers' uniforms. Airey, after all, had had an apprenticeship! But for two reasons they needed Dutch assistance, so with Vandy's agreement two Dutch officers were selected to make the team up to four. Of course it was a great help that the Dutch spoke German fluently.

Dutch greatcoats, with minor alterations, could pass in electric light as German greatcoats. Dutch supplies of lead piping (most of ours had been used to construct a distilling apparatus!) were melted down to produce, with the help of molds, the various metal parts of German uniforms: swastikas, eagles, buttons and buckles. Leather parts such as belts and revolver holsters were made from linoleum, and leggings from cardboard. Excellent service caps were created by our specialists.

And so it was that after evening *Appell* on 5 January I led Airey and Lieutenant Tony Luteijn (Royal Netherlands Indies Army) up to the *Saalhaus*, through the hole beneath the stage and eventually to the attic above the guardhouse. I left them and returned to cover up our traces. Watchers reported a perfect exit from the guardhouse and the two were last seen heading for the moat bridge where there was a gate leading down into the moat.

The next day the two *Appells* were covered. Van den Heuvel arranged this with equanimity. He still had at least one dummy saved in his secret hideaway.

In the evening, I repeated the performance of the night before. Hyde-Thompson and his Dutch colleague, 2nd Lieutenant H. G. Donkers, departed from the camp.

Eggers persevered with his search for the secret exit. Little did we know how Giles Romilly's incautious remark had improved his chances of success. After much fruitless searching, including the wine cellar and the chapel, he came to search the *Saalhaus* on the 13th. A corporal prised up one of the floorboards of the steps up to the stage and Eggers ordered the smallest man from the guardroom to squeeze through and see what he could find. What he found was our hole in the ceiling. Eggers reports:

> So confident had the escapers been over this exit that no camouflage to speak of had been used to cover the framework on the top side, and close alongside, under the stage, we found hidden a rope made of bedsheets, for lowering the escapers to the floor underneath [in fact the wooden frame was carefully covered and camouflaged, as were the bedsheets]. This was obviously how the four of them had got out the week previously.
>
> We checked back, interviewing guards. Naturally no one remembered anything a week after the event, but someone or more of them must have let four prisoners past.
>
> More precautionary measures were once again forced upon us. . . . The door at the top of the guardroom stairs . . . was doubly bolted. The

horses, however, had gone. Two never came back. But I got a week's leave and a bottle of champagne from the *Kommandant* for my discovery up in the theater.

On 10 January, Hyde-Thompson and Donkers were back. They had been trapped at Ulm—a railway junction necessitating a change of trains. But their recapture exposed a serious flaw in my escape strategy which becomes evident from Airey Neave's account of his progress out of the Castle and through Germany. Changing at Ulm they had asked for tickets to Singen. The ticket clerk frowned at their papers and called a railway policeman:

> The policeman took us to an office in the goods yard where a thin, tight-lipped German railway police Lieutenant sat at a desk. He examined our false papers with bewilderment. It appeared to me that the writing on it did not make sense to him. I could hardly stop myself from laughing as he lifted them to the light, looking, no doubt, for water marks. He was, however, impressed by Luteijn's Dutch passport and there seemed no inkling in his mind that we were escaped prisoners of war.
>
> "I don't understand these men at all," he said helplessly. "Take them to the Labor office. I wish someone would control these foreign workers more efficiently."

Escorted to the Labor office by another armed policeman, they escaped through a back door. After this incident and a few more risky encounters, the two, traversing forests and fields in deep snow near Singen, on the same route that Larive had taken, crossed the frontier safely into Switzerland.

The Ulm policemen were not going to be taken in so easily again, so that when Hyde-Thompson and Donkers arrived the next day with similar identity papers and travelling to the same destination the police pounced on them.

In future the route to the frontier would have to be varied.

Airey Neave had progressed from the Eton Officers' Training Corps through Oxford Territorial Army—an infantryman. Then, at the outbreak of war, he became a gunner in a searchlight training regiment in Hereford. From there he crossed to Boulogne in February 1940 in charge of an advance party of rugged old veterans of the First War. During the *Blitzkrieg* in May 1940, Airey moved from Arras to the outskirts of Calais with his battery to take part in the last stand before Dunkirk. On 24 May he was wounded. "A field-grey figure appeared shouting and waving a revolver. Then a large man in German uniform and a Red Cross armband put me gently on a stretcher. I was a prisoner-of-war."

In August, Airey was in *Oflag* IXA/H, a castle high above the town of Spangenburg, near Kassel. From there he was transferred in February 1941 to *Stalag* XXA, a vast POW camp in Poland, at Thorn, on the banks of the Vistula. Here he found himself with hundreds of other officers living in damp cold vaults in an old Polish fort surrounded by a moat. This was a measure of reprisal for the alleged ill treatment of German POWs in Canada. From here Airey made his first escape, on 19 April, only to be recaptured a few days later when frontier guards found a small map of Grandenz Aerodrome in his pocket (his fellow escaper was Flying Officer "Bricky" Forbes, and they had planned to steal an aircraft). They were returned to Thorn, and shut up at first in filthy underground storerooms, with rotting swedes and fetid air.

Then, one morning in the early hours, Airey was led from his cell towards some lights on the fort's drawbridge; as he drew closer he noticed shadowy figures stamping their feet, talking in English and even laughing. He recognized Forbes and then Squadron-Leader Paddon and Lieutenant-Commander Stevenson, who a short time before had tried to escape in a dust cart.

"Where in hell are we going?" Airey exclaimed.

"To Colditz."

Airey, with Tony Luteijn, had made the first British home-run from Colditz. For the men he left behind he was like the dove released from the Ark which had found land.

The Germans found it difficult to believe that four officers had got away without trace. On the morning of 10 January when Donkers and Hyde-Thompson returned they made a further search of the British quarters, thinking two men were concealed. Then on 14 January, after the discovery of the *Saalhaus* exit, the whole British contingent was marched down from the Castle to the *Schützenhaus*.

A march of about half a mile brought them to what had long been regarded as a *Mitarbeit*—collaboration—camp. The presence of decorative electric bulbs on two Christmas trees; a domestic cat purring by a hot stove; a quantity of *Mitarbeit* propaganda, together with spacious grounds in which to walk, play at football, grow vegetables, and keep about forty Angora rabbits, appeared to confirm the suspicion.

The residents of the *Schützenhaus* were occupying the upper portion of the building, and the POWs on the ground floor were prevented from having any contact with them by armed sentries posted on the stairway. A wise precaution!

Few people were quite so detested as *collaborateurs.* Officers therefore experienced none of the restraints of conscience in availing themselves of *Mitarbeit* flex, lamps and fittings. An intention to introduce pussy to more of the "best people" of *Gefangenschaft* (captivity) was frustrated by a prescient orderly who evidently sensed the impending depredation and removed her to the safety of the upper story.

The floor of the British subalterns' dormitory had received considerable attention in their absence from the Castle, and the one remaining tunnel found.

10

'Tis All a Checker Board

Winter to Spring 1942

EARLY IN JANUARY, about the 9th, thirty-one French officers were transferred from Colditz to *Oflag* IVD at Elsterhorst. The reason for the transfer has never been clearly explained. Eggers gives no reason for it. The fact that Lieutenant de Bykowitz, a White Russian (French Army), tried to jump train on the way is of only passing interest. He was recaught, trapped by Germans, on the ice-covered buffers at the end of the train. Nevertheless there may have been a reason for their transfer because amongst the thirty-one were some members of the team who had been working on the great French tunnel, a truly prodigious undertaking, since May 1941. The Germans knew a tunnel was being excavated. After 7 January, according to Eggers, the OKW were wondering if the tunnel wasn't finished and men being trickled out by a secret exit. There had been visits by experienced police inspectors from Dresden prior to this—every month—to find the tunnel, but with no success. The *Kommandant* became very nervous and, as soon as Eggers had returned to Colditz by Christmas, he had been given the special task of uncovering the secret. Stabsfeldwebel Gephard and Obergefreiter (Corporal) Schädlich were his assistants.

The French architects of the tunnel consisted originally of a team of nine officers who constituted themselves the original "*Société Anonyme du Tunnel de Colditz.*" To make sure that it was *anonyme*, the tunnellers had no chief. "*Liberté, égalité, fraternité*" was the motto they lived up to. They were: Jean Bréjoux, a professor of German; Edgar Barras, the strong man and the champion French "stool-ball" player; Lieutenant Bernard Cazaumayou, the weightlifter; Lieutenant Roger Madin, an engineer who was the tunnel electrician; Lieutenant Paillie,

French Sappers and Miners; Lieutenant Jean Gambero, the astute Parisian; and Lieutenant Léonce Godfrin, from the Ardennes. Lieutenant "Fredo" Guigues was a kind of consultant.

Their conception was brilliant and typical. The French are a logical race. They had read in the German press that the Leipzig Fair was to be held in spite of the war. Leipzig was only twenty-two miles away. The thronging visitors would provide wonderful cover for the escape of a large body of prisoners. The only way, it seemed, to despatch a large body of prisoners out of the Castle was by tunnel. Having decided where they would like their tunnel to debouch so as to provide a safe get-away, they worked backwards into the Castle to see where the entrance should be. Eventually they decided on the top of the clock-tower!

The clock-tower provided them with a means of access to the cellar. The clock had not worked for years and the weights, with their long ropes, had also been removed, leaving empty cylindrical sleeves lined with canvas between the floor and ceiling below at each floor level. There were four floors above ground-floor level. The sleeved floors were in small inspection chambers, originally with access doors by the circular staircase at each floor level. The access doors had long ago been bricked up by the Jerries. A heavy steel door on the top landing of the French quarters, at fourth-floor level, gave access to the clock itself. With men like Lieutenants "Fredo" Guigues and Roger Madin in the camp, the padlocks, mortice locks and cruciform locks (like four Yale locks combined) securing this door were soon provided with keys. Once in the clock-room, a camouflaged opening was constructed in the floor and in the ceiling below, which let the Frenchmen down into the chamber on the third floor. The sleeves were a tight squeeze for any adult, being only sixteen inches in diameter, and climbing up again would have been difficult. They constructed ladders instead, using bedboards (taken from their bunks), piercing holes in each chamber floor down to ground level. Electric cable was led in and light provided at each floor. Now the first serious tunnelling began. It consisted of a vertical shaft through the stones and mortar of the arched roof of the Castle cellar.

The masonry defied all the earlier tools. It was clear that probes, levers and drills were essential. These were made from the steel axles of the clock mechanism. They were tempered, then the tips hardened. A crowbar was needed to shift large blocks and slabs of stone weighing as much as two hundredweight. The British managed to steal one and lent it willingly to the French for a few hours every day.

On 15 August 1941, the three strongest of the team managed to shift one of the massive marble slabs which were part of the foundations' ventilating system. They were exhausted, but the cellar had been reached!

Once in the cellar, which, of course, was subject to examination by German patrols, the Frenchmen had the choice of digging in any direction they wished. They started breaking out a hole, four feet from the ground, in the wall facing the chapel. They had been given an indication from a British plan of the Castle (which had come from England) that there was probably a vault under the chapel.

Having made an entrance door on pivots out of the original stones from the wall, they continued, digging a horizontal tunnel behind it, through the heavy foundation which supported the dividing wall between the chapel and the spiral staircase to the French quarters. This continued for a distance of fifteen feet.

Once under the chapel, they dug a vertical shaft upwards for a distance of nine feet, removing some massive masonry, until they met the beams of the chapel floor. With no means of getting round them, lengths were cut from each beam with saws made from kitchen knives. Seven beams in all were breached over a distance of twenty yards, until finally they were under the sacristy. But still no sign of a crypt. They were getting nowhere. And the foundations resisted every effort to tunnel through.

The team realized, at last, that there was no short cut and that they would have to continue the tunnel until they were outside the wire. They decided to increase the number of tunnellers. They had been working by day and night for two months and were ready to welcome new blood. So the numbers rose from nine to thirty. Tunnelling would continue in three shifts throughout the twenty-four hours.

They decided to go under the foundations, and commenced digging a shaft. For six yards the masonry continued downwards. They kept on digging. The fat lamps were changed for electric light connected to lighting switches in the sacristy. An electric signaling system was installed. Then the Germans closed the chapel, destroying the stooging arrangements. Abbé Jean-Jean, the French chaplain, protested vigorously. It was impossible, he said, to initiate novices into the mysteries of the faith they wished to embrace! They knew very little of the Catholic faith. They had to be taught the catechism, the prayers, the gospel. The chapel was the only appropriate place in which to do so. As a result he was allowed to use the chapel for two hours a day.

Seated inside, near the half-open door, he was able to keep watch. If a Goon looked like entering, the tunnel electrician and others engaged on illicit work were quickly kneeling and praying near Abbé Jean-Jean. Faced with such an edifying picture, far removed from escape activities, the Goon usually tiptoed out. As soon as he had disappeared the "novices" resumed their work.

One day Gephard ("Mussolini") himself entered the chapel. The electrician abandoned the wires which were hanging loose and rushed to a *prie-dieu*. Mussolini indicated that he wished to talk to Jean-Jean and walked towards the sacristy. All seemed lost. But the curé gave more signs of the cross, more blessings, more prayers. He and the "novices" were so taken with the Holy Spirit that Mussolini, much impressed, turned and tiptoed out of the chapel.

The chapel was Abbé Jean-Jean's domain. He organized its use by each of the various "cults," to the satisfaction of all except perhaps the Polish curé. But it was not entirely a question of religious services! Far from it!

The chapel did not escape searches, although usually there was sufficient warning to cover up. On one occasion, with only seconds to spare, important items of civilian clothing were pushed into three of the organ tubes and got through the search. The Germans' suspicions were aroused so for the time being the clothing had to stay where it was. Hymns had to be chosen carefully, avoiding notes corresponding to the "hidey-hole" tubes. A couple of the guards attended services regularly.

One search produced a tricky situation. It was normal after a search for things to be taken away for closer examination. On this occasion the monstrance, in which were already consecrated Hosts, was removed. Abbé Jean-Jean demanded its immediate return, accusing the Germans of sacrilege and profaning the Holy Sacrament. Such was his anger that the *Hauptmann*, abashed, went off to find it. When he returned with the monstrance the Polish and French contingent were in the courtyard, prostrated on the cobbles in quiet, pious adoration, leaving only a narrow passage which led to the chapel door.

The religious choirs were international; organized and directed by Jean-Jean. The Poles, always eager to take part in Catholic services, contributed not only their deep faith but also their splendid singing voices. They were most moving. Their country had been wiped off the map. They were not even allowed to write the name "Poland" on their letters. Should they rejoice or should they not over Russian victories? Refusing to be discouraged, their faith in their fatherland inspired admiration. Their fervor was impressive. Their splendid songs, in which the whole choir joined, affirmed their faith in the resurrection of Poland.

The irrepressible Padre Jean-Jean had his own ideas about the French tunnel. He was not going to be left behind. On 10 January he and the French doctor, Le Guet, made a break for it while out in the Colditz woods for a walk. Medical and religious personnel were to some extent privileged under the Geneva Convention. Doctors and ministers, as well as Red Cross orderlies, were allowed to go outside the limits of the park for exercise. They went out on walks "escorted" by one guard. The Germans certainly did not think that these two would try to get away. There was only one guard to the group of five, and he could not, of course, stop them. They got as far as Saarbrücken before recapture, in civilian clothes, with the usual false papers on them and German money. Eggers felt this escape to be a breach of trust. In any case, privileged or not privileged, the two took their twenty-one days' cells without protest!

Dick Howe once told "Fredo" Guigues: "We've heard you digging away for months, and of course your own people have, too. Haven't you been running a tremendous risk all this time? The Germans must know well enough that a tunnel's in progress." It was a fact that at all hours of the day, but more especially at night when the Castle was wrapped in silence, tunnelling could be heard.

"The Jerries may know it well enough," said Guigues in French, "but as long as they can find no entrance we are safe."

"But the Germans will persevere. . . ."

It wasn't until the end of December that the diggers finally reached the foot of the chapel wall foundations. Hope was reborn! Levels and direction were assessed. A tunnel, about thirty yards long, would emerge beyond the cat-walk, out of sight of the sentries. They would be on the slope into the moat on the north-east of the Castle, at the bottom of which was a fast-flowing, noisy stream. The work continued with renewed vigor.

Digging this final section of tunnel required great care. There were loose rocks and stones. Protective headgear was worn and the roof supported by timbers. The tunnel jinked and turned to avoid unmovable obstacles. The disposal of earth and rocks was particularly arduous. Readily available spaces were quickly filled. Soon, bags of soil and rock filled the tower-chambers right up to the fourth floor. After that the only solution was to go even higher. Above the chapel was a large attic with spacious cavities under the eaves. There the rubble could be hidden from the "ferrets," who rarely went there as it was believed to be inaccessible to the prisoners. Access was through a camouflaged hole in the celling of the fourth floor.

Transporting sacks of rubble weighing forty to fifty pounds from the depths of the foundations and from the end of a narrow tunnel to the attic, involving nearly forty yards of horizontal travel and twenty yards of vertical shafting, was far from easy. Apart from manpower, a lot of equipment and efficient organization were necessary. A workshop in the clock-tower was used for making sacks, ropes of various sizes, string for tying them, hooks, pulleys, "rolling carpet" for maneuvering the sacks under the chapel floor, track and trolley repair parts. All equipment wore out rapidly and had to be made good repeatedly with whatever materials the team could lay their hands on.

The disposal of rubble required twenty-two men, spread out along the route, each with a clearly defined role. Their actions became mechanical. Pull or lift a sack; hook it on, or unhook it; signal "ready" to the next chap. Then the same again. At peak periods over a ton of rubble per shift was safely transferred from the tunnel to the fifth-floor attic.

Over Christmas and New Year the French tunnellers were in good spirits. Less than twenty yards to go before reaching the exit! There was a fever of preparation. Tailors, hat-makers, forgers, map- and compass-makers, all worked long hours. German money was distributed; lots drawn for the order of leaving. Even the rope necessary for descending the ravine was ready. Emerging two by two they would walk in the stream some distance so as not to leave footprints. Half an hour after the last of the escape team had left the tunnel would be available for all. About 200 expressed their intention of using it. . . . And, as the final few yards of the tunnel were being dug, the tunnellers had the satisfaction of hearing over their heads the tread of the cat-walk sentries.

Then came the departure of the French officers early in January, including members of the tunnel team. The Germans, encouraged and goaded on by their discovery of the theater exit, were on the warpath for the tunnel. The French ceased all work.

Then there was peace for three days. Work started again—cautiously. But the Germans had not finished. On 14 January, searching of the upper floors began. Mussolini made a surprise attack on the 15th. He probed the long weight sleeves in the clock-tower; he could see nothing as he flashed his torch down into the darkness. He let one of the clock weights fall. It dislodged some camouflage. Then he saw a light below and heard movement. He sent a message out to the *Kommandantur* by the hand of the sentry who was with him.

Within ten minutes several Goons appeared with a small boy amongst them. A coil of rope was tied around his waist, and he was lowered slowly through one of the sleeves into the blackness below. In his hand he carried a torch which he aimed at the floor beneath him. As he landed he flashed the torch around him and screamed in terror. "*Hilfe! Hilfe! Hier sind Leute!*" ("Help! There are people here!")

There were three Frenchmen in the chamber. Mussolini was occupying the only exit. The Frenchmen knew of a last desperate way out. At one corner of the chamber, a comparatively thin wall, nine inches thick, separated them from a bathroom used by patients from the sick ward.

As the terrified youth, sobbing with fright and shouting "*Hilfe!*," was hauled up again through the sleeve, the Frenchmen attacked the dividing wall with crowbars like demons, and in five minutes had battered a hole through it. The noise they made was deafening, yet the Germans above them were so occupied with the youth that, when they awoke to reality and sent search parties in frantic haste to locate the new hole being pierced with all the publicity of a battery of pneumatic drills, they were too late. The birds had flown.

A Belgian Army major, Baron de Liedekerke, was peacefully reading a book, lying in his bath, on the other side of the wall, when the earthquake started. A brick landed on his stomach. It was time, he thought, to evacuate. He rose and reached for his towel. A jagged hole suddenly appeared. Iron bars flayed the opening, enlarging it. As he stepped from the bath, a head and shoulders came through the opening. Then a half-naked body scrambled over the bath on to the floor, bespattered, sweat-stained and filthy. Another body followed and then a third, more bulky than the others. It had difficulty in squeezing through and fell into the bath.

Major de Liedekerke picked up his belongings and rushed from the room shouting: "*Mon Dieu! Mon Dieu! C'est le comble!*" Which means, "My God! My God! This is the end!"

It was indeed the end of the French tunnel.

The French were certain that the tunnel had been given away through injudicious talk by some of the officers who had been transported to Elsterhorst. Eggers says that this was not true. He writes:

> The circumstances of the start of our inspection of the clock-tower that morning showed that we had had absolutely no idea of what was waiting for us. We certainly never expected to find the entrance to a tunnel right up under the roof. If we had indeed had a tip-off about this, we certainly should at least have put sentries on each floor up against the bricked-up tower entrances. This find was one of those lucky chances that happen occasionally if one follows a sound principle long enough. In this case our rule was to close in slowly and methodically upon a suspected danger spot, ignoring lack of results until the job was finished, whether successfully or unsuccessfully. This was indeed a find—at least six months of work must have gone into this tunnel project. I crawled to the working face myself and could hear the sentry above me and they had only thirty feet to go! We were only just in time. We were all cock-a-hoop—especially the *Kommandant*. He gave our search party special leave as a reward.

The discovery of the tunnel coincided with the visit to the Castle of the *Gauleiter* (area commander) of Saxony, Herr Mutschmann. Not only was this gentleman given a riotous reception by the resentful French in particular and the remainder of the camp in general, but Eggers' life was made unbearable with howls and catcalls whenever he entered the courtyard.

As heaps of tunnel debris began to pile up alongside other piles of escape material of all kinds which had been concealed in the tower, the *Gauleiter* expressed his astonishment at the siege conditions under which, to him, the camp appeared to exist.

It is not inappropriate at this point to mention something about POWs' pay, which was given to them in *Lagergeld* prisoners' money—i.e. paper money of small denominations which could not be used outside the prison walls.

The Germans wrangled long and loud with the prisoners over the repairs to be done in the clock-tower, under the chapel and in the attics. Who was going to pay for this and for the removal of several tons of rubble? A local contractor wanted 12,000 marks—nearly a thousand pounds—for the clearance job! He had to fill up the holes with concrete as well. The *Kommandant* made a forced levy out of all prisoners' pay. Prisoners were entitled to half their home rate of pay at an exchange rate of so many *Lagermarks* to their own currency (fifteen marks to the pound sterling). The Swiss government held the real cash, which both the Germans and the Allies paid up as backing for camp money issued on both sides. The OKW came into the tunnel dispute at the prisoners' request, and ruled against this collective fine. They ordered the repayment of the forced levy to the prisoners, arguing that this was a collective punishment and the *Kommandant* had no authority to inflict it. They said it was illegal under the Geneva Convention. The Germans lost face at first, but regained it, and the money, by another interpretation of the same Convention, supported this time by the barrack-room lawyers of the OKW: the *Kommandant* levied the canteen profits, which under the Convention might be used "for the benefit of the prisoners." Obviously, he said, it was to the prisoners' advantage that the roof should not collapse upon them or the floor in their so valuable chapel should not subside beneath them!

As to other measures—the chapel was closed indefinitely. The Germans buried microphones every thirty feet all round the outside of the prisoners' buildings. Brand new tools found in the clock-tower showed the Germans that the bribery and corruption of the guard company was rampant. The OKW ordered the replacement of the whole company.

Some arrivals and departures took place around this time. On 23 January Howard Gee, the civilian, turned up again. He had been despatched from Colditz almost as a menial in February 1941. Howard Gee had the following to say of his adventures:

> I was in Colditz on two separate occasions, arriving first in 1940 as orderly to a group of British officers who had escaped by tunnel from a camp at Laufen near Salzburg. At the time I was rated as an other-rank prisoner, having been picked up in Oslo with several other Englishmen. The Germans did not believe that we were returning from Finland where we had been volunteers for the Finnish International Brigade. They thought that we were British troops in civilian clothes, waiting for the British invasion of Norway, which they had just forestalled. There were some sharp exchanges as to the fate we might deserve. I left Colditz at the beginning of 1941, on being recognized as a civilian.

He returned to occupy officers' quarters on a somewhat similar basis to Giles Romilly. He had made the circuit of several *Ilags*, i.e. civilian prisoners' camps, and having escaped from one of them he was given the final accolade of a red tab on his papers, *Deutschfeindlich*, and despatched to his natural habitat—Colditz.

Guy German and Padre Hobling left for Spangenburg *Oflag* IXA on 21 January. The reasons for Guy's dismissal from his duties as SBO were not far to seek. Over a long period of stewardship it was finally driven home to the Germans that Guy German was totally committed to promoting the escape of officers and also to collusion with disruptive and non-cooperative practices amongst the POWs. He was universally popular but greatly respected at the same time. Undoubtedly he was a scourge to Oberst Schmidt, who must have engineered his removal. With him went his batman, the irrepressible Solly Goldman.

The discovery of the French tunnel was a major setback for the French, but the camaraderie that existed between the nationalities was such that the whole camp felt the loss and were inwardly seething at the success of the Germans. The French would never forgive Eggers.

The first confrontation in the "saluting war" had taken place in September when the Polish Lieutenant Siefert had won a resounding victory and the German side had been greatly discomfited. Now the mood of the whole company was such that another round in the war was imminent.

On 19 January the twenty-two-year-old Belgian Lieutenant Verkest (he had stood in for Mairesse Lebrun in the park-walk count) crossed the path of Hauptmann Eggers without saluting, on his way to fall in for *Appell*. Eggers stopped him and requested the salute prescribed by the Geneva Convention. Verkest refused to comply. Eggers then said: "Will you not take your hands out of your pockets? It is not the custom in Germany to speak to a superior officer with your hands in your pockets."

Verkest replied, "Neither is it so in Belgium."

This was the last straw for Eggers. He reported the incident to the *Kommandant.* Normally the cells were overflowing with officers doing a week's *Arrest* for not saluting. On this day the war came to a head. The *Kommandant* ordered a court-martial and Verkest was "clapped into jug" pending. . . .

The court-martial was ordered on a charge of disobeying an order. The local lawyer, Dr. Naumann, the ex-POW from England, undertook the defense. The hearing was put down for March. In the meantime Verkest remained in "solitary."

On 29 January Oberst Schmidt summoned all the Senior Officers to a meeting in order to convince them of the necessity of obeying the OKW order. At the end of the meeting a copy of the *procès-verbal* was handed to each. The outcome of the meeting was to establish a sort of *modus vivendi.* For their part the Germans turned a blind eye unless it seemed that prisoners were being blatantly insubordinate. At *Appell* for instance, the prisoners "adapted" to the new order: the French and British saluted "casually"—at the very last minute; the Senior Polish Officer waited until his interpreter had saluted the German and the salute had been returned.

Both sides seemed to accept that approach. The exception was the German Doktor Rahm, who insisted always on being saluted by every prisoner. Every failure to do so was punished, and the cells were full of his victims. The hatred that this inspired, added to his attitude towards sick prisoners, led to demonstrations.

Unknown to the prisoners, on 8 February, a German soldier purloined the revolver of Hauptmann Vent and shot himself through the head whilst the *Hauptmann* was absent. According to Eggers the motive was not discovered. But all the indiscipline in the camp had one significant consequence. Eggers replaced Priem:

> The indiscipline in the camp never ceased to have its effect in the cold war between staff and prisoners. L.O.1 [Priem] was held largely responsible for this. We had some argument about it. As senior Duty Officer, had he not started off, right back in 1940, on the wrong foot? This sort of life was no joke, and we felt it was he who had set the tone of our relations from the beginning, and that it was the wrong tone entirely. Besides, he liked his drink, and everyone, the prisoners and ourselves, knew it. There were some

> stand-up rows in the Mess about him, and in the end, although he was well in with the *Kommandant*, L.O.1 was helped upstairs to the post of Deputy *Kommandant*, which kept him out of the prisoners' yard pretty well altogether. At the same time, his sharpest critic, L.O.4, was posted down in the town, in charge of the Indian prisoners in the *Schützenhaus* camp there. Two hundred and twenty of them arrived on the 28th of January.
>
> It fell to me now to bear the maximum brunt of contact with the "bad boys," with three roll-calls and several arguments per day to work from. I had been doing this work while L.O.1 was on leave, and shortly after his return and promotion (on February 14th) I found myself in his shoes, the new "*Lageroffizier* No. 1."

One amelioration of the POWs' regime resulting from Eggers having taken over the duties of senior *Lageroffizier* from Priem was the installation of an electric bell controlled from the guardhouse for announcing *Appells*. This rang loud and clear giving half an hour's notice of *Appell*, followed by a second bell at five minutes before. The POWs were grateful for the half-hour's notice to wind up their nefarious activities and, in order to retain this advantage, consented to put a little order and punctuality into their own attendance, which benefited everybody. The result was thus beneficial in another direction. Eggers in return had to agree to speed up the *Appell* routine. The time taken was reduced from between twenty and twenty-five minutes to ten minutes.

Temperatures throughout January had been appalling, from 17°C to –33°C. On 28 January the coal shortage necessitated cutting off all hot-water washing facilities for a fortnight. A short thaw actually occurred at the end of the month and to illustrate the effect on the British POW quarters Padre Platt reported that he started de-icing his "Priests' Hole," collecting four buckets of ice from inside the windows and three buckets of water mopped up from the floor. After the thaw, snow began to fall again and it grew colder.

11

Physician Heal Thyself

Spring 1942

THOUGH IT HAD PROVED expensive for the prisoners, the clearance of the rubble from the French tunnel at least offered a couple of escape opportunities.

Jacques Hageman and Cadet F. V. Geerligs walked out of the main gate early in March 1942 dressed as German laborers who were busy removing debris. They got as far as the moat bridge, one of them pushing the Germans' wheelbarrow. Unfortunately, "Little Willi," a German electrician, was coming the other way. Little Willi would know these two German laborers well. Alas! Hageman and Geerligs had not disguised their faces, relying on their civilian caps as sufficient. Little Willi was about to pass the time of day with them. He hesitated and then he shouted to the guard at the last gate, "Guard! Those two are not our men. They are prisoners!"

Later a cart was being used for the clearance. On 20 March, Lieutenant Desjobert, a Frenchman, managed to climb on board and hide under the rubble. He got as far as the town, but was being slowly smothered so he crawled out from under it. A woman, looking out of an upper window, saw him and warned the driver.

Hageman next was involved in the Dutch tunnel. The Dutch occupied the third floor on the east side of the Castle above the British quarters. Outside on the east wall was a buttress, extending up to the third floor with a balustraded balcony at the top of it. Amongst the prisoners it had always been a question of conjecture. Was the buttress hollow? Van den Heuvel decided to find out.

Inside the main wall, which was about two yards thick, there was a three-man-wide urinal and a WC off one room. This room led to a further room through a large and deep opening. Could the wall between the opening and the main wall be hollow?

Vandy persuaded the Germans that for sanitary reasons the urinal must at all times be thoroughly disinfected. A bucket of liquid tar and a large brush were provided by the Germans. A hole, about eighteen inches square, was started at waist level, lined with bedboards, cut to fit, and cemented in place to form a frame. A close-fitting concrete slab was made to join the frame. Slits were filled with a soap mixture and the whole wall then coated with liquid tar.

From the square hole a short tunnel was dug, turning sharply to the right in the thickness of the external walls. After about six feet the tunellers reached, as they had come to expect, a completely sealed-off cavity, a chamber in the thickness of the dividing wall between the two rooms. It became clear that the chamber was a hall or corridor leading out to the balcony through a doorway which was walled up. From here, the tunnellers dug downwards, through the floor diagonally and outwards.

Eventually they came out at the top of a hollow shaft immediately under the balcony floor. The shaft inside the so-called buttress was about seven feet wide by three feet deep. There is little doubt that this buttress was a medieval lavatory for bedrooms on the second floor. This is further borne out by the fact that the tunnellers, having manufactured a rope ladder to reach the bottom of the shaft, found that the bottom was several feet below the ground level outside, forming a pit.

Starting a tunnel horizontally from the pit bottom, with plenty of room for spoil, they were now only nine yards away from that same steep slope to the ravine which the French had so nearly reached.

Dames and Hageman were on digging shift, Hageman at the face and Dames on watch, when the balloon went up. Eggers had decided to investigate the buttress. It was last on his list of "unoccupied quarters," and he had asked the paymaster, who knew the Castle from before the war at the time when it was an asylum, whether the buttress was solid or hollow. The paymaster's assurance that it was solid was not enough for him. It is more than likely that his sound detectors had picked up some scraping noises—though he does not admit to that.

With his team, equipped with pick-axes and sledge-hammers, he went straight to a room on the ground floor which backed on to the buttress and began opening up a hole. The tunnellers had already been signaled to stop work. When the hammering began, they climbed up the ladder fifty feet, one at a time, back into the chamber. There was a race to haul up the ladder before the Germans broke through. They were not quite quick enough. A torch beam glinted on the ladder swinging upwards.

The Dutch had now been cleared from their quarters and counted, and there was complete silence outside the chamber. Then a German was climbing up the buttress inside. He must have had crampons. The tunnellers threw everything they could by way of debris at him down their chute entrance. They burnt incriminating papers and materials and threw them down. Still he persevered. So they decided to break out through the secret sealed entrance, only to be confronted by a German guard. The Germans then made a big haul of escape paraphernalia, including dummies and uniforms, from the chamber.

This period saw a further blow to the prisoners' supplies of contraband. One of the German censors worked in the book trade in Leipzig. In the early part of 1942, he noticed that the covers of some of the books that he was handling seemed rather thicker than usual, especially as paper was in short supply all over the world. At his suggestion the covers of half a dozen books sent by the Prisoners' Leisure Hour Fund from Lisbon were opened up. They were found to contain in every case either 100-mark notes, or maps on silk of, for example, the Swiss frontier, the Yugoslav frontier, the Dutch and Belgian frontiers, the layout of Danzig harbor, and so on. They even found tiny hacksaw blades and compasses in these covers as well. Eggers said that it then struck them that they had recently received and passed on to individual prisoners several other parcels from this same source in Lisbon. So, something had to be done. At least these books had to be taken back. That meant a visit from Eggers to the British library.

The British librarian was now Padre Platt. Eggers went over to the prisoners' library and got Platt to give him back several of these Lisbon books. Eggers said he wanted them for "statistical purposes." Some of these books were out on loan to readers, but Platt promised to get them back.

Back in the censor's office it was found that the books that had been collected also had unusual covers with valuable contents. But when Eggers got the rest of the books that afternoon, he found that the covers had all been cut open and emptied, and the endpapers stuck back on again. Quite naturally the British realized what Eggers was after, and removed the contraband from what till then had been a first-rate hiding place. Eggers concludes:

> From then on, no book covers at all were allowed, and to save ourselves trouble we put it through to the OKW, and they agreed with us, that the

prisoners should be allowed to receive only books with paper backs. For once there was no argument in Colditz.

Under a new order in March all *Antrags* (requests) of a general nature had to be submitted to four representatives of the *Kommandant* who sat in the *Evidenzzimmer* for that purpose at 3 p.m. on Wednesdays. Padre Platt attended with Colonel Stayner, the new British SBO since the departure of Colonel German, to enquire about the stopping of the non-combatants' walks. For answer he was not told, as he had expected to be, that they were now foregone because Le Guet and Jean-Jean had escaped from one, but that a recent OKW order declared that British chaplains were now to be regarded as combatant officers. Platt commented: "this ruling surely awards to weary chaplains the privilege and excitement of engaging in escape rackets and making good the racket should opportunity occur. I think it is rather a good exchange!"

In mid-March the British had a small new intake: Lieutenants Michael Sinclair and Grismond Davies-Scourfield and Major Ronald Littledale (somewhat later as he was held in hospital in Czechoslovakia), all of the 60th King's Royal Rifles. These three had escaped from the reprisal fort at Posen on 28 May 1941. Sinclair and Littledale had been in Poland, where they were looked after by the Polish Underground. They were eventually passed on and ended up in Bulgaria. After five months of freedom they were caught and handed back by the Bulgarians to the Germans. Grismond remained at liberty for nine months in Poland.

On 16 March Flight-Lieutenant Peter Tunstall and flying Officer Dominic Bruce arrived from *Oflag* VIB.

Doktor Rahm, the German camp doctor, came into prominence once more at this time. The sickroom tunnel, in which Airey Neave had once been involved, had progressed quite a distance under the parcel office when it was betrayed to the Germans on 18 March by a Ukrainian orderly. The orderly was badly beaten up by the Poles, and Rahm was furious that allegedly sick patients, treated by him with care and consideration, should take advantage of their situation. He closed this lower "cellar" sickroom, transferring the beds to another room on the first floor on the park side of the Castle.

On 25 March Admiral Unrug and General Le Bleu were scheduled to leave Colditz after the morning *Appell*; General Le Bleu for the generals' camp IVB at Königstein and Admiral Unrug for camp VIIIE at Johannesbrun in Czechoslovakia. So the Polish and French contingents all remained in the courtyard after *Appell* to give their Senior Officers a good send off.

On that same morning, news had come through of the court-martial verdict on Verkest the day before. Verkest pleaded guilty and was awarded a three-year sentence for "disobedience" on the "saluting" count. However, during the *procès* Verkest revealed in cross-examination that the whole Belgian Colditz contingent, thirty-three of them, had agreed together to refuse to salute; and according to Eggers:

> They had also passed a resolution [not to salute] concerning those members of the Belgian Armed Forces who had given their parole to us and returned to freedom. The Court held this, as well as the group refusal to salute, to be an "agreement to disobey orders concerning duty matters," and therefore mutiny. Verkest was sentenced to death, in spite of Naumann's pleadings. Sentence was suspended for three months. The Head of State must confirm it.

While the Poles and the French were waiting in the yard, Stabsarzt (Surgeon-Major) Rahm entered through the main gate, the "eye of the needle." He was always punctual. It was exactly 9 a.m. Many officers were walking round. With a large number of potential salutes before him, he scented blood. The "horse doctor" made straight for the nearest group, whose attitude promised a rich harvest. The group split in two, one going towards the left-hand door, the other to the right. Rahm went after the group on the left, but they had disappeared through the door, leaving him alone in that corner. The other group had followed, shouting "*Tierarzt, geh' nach Moskau!* (go to Moscow!)" and other insults. Those prisoners in their rooms crowded the windows.

Rahm turned and rushed at his assailants, but they in turn disappeared through the right-hand door just as the first group reappeared and recommenced their shouts, backed up by the spectators at the windows. "*Tierarzt, T-i-e-r-a-r-z-t!*"

This continued until the German duty officer arrived, followed by the inevitable Riot Squad (party of Goons with fixed bayonets called to a trouble spot). He cleared the courtyard. The *Tierarzt,* still suffering booing from the windows, made his way to the sick-bay.

Not all the prisoners approved of this demonstration; among them Colonel Stayner and Padre Platt. The first consequence was the stopping of the park walk. Major Engles for the Dutch and Colonel Stayner for the British made a joint complaint that their officers were not in the *Hof* at the time, and the exercise ban should not therefore apply to them. The *Kommandant* agreed. But when Stayner acquainted British officers with these findings, it was pointed out that certain of the British contingent did share in the demonstration from the windows of their quarters, and had no wish to receive treatment discriminating them from their fellow-prisoners. Whereupon the colonel drew up another *Antrag* in which he disclosed to the *Kommandant* that British officers had shared in the demonstration after all, and that he wished to withdraw his plaint. He then repeated to the British his disapproval of shouting and booing, and hoped that officers might not be found doing so again.

At about this time (March), Colditz had one of its periodic visits from members of the International Red Cross. They came to see that all was well with the supply, either indirectly, or as directed by them, of food parcels to the prisoners from the different Allied countries on the one hand, or from relatives on the other.

Food parcels were more or less standardized in weight to about ten pounds each. They came from different countries and the British prisoners received them from England, Australia, Canada and the United States, in bulk. Besides food, the Red Cross also sent bulk consignments of cigarettes and tobacco for distribution among the inmates of the camps. From 1941 onwards the supply of parcels of different kinds was regular enough to keep all the British prisoners decently clothed, and sufficient also to provide one food parcel per fortnight for each prisoner, as well as about forty cigarettes a week.

In addition, four private parcels could be sent per annum to each prisoner, from families or friends, and the Germans controlled the arrival of these parcels by an arrangement whereby they might only be sent against a special type of label which was issued in the permitted quantity to the person authorized. Private parcels usually contained clothing or books. Cigarette parcels were also allowed to individuals in unlimited quantity.

The French received food parcels mainly from private sources, but they did have a certain amount of bulk supply in the form of what they called *singe* or "monkey," which was tinned meat from their Army reserve. It came from Madagascar. They also had large quantities of *Biscuits Pétains*, French Army biscuits, which they exchanged with the British for cigarettes at the rate of one for one. The Poles and Dutch had private food parcels but in no such quantity as the British supplies, so that they were not particularly well off for food or clothes or cigarettes at any time during the war.

From 1942 onwards most of the Colditz prisoners were nearly as well fed as the German civilians in the town, at least as regards calorie intake. They had chocolate, sugar, butter, tinned meat and dried food in quantities. They made wine from their sugar and raisins and distilled from this wine a highly intoxicating alcohol which they called firewater. What they did lack, of course, was fish and fresh fruit.

All the parcels, together with the mail, were subjected to a strict censorship on the German side. They were after contraband. Eggers states categorically:

> We never on any occasion found any contraband, or anything that could be described as contraband, in the bulk supplies which came from, or through, the International Red Cross. We did, however, find a tremendous amount of forbidden goods in private clothing parcels and in private food parcels, in particular, those which came from France. We also found a lot of contraband in the "Welfare" parcels which were sent out from England either individually or by undercover organizations.

The Germans were late in the contraband stakes. Now they began to take a much closer interest in parcels from sources other than the International Red Cross. They installed an X-ray apparatus and subjected every incoming object without exception to its revealing gaze. They found in particular that the Licensed Victuallers' Sports Association was effectively helping to replenish the prisoners' stocks of escape material. Hollow-handled tennis rackets contained tiny compasses and hacksaw blades. Gramophone records contained maps and yet more money in the center. Playing cards had maps inside them. Jumping ahead in time, when Wing Commander Douglas Bader arrived in 1943, his chess set produced 1,000 *Reichsmarks,* three compasses and seven maps!

The Germans felt that this X-ray machine would soon put a stop to all this, but while it blocked one smuggling route used by the British, it merely served to open another and better one for both the English and the French.

On Good Friday, 3 April, there was a lightning search of the British quarters in the late afternoon. The stooges had failed on their job. This time the Germans suddenly erupted from the *Evidenzzimmer* door which was close to the British quarters staircase door. The stooges had focused their attention on the main gate. How had they failed? According to Platt, the Germans had entered the *Evidenzzimmer* in small groups at various intervals during the day. When the groups came out, each group left one behind, whose absence was not noted. This story is to be doubted. It is more likely the Germans used a secret passage which they had constructed from their quarters into the *Evidenzzimmer*. Eggers says he can't recall that they ever used this route (he may have been away on leave at this period), but having gone to the trouble of building the route why should they use the clumsy, time-consuming method suggested by Platt?

The only notable outcome of the search was that Flying Officer "Errol" Flynn was caught at work on a new tunnel. He had only come out of solitary the previous day after twenty-eight days for a three-day break before a second twenty-eight days he was due to serve for making a break while on his way to the cells. This new tunnel offense would earn him a further twenty-eight days. This brought his total to 170 days with previous sentences accumulating.

The chapel was still closed at Easter due to the French tunnel repairs—so the Easter Catholic services were held in the courtyard. The weather was kind. Platt records:

> Their services were in Latin. The Protestants or sectarians celebrated their Easter without saints and song, and much more simply. They had their own services, each in his own quarters and each in his own tongue. The Jews in Colditz had apparently no particular observance of the day of this Christian feast. There was no Rabbi among them anyway.

Then on 8 April five French Jewish doctors of the Jewish contingent were sent off to work in Russian POW camps in Poland to deal with typhus epidemics (cholera was also rumored). According to War Office records, during the winter of 1941–1942 typhus, thought to have been brought in by Russian prisoners, broke out in six POW camps where British prisoners were held.

When large numbers of Russian POWs were taken they were kept under appalling hygiene conditions, and were soon decimated by typhus. The Germans, who until then had refused to make use of the Jewish doctor POWs, sent the French Jewish doctors in Colditz to one of these camps. Later, at the end of April, a few of them returned. They were very ill. Despite their fever, which could leave no doubt as to what it was, Dr. Rahm refused categorically to see the gravity of the situation, or to send them to hospital. He was immediately given another pseudonym, "Doctor Typhus."

The Red Cross were alerted. This led to an inquiry *in situ* by the German Medical Service. They saw immediately that these prisoners had typhus, which they had caught whilst caring for the Russians. This created panic in the *Kommandantur*. The *Tierarzt* and the *Kommandant* were punished. The Jewish doctors with typhus were removed to hospital. The Jewish quarters were isolated in an effort to prevent a spread of the fever. The prisoners lived in such crowded conditions that the risk of an epidemic was serious.

The effect produced by the intervention of German top brass was clearly seen in the changed behavior of Rahm towards the Jews, whom he had always treated with contempt. He begged them to adhere rigorously to the "isolation" order, promising to ensure that food would be sent to their quarters; to have everything disinfected; and to provide them, within reason, with whatever they needed. This incident, however, spelled the end of Dr. Rahm. He left Colditz early in May and was replaced by the German doctor from the French generals' camp at Königstein.

The "saluting war" warrants a moment's reflection. Today, perhaps, it seems to bear little relation to the realities of a world at war. With full knowledge of the events of forty years ago, we may feel tempted to condemn the fact that officer prisoners—an internationally privileged class in a walled-off, even protected, enclave—should be allowed the luxury of playing childish games with an unpopular German Army doctor.

We must remember, however, that the prisoners in Colditz were ignominiously constrained while at the same time honored by being set apart—a contradiction brought about by a conglomeration of military considerations. The prisoners had no conception of war crimes perpetrated around them; had they known, it would not so much have brought humility into their own attitudes as a boiling fury into their reactions. Knowledge of world events such as they did possess produced two reactions: impatience and a feeling of impotence in their situation. They can be excused their apparent frivolity.

The success of the saluting war—the dismissal and departure of Rahm—was ultimately the achievement of the French. The British, Poles and Dutch played little part: the British because of their own weakness—a sentimental softness for the underdog; the Poles because the climb-down of the OKW had already given them a moral victory; the Dutch because their honor demanded that they uphold the respect due from one officer to another, even though they be enemies—the age-old code of the officer and the gentleman. For when that code was infringed by one side, what might the other side not do—with honor if not justice on their side? The Germans were the victors and the captors. They could rebound powerfully.

There were about twenty officers in the French contingent who were known as "*Les Innocents*," because, although they had racked their brains, they could not establish to anybody's satisfaction why they bad been sent to Colditz. Possibly they had been denounced out of some spite by fellow prisoners.

The French Jewish officer contingent increased considerably in the spring of 1941 until by mid-June they numbered about eighty officers. Because their number had grown so much, the Germans insisted on their forming a separate group from the other French at *Appell.* They also allocated them separate living and sleeping quarters. There was considerable doubt in the minds of the members of the other nationalities as to how the French Jews came to be "hived off" from the other French. In the French contingent there was already a division of loyalty between Pétainists and de Gaullists. Several senior French officers, presumably Pétainists, had been repatriated on 9 August 1941. Pétainists would be more likely to succumb to wily German propaganda. Either the Germans in Colditz made the suggestion to some of the French or some of the French made the suggestion to the Germans, that as they were becoming overcrowded in their quarters, would it not be better for everybody if the top floor—i.e. above the French quarters—were employed and how better than by giving Jewish officers their own quarters? The Germans, whether they were the initiators or not, were the delighted perpetrators of this subtle move, calculated to disrupt the universal harmony between the nations.

Eli de Rothschild, who had arrived in Colditz on 1 July 1941, had been heard to express considerable pleasure that "at last he was in a camp that had a British community." Padre Platt comments that the remark had little significance, unless the Ghetto, to which the French officers had given their acquiescence, was in the background of his thoughts. Many of the British regarded this segregation as disgraceful, among them Airey Neave and Squadron-Leader Paddon, who spear-headed the expression of outrage. Jewish officers were regularly invited to dine and share British Red Cross food with certain British messes. The effect on the French was salutary—to some extent.

Albert Maloire in his book *Colditz—le Grand Refus* (published in 1982) places the responsibility for the segregation of the Jews squarely on the shoulders of the Germans. Significantly, though, Le Brigant does not mention the subject in his book *Les Indomptables.*

Most of the Jews were there because they were Jews—for political reasons. A few were there because they had some value as hostages, and a few because they had been recaught after escaping or had otherwise been labelled as *Deutschfeindlich.* Amongst them were some famous names: the Baron Eli de Rothschild, Dreyfus, Captain Robert Blum (French Artillery), and Captain Count André Hirsch. Hirsch, the balding and well-known Paris banker, was more than an astronautical enthusiast. In the "little book" which I have mentioned in Chapter 3 (*Stratosphere and Rocket Flight* [*Astronautics*]) the author, Charles G. Philp, referred to Hirsch's establishment of the International Astronautical Award for the promotion of interstellar navigation. Hirsch gave a brilliant after-lunch lecture lasting one and a half hours on this subject at the end of December 1941. Robert Blum was a classical pianist. His sensitive features were set off with a neat professorial beard. Unenviably, he was the son of a famous father, Léon Blum the Socialist leader and former Prime Minister of France. Léon Blum was held under house arrest in the Pyrenees. Messages from his father reached Robert rarely, many times censored and long delayed. Robert's mother was under house arrest in the Hôtel des Voyageurs in Urdos below the Fort du Portalet where Léon was incarcerated.

Lieutenant Rémy Lévy had escaped (as I have described in Chapter 8) on an Elsterhorst hospital party from Colditz on 4 October 1941. He was recaptured 500 miles away at Aachen (Aix-la-Chapelle). He was placed in a cell at a prison at Arnoldsweiler where he spent the rigorous winter of 1941. He nearly died of polio-arthritis and remained thereafter a complete invalid. There is a story that a German guard, while searching his meager belongings, found a handtowel marked *Polizeigefängnis Aachen*, meaning "Police prison Aachen." The German guard commented, "That is the last straw! He continues to steal even in prison!"

12

Never a Dull Moment

Late Spring and Early Summer 1942

WITH SPRING IN THE AIR the escaping season would soon be accelerated into top gear. The German counter-attack took the form of the biggest search organized so far. On 16 April at 6:30 a.m. the "spring-cleaning" started. At 10:30 the "personal" search began, everyone being herded into the day-room, then taken out one by one to the kitchen where all clothing was removed and subjected to close scrutiny. Finally there was the "body search," including the soles of the feet and a torch-light examination of the hair, the ears, the mouth (false teeth removed), the armpits, the crotch and, bending down, the backside, which the French called the *codette du Légionnaire*. By about 1 p.m. everybody was dressed again and slouching in the courtyard while the day-rooms were put through it. Books, papers, toilet requisites, cupboards, tables, chairs and stools upturned, beds shifted, bedding removed, floorboards torn up. The British quarters were left in such confusion and wrecked disorder that a placard was erected outside them. It read: "You are invited to visit an example of Nazi culture."

To relieve the monotony, Lieutenant Monty Bissell refused for obscure reasons to undress except in the presence of a doctor or a priest. The Germans were bemused. They produced the Indian doctor Mazumdar, who saw the point at once and reinforced Monty's prejudices by insisting on further ritualistic observances during the body search to the dumbfounded amazement of the Goons.

Early in April, fifty Upmann Havana cigars arrived in two cedarwood boxes of twenty-five each addressed to me. In 1932 some engineering graduates of that year from King's College, London University, had formed a "13" Club, just to keep in touch with each other as the years went by. We had been close friends at King's. Then the war came, and in 1941, when they learned that I was a POW, they decided to send me a private parcel containing what they knew I was most fond of. The cigars were three months in transit, but they arrived safely in Colditz. This says much for the International Red Cross Organization and something for the honesty of the Germans, who treated Red Cross and next-of-kin parcels with the utmost respect. The cigars were each contained in their aluminum tubes, sealed and in good condition.

As each cigar was smoked either by me or by one of my friends, I felt like the little girl at school who had a box of chocolates, the most popular girl in the school until the box was empty! In this case there was a difference because the aluminum tubes were far more durable than the ephemeral cigars and they were greatly sought after and treasured for one purpose for which they were uniquely adaptable—namely as "arse-creepers."

There is nothing new about the concealment of contraband in the body. However, a package containing a button compass, 100 *Reichsmarks* in notes of various denominations, a route map from Colditz to Singen, a workman's *Ausweis* (passport) in stiffish card and a leave permit on foolscap paper, presented a formidable problem. Before the advent of the cigar tubes, and there were only fifty of them, the ingenuity of the POWs had been seriously taxed. There was a great scarcity of any kind of waterproof packing paper. Cellophane did not exist. The nearest was an oiled or greased toughened paper, very difficult to come by. Occasionally the canteen produced a small stock of some articles in a container which could be adapted.

The French were very keen on the body-concealment idea but also not a little worried about the effect of such foreign bodies on the intestines. They consulted their doctor, who reassured them provided they followed some simple rules as to cleanliness. As many of the creepers were home-made affairs, he also advised them as a precaution to attach a thread to the lower end, so that their withdrawal would not be a matter of uncertainty. The French were particular about this to such an extent that on a major French search it proved their undoing. An astute German searcher, when it came to the body search, noticed a thread. When he had registered its presence in some half a dozen Frenchmen, he demanded their recall—and pulled on the threads with disastrous results thereafter for a large number of the French contingent.

The British doctor, on the other hand, had not specified this accessory, and the British body search revealed nothing.

By now the reader should appreciate not only the significance of the cigar tube but also of the name of the brand of the cigar, printed indelibly in blue on the tube. My engineering colleagues back in Britain had done their research well. The tubes could be cut to an appropriate length, and the cap could be hermetically resealed usually with sticking plaster. It is a fact that all the necessary escape items listed above could be and were so rolled as to fit snugly in the tube.

Another light relief which went the rounds was the story of a complaint voiced by one of the German guards to his *Unteroffizier* that his relief had not turned up and he had missed his mid-day meal and was very hungry. Peter Tunstall immediately produced a German coin and offered it to the German with the words, "Here you are, my good man, go out and get yourself a good meal." The guard in confusion replied, "*Nein, danke. Nein*," and refused the coin. The point of the story is that one of the main aims of the search was to find and confiscate every vestige of German money.

The French General Giraud escaped from *Oflag* IVA, the castle of Königstein, on 17 April 1942. This was a sensational escape—a serious blow for the Germans. They tried to conceal knowledge of it from the public for many days. General Le Brigant recounts the joy with which the French received the news through their clandestine radio on 5 May, four or five days after the departure from Colditz of the French Lieutenant Raymond Bouillez for court-martial at Stuttgart (Bouillez had been sent to Colditz from *Oflag* XC to await his trial). Bouillez had jumped his train at night as far south as was possible. He was found unconscious by the railroad next day with broken jaw, broken arm and head injuries. In this condition he was taken before the judges, acquitted and then returned to the infirmary ward in Colditz. Le Brigant immediately paid him a visit and told him the good news of Giraud's escape. Bouillez took a little time to pull his bemused mind together and replied that he knew of it already the day before he was returned to Colditz; a French prisoner in the booking hall at Leipzig station had told him! Le Brigant's reaction was "Here is a man who has possessed the most sensational news of the war for a whole twenty-four hours in Colditz without telling anybody!" Bouillez was indeed in a bad way. He was removed to hospital. He escaped from there on 25 June and reached France successfully.

Giraud's escape had repercussions in Colditz. Eggers was seconded to Königstein to discover Giraud's trick. He stayed until the end of July 1942, and was able to establish that the general had slid down a cliff beneath the Castle on a length of telephone cable. Königstein's *Kommandant* and his security officer were both punished with six months' imprisonment at Gollnow in Pomerania. "We thought they were lucky to get away with that," remarks Eggers, "because

Romilly, our civilian hostage, was a standing death sentence to the two officers in the same position at Colditz."

Before the month of April was out (on the 26th), a further major escape of five Colditz officers took place from the military hospital at Gnaschwitz, near Dresden; three Poles, one Belgian and one Englishman. The *Tierarzt* had sent them for treatment as "serious cases." He was wild with fury!

Two of the Polish officers, Lieutenants Wychodzew and Niestrzęba, coolly sent the *Kommandant* a picture postcard from Hof, a town on the road from Dresden to Stuttgart. The Germans warned the Stuttgart *Kriminalpolizei*, and they picked up the first-named at the station after two days at large. Niestrzęba was caught in a train the next day at Singen, disguised as a Belgian worker, with papers in the name of Carl Winterbeck. Unfortunately he also had on him his POW number plate, with *Oflag* IVC on it.

The other three "sick" were the Polish Lieutenant Just (yet again!), the Belgian Lieutenant Rémy and the British Squadron Leader Paddon. These three all posed as Belgian workers. In Leipzig they came under suspicion. Just and Rémy were being watched when Rémy suddenly made a dash for it. Paddon and Just, who had intended to travel separately, met again by chance. Eggers reports as follows, though his memory cannot be considered faultless; Rémy, for instance, disagrees radically with his version of paragraph (11):

> We discovered among papers during a search, the Paddon Escape Rules—a memorandum written up after this escape. Born of experience, this is what they said:
>
> (1) Travel in slow trains, not by expresses or specials, as no passes required when buying tickets. No control of passes on slow trains under the first 100 kilometers.
> (2) Express trains—between Leipzig and Dresden the control is carried out by a German sergeant. He requires only our identity cards.
> (3) Passes recognized by police as forged because
>   (a) they had seen this type of phoney pass before;
>   (b) there is no such thing as a *Nebenbauamt* (Branch Works Office) stamp;
>   (c) no such thing as *Bauinspektor* (Building Inspector);
>   (d) the signatures on Lieut. Just's identity card and mine were different, but in the same handwriting;
>   (e) the stamp was poor—it was weak and hence illegible;

(f) same handwriting in both my passes, although one was issued in Leipzig and one in Dresden.

(4) Brown pass O.K. for identification only. Not for travelling. For 24 hours the police thought I was a Belgian. The interpreter in French at Leipzig police station spoke worse French than Just and I together!

(5) Best of all is a leave pass. Everyone asks for it and it commands fare reductions. This is the key to everything, and it must be a pleasure to travel with a good one.

(6) Tuttlingen is in the frontier zone. Tickets to Stuttgart issued sometimes with and sometimes without identity cards being demanded.

(7) We went from Dresden to Stuttgart via Leipzig. Wish I had followed my own intention and not taken the advice of the train conductress.

(8) German civvies better clad than we had thought, especially on Sundays—a bad day therefore for travelling.

(9) It is always possible to get something to eat without having to produce coupons. I'll never again carry chocolate or Red Cross food.

(10) Remove all names from clothes, or sew false ones on if you have none. Lieut. Just had his name and "*Oflag* IVC" on his trousers! That's why they were so suspicious about my story of having just been shot down. Just and I met in Leipzig quite by chance after our initial escape.

(11) Rémy, who travelled with Just, made himself conspicuous. Both were watched in the train by a civilian (? Gestapo) after they had been checked by the sergeant. Rémy disappeared suddenly when they got to Leipzig, while Just was left trying in vain to get rid of the overcoat that Rémy had left behind in the compartment. Although he pretended not to see it, people pressed it on him as belonging to his friend. I was picked up half an hour later as I was speaking to Just, thinking he was by then clear of suspicion.

(12) He travels best who travels alone!

Rémy, the Belgian, made a home-run.

On 28 May the French Lieutenant Michel Girot disappeared during a park walk. He was the Benjamin—the youngest of the French company. He was caught on a train going to Frankfurt but the Germans never found out how he escaped. A bar in one of the French rooms had been sawn through. Actually he had concealed himself under a *planche* during the walk. This was his second attempt. He made three further attempts of which the last was from the French tunnel at Lübeck on 27 April 1944. He was caught by the Gestapo and executed.

May was a busy month in the Castle's administration. Early in the morning of the 19th, some sixty-three Polish officers and four Serbian officers left Colditz. This left a balance of about forty Poles—mostly hardened escaper types. They were followed on the 28th by 125 French and Belgian officers, including the Jews. They were destined for *Oflag* XC at Lübeck. On the 21st the British contingent (but not the colonels and majors) moved quarters from the first floor of the east wing to the fourth story (eighty-eight steps) of the north wing over the chapel. Then the *Kommandant* announced that he would allow parole walks for the British chaplains outside the Castle perimeter. (Padre Platt appears not to have availed himself of the opportunity.) A more serious matter was the attempted suicide on 26 May of Don Middleton, the Canadian RAF pilot, one of the first three of the British contingent at Colditz. He had appeared to be quite resigned and content, pursuing a course of studies for an eventual university degree. Then letters from his wife began to haunt him. Padre Platt and a fellow Canadian, Don Thom, appear to have been his *confidants*. Platt maintains the wife's letters were not calculated to undermine his morale. Nevertheless he became obsessed with the idea that he must release his wife from their marriage. He opened his wrist vein with a razor in the bathroom but was discovered in time. Dr. Playoust (an Australian POW who spent a short time in Colditz) stitched up three cuts on the resentful patient. Then Don attempted to throw a bottle out of a window at a sentry to get himself shot. Next he attempted to cut his throat. From now on he was under constant observation by a roster of POWs. Rahm examined him on 27 May (a day before Rahm left Colditz) and appeared convinced enough of his instability to start proceedings to have him removed to a mental hospital. In the meantime the roster continued twenty-four hours a day. Don Thom remained always close to him, to his own detriment. Before the end of the war, Don himself became mildly but permanently insane.

Don Middleton was removed on 29 May under guard to the hospital at Elsterhorst. At one point he tried to grab a German's bayonet, and when crossing the river bridge in Colditz on the way to the station, he leapt over the bridge parapet in order to provoke the guards to shoot him. He hung suspended over the water until hauled back by a guard, aided by Captain Cyril Lewthwaite who was also going to the hospital.

Two events of note occurred on 2 June. Errol Flynn came out of "solitary," having done three consecutive terms of one month with breaks of three days between. He was starving because no Red Cross food was allowed to POWs in confinement. The second event was the news that Mike Sinclair had escaped from Leipzig hospital where he had been taken for treatment for chronic sinusitis. He reached Cologne a few days later where he was trapped on 6 June in a round-up of suspected British RAF pilots, parachuted survivors of planes shot down during a recent air-raid on the city. Sinclair's disguise was not good enough. He was taken to a *Stalag*, escaped again and was recaught.

On 7 June, 360 Red Cross parcels arrived for the British, together with a large consignment of battledress uniforms. For the first time in the history of the British at *Oflag* IVC the POWs had one parcel each to cover one week. Thereafter the ration was reduced to three-quarters of a parcel and later to half a parcel per head per week.

Squadron-Leader "Never-a-dull-moment" Paddon was called to face a court-martial at a former prison camp in the north-east of Germany, charged with insulting an *Oberfeldwebel* (sergeant-major) by accusing him of theft. He was duly equipped for an escape and left for his destination under heavy guard on 9 June. It was a long journey and he would be away for several days. As the days turned into weeks, Colonel Stayner naturally became concerned, and demanded an explanation from the *Kommandant*. The latter replied with a resigned shrug of the shoulders: "*Es war unmöglich, trotzdem ist er geflohen*"—"It was impossible, nonetheless he escaped!" Paddon eventually reached Sweden and then England safely. He was the second Englishman to do the home-run from Colditz. Eggers states that the Germans never discovered how he escaped, though he goes on to theorize, correctly, that Paddon had joined a party of British orderlies detailed to leave the camp each day at 6:45 a.m. to work on nearby farms. He wore an Army battledress over a makeshift civilian outfit (all items, except his own RAF trousers, borrowed overnight from fellow-prisoners), and slipped into a barn, where he removed the battledress and walked calmly away. According to Platt's diary, the POWs first knew of Paddon's success on 24 July.

On 15 June there had been some excitement caused by a fire deliberately started by the British at the bottom of their staircase. The fuel was provided by a pile of woodshavings dumped by the Germans as filling for the straw mattresses. As anything to divert the POWs from their monotonous existence was welcomed, buckets of water were produced and thrown anywhere but on the flames. Dominic Bruce decided to continue a water battle started some days before when the courtyard had been full of recumbent sun-bathers. A mass of water thrown from a height of three or four stories can cause an almost explosive effect landing on cobbles (or on human beings). The evening *Appell* was long delayed, Bruce was caught red-handed and the acrid smell of damp cinders polluted the staircase for days.

Saturday, 20 June, was the first anniversary of the German attack on Russia. Being high summer and the news from the front being optimistic, youthful spirits amongst the nationalities developed another water-bomb-bucket battle. Anything that held water—bowls, tins, buckets and best of all home-made paper containers filled with water—came into their own. The younger officers, Poles, French, Dutch and British, were soaking each other indiscriminately and hilariously. Even the sentries were laughing. Then suddenly the Riot Squad (fifteen-strong) entered the yard led by the aging Hauptmann Müller who was the post officer and evidently on guard duty that evening. It appears that the noise from the courtyard was loud enough to be heard in the town and had alarmed the townspeople, who appealed once again to the *Kreisleiter*, who in turn telephoned Oberst Schmidt, who ordered the duty officer to restore order.

Müller ordered the horseplay to stop, which only caused the players to use their ingenuity from windows, corridors and staircases, while the "barracking" started up from all the windows where spectators had been enjoying the fun. With "*Où sont les Allemands? / Les Allemands sont dans la merde*," this now well-rehearsed Colditz chant of derision swelled to an anthem. Müller gave incomprehensible and incoherent orders to the POWs, presumably concerning retreating from the windows and piping down. All to no effect. The Riot Squad opened fire at the windows. A French officer, Lieutenant Maurice Fahy, a spectator leaning out of a third-story window, was shot through the neck and shoulder. Eggers says that Fahy was wounded by a shot from Hauptmann Müller's revolver. He returned from Elsterhorst, where he was sent for treatment, on 23 July. The fingers of his left hand were paralyzed.

André Perrin, Lieutenant French Army, arrived in Colditz on 18 June from *Oflag* XB.

The Verkest trial papers had all gone to Hitler, as they involved the death sentence. They were returned with Hitler's marginal note "Loss of freedom sufficient." The court therefore sat again at Leipzig on 21 July. Verkest's sentence was now reduced to two years. By the time he was out, the Belgians had left Colditz. Verkest served his sentence at a prison in Graudenz. When released he rejoined the Belgians at Lübeck.

On 6 July the whole camp was shaken by an action of the Poles. At morning roll-call Colonel Kowalczewski gave the customary order for "attention." He then turned to the German Oberleutnant Püpcke and, reporting the number of Polish officers present, said, "Forty-seven officers and one traitor." Ryszard Bednarski, claiming to be a lieutenant in the Polish Army, was removed at once by the Germans. Bednarski had escaped with Lieutenant Just from the Königswartha hospital on 5 May 1941. Eggers has the following telling commentary:

> Bednarski got as far as Cracow where he should have certainly been quite safe. Although our people could not discover all the underground network in that city, we were able to get our hands on part of it. And so *the Gestapo picked up Bednarski and in due course returned him to us as an Officer Prisoner of War. Naturally he came back with the most valuable information of all kinds from which his fellow prisoners were able to benefit.*

The italics are mine! Can anyone in their right mind believe that Bednarski would be allowed by the Gestapo to return to Colditz to give the prisoners valuable information without holding him on a long leash?

Bednarski had arrived back from Cracow in May. An eye-witness of Bednarski's "drumming out" after a Polish court-martial in Colditz relates that on a certain day (probably 5 July) all the Polish officers were told by their adjutant, Captain Lados, to assemble in the largest room of the Polish quarters. The roll was taken. Colonel Kowalczewski, the Senior Polish Officer at that time, entered. Everyone stood at attention. Ladas reported all present.

Kowalczewski ordered Bednarski to step forward. He then pronounced him a spy and a traitor, unfit to wear a Polish soldier's uniform or insignia—and called upon Lieutenant Kępa to remove the insignia from his uniform. Kępa then ceremoniously, but also with force, tore the epaulets from his tunic. Bednarski was ordered to leave the room. Colonel Kowalczewski had to restrain some officers from beating the traitor up. It is not confirmed, but likely, that the Senior Polish Officer asked the Senior British Officer to accompany him and that they went to the *Kommandant,* informed him of the trial and conviction and demanded Bednarski's removal the next day, on the ground that the SPO would no longer accept responsibility for his life. Bednarski would certainly have been hanged or killed if he had remained in the Castle. A Pole who was at the trial reports that it was a legally constituted court-martial. Bednarski was to be thrown out of a high window to simulate an accident.

From the trial itself it appears that Bednarski had been suborned by the Germans long before he went to Cracow. In the prison camp of Murnau he had been ordered by the Germans to simulate an escape so that he could be legitimately sent to Colditz. He was not a Polish officer and had not been in the Polish Army. The Poles attributed several failed escapes to his "informing": in particular, the attempted escape or prospecting for an escape by four Polish officers on 24 April 1941. The four officers had already made sorties into the courtyard late at night. On this night, one of them was indisposed and remained in bed. That night the Germans surprised and caught them, and asked, "Only three? Where is the fourth?" This was just another piece of circumstantial evidence at the time, but it kept the Poles on the scent of a spy.

On the occasion of the escape of some Polish officers from the hospital at Elsterhorst, a Polish captain, Aleksander Ligęza, was a genuine sick case—in fact the only one. Remaining behind, he managed to steal from the hospital office a report by Bednarski to the German *Abwehr* officer, pleading that it was not his fault that they had escaped, because he had reported the preparations for the escape to the *Abwehr* officer, who had done nothing about it in time to prevent it.

On 21 July, Priem took the unprecedented step of announcing on *Appell* that Bednarski had disclosed no POW secrets to the German staff.

After the war, Colonel Mozdyniewicz met Bednarski one day in a city street in Poland. He immediately informed the public prosecutor. Bednarski committed suicide.

13

No Coward Souls

Summer and Early Autumn 1942

AT THE END OF JULY Oberst Schmidt, the *Kommandant*, retired at the ripe age of seventy. His soldiers considered him a great soldier, austere, harsh but just. Although a Saxon he was a soldier of the old Prussian school. Punctual always, and at his office by 8 a.m., he inspected his staff daily and the POW camp more often than any other *Kommandant*. He was anti-Hitler before the war. He was intolerant of any officer who behaved in any way unbefitting his rank, and reduced one officer to the ranks for dishonesty. He never gave the Hitler salute. But he was known to have said: "The NSDAP [the Nazi Party] has given the German officer a status he did not have even in the reign of the Kaiser, so our loyalty is assured."

During the 20 June courtyard riot, the *Kreisleiter* had demanded that Schmidt give the order to open fire on the mob. Schmidt had replied, "Before I give orders like that I shall make sure from a legal expert that such an order is lawful."

His appeal to the Senior Officers of the different nationalities to maintain military discipline fell on rather stony ground. In his eyes only the Dutch and the Poles lived up to this. Eggers has written that "eventually the OKW was compelled to put an end to the mutinous situation by partially dissolving the Camp in 1943."

He retired to Dresden but had to move after the terrible air-raid in 1945. He was arrested by the Russian OGPU and imprisoned in no less than six different prison camps. He was never tried by the Russians and died in a hospital in Riga—Russian-controlled Estonia—in 1946 or 1947.

The new *Kommandant*, Oberst Edgar Glaesche, was very much a new broom. He was born in 1899. He was of medium height, with a slight squint in one eye, much less imposing than Schmidt. He insisted on great thoroughness in all work, down to the last detail, and gave frequent pep-talks. It was an officer's duty, he said, to set an example to the men. Correct application of the Geneva Convention and all its rules as regards the treatment of prisoners of war was insisted on. Prisoners must be made to behave themselves correspondingly. He required "watchfulness, circumspection, presence of mind, calm, and persistence" on the job. He would set an example. But he would not frequent the prisoners' yard overmuch. He must seem to be what he was—the symbol of ultimate authority!

One idea that Glaesche put into practice was calling special parades at any time of the night. It was asking for trouble. It started the "*Appell* war." One night (29/30 July) there was a *Strafappell* (punishment *Appell*) for the French, who duly paraded. A general *Appell* called for 1 a.m. had just concluded, and the Goons had been greatly upset by its disruption. This took the form of loud animal and bird calls, a cockerel here, a cow there, mixed with wailing sirens and the sound of falling bombs. Far from stopping after the summoning of the *Strafappell*, the uproar grew noisier and noisier as the British, Polish and Dutch yelled from their windows. It was absolute pandemonium. The entire guard was called into the *Hof* and lined up facing the windows. Then the duty officer ordered them to take aim. A moment later a volley of shots rang out, smashing through the windows of the various quarters. Vandy earned ten days' "solitary" for storming down in his pajamas to protest about the use of firearms on unarmed men.

Eggers explains the shooting in this way:

> One of the guards, more weary than the rest at that time of night, did not hold the muzzle of his rifle high enough. In fact he let it droop so far that it was aimed at the head of a French officer standing close in front of him.
>
> "*Höher*," bawled the Frenchman ("Higher").
>
> His accent was wide of the mark, and so a guard down the line thought he heard the order "*Feuer*" ("Fire").
>
> He let go. They all did.

An inquiry was held at which the *Kommandant* presided and the story about the mistaken order to fire was given out as the official explanation. The *Kommandant* added that another midnight *Appell* would be called that night and, if a demonstration took place, midnight *Appells* would continue. Colonel Stayner then asked British officers to desist from vocal exercise at *Strafappell* that night.

The *Appell* was not called. Some thought wiser counsels had prevailed and that the clause in Article 47 of the Geneva Convention, "collective penalties for individual acts are also prohibited," would be observed. But at evening *Appell* Priem announced an *Appell* for 1 a.m. No sound of any kind greeted the announcement. Padre Platt wrote:

> The bell rang at 12.30a.m. and at a few minutes to one we (all nationalities) trickled down the staircase in stony silence. Priem counted the five companies and his usual dismissal, "*Danke, mein Herren*," echoed hollowly on the huge walls. With soundless tread we glided back to quarters in a silence as solemn as a funeral.

After this good behavior, Colonel Stayner expected the end of the matter. He was disappointed. On Saturday night an *Appell* was called for 11 p.m. This was attended in stony silence. It was over in two minutes. No count was taken. This ended the "*Appell* war." Stayner nevertheless drafted a letter to Switzerland, our Protecting Power under the Geneva Convention, setting out a complaint.

Lieutenant-Colonel David James Stayner of the Dorset Regiment was born in 1896 and he was familiarly known to the Colditz inmates as "Daddy" Stayner. White-haired, tall, erect and slim, his speech was always quiet and considered. He would give the impression of being a man of peace almost at any price. That does not do him justice because he was not a weak man—simply a man of experience—a diplomat. He had fought in the First World War from 1914, a Regular soldier, promoted to captain in August 1917, mentioned twice in dispatches, wounded. In 1919 he served with British forces in Russia.

The Germans had selected him to replace Guy German. From their point of view it was not a bad choice. He did have a calming influence but he certainly did not try to curb or reduce escaping activity. He approached the problem of Colditz rather more as the Dutch did. Comparing him with Guy German, he was the shaped, formed, molded officer of the regular Army, whereas Guy German was the natural, respected leader for any guerilla campaign. Both aspects of character added richness to the alloy forming in the crucible of Colditz.

The exact date of the discovery of a Polish-initiated tunnel under the paving stones in the ground-floor corridor of the *Saalhaus* is uncertain but its repercussions were serious. Eggers in his diary says it was "one day in August." Padre Platt mentions the discovery, writing: "two Polish and one Belgian Officer were in cells . . . their tunnel was discovered on Sunday [i.e. 19 July]." Moreover, Priem's announcement about Bednarski on *Appell* on 21 July had included an express denial that Bednarski had revealed this tunnel. The Poles were fully alive to Bednarski. It is not likely he gave the game away. Eggers' story, here summarized, is almost certainly true.

The special squad employed by Eggers to keep a constant watch on the movements of "Emil" spent much of its time "searching" as well. They were searching the *Saalhaus* corridor for "hides" and finding a likely paving stone, they lifted it and found a tunnel. There seemed no point in the tunnel. It led inside the Castle—not out. Only much later did the Germans realize that this tunnel was only the first of three tunnels all of which in their time headed for the main sewer under the POW courtyard.

The Poles unfortunately had hidden some valuable escape aids in the tunnel which were promptly removed for examination. Eggers gives this account:

> It was used as a hiding place for various items, such as a homemade typewriter, some glasses with pieces of paper etc. The stuff was taken to Captain Lange and when he examined the pieces of paper he found that many different figures had been written. Captain Lange rightly assumed that this was some sort of code and after some trouble he managed to decipher the code and read on one of the pieces of paper, "If you escape, avoid the Central Station at Leipzig. Leave the train in time and take a tram to Wahren Station. There go back into the train." Another read, "Phone Leipzig . . ." and gave the number. Other pieces were bills for tools delivered to the prisoners. Captain Lange checked the telephone number and found out the guilty person who had supplied the tools to the POWs. He was a soldier of the former Guard Company. We had often found new tools and now we knew who had supplied them. Later the Police searched his house at Leipzig and found more bills. His partner in crime was the Polish Lieutenant Niedenthal. The soldier was arrested at Mühlberg where he was then stationed and after being Courtmartialled he was shot at Torgau.

According to Eggers, the German soldier had been, prior to the war, an electrical-equipment tradesman and had had business connections with Niedenthal. The prices he charged in the form of coffee and cigarettes seemed to the Germans very small compared to the risk he was taking (but see Chapter 15).

Early in August some Russian POWs arrived in the Castle for delousing prior to going to work in the country. Their untoward appearance in the delousing shed near the *Saalhaus* corridor led to the discovery of two British officers, namely myself and Rupert Barry, who had started a tunnel in one corner. The reader need hardly guess where the tunnel was to lead!

The German censors who also scrutinized all photos connected with Colditz Castle which were allowed to the POWs had overlooked one point. "Lange, the photographer, had presented a pre-war photo of the cobbled courtyard which could be purchased by the prisoners. Near the main archway, and the gates into the yard, a large manhole cover was plainly visible amongst the cobblestones. Now, and since before 1941, the manhole cover had disappeared. In other words it had been cobbled over. I, as a civil engineer and with my previous knowledge of the run of the drains from my canteen tunnel, knew precisely where the main drain led—namely out of the courtyard under the main gates. If I could get into this drain, big enough to take a man on his hands and knees, I would be able to get outside those courtyard gates.

However, I knew of the stout brick wall built across the drain just beyond the corner of the delousing shed. This decided the location of the new tunnel entrance in the delousing shed—only a matter of three or four yards from the drain and beyond the wall.

The Poles had evidently worked out this information too. They had not told Dick Howe, who had taken over from me as escape officer in the spring. From Eggers' statements, it appears that at first the Germans did not realize what the Polish tunnel was heading for. They certainly did not appreciate where the Lazaret tunnel (in which Airey Neave was at one time involved) was vaguely heading for. When however they found my tunnel entrance—it became clear what the POWs were after.

The delousing shed was a temporary structure in the courtyard built to house the portable ovens, which looked like huge boilers and into which clothing was put and baked in order to kill lice and other pests. The sudden arrival of the Russians necessitated the use of these portable ovens, and Rupert and I were caught red-handed. The boilers were hardly used once in six months. It was unfortunate the Russians arrived just during British working hours!

The incident, however, enabled the British to make the first contact ever with Russian soldiers, who were to be housed in the town. They were a sight of which the Germans should have been ashamed. Living skeletons, they dragged their fleshless feet along the ground in a decrepit slouch. These scarecrows were the survivors of a batch ten times their number which had started from the Eastern front. They were treated like animals, given no food and put out into the fields to find fodder amidst the grass and roots. Their trek into Germany took weeks.

With tunnels discovered, the "do or die" attempt appeared the only way—or so it did to Flight-Lieutenant "Bag" Dickinson. Because there were so many POWs doing "solitary" confinement sentences, the Germans had to supplement the seven prison cells in the Castle precinct by hiring more in the town—as I have explained in Chapter 8. The normal Castle cell was about ten feet by six feet, and two to a cell was nowadays the norm. So Colditz could only house fourteen POWs at a time doing prison sentences of anything from five to twenty-eight days. The waiting queue was getting longer and longer. The old town jail provided the answer. It was not in use, but on the first floor were ten "good," old-fashioned cells and a guardroom. There was a small exercise yard. It was ten minutes' walk from the Castle. On 18 August after an hour of "exercise" in the diminutive yard, with a sentry in front and one at the rear with revolvers in their holsters, a procession of ten POWs walked back through the prison door. The sentry in front proceeded to mount the stairs. This was Bag's moment. From the middle of the procession, he ran a few yards to a side wall with a locked door in it. The lock handle gave him a foothold. He leaped and grabbed the top of the eight-foot wall. He swung over and dropped into an orchard beyond. Over another wall and out on to a street. He grabbed a bicycle—miraculously unlocked—and was away like greased lightning. The second sentry had hesitated to shoot because the prison was surrounded by houses with windows close by. He was also slow on the draw.

Unfortunately "Bag" was not properly equipped for his escape. The Germans issued their codeword "*Mäusefalle*" ("Mousetrap") to all police stations up to 100 miles around. Dickinson was caught by the police that evening in Chemnitz about forty miles away.

Wing Commander Douglas Bader (WingCo) had arrived on 16 August.

On 20 August the French Lieutenant Delarue, dressed as a German painter, unsuccessfully tried to bluff his way out of the garrison yard after side-stepping from the park walk. He did not possess the correct pass. On 25 August Flight-Lieutenant Forbes and Lieutenant Lee tried a "break-away" from their guards in the streets of Leipzig.

In England Paddon, after a short leave and promotion to wing commander, was sent off on a tour of operational units to give advice to the many aircrews soon to face the possibility of capture. One day late in August he was called up by MI9. An alleged Belgian was being held in custody under grave suspicion of being a spy. The man was claiming to have escaped from Colditz. He had swum to a British ship off the coast of Algeçiras and stowed away. On arrival in England he was handed over and had been in prison a month. Would Paddon be prepared to see this man and identify him?

Paddon entered the man's cell and faced none other than his Belgian friend Lieutenant Louis Rémy who had been the one to get away, when he, Paddon and Just had made the escape bid from a Colditz hospital visit in April of that year, 1942.

At his own request, Paddon returned to an operational unit, but was not allowed to fly over enemy-held territory for fear of torture and perhaps death if the Gestapo got him. He commanded several airfields, was again promoted, and as Group Captain Paddon controlled the great Coastal Command base at Thornaby, Yorkshire.

Later he wrote his autobiography of the war years. His memoirs make fascinating reading and it is sad that permission for their publication has not been granted by his widow. Hopefully she will soon relent.*

On 1 September, "the Navy" arrived in Colditz from Stalag VIIIB, Lamsdorf, in Silesia, where they had got to know Douglas Bader. The group consisted of sixteen when they set out and fifteen when they arrived. Lieutenant-Commander W. L. (Billie) Stephens, who had been captured during the St. Nazaire raid in March 1942, was missing. He had climbed on to the roof of the train they had changed from at Gross Bothen. This train took off in another direction. But Stephens was caught later, still on the train roof. Among them were three ERAs (Engine-Room Artificers), Lister, Hammond and Johnson, who as chief petty officers should not have been in Colditz at all. But at Lamsdorf they had simply been promoted in order to increase their chances of staying with the officers they had befriended.

Mike Moran recalls the following story about Bader, whom he first met in Lamsdorf, where Douglas had been sent for medical treatment. Characteristically, he was determined to escape, despite his obvious disadvantages. Shortly after his arrival at Lamsdorf, however, luck seemed to come his way when a working party was required for a job alongside a *Luftwaffe* air base.

The working party was selected and the *modus operandi* planned with infinite care. But the difficulties were all too obvious—not least among them Bader's "fame" in Germany. When news got round that he was in Lamsdorf, the *Kommandant* was deluged with requests from local bigwigs who wanted a chance to see him. Clearly Douglas wouldn't be away long before his absence was discovered.

The sick bay was the second hut in from the main gate; the first was a guard hut, where outgoing working parties were checked. Before daylight the air-field party went through the usual routine at the guard hut: an argument was started

* Editors were not able to verify further updates to this information as of publication.

and became a free for all. Bader slipped out of the sick bay; his replacement slipped in. The party marched off to the station and reached it and the hut at the air field without incident. Douglas was to be the "duty-room stooge" while others spied out the land.

About mid-day a staff car pulled up outside. Two *Luftwaffe* officers entered the hut, bade Douglas "*Wilkommen*," and took him to their mess, where he was wined and dined, enjoying every minute of it. Lamsdorf was informed by telephone. The *Luftwaffe* refused to return him until the next day. "He's ours until tomorrow!" He got his spell in cells, of course.

Bader arrived in Colditz a fortnight before "the Navy." Mike Moran remembers well the shouts of welcome from the windows of the French, "*Vive le Royal Navy!*," and the bugles blowing through the iron bars of the windows in the British quarters. He wondered what sort of a bedlam he had entered.

At 8 a.m. next day they wearily descended the eighty-eight stone steps to the courtyard for morning *Appell*. When the count was over the German duty officer read out the names of those who had arrived the previous evening. Everyone back to their rooms, except them.

Into the courtyard came a civilian with a camera, guards carrying a small table, fingerprint equipment and other items, and a *Hauptmann* with a large folder. In a corner of the courtyard, between the chapel and the entrance to the British quarters, the equipment was set up. Mike was the first to be dealt with. For the photograph, he stood behind the stand which already held a card with his number—110599. He wasn't asked to smile!

Through the window bars the other prisoners were looking down. As the photographer pressed the button on his camera—*crash!* Two water bombs landed on the fingerprint table, breaking the glass slab, sending cards and ink-pad flying. More water bombs came down, one hitting the photographer, another one of the guards. From the windows came shouts and cat-calls. The guards shouldered their rifles, pointing them at the windows. The German officer shouted the usual threat, "*Von den Fenster zurück, oder ich schiesse!*" It was ignored—the cat-calls continued. The order came to shoot. Two or three shots were fired at the windows, but by then they were empty.

Mike was still standing behind the number board, wondering for the umpteenth time since the previous evening what sort of place he had arrived at. Guards were placed at the entrance doors to the prisoners' quarters. The naval contingent were hustled through the gate to the German courtyard. There the remaining identity photographs were taken.

That was his introduction to *Oflag* IVC. But it had not yet finished.

The Colditz "old lags" decided to have some fun at the new boys' expense. Howard Gee, who spoke German perfectly, was togged out in the best pieces of home-made German officer's uniform, converted from a Dutch uniform for the occasion (and removed from its hiding place). He was accoutered as the German camp doctor, complete with stethoscope, accompanied by his medical orderly, alias Dominic Bruce, in white overalls, carrying a large bowl of blue woad—mainly theater paint—and a paintbrush. No sooner were the fifteen new arrivals let loose in the British day quarters than Gee and Bruce entered. Gee, in a stentorian voice, demanded that the newcomers parade before him. He inspected them, condemned them as lice-ridden, bellowed at them to remove their trousers, condemned them again in insulting language as being ridden with crabs and indicated to his orderly that their offending body areas and other excrescences be generously painted with the blue liquid, permeated with high-smelling lavatory disinfectant. The "Navy" seethed with suppressed indignation—but were covertly informed by the crowd of onlookers that what was being done to them had to be endured because any resistance, not to mention defiance, would bring diabolical retribution on everybody.

To be fair to the newcomers, they had by this time divested the "doctor" of his stethoscope and they were about to smash it to smithereens when they were alerted to the horrors of immediate German revenge. The stethoscope happened to belong to the British camp doctor—and was the only one in the region. The fake camp doctor then retired from the scene with his orderly, leaving the Navy standing at ease with their trousers down, but not before he had harangued them once more in the most insulting language his German vocabulary could rise to.

The Polish Lieutenant Żelaźniewicz escaped on 2 September from the park walk but was recaptured near Podelwitz, a local village.

On 8 September, Colditz was inspected by a senior German officer, General Wolff, who was in charge of prisoners of war in Army District No. 4, Dresden. He inspected the camp and found everything to his satisfaction and the German staff efficient and in control. Fortunately for everybody, when he was driven away his back was turned to the Castle wall beside the moat bridge. If he had turned his head, he would have seen a sixty-foot length of blue and white checked (bedsack) rope dangling from a remote window high up in a *Kommandantur* attic. It was seen by a housewife from the village, who reported it to the duty officer.

The day before, following upon an earlier order issued from General Wolff's office, the *Kommandant* had instituted a reduction of surplus prisoners' baggage. The British POWs had accumulated a substantial horde of private belongings which tended to clutter up the dormitories and also impede German searches. They were told to pack unwanted gear in large tea-chest-sized boxes, ex–Canadian Red Cross. These boxes were to be carefully labelled and stored until required. Some of the boxes contained books and were correspondingly heavy. Flight-Lieutenant Dominic Bruce, always known as the medium-sized man, fulfilled the role of a consignment of books complete with blue-check bedsack rope and equipment for an escape. All the boxes were duly carted away and manhandled by orderlies up a spiral staircase into an attic in the *Kommandantur* buildings. The doors were locked and Bruce was left to his own devices. During the night, he escaped, but not before he had inscribed on the empty box: "*Die Luft in Colditz gefällt mir nicht mehr. Auf Wiedersehen!* [The Colditz air no longer pleases me. Au revoir!]"

Bruce reached Danzig and tried to board a ship, as Paddon had done. He wasn't caught until a week later, near the harbor basin at Danzig. He had made use of one of those silk maps from the cover of a book from the Lisbon "agent." His story there was that he had jumped from a British plane over Bremen and had arrived in Danzig on a stolen bicycle. His bicycle, unluckily, had a local number on it. He was, however, sent to the RAF camp at Dulag Luft near Oberursel. There he was recognized by members of the German staff and for the second time he left for Colditz. It was perhaps artless of Bruce to write "*Auf Wiedersehen*" on the box when he really had "Goodbye" in mind. It was tempting fate.

Things were hotting up for the new *Kommandant.* On 9 September, ten officers were found to be missing after the morning roll-call had been delayed—the count fudged, the parade recounted, dismissed and recalled—while Hauptmann Priem raged up and down the ranks. An identity check of all the POWs had to be instituted to confirm who exactly had got away. This took several hours. The "confusion" ploy was used because there was no way of properly concealing a number of absentees at one time.

The escape plan had arisen one hot day in August 1942. Captain "Lulu" Lawton complained to me that a half-starved rat couldn't find a hole big enough to squeeze through to escape from Colditz. If only, he lamented, he could think of a way. I told him to look for the enemy's weakest point. Thinking aloud, I said, "I should say it's Gephard's own office. Nobody will ever look for an escape attempt being hatched in the German RSM's office."

Lulu procured the services of the red-bearded Lieutenant van Doorninck to manufacture, with formidable skill, a key to open the intricate cruciform lock on the door to Gephard's office. The plan evolved. Lulu had teamed up with Flight-Lieutenant "Bill" Fowler, and they made a foursome with van Doorninck and another Dutchman. Dick Howe, as the new British escape officer, was in charge.

I inspected the office. I saw that it was possible to rip up the floor under Gephard's desk, pierce a wall eighteen inches thick, and have entry into a storeroom outside and below the office. From there, simply by unlocking a door, the escapers would walk out on to the sentry path surrounding the Castle. The plan was based on the fact that German NCOs occasionally came to the storeroom with Polish POWs who were working in the town of Colditz. They brought and removed stores, etc., arriving at irregular hours, mostly in the mornings, sometimes as early as 7 a.m., and seldom coming more often than twice a week.

The escape party was increased to a total of six. Two more officers were therefore selected. They were Stooge Wardle and Lieutenant Donkers, a Dutchman. It was arranged that Lulu should travel with the second Dutchman, and Bill Fowler with van Doorninck. Sentries were changed at 7 a.m., so the plan was made accordingly. Van Doorninck, who spoke German fluently, would become a senior German NCO and Donkers would be a German private. The other four would be Polish orderlies. They would issue from the storeroom shortly after 7 a.m. Van Doorninck would lock up after him. The four orderlies would carry two large wooden boxes between them, the German private would take up the rear. They would walk along the sentry path past two sentries, to a gate in the barbed wire, where van Doorninck would order a third sentry to unlock and let them pass. The sentries—with luck—would assume that the "fatigue" party had gone to the storeroom shortly before 7 a.m. Once through the barbed wire the party would proceed downhill along the roadway which went towards the park.

The plan necessitated the making of two large boxes in sections so that they would be passed through the hole into the storeroom, and yet of such construction that they should be very quickly assembled. This escape was to be a blitz job. The hole would be ready in a matter of three days. Experience was proving that long-term jobs involved too much risk.

The hole was duly made, leaving a little to be knocked out at the last moment. The evening before the "off" (8 September), the six escapers, with myself and Lieutenant Derek Gill (who had been helping me dig the hole), were locked into Gephard's office.

At midnight there was an alarm. Germans were unlocking doors and the voice of Priem was heard in the corridor. He approached Gephard's office door. The night-duty NCO asked: "Shall I open this door, Herr Hauptmann?"

"Yes, indeed, I wish to check everything," answered Priem.

"It is the office of Oberstabsfeldwebel Gephard, Herr Hauptmann."

"Never mind. Open!" came the reply.

There was a loud noise of keys and then Priem's voice: "Ah, of course, Herr Gephard has many locks on his door. I had forgotten. Do not open, it is safe."

Between 3 a.m. and 6 a.m. we finished off the hole and carefully conveyed the men and their equipment through. Derek and I then left the office having patched up the hole. A little later Dick Howe reported a perfect take-off.

The morning *Appell* at 8:30 was going to cause trouble. By now, Dick had temporarily run out of inspiration. The Dutch dummies were no more. He might manage to conceal one absence, but six was an impossibility. So he did the obvious thing. He decided to lay in a reserve of spare officers for future escapes. Four officers were concealed in various parts of the Castle. There would be ten missing from the *Appell*. With luck the four hidden in the Castle would become "ghosts." They would appear no more at *Appells* and would fill in blanks on future escapes. The idea was not unknown to the Germans, but it was worth trying.

The 8 a.m. *Appell* mustered and, in due course, ten bodies were reported missing. By 11 a.m. the Germans had discovered the four ghosts and were beginning to conclude, after their first impression that a joke was being played on them, that six men had in fact escaped.

Dick was satisfied at having increased the start of the six escapers by a further three hours. Later in the day the Jerries, after questioning all sentries, had suspected the fatigue party, and working backwards to the store room, had discovered the hole. There was much laughter, even among the Jerries, at the expense of Gephard, under whose desk the escape had been made! The reader can imagine the disappointment and fury of Priem at the escapers having eluded his grasp so narrowly during the night!

Geoffrey Wardle and his Dutch colleague, Lieutenant Donkers, were unlucky. They were recaught and back in the Castle before the tumult of the roll-call was over. They were noticed by the *Bürgermeister* of a nearby village called Commichau as they passed through. He knew everybody in the village and immediately became suspicious. A local peasant woman found a number of discarded uniforms in a nearby wood and reported this at once. Thus the Germans knew that more than two had escaped. Eventually, they established the correct number at six. Lulu Lawton and Ted Beets were accosted and arrested at Döbeln railway station later in the day. Meanwhile van Doorninck and Bill Fowler carried on and reached Switzerland safely eighty-seven hours after leaving the Castle.

14

Swift Be Thy Flight

Late Autumn 1942

THE OKW SHOWED DISTINCT jitters at this time. Normally by September the "escaping season" was considered by them to be over. Instead it now appeared to be hotting up. General von Schulenburg was sent to tighten up discipline amongst the German garrison and impose stricter discipline on the POWs. "Otherwise," as he said, "different methods would have to be adopted." His influence had no appreciable effect. During October and November escapes continued at irregular intervals. Even Hitler's order that all commandos and parachutists were to be regarded as outlaws and to be shot when taken prisoner (which became public knowledge by the end of October) did little to deter initiative or dampen enthusiasm. Eggers reports that the *Kommandant* received Hitler's above orders from the OKW in writing on about 14 October.

Actually, on the evening of 7 October—unbeknown to the prisoners in Colditz—seven commando prisoners from the expedition code-named "Musketoon" arrived in Colditz. The *Kommandant*, taken by surprise and knowing nothing about them, telephoned the OKW for instructions. The commandos were locked up for the night in the guardroom, away from the other prisoners. The next morning they were being photographed in the *Kommandantur* courtyard when Peter Tunstall and Scorgie Price, who had entered the *Saalhaus* overlooking them, called out to them and discovered they were commandos captured in Norway and were en route to another camp. Later Rupert Barry obtained their names through an orderly who took food to them, and the information was passed on in a coded message to MI9 in London.

Two of them, including their leader, the Canadian Captain Graeme Black MC, were taken to cells in the town jail. There Peter Storie-Pugh and Dick Howe managed further conversation with them, and Dominic Bruce did so the following day. The next afternoon Eggers escorted four Gestapo men to the jail and the two commandos were removed.

The seven commandos left Colditz on 13 October. Hitler's order that captured commandos should be shot was not issued in Germany until 18 October, nor in Norway (where the commandos had blown up a hydroelectric power station) until 26 October. Yet at dawn on 23 October all seven were killed by the SS, shot in the back of the neck at camp Sachsenhausen. The German government then told the Swiss that the men had escaped, and Colditz *Oflag* IVC was instructed to return any letters to their senders marked "*Geflohen*," "escaped." Six were so returned.

It was a grim episode in the Castle's history. At the Nuremberg trials after the war, where the crime formed part of the indictment against General Jodl, it was seen that the date on the German document recording the executions had been altered from 27 to 30 October in an attempt to disguise their retrospective nature.

This is an appropriate moment to enlarge upon the code system developed at Colditz.

Rupert Barry became OC (Officer Commanding) Codes in Colditz at a very early date. It is generally thought, but not completely documented, that the War Office had already by May 1940 instructed a scattering of officers in the British Expeditionary Force on a code system for communication by letter in the event of their being taken prisoner. For instance, from *Oflag* VIIC at Laufen a message dated 4 March 1941 was received by the War Office on 22 March. However, the first British inmates at Colditz had no such code. Rupert and I set to make our own. I had actually invented a primitive code with my friend Biddy O'Kelly in Ireland. I wrote some letters in this code, but she could make nothing of them. Rupert had much more success. His wife Dodo was a highly intelligent girl who could do the *Times* crossword puzzle while she had her morning cup of tea. The first message he sent was: "Go to the War Office, ask them to send forged Swedish diplomatic papers in shovehalfpenny boards for Reid, Howe, Allan, Lockwood, Elliott, Wardle, Milne and self." His wife's immediate reaction on receipt of this letter was that he had gone mad, but before long she had decoded it. Rupert says:

> At nine o'clock next morning she presented herself at the War Office main door and asked the commissionaire if she could see an officer in the

Military Intelligence Department. She was presented with a form to fill in in which she was asked, among other things, for details of the subject she wished to discuss. This she refused to state, saying that the matter was secret. A violent argument ensued and as it became clear that she was not going to be allowed in, she explained her difficulty to an officer in uniform who came by, and told him that she had come to discuss a secret matter with an officer in Military Intelligence and not with the commissionaire, and could he help her. It so happened that he could, he would, and in fact did help her. My wife was instructed to write back to me in clear saying that she had met an old aunt of mine called Christine Silverman who had not seen me since I was a child and was distressed to hear where I was and that she would write to me. I, of course, had no aunt of that name and, as things turned out, I in fact received "Christine's" letter before my wife told me of her chance but happy meeting. However, it only took me a few seconds to rumble what had happened. We set about the letter with great expectations only to have our hopes destroyed by the message, "The War Office considered the use of Swedish Diplomatic papers to be too dangerous." Our reply to this was, "We will consider the danger and not the War Office. Would you please expedite." Suffice to say that after this somewhat unnecessary delay and because shovehalfpenny boards were no longer acceptable to the Germans as they had already found naughty things hidden in them, we never received our Swedish papers! However, communications had been established and these grew and grew.

But this single code could not be secure for long. Soon one coded message told us that some private (not Red Cross) parcels had been sent:

> One contained amongst the clothing a packet of Smarties, and the other six handkerchiefs each with a different coloured border. We were further told what we had to do with these, which was to place the yellow Smartie in a mug of water, then place in this water the handkerchief with the green border, stir for a few minutes, take out, read and destroy. The developed handkerchief contained detailed instructions for the operation of two really quite complicated codes. These were immediately taken into use, discarding the previous simple one. [See Appendix 3.]

With these codes we could say anything we liked. Our primary need was items for escape kits, and we would suggest ways of concealing these in private parcels. Later when Dick Howe had perfected his technique for stealing whole parcels before the Germans opened them (in fact inherited from the French—see below) it was only necessary to specify our requirements. We had nothing but admiration for the department of Military Intelligence (MI9) which dealt with us. The department also sent us information about enemy activity on frontiers, sentry positions, and so on. At one point they even boosted our morale by appearing to consider our suggestion that a splendid propaganda *coup* could be achieved by landing a light aircraft on the *Autobahn* near Colditz and so rescuing Douglas Bader.

As the system developed we were able to receive messages in certain BBC programs. We never had a transmitter, however.

> Life was full of surprises—for example, we asked for and received from London by the magic handkerchief method a plan of Colditz Castle floor by floor. We required this because at the time we were interested in possible old drainage systems and possible bricked-up cavities in the massive castle walls. Each room was shown under the name of the then occupant, Graf von So-and-So, Gräfin von somebody else. Enquiries after the war revealed that these plans had been obtained from the archives of the British Museum.

On 1 October, thirty-one French officers left Colditz for Lübeck, including "Fredo" Guigues. There were four expert lock-pickers in Colditz, one for each of the four principal nationalities. The Poles had Miki Surmanowicz. The British had me first of all, amateurish, taught by Miki; then Paddon, who was good but did not remain in Colditz long enough to be of much use to escapers. However, Bush Parker, an Australian, took over his role and became very capable. Van Doorninck was the Dutch expert and with Guigues was the king of all the lock-breakers. Fredo succeeded in gaining entrance at will through several locked doors into the parcels office.

Everyone had readily appreciated that free access to the parcels office would be an inestimable boon, but there was a formidable obstacle: on the door in the courtyard leading to the office the Germans had fixed to the old lock a cruciform key device which prevented it from being picked. Operating the device—which in turn operated the old lock—required a small key in the form of a cross, which when inserted moved several tiny pistons in their cylinders. Each piston moved a different distance, the accuracy of which was gauged to a thousandth of an inch. When all the pistons were moved accurately a circular drum could be rotated by the key to operate the lock.

Fredo managed to study one of these devices until he understood its mechanics completely. But a key was indispensable. He would have to make one. He cut out a key blank from one of the spindles stolen from the clock-tower, and a colleague had the idea of turning razor-blades into metal saws by cutting along the chamfered edge of the blade with a pair of scissors, to give a finely jagged effect. With such a saw Fredo was able to tool the appropriate notches on the key blank.

In one highly organized lightning operation, the actual lock was removed and the notches in the key blank were sawn to the exact depth required. The key worked and the lock was replaced. Having opened the principal door with his cruciform key, there were two further doors and more lock-picking before Guigues reached the actual parcels store. Every visit was a major operation involving seventeen men each with a different role to play. Fredo's first ploy was to order from his wife two parcels of tools. When they arrived he intercepted them, replacing them with innocent parcels before distribution (and examination by the Germans) took place. To celebrate this remarkable success, Abbé Jean-Jean had to open a bottle of communion wine.

Now the French could smuggle in anything they liked, but the process did not evolve without the occasional crisis. Once Fredo found a terrified cat with its kittens in the first room which fled from him as he opened door after door. When the time came for him to return, the cat evaded his grasp, with the result that the next day the Germans found the cat's kittens dead in the first room and the mother locked up in another.

Eventually the Germans installed an electric alarm on the locks of the parcels office. But this was no threat to Fredo and his clandestine visits because he intercepted the circuit before the installation was complete, carrying it through to the floor above. This particular achievement took place in May 1942 and was eventually put to bizarre use. Noticing a burly British officer ineffectively trying to pick the locks of the parcels office with a piece of wire (it was Errol Flynn, who, sadly, by this time was "going round the bend"), Fredo went straight to Dick Howe and demanded Flynn's removal. The last thing he wanted was a new set of locks. Dick indicated that Fredo could easily end Flynn's intervention himself. At once Fredo signaled to a colleague (looking down from the French quarters) to activate the alarm. Seconds later a squad of Goons rushed into the courtyard and carried Flynn off.

When Guigues left Colditz on 1 October, his keys, his picks and sundry instructions were inherited by two colleagues, Yves Desmarchelier and Robert Lalue.

At morning *Appell* on 15 October no fewer than ten British officers were found to be missing. This is what had happened.

Dick Howe had come to me towards the end of September to tell me of a scheme hatched by Ronnie Littledale and Billie Stephens. The idea was to sortie from one of the windows of the kitchen over the low roofs of various store buildings in the adjoining *Kommandantur* courtyard (which were in full view of all the windows of the *Kommandantur* above the ground floor), descend to the ground and cross the path of a sentry when his back was turned. The next thing was to crawl across the dimly lit area in front of the *Kommandantur* to a small open pit visible from the POW windows. At this point the escapers would still be in the bosom of the enemy, yet the plan went no further! I said the scheme was lunatic, but Dick confessed he wanted to let them have a shot. "And I want you to go with them, just to see they don't get into any trouble." I could see no prospect other than another month in the cooler, but I thought I might as well agree to join them.

I wondered if it would be possible to break into the tall block of buildings from which Dominic Bruce had escaped on 8 September. Bruce was doing his resulting solitary at the time, but I smuggled a message to him with his food and in due course had an answer. He pointed out that once inside this building one could descend from unbarred windows on the far side into the Castle's moat. The top floors were empty, but Germans occupied the floors below. There was a large door into the building which led to an unused staircase, but it was visible from almost everywhere and in full view of the *Kommandantur* sentries. This door was also locked (albeit not with a cruciform device). It was true that the floodlights at night threw the doorway into shadow, but the main thoroughfare from the outer Castle gateway to the entrance of the *Kommandantur* passed within a yard of it.

Using a stooge I entered the kitchen and examined the window giving on to the flat roofs. Working on four successive evenings I sawed through the head of a rivet on one of the bars (taking enormous care not to alert a sentry on his beat a mere fifteen yards away), and on the fifth evening removed the rivet itself with a silent working punch made for me by ERA Wally Hammond. Once the rivet was removed, the bar could be bent back to allow a man to squeeze through the window. I camouflaged the joint with a clay rivet.

I invited Hank Wardle to join us (he agreed we hadn't a chance), making a party of four. A further six men would be concealed about the Castle as ghosts to cover our escape. We four all had our identity papers, general maps, money and compass, kept usually in our "creepers." The map of the Singen border-crossing into Switzerland we had to commit to memory—I had forbidden frontier maps to be carried many months before. Clothes had long since been prepared. I had one of my cloth caps, converted RAF trousers, a windjacket and a German civilian overcoat which I had bought off a French officer who had obtained it from a French orderly who in turn had access to the village. I also had a pair of black shoes.

Hank and I decided to pose as Flemish workmen collaborating with the Germans. As *Flamands* we could pass off our bad German and our bad French, and we would be unlikely to run into someone who spoke Flemish. We constructed elaborate case-histories.

We also carried cardboard (ersatz leather) suitcases which had been sent for from Britain containing Army clothing. The value of a suitcase was that a man without one travelling across Germany on main-line expresses looked like a fugitive. It would be hell lugging them out of the camp, but well worth the effort in the end. We would need to wrap them in blankets to muffle sound; in any case, we were to take enough sheets and blankets to make a fifty-foot descent.

After evening *Appell* on 14 October we all made the highly dangerous run to the kitchen; Malcolm McColm was with us to cover our traces. Balaclava helmets and gloves covered our white skins.

Hank and I got through the window, made our way across the low roofs and dropped to the ground. A British orchestra—which the Germans had had several nights to get used to—was playing in the *Saalhaus*, conducted by Douglas Bader. Bader had a clear view of the sentry for the whole of his beat. The idea was to use the music for signaling: when they stopped playing it meant the escapers could cross his path.

The orchestra was playing as arranged, but each time I started across on the cessation of the music, it started again. Then I heard German voices. It was the duty officer on his rounds. Suspicious, he was questioning the sentry. Five minutes later the music stopped again, but this time I was caught napping, and I dared not risk a late dash. I waited a long time and the music did not begin again. Obviously things had gone wrong for the orchestra. I decided to wait an hour, to let suspicions die down.

In the hope that we could hide in that time from any passing Goon, I tried the handle of a door in the angle of the wall where we were hiding. It opened, and we entered warily. It was pitch-black inside. We went through a second door and took refuge in a room which seemed to contain no more than rubbish.

When the hour was up, we crept out again, and moved to the end of the wall as the sentry's footsteps indicated that he was turning on his beat. I peered round the corner, saw the soldier ten yards off marching away, and with Hank close behind tiptoed across the pathway (we wore socks over our shoes). Soon we were hiding in a small shrubbery near the entrance to the *Kommandantur*. Ronnie and Billie clambered across the roofs from the kitchen when they saw us cross the path, and in no time we were all in the pit.

My next job was to see if I could open the door into the building from which Dominic Bruce had escaped. It was fifteen yards away. I reached it, and apart from a hair-raising interruption when I heard Priem returning from an evening in the town, I worked for an hour without success. We would have to find another way out.

A tunnel led from our pit under a verandah. We felt our way along until we came to a cellar. At the far end was an air-vent or chimney flue. At first it seemed impossible for a man to negotiate this shaft, but after a few moments of despair I found that by removing some of my clothing I could slide up easily enough. I could see that it led to a barred opening at the level of the ground outside—that is, on the far side of the building, where lay the moat for which we were heading. One of the bars was loose in its mortar socket; I freed one end and bent it nearly double. We could just squeeze through!

It was an enormous struggle, and we each had to strip naked, but by 3:30 a.m. we were all lying in bushes on the moat side of the *Kommandantur*. Indeed we were on the very edge of the moat. We peered over. Luckily the moat wall was stepped into three successive descents; the drops were about twelve feet and the steps were about two yards wide. We made a couple of sheet-ropes and climbed down, fully clothed once more. It was 4:30 a.m. By 5:15 a.m. we were over the outer boundary wall—none too soon, because we had a long way to go before dawn.

Eggers was in Dresden attending a conference called to discuss the use of as many POWs as possible in German industry, a need arising out of the heavy losses Germany was suffering on the eastern front:

> I returned from Dresden on October 15th and found all passengers being checked by the police when I changed trains at Dobeln. My heart sank. I knew without asking. "Yes," they said. "Four prisoners missing from that *verdammten Sonderlager* of yours!"
>
> That morning four British officers had been found missing after the usual hullaballoo.
>
> Once again it was a report from a civilian coming up through the *Tiergarten* which had warned us that something was up. She had found some suspicious blue and white material (the usual bedsheets) under some bushes.

Although they found plenty of evidence to indicate the route we had taken, they simply could not believe that we could have done so and not been seen by the sentry. Eventually they concluded that somehow or other we had escaped via the *Saalhaus*.

News of the record-breaking success of the four escapers in reaching Switzerland became known in Coiditz—according to Platt's diary—on 9 November. Hank and I crossed the Swiss frontier on 18 October, a Sunday night. Billie and Ronnie arrived safely over the frontier the following evening at 10:30 p.m.

On 23 October, Colonel Breyer of the OKW, Leipzig, visited Colditz with the object of showing two high-ranking Italian officers, in typically festooned flamboyant uniform, around the prison. Eggers records that they realized this would provide a festive occasion for the POWs. In fact, the Italians had already been spotted from a prison window and loud cries of "Macaroni" were already wafting into the *Kommandantur*. Eggers persuaded the *Kommandant* to show the visitors around the outside of the Castle only.

News concerning the men who escaped successfully from Colditz in 1941 and 1942 trickled into the camp slowly, and was sketchy when it arrived, to say the least of it. Nevertheless, when it came it boosted the prisoners' morale considerably. A first wave of elation started about a week after an escape, when, with the continued absence of the escapers and glum reactions from the Germans upon questioning by the SBO as to their whereabouts, it was reasonably safe to assume that the men were out of enemy territory, provided they had not been killed en route.

Reliable confirmation arrived by various routes: sometimes a picture postcard slipped through the censor's net, written in a disguised hand from a fictitious character, but leaving no uncertainty in the mind of the recipient as to the meaning of the seemingly innocuous phrases in the text.

Hank Wardle, often called Murgatroyd by Rupert Barry, thus wrote to him from Switzerland in November 1942:

> We are having a holiday here (in Switzerland) and are sorry you are not with us. Give our dear love to your friend Dick. Love from
>
> Harriette and Phyllis Murgatroyd.

"Harriette" and "Phyllis," with the H and P heavily emphasized, were obvious cover-names for Hank and Pat.

At the end of November 1942, ERAs Wally Hammond and Tubby Lister, both submariners captured in 1940, made a formal application to the *Kommandant* to be removed from Colditz and sent to their rightful camp—after all, they were not officers but petty officers. Having had their training at Colditz they knew that to escape from a troops' camp would seem child's play. This was because troops went out daily from their moderately guarded cantonments to work (as the Geneva Convention permitted for other ranks), often unguarded, in factory or field. Eventually, their request granted, they set off for the troops' camp at Lamsdor. From there they escaped in no time at all, and after a hilarious and exciting journey, they crossed the Swiss frontier safely on 19 December.

They arrived in Berne for Christmas and for a reunion party that will long be remembered by the participants. The others were Ronnie Littledale, Billie Stephens, Hank Wardle, Bill Fowler and myself.

15

Of Whom Each Strives

Winter and Early Spring 1943

AFTER HIS ESCAPE, Pierre Mairesse Lebrun arrived back in France on 14 July 1941. In the area south of the Loire, still unoccupied by the Germans and known as the *zone libre* (or "Vichy" France) he celebrated his freedom in riotous fashion for three weeks. But his reputation had spread and in August he was recruited by *l'Armée de l'Armistice* to assist in setting up the French Resistance movement. For fifteen months he was actively engaged in making contacts, stocking arms, organizing an intelligence network, and in the clandestine passage of men across the Spanish frontier. Then in November 1942 the Germans marched into the *zone libre* and Pierre was forced "underground." A fugitive, always on the move, he nonetheless continued his Resistance work for another month: he felt a personal duty to execute his responsibilities to the full. Finally he left for the Pyrenees himself, crossing the border on 5 December.

On 16 November Peter Tunstall went for court-martial at Leipzig. On the 19th the Senior British Officer got five days' "room arrest," allegedly for providing Tunstall with "aids to escaping."

Flight-Lieutenant "Pete" Tunstall had arrived in Colditz on 16 March. Nearly six feet tall, he had a boyish, open face with large innocent pale-blue eyes. There was only a hint of a twinkle in them when he approached anybody with his impish smile. That smile could soon spell turmoil for the Goons and another court-martial for Pete—as well as for anybody ensnared by him into his "Just William" escapades.

He had been taken prisoner after a forced landing on the beach of the Friesian island of Vlieland on 28 August 1940. Since then he had escaped many times from many camps. He was like the Wandering Jew in his meanderings, always under heavy guard and all over Germany from one prison camp to another. After many long bouts of "solitary" and as many transfers he had eventually arrived. At Thorn he had gone down with meningitis. In prison conditions it was a wonder he survived. That, together with the fact that he felt compelled to continue his war against the Germans wherever he found himself, turned him into the most redoubtable Goon-baiter in Colditz.

In one of his first prison camps he had been briefed by his Senior Officer "to be as big a bloody nuisance to the Germans as possible." Pete took this as an order. When he came in contact with Douglas Bader at Warburg, he was greatly encouraged by the aggressive example that Bader gave in unmercifully baiting the Germans on every possible occasion. Pete became an ardent follower of this principle and method of continuing the war here in the middle of Germany.

Now he had to go to Leipzig to stand court-martial—this was his third—for a "water-bomb" incident which had occurred at the time of the escape of van Doorninck and Bill Fowler (9 September). In order to prolong the German identification parade he had thrown a bucket of water out of a window aimed at the table on which the POWs' identity papers were arranged.

Hauptmann Priem saw Tunstall throw the water out of the window and came upstairs and arrested him on the spot, saying that he had assaulted the German state! Tunstall was taken off to the cells where he remained in preventative arrest until the date of trial.

Despite the help of Dr. Naumann and of Lieutenant Alan "Black" Campbell (Colditz's "legal eagle" and a barrister in civilian life), Tunstall was found guilty in Leipzig of a breach of Camp Order No. 2 (which prohibited the throwing of water out of windows) and sentenced to four weeks in solitary confinement. But he was released at once because the time served in preventative arrest counted against sentence. He was given honorable acquittal on three other charges: assaulting his superior in the course of his duty (but there was no intent, nor was any German hit); causing a superior to take cover (but Hauptmann Eggers, the superior, was already in the cover of a staircase); causing confusion on a roll-call parade (but there was no proper military parade at the time and if there was Tunstall was within his rights to confuse it in order to aid an escape—Article 51 of the Geneva Convention).

Colonel Stayner and the Dutch Captain Moquette were the only witnesses allowed for the defense. Herr Naumann was engaged by Tunstall at a cost of nearly 400 *Reichsmarks* of which 200 were paid by the Protecting Power. The outstanding cost was borne by British mess funds. Naumann's charges were considered heavy but he was trusted to act conscientiously. Stayner reported that he was greatly impressed by the impartiality and correctness of the officer presiding at the court-martial and with the gentlemanly way in which the witnesses were received.

After this case Priem posted a sentry to cover the windows of the British quarters with orders to fire without warning. When Colonel Stayner requested the removal of the sentry if he himself gave his word of honor that nothing would be thrown out of the windows, Priem refused on the grounds that he could not accept Stayner's word of honor as a British officer.

On 25 November Mike Sinclair, along with a Frenchman, Captain Charles Klein of the French contingent, carried out an escape via the light well in the theater block. They debouched from the German kitchens into the *Kommandantur* area during the break after the mid-day meal. Sinclair very nearly made Switzerland, being trapped at Immendingen near the Schaffhausen frontier on 30 November. Klein did not get so far. He was recaught at Plauen.

Rupert Barry and another Frenchman, Aulard, had a real piece of bad luck when they followed the next day. They had managed to procure by bribery two Goon uniforms. Unfortunately Eggers chose that moment to inspect the German kitchens. Rupert had seized a wheelbarrow and was wheeling it away, when Eggers accosted the two "unknown" Germans. Eggers states that he failed to recognize Rupert Barry, who had shaved off his handlebar mustache for the occasion.

On 3 December, Thibaut de Maisières, a Belgian, arrived, making sixteen Belgians in all. One of them, Lieutenant Jan Scheere, was an Olympic pentathlete. He had beaten up a *mouton* (informer) for having betrayed an escape elsewhere of two Belgian officers and then had been posted to Colditz where he was pointed out to newcomers with admiration as *l'assassin belge*. Another, Lieutenant Le Cocq, had one day impulsively written to his wife in Belgium from his previous camp that he hoped that she would soon be rid of the "*vermine grise*." Conscientious German censors translated this as *graue Pest*. When they grasped that what appeared to be an allusion to a garden insect was an insulting description of themselves they reported the lieutenant, who was awarded two months' imprisonment, Colditz to follow. "Inflammatory sermons" had qualified the Aumonier Schmickradt, a Jesuit priest; and the other had come from mild Eichstatt, adjudged of "*mauvais esprit*." The Belgians' Senior Officer, Colonel Desmet, had been put on a train in France (after the capitulation) in order, as had been promised, to be repatriated to Belgium. The train made a detour in the night however and next morning Colonel Desmet woke up in Germany a prisoner. The Germans explained that the train had entered Belgium after 23 August, which they had appointed as the final date for free repatriation. Irritated by this duplicity, Colonel Desmet made a tart speech which brought him inevitably to Colditz. His aide, L'Officier Adjutant Leroy, had lived freely at home until December (1940) when he was suddenly arrested and sent to join the colonel on the strength of a police card stamped "*très dangereux*."

On 1 December Fredo Guigues escaped from Münster where the thirty-one Frenchmen had ended up, along with seven others. Of the eight who escaped, five were recaptured, including Guigues. Fredo and Pierre Boutard were caught in the middle of a wild-boar hunt. They were savagely beaten up, hospitalized in Soest and then sent back to Colditz where they arrived before Christmas. (Boutard died in hospital on 18 August 1944.)

Guigues learned of the discovery of his wireless set "Arthur I" by Eggers during a great search on 15 December. He was certain that a traitor must have given the game away. He was right.

Eggers revealed to Guigues in 1970 that a French soldier had offered to betray the place of a secret wireless in exchange for his freedom. The OKW had accepted the offer provided the set were found as directed by the POW and found in working order. He declared himself a collaborator and, because they were Anglophile, an enemy of the other French officers. He told Eggers that the set could be found behind Tunisia in a map of Africa on a wall in room 305, and Eggers, after a full-scale search of the whole French quarters to disguise his intentions, discovered it exactly as described. The traitor left Colditz with some orderlies. In 1970 Eggers revealed the man's name to Guigues but his identity was to be kept secret until the year 2000.*

Willie Pönert, the German civilian electrician attached to the Colditz garrison, was well known by the prisoners. He was a frequent visitor to their quarters repairing damage of many kinds—not confined to electrical faults.

Early one evening at twilight, on 28 December to be precise, the French conveniently short-circuited their lighting system so that Willie could be called in to repair the fault. Now Willie was such a frequent visitor that he seldom bothered to show his identity disc on entering or leaving the courtyard. The French Lieutenant Perodeau had noted this. He had also noted that he corresponded in height and build with Willie and that Willie wore glasses.

---

* Editors were not able to verify further updates to this information as of publication.

When Willie was fully occupied in the French quarters, Perodeau (looking exactly like Willie, complete with yellow distinguishing armband) headed for the main gate. To the security guard there he said "*Ich habe etwas vergessen* (I've forgotten something)." The guard allowed him through, but at the next gateway the guard demanded to see his identity card. So near and yet so far!

During the Christmas festival at the end of the year a truce was declared between the German staff and the prisoners. They promised not to escape and the Germans left the lights on until 1 a.m. Some of the prisoners contracted bets that this would be the last Christmas of the war.

The saluting war reared its head again in the camp. More trouble had been caused by Colonel Glaesche's Order No. 38 of 20 December 1942, in which he reminded the prisoners of their obligations under the Geneva Convention which called upon them to salute all superior officers and officers of equal rank. He also demanded punctuality and discipline at all roll-calls. A bell was installed to signify the commencement of roll-call. Anyone late was noted. The end product, naturally, was tumult.

So 1942 came to its end with the following result:

Home-runs 1942: 7 British; 5 French; 1 Belgian; 3 Dutch.

All together eighty-four men were involved in forty-four escape attempts and of these the above sixteen were successful. Thirty-nine were caught in the process of getting out of the Castle. Men who escaped in transit to and from Colditz including hospitalization numbered nineteen, of whom three made home-runs.

For 4 January 1943, Eggers had the following to report in his diary:

> The prisoners, the British and the French in particular, are doing all they can to get me out of the camp by making life unbearable for me. They have reason enough—I discovered the church tunnel and their attempts to get out from under the stage; I was their main antagonist in the saluting war; I discovered one of their radios. Today Colonel Stayner began a definite attack against me. I had recently brought Lieut. Sinclair back from Weinsberg and the Colonel complained that I had not treated Sinclair well during our train journey for when I ordered a meal in a station restaurant I did not invite him to dine with me. This beats everything! Such arrogance surpasses all my experience!
>
> The difficulty was later smoothed over and explained away as a misunderstanding due to language difficulties.

When Eggers found the wireless set called Arthur I he removed it triumphantly from its hiding place. What he did not know was that, well camouflaged, Arthur II was hidden nearby! That very evening, whilst being congratulated by their superiors, Eggers and his cohort were blithely unaware that Arthur II had arrived some days earlier and had been "switched" from the parcel office. Unfortunately, it arrived with one valve broken. A replacement was ordered. In the meantime Arthur III arrived. It was "switched" and given a very good hiding-place on the second floor of the French quarters (later occupied by the British) in a recess on the stone staircase behind a ventilation grille. A dug-out was built into the shaft behind and Arthur III was installed. By 17 January 1943, the POWs were once more listening to the BBC news.

On 8 January, while there was much snow about, Eggers was nearly hit by a snowball after an *Appell.* The snowball hit a door behind him, collapsed to the ground and revealed a broken piece of beer-bottle glass which had been packed inside it. As retribution, the Germans started taking photos of the courtyard *Appells* from an inconspicuous window in the kitchen gallery (the "Witches' Corridor"). They also installed a machine-gun there which was manned during *Appells.* Neither the machine-gun nor the photographer was visible to the men on parade but Padre Congar somehow found out what was happening. A protest was lodged.

The *Kommandant* revealed that the purpose of the photography was to provide evidence in the case of any mutinous behavior contrary to his Order No. 38. Of course this revelation made matters far worse. Eggers admitted that from then on there was mutiny at every roll-call. Order No. 38 was openly transgressed by smoking, howling, whistling and cat-calling. Names were taken, arrests were made and the cells were full for months.

The invasion of North Africa in November 1942 by the Allies and the subsequent entry of the Germans and Italians into Vichy France (in the same month) had upset all the recognized ways of travelling to Spain from Switzerland. With the Germans present, new and much more clandestine "tourist" routes had to be organized.

Bill Fowler and Ronnie Littledale were the first of the Colditz colony in Switzerland to leave. They crossed the Swiss frontier into France on 25 January 1943. The British consular staff in Geneva arranged this crossing into France at Annemasse. A guide took them in hand. They crossed the Spanish frontier on 30 January. They marched the whole day, reaching the La Junqueras–Figueras road at 4 p.m., and, while crossing it, they were arrested by Spanish soldiers who were patrolling the district in a lorry picking up the numerous refugees in the neighborhood. They seemed familiar with this routine and were not even armed.

They were taken to Figueras, where their heads were shaved and they were inoculated (Bill was tenth in line for the same needle). They were locked up in a cell with fourteen other men for almost three weeks. There was no furniture and little light; a single bucket, removed once every twenty-four hours, was provided for all natural functions. Prisoners were sick intermittently all day long. Two men died. Not until 22 February were they turned over to the British consul.

The POWs of Colditz saw and heard their first air-raids in January 1943—a strange excitement gripped them as they heard the throbbing of machines overhead, manned by men of their own nation who would mostly be home for breakfast in England. The Leuna Synthetic Oil from Coal Works, to the west of Colditz and south of Leipzig, appeared to be the target.

There was a big search on 21 January. The Germans retrieved German and French money and a lot of German accoutrements made out of linoleum, also false document stamps—carved from linoleum. They removed all the floor lino they could find from the prisoners' rooms.

Our Indian doctor Mazumdar started a hunger strike on 7 February. Captain Mazumdar, the only Indian in Colditz, had repeatedly asked to be moved to a POW camp for Indians to practice his religion there. This was his entitlement under Geneva Convention rules. The OKW repeatedly refused his request. He was *Deutschfeindlich*. He decided to go on hunger strike, following the example of Mahatma Gandhi who was also allegedly on hunger strike at that time in India. Mazumdar lost a lot of weight and after a fortnight the OKW gave in and he was moved to a camp for Indians near Bordeaux. True to Colditz tradition he escaped from there in 1944 and reached Switzerland safely.

On 13 February the *Kommandant*, Oberst Glaesche, was transferred from Colditz to the Ukraine, promoted to take charge of all POW camps in that region. Born in 1899, he died at Stuttgart-Degerloch in 1968.

Glaesche was really unable to control the Colditz POWs. At a loss, he avoided their contact. During his reign, escaping reached a climax and the punishment cells could not house the queue of those awaiting punishment. After six months he had to go. Eggers says they lost a man they all respected.

His successor was Oberstleutnant Prawitt, a more active man than Glaesche. He had been at Colditz for some weeks learning his job. He was forty-three years of age, a Regular infantry officer, and a Prussian. He claimed he had been promoted to full colonel in February 1943 in a telephone message from the *Generalkommando*. He was a martinet, and once publicly admonished the guard commander, Hauptmann Thomann, for allowing one of his men to go on duty with his collar up to keep out the snow.

Oberst Prawitt often attended the parties given by rich families of Colditz, partaking to the full of the food and wine available. (When offered a cigar, for instance, he sometimes took more than one.) Although his outward appearance and bearing were generally those of a model German officer, he was in fact openly in opposition to Hitler, concealing his attitude only after the assassination plot of 20 July 1944.

On 15 February, a second *Prominenter* arrived in Colditz in the person of Lieutenant Michael Alexander to keep Giles Romilly company. He was the nephew of Field Marshal Alexander. He was awaiting court-martial because he had been captured in Africa while wearing German uniform.

The first four prisoners who officially called themselves "Gaullists" arrived on 25 February. They were counted as soldiers of the British Army with the same status as the British prisoners.

There were triumphant demonstrations around this date because of the defeat at Stalingrad, although the last Germans had surrendered on 2 February. It was therefore three weeks before the news was public in Germany, although the POWs in Colditz heard it on the wireless as soon as the BBC broadcast it.

On 1 March General von Block became Commander of Prisoners of War, District No. 4, Dresden.

Bag Dickinson managed to evade his guards once more, during an exercise period in the town jail. It was 7 March. On the exercise walk while screened by two POWs lighting up cigarettes, he dived under a table in the dim-lit hallway. He managed to reach Chemnitz for the second time on another bicycle, where he was again caught. The Germans' "Mousetrap" code signal to all the main cities, towns and villages within a large radius appeared to be effective. But Eggers says he was caught because of "abject carelessness."

On 16 March there were 103 British officers in Colditz, forty-six Army, twenty-one Navy and twenty-one RAF, and fifteen orderlies. There were also two civilians. The Germans decided to send twelve officers back to Spangenburg. Some of them were Royal Engineers, not actually caught escaping anywhere, others had behaved themselves at IVC by committing no offense warranting "solitary." One—Black Campbell—was obviously removed because of his fine advocacy on behalf of British POWs on court-martial charges.

A bold attempt to climb out of the Colditz prison yard and over the roofs of the *Kommandantur* for an exterior descent was made on 2 April by two French lieutenants, Edouard Desbats and Jean Caillaud. The idea for this attempt was born one rare foggy winter's day when the high roofs of the Castle were completely blanked out of sight. But how to take advantage of it? Soon after, and for the first and last time, the Germans held a cinema show for the prisoners in a building outside of the Castle. On the way back a lightning conductor was spotted, leading from the end of the roof of a *Kommandantur* building down to the moat, which did not appear to be guarded. The other end of the roof linked up at right angles with the coping of a building which gave on to the prisoners' courtyard.

But to climb up sixty feet on to roofs that were floodlit was a very dangerous business, particularly when there was no fog. So there was no point in being impatient. The roof project was studied with care. The fact was that those roofs, and the lightning conductor, were only two elements in the scheme, albeit very important ones. A way had to be found to get clear of the courtyard. A window in the Gaullists' quarters was within about two yards of a flat ledge of roof which abutted a square brick-built chimney. This rose above the gable of the roof they needed to reach. The gap between the window and the ledge could be bridged with a stout plank.

The chimney was the problem. There was a powerful lamp fixed to it on the courtyard side, so that sentries could see it as clearly at night as by day, and barbed wire was coiled around it, just above the kitchen roof. Later, returning from exercise in "the park," another lightning conductor was noted on the face of the chimney, where there was no flood-lamp. It could be reached once past the barbed wire. Whether it would stand up to the weight of a man for the twenty-five to thirty-foot climb, with a sixty-foot drop below, was anybody's guess.

However, there was a lightning conductor in the prisoners' courtyard, leading down from the kitchen roof, which was built out from the main building, and about twelve feet high—an obvious place to test the strength of the conductor tube. A tennis ball got conveniently lodged on the roof, in the guttering. Caillaud, heavily built, hauled himself up and retrieved the ball safely. That problem had been resolved.

March was almost over. The days were getting longer. Fogs were few and far between. They could be ruled out. Caillaud and Desbats were getting impatient. Having convinced themselves that the sentries would not normally keep their eyes on the roofs they decided to take advantage of the period between the evening *Appell* and lights-out at 10 p.m. The floodlight unfortunately would be on. During that period lots of rowdy prisoners would be in the courtyard, so covering up any noise from the escape attempt. There was a light covering of snow on the cobbles which had melted higher up.

With everything ready for that evening, 2 April, and with the escapers on the point of making a start, the bell rang at 9 p.m. for an extra *Appell* following an abortive escape attempt by a British officer. Desbats and Caillaud still felt they had to go, so immediately after *Appell*, wearing the minimum of clothes and rubber shoes, they hurried to the Gaullists' room, carrying a bundle containing civilian clothes and a long rope made from strips of palliasse cover.

The window bars had been sawn. First out was Desbats. Climbing on to the ledge, he ignored the plank that had been so laboriously placed across the void and jumped to the flat ledge. Caillaud followed having tied the rope to the bundle. The other end was attached to Desbats' belt. Desbats managed to get past a brick projection and the barbed wire. Conveniently there were metal hoops around the chimney, secured by large bolts. These served as securing points for the rope. "Lights out" was sounded in the courtyard. Soon it was empty of prisoners and the noise dwindled to silence.

Desbats continued his climb to a point about sixty feet above the German courtyard, from where he could see a guard on the far side. Caillaud had by now got on to the ledge, from where he eased the rope as Desbats made progress. Desbats had made his way to the other side of the chimney.

But in climbing the lightning conductor he dislodged a piece of brickwork. It fell on to the roof of the kitchen and from there into the German courtyard, making a frightful noise. Realizing the danger, Desbats tried to hurry his climb, but the rope with its bundle was a nuisance. If he could reach the roof he would be safer and out of sight of the sentries. He was getting tired. Effort was required to haul in the rope and secure it each time to an iron bolt before each upward step.

The sentry had heard the falling brick. Desbats, still making very slow progress, watched from the corner of his eye. Caillaud, who had heard the noise, but couldn't see Desbats, continued to release the rope, hoping all the time that they hadn't been spotted. But it was a vain hope! The sentry in the German courtyard shouted to another guard, and both of them, looking up, saw Desbats dangerously situated about ten feet below the roof that was his objective.

Shouts of "*Halt!*" were followed immediately by a shot, which gave the general alert. Desbats stopped climbing. He called out, "*Schiessen Sie nicht! Ich ergebe mich.* (Don't shoot! I'll give myself up.)" But it didn't stop the Germans.

With Desbats in the full light of the powerful floodlamps there was a hail of shots, hitting the brickwork above his head; one bullet was a very near miss. Püpcke quickly arrived and ordered the shooting to stop and assured Desbats that he could come down without danger. So down he came, down the sixty feet of lightning conductor to the ground.

Now the sentry in the prisoners' courtyard had also been alerted, and he could see Caillaud on his illuminated perch. As he raised his rifle to fire, a Frenchman rushed out of the French quarters, despite it being forbidden after dark, and persuaded the guard to lower his rifle.

Then the bell rang again for another *Appell*. After the previous *Appell* that evening at 9 p.m., the British retired to their bunks and most of them were soon asleep. Then shots rang out in the stillness. Men stirred and turned over; some sat up. Scarlet O'Hara was heard to remark, "Coo, did you hear that? Three *gros coups de fusil*!"

More shots followed.

Black-out blinds were raised. (Although the outside of the Castle was floodlit, prison orders were to the effect that blinds must be drawn. It was a precautionary measure in the event of air-raids, when the floodlights were always extinguished. The order was, needless to say, flagrantly disobeyed.) Lights went on in the courtyard windows like patches in the quilt of night. Windows opened. There were shouts, orders, jeers, counter-orders and laughter. Windows shut again, blinds were lowered, and the lights went out one by one.

The annual "Day of the *Wehrmacht*" was 4 April. In the town of Colditz peas and bacon were sold for the last time. The *Oflag* IVC museum was opened to the public, and visitors were asked to give money for the WHW (Work for Help in Winter). Many visitors came to see the rich collection of escapers' contraband. For a year now the Germans had been X-raying the prisoners' parcels. They had discovered compasses, money, saws—all concealed in brushes, games, sports goods. Also exhibited were the home-made uniforms and ropes, and general carpentry and tools.

On 5 April more than 150 prisoners wanted to take part in the exercise walk in the park. This in itself should have aroused the curiosity and suspicions of Hauptmann Lange, the security officer. The POWs as usual did not march in any sort of military order but ambled along in disorderly fashion.

When they arrived in the German yard somebody called out from one of the windows that all the Dutch officers were to return to their quarters for a lecture. The result was that prisoners milled all over the place causing total confusion. The German duty officer ordered everyone back to quarters. Amidst all this chaos two German officers stood watching the shambles with supercilious smiles on their faces. A guard asked them for their identity papers and one of them produced a document stamped and signed neatly by the German adjutant stating that the two officers were from the OKW and had permission to inspect all parts of the Castle. Purely by chance "Beau Max"—*Feldwebel* Grünert who was in charge of the camp parcels office—arrived on the scene. He was the best man to recognize every prisoner in the camp and as soon as he saw them he exposed them as a Dutch officer and an English officer. They were taken to the guardroom and positively identified as Captain Dufour and Flight-Lieutenant van Rood.

In the meantime all the prisoners had been returned to the yard and a special roll-call was ordered by Lange. It was then discovered that two prisoners were missing. They were Flight-Lieutenant Jack Best and Lieutenant Michael Harvey RN. They had disappeared, the Germans thought, in the park parade chaos. In due course, the OKW in Berlin were told that these two had escaped successfully. In fact, they were being concealed in the camp as ghosts.

The *Appell* lasted from 5 p.m. to 9 p.m. and was a riot. Pete Tunstall and Don Thom were hauled off to the cells. They were let out again later in the day awaiting "charge." At morning *Appell* the next day Don Thom was charged with doing something odd with his arms and legs and thus behaving himself incorrectly on *Appell*. He was sentenced to ten days, which he carried out in May.

On 11 May as usual the half-dozen prisoners in the solitary cells in the Castle were given their hour of exercise. Escorted by a corporal in charge and a sentry in front and behind, in single file, they passed through the guardhouse, to the turret staircase (the same one that Airey Neave had descended), and sortied out through a small door on to the terrace. The corporal took up the rear of the procession descending the staircase. Bag Dickinson sortied first and marched on behind the leading sentry towards the far end of the terrace. Don Thom was second out. As soon as he sortied, van Rood, who was third, stopped in the doorway and blocked it. Thom leaped over the parapet of the terrace, down a drop of thirty feet. He broke his fall twice by gripping the bars outside two small windows, one above the other, which gave light to the lower part of the circular staircase. There was a machine-gun post in a pagoda facing him as he landed. It was forty yards away at the corner of a small garden. The sentry saw him immediately and fired his rifle once, missing him, before springing to his machine-gun. Thom had run thirty-five yards by then and was almost under the pagoda. The sentry in it was powerless. But two more sentries on the beat in the garden and round a corner heard the shot and the sentry's shouting. So also did the corporal (who had dived out through the door) and the two sentries up on the terrace. They started shooting. The two sentries in the garden ran to the scene and joined in.

By this time every prison window facing the terrace was crammed with Frenchmen in their quarters. They went mad and tried to upset the concentration of the sentries. While on the terrace, Bag Dickinson and van Rood obstructed their guards in every way possible.

Don Thom was now climbing over two barbed-wire fences each six feet high. A fusillade of shots surrounded him—one grazed his scalp and a second tipped his heel. He was soon over the fences and tumbling down a precipitous slope to the stream. Bushes helped break his fall. He was over the stream and climbing its steep bank before sentries in the park spotted him. They fired at him as he passed between the trees and the sentries from the garden joined in. Luckily the machine-gun was now useless, being above the trees. Thom now had 100 yards to run, uphill, to the final obstacle, the high park wall with wire on top. He was nearly exhausted, his heel and scalp bleeding. The park sentries coming from another direction were on his level and closing on him. He could not find footholds in the wall. He could not climb it. He turned and raised his arms. The firing had already stopped.

Pete Tunstall was soon up again for court-martial. Black Campbell's précis report of the proceedings is a gem of understatement. The trial took place at Leipzig on 7 May.

Circumstances: Tunstall had just completed one of his many visits to the cells and being fairly dirty asked a German officer if he could have a bath. He was told that this was all right so he went off to the bathroom, which at that time was in the charge of a most unpleasant German bathroom attendant who refused to allow Tunstall to have a bath, or to listen to his explanations as to why he should have one, or to heed the authority of the German officer who said he could have one.

A quarrel ensued in which Tunstall told him to check up with the duty officer, and much else besides, and to emphasize some of his points touched the German with a rapidly gesticulating index-finger.

Charge: Assault against a superior in the course of his duty.

Award: The court offered Tunstall an honorable acquittal if he would agree that there had been a misunderstanding.

	Tunstall said that there was no question of any misunderstanding and that the witness for the prosecution was lying: so the court ordered a retrial.
Defense:	No assault, the incident was provoked by the stupidity and improper attitude of the bathroom attendant.
Witnesses:	Pte Brooks Pte Doherty — No assault L/C Hallen
Retrial later:	On retrial, the prosecution witness fainted under cross-examination and was revived by Tunstall, who took the carafe of water off the Judge's desk and administered it to him; asking the Judge not to press the poor fellow with awkward questions until he had fully recovered. The defense evidence was in substance that of some British orderlies who witnessed the alleged assault: an attempt was made by the prosecution to tamper with this evidence before the date of the retrial; fortunately this attempt did not succeed.
Award:	Acquittal.
Note:	O'Hara R.T.R. [Royal Tank Regiment], one of the camp wags, on hearing of Tunstall's acquittal is said to have observed with some ardor: "Is there no justice in this country?"

The "solitary" he had served as a result of his court-martial in November for the water-bomb did not prevent Peter Tunstall from doing it again. On the second occasion he used an over-size water bomb. It was high summer and the *Kommandant* appeared in a spotless white duck uniform, followed by five Germans in the brown uniforms of Nazi politicians, with massive leather belts encircling their paunches, their left arms swathed in broad, red armbands carrying the black swastika in a white circle. Their shoulders, collars and hats were festooned with tinsel braid like Christmas trees. They were *Gauleiters* from Leipzig and Chemnitz.

The *Gefreiter* called "Auntie" ran ahead of them, up the British staircase and burst into the mess-room. Prisoners were having their tea and his shouts of "*Achtung! Achtung!*" were received with the usual complement of "raspberries" and rude remarks. Tea continued and his more frenzied "*Achtungs!*" were ignored. The *Kommandant* walked in at the head of his procession. He had expected everyone to be standing glassily at attention. Instead he had to wait three minutes—the time it took for the more ardent tea drinkers to note his presence "officially."

Benches and chairs scraped, mugs and plates clattered and men rose to their feet, wiping their mouths and blowing their noses with large khaki handkerchiefs in a studied display of insolence of finely calculated duration.

The *Gauleiters* raised their arms in the Nazi salute with their arms slightly bent—Hitler-fashion. The salute was returned by the members of one table, including Scorgie Price and Peter Tunstall, in a manner which appeared to please the *Gauleiters*. The prisoners saluted with a variation of the "V" sign in which the fingers were closed instead of open and the thumb facing inwards. The *Gauleiters*, happy to think that their importance was appreciated, saluted again, and the salute was acknowledged again but with greater vigor. As the procession passed between the rows of men standing to at their tables, the cue was taken up and prisoners everywhere gave the new salute, which was acknowledged punctiliously at every turn by the *Gauleiters*.

They turned, retraced their steps, saluting and being saluted, beaming with smiles at their pleasant welcome and finally left the quarters.

A water-bomb just missed them as they emerged from the British doorway, but spattered the *Kommandant*'s duck uniform with mud. He shouted for the guard, hurried his visitors through the gates and returned alone. A posse, dispatched upstairs at the double to find the culprit, was not quick enough. Pete was learning: nothing could be pinned on him. The *Kommandant* left the courtyard followed by cries of "*Kellner!* (Waiter!) *Bringen Sie mir einen whisky soda!*"

His exit signaled the arrival of the Riot Squad. Windows were ordered to be closed; rifles were levelled upwards at those delaying to comply with the shouted commands. Scarlet O'Hara, sleeping peacefully beside an open window, awoke from a siesta in time to hear the tail-end of the shouting. Poking his head out as far as the bars he cautioned the squad: "*Scheissen Sie nicht*, my good men, *scheissen Sie nicht!*"—all to no avail. A bullet zipped through the opening and he closed the window from a kneeling position, cursing the ill manners of the "uncouth b— Huns." The word he had pronounced was *scheissen* (shit) not *schiessen*.

The *Kommandant* never appeared again in his white duck uniform.

An interesting unsolved mystery, which will almost certainly never be solved now, is introduced here by an entry in Platt's diary for 25 May:

> In a conversation with Dr. Eggers after evening *Appell* he referred to an entry for November in the portion of my diary now being *geprüft*. The

> point raised was my account of the case of "Sheriff" and the Leipzig general dealer. He, Dr. Eggers, was surprised that the prisoners had regarded the "general dealer" as having filled the inauspicious role of stool-pigeon and assured me it was not the case and that sentence of death had been carried out.

First, it may be noted—as an aside—that Eggers is reading of events recorded in the diary in November, in the month of May following—that is five months later. Throughout the diary there appear to be several such instances in which the "interval" would appear to be less than five months. Platt was running a risk here. The information and its availability to the enemy comes within the scope of that "gray" area in intelligence matters where information revealed which deals with the past may nonetheless betray pointers or clues in the future. Further, the OKW issued a "News for Security Officers"; Eggers, in his diary, says that from this they learned that at another camp the laundry had been used for communications between prisoners and people on the outside. Lange, the security officer at IVC, ordered an immediate check on the laundry and found chocolate, love letters and cigarettes going out, and *Schnaps* coming in. This was soon stopped. There can be little doubt that extracts from Platt's diary were submitted for this journal.

As for "Sheriff" (Lieutenant Adam Niedenthal), the reader will recall that the so-called "general dealer," or the "Leipzig wholesaler," the German sentry, was reported to have been shot by the Germans (see Chapter 13). Are Eggers' words to be trusted in this matter?

Logging backwards, after the discovery of the *Saalhaus* tunnel and the coded messages, Sheriff was in solitary confinement for four months. He had a lot to say when he came out on 23 November. Unfortunately the only report extant comes again from Platt who in his diary for that day (the entry he discussed with Eggers) adds a lot more about the British connection with the "general dealer":

> Sheriff Lt. Niedenthal, came out of confinement today after sixteen weeks. He was taken to the cells in July for questioning re the Heath Robinson typewriter which had been found and confiscated. And thereby hangs a tale. Sometime about the end of March this year a new German sentry appeared in British quarters guarding the *Tischler* [carpenter]. He was keen to converse with us and at once declared himself willing to assist with our escape schemes, if the pay were good enough. It was, and arrangement was soon made whereby he would furnish us with a quantity of tools and

> equipment for general escape work. He received a personal rake-off of 100% of the value of anything he produced and was paid in R.M. [*Reichsmarks*], cigarettes, coffee, chocolate, or whatever currency he chose. Usually he took as much chocolate, coffee and cigarettes as he could get. There were several things, however, about his dealings with us that suggested to the oldest inhabitants who had been bitten before, that his interest was a little farther reaching than personal gain would require. He was a shade too eager to know the exact nature of certain schemes that were then afoot and showed more than a passing interest in the time and place at which they would mature.

Knowing that the last thing the Germans wanted them to have was a radio, they tested him by asking him to get them one. Despite his many promises, he never complied. Then he hardened their suspicions enormously by offering his address in exchange for the one in Leipzig from which he knew (and he claimed Authority also knew) escapers obtained assistance. Further he advised escapers to leave the train before Leipzig general station and catch a train to his house.

Then he disappeared. The Polish tunnel was discovered, and Niedenthal was arrested, and interrogated by the Gestapo. Platt goes on:

> Sheriff made it known that he believed the Wholesale Dealer to have been a stooge, at which the Gestapo, he thought, laughed rather too heartily. This interrogation lasted six hours! Sheriff was not proceeded against, i.e. he was not court-martialled for bribery, nor was he sentenced by the Camp *Kommandant*, but he has been in the cells since the 21st July until today.

As I have said, Eggers writes that Niedenthal (or a friend of his in Colditz) had been a business partner of the "Leipzig wholesaler" before the war. This had started up the connection. Yet Platt does not record this at all. Again therefore the question arises, is Eggers telling the truth? Is he once more trying to hide the fact that, willingly or unwillingly, he was co-operating with the Gestapo?

The principals in this drama are all departed: Eggers, Platt and Niedenthal. But perhaps the "Leipzig wholesaler" is not!

With spring turning to summer, Peter Tunstall found another opportunity for Goon-baiting. Little Willi appeared in the courtyard carrying a long ladder. A sentry was with him. Crossing to the chapel, where he had to repair a window, Little Willi propped the ladder against the wall and, leaving the sentry behind to guard the ladder, returned through the gate to fetch the glass. While Don Donaldson distracted the sentry by sitting on the cobbles nearby and embarking on a series of extraordinary tricks with his hands, Pete and Bag Dickinson removed the ladder. Starting up the spiral staircase to the British quarters they found that the twenty-five-foot ladder could not get round the curves. Bag fetched a saw (made out of gramophone spring) and they shortened the ladder by five feet. Moments later the five-foot length of ladder was standing where Little Willi had left the twenty-five-foot one. The electrician returned with the glass, stopped, and stared incredulously at his new ladder. The sentry joined him. Willi asked what had happened. The sentry blamed a poltergeist. Then, picking up the ladder and the pane of glass, they marched forlornly out of the courtyard.

16

A Measure of Sliding Sand

Spring and Summer 1943

DURING MAY THE INADEQUATE diet of the prisoners began to show up in numerous skin complaints. Vitamin deficiency was almost certainly the cause. Padre Platt's feet and later hands became swollen and septic. On 26 May he went to bed sick in his Priests' Hole. He remained there till the end of July. His sickness was diagnosed as vitamin deficiency. The POWs had not seen a fresh vegetable for years. Everybody was affected in various degrees. Padre Platt, being probably the oldest POW, felt the brunt of it.

On 13 May came the visit of the Swiss Red Cross delegate. He entered the courtyard accompanied by German officers and went to the *Evidenzzimmer*, where he listened to the grievances of the various POW Senior Officers.

Whilst the Polish Senior Officer was there, Prawitt went out to the courtyard. It was about mid-day. A group of prisoners were taking advantage of the brief period when the sun could be seen. Prawitt's adjutant shouted "*Achtung!*" It was ignored. Prawitt was furious. He ordered the guards to clear the courtyard. The prisoners, angry at being deprived of a brief sight of the sun, gathered at the windows, booing and shouting. Ordered to leave the windows, they continued howling. Prawitt ordered the guards to fire at anyone appearing at the windows. Shots were fired, fortunately not finding a target.

Hearing the shots the Swiss delegate came out of the *Evidenzzimmer* and asked what was happening. The Polish Senior Officer said, "Just shots at the windows. We don't take any notice. It happens so often."

The Swiss expressed his surprise to a German officer, who replied: "There is such a hostile attitude adopted by the prisoners that the *Oberst* has no alternative but to open fire in order to protect himself." As the Swiss turned to re-enter the *Evidenzzimmer* he saw a stretcher near the entrance. He asked why it was there.

"Oh," replied the Pole, "we always have a stretcher ready for the wounded."

The delegation then visited the Dutch and Polish quarters where the reception was very military and everything was in order. On coming downstairs again they found someone had removed the handle from the door, effectively locking them in. A sentry had to be called to produce a French bayonet from the guardroom. These bayonets were in the form of a cross, and when the point was inserted in the hole left by the missing handle, and then turned, it opened the door.

On 30 May, the blind French General Scapini, a deputy of Field Marshal Pétain, visited the French contingent to speak to them. It is time to speak of the problems of loyalty and conscience that faced the French at Colditz.

When, with the assent of the French government, officers were asked to volunteer for work in Germany, nearly everyone put his name down, not wishing to neglect an opportunity of getting out of the Castle. But when told the conditions (word of honor not to escape; not to bear arms against Germany), everyone refused to sign; it was only in order to escape and fight again that they had volunteered. But later, one officer changed his mind. He would not listen to argument. "I want to escape," he said. "It's impossible to do so from here." The French Senior Officer replied, "But if you sign the paper and are recaught, you'll be shot." "Yes, but I'll risk it. In any case, I don't consider that my word of honor to a German has any validity." "Your word of honor perhaps, but it is the word of honor of a French officer that you would be breaking. That I cannot permit." Shortly after, the officer refused to sign and took his place again amongst his comrades. But they did not find it easy to pardon his weakness. Working in Germany was thought of as treason by every prisoner in Colditz, although the Vichy War Ministry encouraged the French to work for the Germans.

In 1942 or early in 1943, the French were permitted, for the first time, to attend a cinema show in a hall just outside the Castle. Everyone wishing to go had to give his written word not to try to escape. This was valid only for the time between starting off and returning. No sooner were the French seated than a small gang of French officers whom they did not know entered from an opposite door. Either of their own free will, or as a result of ministerial exhortations, they were working in Colditz town, almost certainly in the porcelain factory. They were hardly in the room before they were received with roars of disapproval. Everyone stood up, fists clenched and raised, shouting, "*Salauds!*

. . . *Cochons! . . . Traîtres! . . . Fabricants de pots de chambre!"** The lights were switched off to quiet the noise. Eggers was choking with suppressed anger, but still wearing a forced smile.

There were no more trips to the cinema!

Were all the French officers pro–de Gaulle? A certain number, yes! And those, 100 percent so. The rest found themselves with split loyalties. All their training, all their discipline, had instilled a strong loyalty to Pétain, the commander-in-chief of the glorious French Army of 1918.

How could these men be reproached? Deprived of contact with their country, closely confined, subjected to insidious propaganda by the Vichy government which had accepted the "*double jeu*," their lives as prisoners had been a long and tenacious resistance to the Germans—the *Boche*. How many true French, who certainly did not need lessons in patriotism from anyone, asked themselves with anguish where their duty lay? How could they choose between General de Gaulle and the man who, unless it was proved otherwise, also had the best interests of France at heart? Whatever their differing approach, all were united in one thing, hatred of the *Boche*. It was this hatred that bound them closely.

Colditz was probably the only camp that did not have a "Pétainist Group," or where Vichy propaganda was not distributed, where messages from the Maréchal were not read; from where no messages of loyalty were dispatched. All these germs of disunity were taboo. Nothing can illustrate this better than Scapini's visit on 30 May 1943, a few days after the Feast of St. Joan of Arc, which had been marked by the fervent singing of the *Marseillaise* by all the French, including the Free French.

It was his first and last visit. He could hardly have expected a welcome. The previous winter, on a bitterly cold day, one of his collaborators visited Colditz. He took back with him a memory of fanatics who, not content with giving him a hostile reception, had stolen his overcoat and hat. The news of Scapini's visit aroused heated arguments. The more moderate types had a difficult job persuading the objectors not to let the other nationalities witness a hostile demonstration against a man who was blinded in the 1914–1918 war.

Surrounded as soon as he arrived, he was told that, since 11 November 1942 (when the Germans took over Vichy France), the French government including its chief had lost all credibility in Colditz. Their failure to do anything about the violations of the Geneva Convention by German jailers gave the impression

---

* "Bastards! . . . Pigs! . . . Traitors! . . . Chamber-pot makers!"

that in their eyes the Colditz prisoners were outcasts, abandoned to their fate, in exchange for German favors. The view was strongly held that they would be better looked after by a Protecting Power than by their own country.

Stung to the quick, Scapini protested violently. He explained that he was powerless to do anything . . . the tense situation, the lack of goodwill of the Germans. The prisoners taken at Dieppe were still in chains. French generals were subjected to four *Appells* each day and one each night. The best that could be hoped for was a patched-up peace. He asked one prisoner how he passed the time. On getting the reply, "Trying to get out of here," he said, "Why run such risks, since France is not any longer in the war?" To which he got the response, "I can't believe that the fighting soldier you were in 1914–18 would have said that!" "Maybe not," said Scapini after a long pause.

Scapini's entourage wanted him to address all the French, but his reaction was, "What's the use? We haven't a single thing in common." However, he spoke to a gathering of room leaders, older, calmer men. He denied vehemently that he had neglected his duty towards the prisoners. He spoke heatedly about their mistrust of Pétain. He insisted that the spirit of discipline demanded obedience to the chief, and quoted the English "My country, right or wrong." Standing, leaning on the table, he listened to what the room leaders had to say. But visibly uneasy before this audience, he knew that his discourse had produced no echo. Clearly, there was no common ground. Turning slowly, he said to the gathering, "I'm afraid we don't see things in the same light."

Here is a translation of the final peroration of one of the room leaders—a lawyer—who had been a colleague of Scapini in the Paris law-courts:

> You have said that the *Maréchal* [Pétain] has lost all credibility [in Colditz]. That is only partially true. His photograph is still hanging in some of the rooms. He is still respected by some of us.
>
> But what it is essential that you should know is that every prisoner in Colditz has a deep and abiding hatred of the Germans. They cannot forget that the Germanic hordes have on three occasions invaded our country with the intention of crushing it, that they have committed atrocious crimes, that they are a "nation of prey" [*nation de proie*] and that France cannot live in peace as long as Germany is not destroyed.
>
> They wish for her destruction ardently. They applaud anything that contributes towards it. They participate in it with all their heart and within the feeble means available to them. As for those who still respect the *Maréchal*, it is only because they are convinced that he, too, wishes for

> the defeat of Germany. If they were to learn differently it would make them very sad.

Alas for so many Frenchmen: they could not penetrate the mind of the Maréchal. This was their quandary.

About this time at the end of May, the OKW also decided to give the British a "whirl" to improve conditions at the Castle. General Westhoff of the OKW set up a meeting between senior British officers and the *Kommandant* and it was decided that an experiment be carried out: the British should visit the local cinema in town and also the football field. The first visit to the cinema was disrupted by insults exchanged with inmates of the *Schützenhaus* who were collaborators, and by cries of "Propaganda!" from the British during certain parts of the film. The manager of the cinema lost so many things from his building that he declared "Never again."

The football excursions were well attended by the British. They marched in good order. Their pockets were stuffed with chocolate which they distributed to the children freely. There were no guards in attendance since they were on parole but a few supervising officers were there, without arms. This of course became a propaganda march in favor of the British. They intentionally gave the impression that they were better off than the local civilians and their uniforms were by now generally in better condition than those of the German soldiery. The Germans very soon stopped the excursions.

The OKW then decided that Colditz would only house British and American prisoners and that all other nationalities would be transferred to other camps. The French and Belgians were sent to Lübeck, the Dutch to Stanislau, and the Poles, some to Spitzberg, some to Mühlberg and some to Lübeck.

On 7 June 1943, the Dutch contingent received orders to pack up and leave at twelve hours' notice. This did not perturb them, as they had known of the move for a week through information passed inside the camp. Their contraband was safely stowed away in prepared suitcases. One Dutchman packed his suitcase for the last time at Colditz. He had packed it every morning and unpacked it again every night for two years.

The whole camp turned out to see them off.

"We'll miss you, Vandy," said Dick.

"I'm rather sorry to go," replied Vandy, who was obviously moved. "Ve may haf a chance to escape on the vay. I haf many men prepared. Goodbye, Dick. Ve had goot times together. In Colditz ve haf shown those Germans how to behave themselves."

"Yes," said Dick. "It's funny how well they've behaved in Colditz considering the hell we give them!'

"Ach, Dick, that is the secret. You must always give them hell. If you do not, you are finished. I was in camps before I came to Colditz. There I saw vot happened. Germans despised the prisoners and gave them hell. Here it was otherwise. You vere different—and you gave them hell from the virst days. So, they respect you and are afraid to bully. It is a simple qvestion of domination by vorce of the character. Do not vorget! Goodbye, Dick . . . and . . . Gott bless England!"

So, the irrepressible Vandy, the officer in charge of all the Dutch escapes, but never of his own, departed.

The escape record throughout the war, 1940–1945, of Vandy's sixty-eight officers and cadets, mostly of the Dutch East Indies Forces, who were sent from Holland in 1940 to Colditz via Soest and Juliusburg, is here set down: thirteen made home-runs, two others reached Russia and died there, and in addition this company can lay claim to twenty-seven "gone-aways," i.e. escapes.

There is an interesting aside to be made at this point. In June 1943 I was working at the British Legation in Berne as 2nd assistant military attaché. Intelligence reports were filtering through about Hitler's secret weapons. I noticed that the location of this secret work was often given as Peenemunde. I remembered well the little book I had read at Colditz, and in particular that the Island of Rugen was cited in it as a center of German rocketry research. I studied a map of the Baltic and what should I find on the Island of Rugen but the small town and district of Peenemunde. Thus the likelihood was that Hitler's secret weapon was a rocket! I reported this link to my superior, who in turn told the military attaché. Whether he passed it on to London I do not know, but this story has a conclusion which finds its place appropriately in Appendix 4.

On 17 June Colonel German arrived back in Colditz from Spangenburg where he had tried to escape. Padre Platt's diary refers to stories from similarly returned officers that Spangenburg IXA was "a deadbeat's camp," where escape activity was constrained by a host of committees. "The moat," says Platt, "which in the early days was the domain of 3 wild hogs and was the one hopeful way of escape, is now a flower, salad and vegetable garden." There was apparently "a vigorous knitting and tatting circle." Hearing of this Harry Elliott tried to find a volunteer in Colditz for "Knitting and Tatting Officer."

From 21 June a total of seventy-six British officers and four orderlies arrived in batches from *Oflag* VIIIB at Eichstatt in Bavaria. Of these, sixty-seven officers and men had taken part early in June in one of the greatest break-outs of the war—the Eichstatt tunnel. This was a beautifully engineered escape, but the officers involved were poorly equipped in respect of civilian clothing and identity papers, and none of them made the home-run. The last nine, including Lieutenant-Colonel W. M. Broomhall, Royal Engineers, had made another escape attempt from the same camp. "Tubby" Broomhall took over as Senior British Officer from Colonel Stayner as he was senior in rank. He had marched out of Eichstatt through two gates, dressed as a German general. His ADC was Lance Pope. The general was allegedly visiting the camp on a survey of its layout. He stopped leisurely to examine plans and discuss alterations with a cortège accompanying him. The Germans at both gates hurried to let the whole party through, overawed by raucous commands and impatient looks. Suddenly one of the sentries realized that the general was still inside the gates and that the one who had marched out must be an imposter. A search was implemented and Tubby was recaptured.

Lieutenant Fahy, the Frenchman who had been wounded on 20 June 1942 by Hauptmann Müller, escaped on 8 July from the hospital at Hohnstein-Erstthal and was caught at Kaufungen. On 12 July the French Lieutenant Elisée-Aiban Darthenay escaped from the same hospital and succeeded in making a home-run. He joined the French Resistance. He was arrested by the Gestapo on Good Friday, 7 April 1944, and imprisoned in the local school at Oyannax. On 11 April, with four others, he was led to a small village, Sièges, in the Jura, seven miles away. The Germans held an identity parade with the villagers. None gave the Resistance men away. The Germans thereupon collected every man in the district, and some of the women and children, and transported them into Germany. The five Resistance men were machine-gunned against the wall of a farm. The whole village was then set on fire.

In fact the French contingent were in the process of leaving Colditz. Among them of course was Fredo Guigues, leader of the French tunnellers and master lock-picker. Algerian-born and nicknamed "Scarface" because of an enormous sword scar on his face, Guigues had already left Colditz, only to return. In the summer, stripped to the waist, chest bronzed, a red silk handkerchief around his neck, long black hair, sunbathing in the few square feet touched by the noon sun, he conjured up visions of Mediterranean skies and happier days.

Although gifted with a vivid imagination he was remarkably cool and collected, and could set his hand to anything. Not content with his genius at lock-picking, he was a first-class forger, master schemer, radio expert and electrician. He also served the bearded Abbé Jean-Jean at Mass. Lieutenant Guigues had spent most of his life in Marseilles. He had the typical accent of the region. A pair of mischievously flashing dark eyes and a ready grin completed an appearance of good-humored energy. He understood no English but the British had no better friend among the French contingent. Long before the French left Colditz, Dick Howe and he had become close collaborators, and the friendship between them paid dividends. There was no need even for the British to construct their own wireless hide. Guigues presented Dick with a French set in its stronghold, lock, stock and barrel. Although towards the end of the war the Germans knew the British had a set in action they never found it. They searched until they were blue in the face without success. Eventually the British prisoners made no concealment of the news' bulletins, which were read publicly at the evening meal. The war situation was discussed openly with the Germans, their arguments controverted and their alleged facts and figures contradicted. The receiver was concealed in the eave of the sloping roof above the French quarters—which became British on the departure of the French. This set was Arthur II, with the broken valve replaced.

When a roof is forty feet high from gutter to ridge, it can be appreciated that at least two floors may be built inside it, having dormer windows and comparatively high ceilings. The floor area of rooms within the roof becomes reduced at each level upwards, not only because the two sides of the roof are approaching each other, but because usually a vertical wall is built around the sides of the rooms so that the inmates do not have the impression they are living in a tent. This vertical wall, in the case of rooms at Colditz, was about five feet high. It concealed behind it a small triangular space bounded by the three sides; slanting roof, vertical wall and horizontal ceiling of the room below. The triangular space had to be enlarged out of the seven-foot-thick walls to provide within it enough room for the wireless installation, complete with electric light, switch-gear for the receiver, earphones, a table and two chairs for the operator and the shorthand-writer acting as news-recording telegraphist. Beside it, a second cavity was enlarged to provide a hide for contraband. Entry to these secret apartments was made from the attic which formed the apex of the roof itself.

Guigues also let Dick in on the secret of access to the parcels office, and the interception of contraband in this way was carried on successfully until the end of the war.

The French—some hundreds—were to travel to Lübeck in two groups, and Hauptmann Lange organized everything. On 6 July, the first group were told to pack their heavy luggage; after it was searched it was taken to the approach yard. From there it was taken by lorry to the station and placed in a wagon in the charge of a sentry. The prisoners themselves with their small kit were taken to the park of the *Schützenhaus* where they were checked for identity and their kit was examined by German security men. They then marched to the station.

The first time everything went smoothly, apparently! A few days later on 12 July the second group, including the Belgians, was prepared in exactly the same way. Eggers was on duty in the *Kommandantur* yard when suddenly a heap of trunks, sacks and blankets, started to move and out tumbled Lieutenant Klein (de Gaullist) gasping for air. He had been rolled up in a pile of blankets and was suffocating.

A second incident occurred when the lorry took the first load of heavy baggage to the station. After it had been unloaded and had returned for the next load one of the sentries noticed the lid of a Canadian Red Cross box move and out came Giles Romilly. Prawitt was furious and Hauptmann Lange was brought to task and later placed under open arrest and transferred to another camp at Mühlberg. He remonstrated in vain that because of his security measures Giles Romilly had failed to escape.

A third incident caused much confusion. Three British officers changed places with three French officers of similar size and features. They passed the identity and the check. The Germans did not find out until two or three days later, even though it had been worked by Lieutenant Fleury about a year previously. So three British went to Lübeck. When these were returned from Lübeck, they turned out to be two genuine British and one Frenchman. And thus it carried on. The Germans took some time to sort it all out.

Eggers remarks that after the last contingent of Poles left Colditz in August, he had a fairly easy time of it with only 228 British and a few Free French officers. But this relative tranquility was disturbed by two interventions by the OKW.

The first arose out of Hitler's need for a further 800,000 troops for the eastern front. The German Home Army was ordered to submit to medical examination, and the fittest one-third would be dispatched to the front. Gephard was sent to Russia, and was killed there by partisans. Priem, on the other hand, though younger than Eggers, was discharged from the Army altogether because it was feared he would collapse at any time. He returned to his post as headmaster near Meseritz and died in August 1943. Eggers, though found fit for active service, remained as LO1. The deputy *Kommandant*, Major Menz, became *Kommandant* of a prison camp near the front at Riga, and was replaced by Major Amthor (whose red face prompted the nickname "Turkeycock" among the prisoners).

The second of the OKW's ideas was to order the Colditz staff to copy the British methods of achieving communication between the War Office and POWs.

Most German POWs were in the United States, and rather than send escape material Eggers was required to send them propaganda and to enquire about POW loyalty to Hitler! Only Nazi Party members were privileged to receive these communications. Eggers commented that the British War Office never thought to boost POW morale with political propaganda.

When the second French batch departed on 12 July a further substitution of officers took place—this time Thibaut (a Belgian) and André Perrin: The Belgian contingent from Colditz went to Lübeck with the French. Then, nearly two months later (8 September), they were transferred to another camp. Now André Perrin escaped successfully—his fourth attempt.

No less than seven Frenchmen left Lübeck on this occasion under Belgian identity. Tragically, the small Frenchman Alfred Gallais was killed when he jumped from a train. It was his third escape attempt.

During this summer, Allied air-raids became a regular and welcome feature of life. The fall of Italy had been greeted with great rejoicing. On 31 August a book was opened on whether the coming second front would be launched from Italy or by landing in Norway.

Captain the Earl of Hopetoun, son of Lord Linlithgow, one-time Viceroy of India, arrived in Colditz with the Eichstatt tunnellers. The OKW promoted him to the category of *Prominenter*—the third now in Colditz. The concentration of *Prominenten* in Colditz gave rise to German rumors of an increase in British military interest in the camp that held them. Swiss papers had reported that a plan was on foot to liberate them by a parachute attack, and get them away by plane. The OKW went so far as to organize a kind of Riot Squad on the Colditz model, on permanent standby, at the training camp at Leisnig. The unit consisted of tanks and lorried infantry to be rushed to Colditz should an air landing be reported in the vicinity.

17

That Dares Send a Challenge

Autumn and Winter 1943–1944

ONE BRIGHT MORNING in August Dick Howe thought of another way out of the Castle. The scheme was daring. He put the wheels of his organization into action.

Lieutenant Mike Harvey RN, officer in charge of stooging roster, was to chart the movements of "Franz Josef," one of the German NCO commanders. Lulu Lawton and Bricky Forbes were to cut necessary bars in two windows, one on either side of the Castle. Bos'n Crisp was to prepare two thirty-foot lengths of rope. "Rex" Harrison would have to produce three perfect German uniforms, one for a sergeant.

Major W. F. "Andy" Anderson RE and Scarlet O'Hara were commissioned to produce two German rifles, two bayonet scabbards and a holster complete with revolver, and Scarlet was to deal also with the foundry work for buttons, badges, medals and belt clasps.

Finally, the principal actor in the whole drama had to be coached and transformed into the mirror image of Franz Josef.

The elderly and somewhat stout NCO (one Rothenberger) who was to be given a twin brother was not called Franz Josef for nothing. He was a living impersonation of Franz Josef, Emperor of Austria, King of Hungary and Bohemia; ruddy complexion, puffy cheeks, gray hair, portly bearing and an enormous ginger-colored white-tipped mustache which covered half of his face. Provided this could be faithfully copied, it would in itself provide a magnificent mask. Teddy Barton was one of the theater past-masters. Besides producing shows and acting in them, he had the professional touch when it came to make-up.

Teddy Barton, Mike Sinclair and Alan Cheetham studied Franz Josef's gestures, facial expressions, manners of speech, accent and intonation for a month on end. They made fourteen mustaches before they had the right one. Franz Josef was dogged every time he entered the courtyard. Mike rehearsed and rehearsed again and again, until he lived in the role of Franz Josef.

His moment was approaching. Two sentries had been chosen to accompany him. They were John Hyde-Thompson and Lance Pope. Both were good German speakers. They rehearsed with Mike the German words of command, and practiced all the movements of guard-changing according to the German routine. (It was Pope who had marched out of Eichstatt prison with "Tubby" Broomhall, the latter posing as a German general.) The idea was simply to relieve two real sentries.

A first wave of twenty men would make the rope descent from the old British quarters immediately once the guard had been relieved and was out of sight. Monty Bissell would lead the first wave. If there was no violent reaction by the time the twentieth had descended the rope, more officers were ready to follow, but responsibility rested with their leaders not to lessen by their action the chances of the first wave.

The main body was to make straight for the park at the double, followed closely by Mike—Franz Josef II—and his two sentries. If a stray Goon appeared they were to keep running. Franz Josef II would give the impression of chasing the party and would intercept any such stray Goons and order them to run in the opposite direction, towards the Castle, with instructions to raise the alarm.

D-day was to be 2 September and the hour was to be immediately after the 9 p.m. *Appell.* Franz Josef I would be the guard commander on that day and a particularly dumb-looking Goon was calculated to be on duty at the crucial gate. The bar-cutting was accomplished successfully and camouflaged.

2 September—a Thursday—arrived. The day passed slowly. There was suppressed activity everywhere, concealed by an overall air of casualness. The men taking part in the attempt were not beginners. What worried most of them more than anything else was the short start. If the first stage—the relieving of the guard—came off, that in itself would be tremendously exciting, but the real fun would start when twenty POWs were out, the first with perhaps a three-minute start, and the last with less than a thirty-seconds start, in front of the pursuing enemy. The hounds would be in full cry. Colditz had never known such an attempt before and the consequences were unknown. Mike Sinclair remained outwardly calm while the turmoil of nervous anticipation was inwardly tearing at his entrails and gripping his throat.

Dick spent his time checking up on everybody's instructions, amplifying them, where necessary, to cover every possible hitch or misunderstanding. The escape was the largest and most daring so far attempted from Colditz. If it succeeded, it would make history. If it failed—"Well!" thought Dick. "It'll still make a good story!'

Franz Josef II could have walked out of the Castle with ease.

The hours dragged heavily towards the 9 p.m. *Appell*. Those in the escaping team lay on their bunks, trying to sleep. They yawned and stretched themselves nervously, finding no relief for the tension around the heart or the nausea threatening the stomach, for the hot flush or the cold sweat.

The *Appell* went off normally. Immediately afterwards, Bush Parker and the guard-relieving party—Mike, John Hyde-Thompson and Lance Pope—faded off towards the sick ward. The second stooging contingent disappeared to their respective posts on the upper floor overlooking the guardhouse. The main escaping party with its stooges, led by Dick, Bricky Forbes, Lulu and Mike Harvey, followed by the members of the second escaping wave—altogether thirty-five strong—passed silently through locked doors into the dark unoccupied rooms of the old British quarters. Dick looked down on to the sentry path below. "The ivory-headed Goon's at his post on the gateway—so far so good," he whispered.

Sounds of life in the Castle died down. Soon a deathly stillness reigned. Thirty-five men waited for the warning signals. The first message came through: "Franz Josef returned to guardhouse," Mike Harvey reported in an undertone. Then came, "All quiet in *Kommandantur*."

This was the signal for Bush to act and release Franz Josef II and his party through the window, down the rope, on to the sentry path.

A silence, vibrant with tension, followed. Then suddenly, Mike Harvey spoke in hoarse excited tones: "Our guard party on their way—past first sentry."

A moment later, Dick, Lulu, Monty and Bricky Forbes, crouching near the window, heard the crunch of marching feet on the path and a loud heel-click as a sentry, out of sight, saluted the passing patrol. Then they came into view, round the corner of the building. This was the crucial moment.

Franz Josef II, followed by his two guards, walked to the gate and spoke to the dumb sentry in German: "*Sie sind abgelöst. Sie werden Ihre Wache diesem Posten übergeben. Gehen Sie sofort in die Wachtstube! Dort sind Sie nötig, denn einige Gefangene sind geflohen* (You are relieved. You will hand over your duties at this post. Go to the guardroom at once! You are needed there; some prisoners have escaped)." Lance Pope took up his post beside the gate. Franz Josef II mounted the ladder to the cat-walk and repeated his orders to the second sentry who started to descend. John Hyde-Thompson took over his post.

"My God!" whispered Dick, in a dripping perspiration, "it's going to work. Get ready!"

The cat-walk sentry had reached the ground and was marching off. Then Dick noticed the gate sentry had not followed. Franz Josef II was talking to him. Dick could hear the gist of it through the open window and repeated it to the others.

"The sentry says he's under orders not to move. Mike's demanded the keys. The sentry's handed them over . . . but he won't move. What the hell! . . . Mike ought to go. He's wasting time. The three of them can make it. He's getting annoyed with the sentry . . . he's told him to get back to the guardhouse. No! . . . it's no good . . . the dumb bastard won't budge . . . why the devil won't he move? Mike's getting really angry with him. . . . He's got to go! He's got to go! Mike's shouting at him." Dick was in a frenzy. "Good God! This is the end. The time's about up."

Mike was having a desperate duel with the ivory-headed Goon and the precious seconds were slipping away. He was thinking of the main party—he was determined that the main party should escape at all costs. He had cast his die—it was to be all or nothing. He was sacrificing himself to win the larger prize.

As soon as he started to raise his voice, Dick's stomach began to sink. The game was a losing one. He wanted to shout at Mike to make a run for it, but dared not interfere with Mike's battle. He was impotent, helpless, swearing and almost weeping with a foreboding of terrible failure. The scheme, within a hair's breadth of success, was going wrong. Mike might possibly have disarmed the offending sentry, but it was too late for violence now with less than half a minute's start. If he had been disarmed at the very beginning it might have been different, but who would have done that when persuasion was the obvious first course? Alas! Persuasion meant time and the precious minutes had flown. Four minutes had gone. It was nearly hopeless now.

The two British sentries stood their ground. John Hyde-Thompson was solemnly pacing his beat up and down the cat-walk.

Mike's voice rose to a typical Franz Josef scream of rage. Even as he shouted, there were sounds of hurrying feet and discordant voices shouting in the distance.

The sentry had asked Mike for his pass. Eggers takes up the story from the German side:

> The pass seemed in order, but was the wrong colour. The guard had a vague suspicion and pressed his warning bell. He also covered Franz Josef

> with his rifle and ordered him to put up his hands. Josef cursed—not very fluently—but did indeed put his hands up. In due course, a corporal Pilz known as "Big Bum" and two men appeared from the guardroom in answer to the buzzer. Franz Josef did not know the password when asked. The corporal Pilz drew his revolver and demanded Franz Josef's. There was a struggle. The corporal swore later that Franz Josef tried to draw his pistol. He himself fired.

Mike Sinclair fell to the ground shot in the chest with a 9mm bullet. The true Franz Josef (Rothenberger) arrived, and the two phoney sentries were marched off, leaving Sinclair unattended on the ground. An *Appell* was called, at which feelings naturally ran high. Lieutenant David Hunter RM accused the Germans of murder, but was himself punished after a court-martial with two months in Graudenz military prison.

Mike was not seriously hurt. The bullet passed out under a shoulderblade. An OKW court of inquiry in Leipzig accepted Pilz's statement that he had fired in self-defense. The SBO also held a court of inquiry which ruled that Pilz had fired while Mike had his hands up. Pilz was later sent to the eastern front.

On 4 September the first news trickled through the German press of an Allied landing in Italy—across the straits of Messina. The POWs were able to read between the lines in spite of the German downgrading of the event.

During this month the "non-belligerents"—padres and doctors—were once more allowed out of the Castle on parole walks; this applied likewise to the *Prominenten*. Padre Platt commented: "I resign my escape interests with some regret."

The largest consignment of Red Cross parcels ever arrived, consisting of 2,000 British Red Cross parcels, forty-five tobacco parcels, forty of invalid comforts, eight surgical, one of 200 tins of toothpowder, one of 144 rolls of toilet paper, plus sugar from Buenos Aires and coffee from Venezuelan Red Cross. The store of food parcels had now reached 5,000, estimated at five months' supply at one per head per week. The impression was that Geneva was anticipating a period of disorganized transport to Germany.

A British orderly refused to carry out an order given around this time by Corporal Schädlich—the "Ferret." Eggers reported the incident to the *Kommandant*. Prawitt was furious: "Read my orders," he roared. "In cases of disobedience push your rifle into their backs. If they further disobey, then use them. Do not report such cases to me." Eggers comments: "I remained determined only to use my weapon in self-defense." The orderly was punished with the German Army standard "glass-house" punishment of thirty days—bread and water diet with only one warm meal. The German corporal in due course was sent to the Italian front where he was killed.

On 7 October the Germans caught Lieutenant Alan "Scruffy" Orr-Ewing in German uniform in a paper dump just outside the Castle. The British orderlies had taken him there in a basket of waste.

Hauptmann Lange, the German security officer since 1939, had gone to another camp after Giles Romilly's attempted escape at the time of the French departure. His replacement was a lawyer who had been severely wounded in Russia. He went about on sticks, but in spite of this disability was determined to go back to the front and win a decoration, and was posted for active service after about six months. This officer, Major Dr. Hans Horn, won the *Ritterkreuz* in February 1945, after breaking out with his troops from encirclement by the Americans at Echternach in the Ardennes area. He died in Soviet hands at Sachsenhausen.

The OKW issued the following order on 15 September calculated to discourage escaping:

> Camp Order no. 23 Colditz 15 September 1943
>
> By order of the German High Command, Prisoners-of-War who cause any harm to the German War Economies will be brought in future before a court-martial instead of being punished disciplinarily. The following actions will be considered, amongst others, as harming the German War Economies: (1) breaking through walls, floors, ceilings, etc., damages to iron window bars, etc.; (2) destruction, damage or theft of furnishings and fittings (such as bed-boards, stove-doors, electric fittings, etc.); (3) altering of uniforms which are not the personal property of the Prisoner-of-War; (4) theft of tools and materials and unauthorized use of electric current when building tunnels, etc.; (5) theft and falsification of identity cards, etc.
>
> Offences against these serious war necessities are considered to be crimes against War Economies and will be punished with all severity.
>
> Signed: Prawitt, Lt. Col. and *Kommandant*

General comment: "Well, that covers everything, particularly the etceteras!"

Major Miles Reid RE arrived on 22 September via Spangenburg from Greece. He had refused to take down his trousers during a search.

On the night of 19/20 September 1943, Polish officers broke out of their big tunnel at Dössel and forty-seven men escaped, of whom seven were former Colditz inmates. Nine, of whom two were from Colditz, succeeded in reaching France or Switzerland or the Polish underground. Thirty-eight were recaught and executed in two batches, including the remaining five ex-Colditz men. Most of them were apparently hanged, naked, one after the other, from butchers' hooks while those to follow witnessed the proceedings before their turn came.

This took place in the Buchenwald concentration camp.

Among those who succeeded in getting away, the two ex-Colditz prisoners were Władysław Zimiński and Władysław Pszczółkowski. Of the thirty-eight recaptured and hanged, the ex-Colditz men were: Mieczysław Chmiel, Tadeusz Osiecki, Jan Stec, Stanisław Stokwisz, Jan Zwijacz.

Lieutenant-Colonel Bronisław Kowalczewski organized this escape, with Major Stefan Pronaszko and Captain Władysław Wasilewski. All three were from Colditz. They arrived in Dössel in August 1943. Before their departure from Colditz, Dick Howe introduced them to two Canadians in the British contingent who had at one time been at the Dössel camp. Their names are, unfortunately, at this date, not available.* However, they revealed the whereabouts and the secret entrance to a tunnel which they had been digging when they left the camp. This became the Polish tunnel and accounts for the fact that the tunnel—thirty-six yards long—was completed within a month of their arrival.

One of the successful ex-Colditz escapers, Lieutenant Władysław Zimiński, sent a postcard to Colonel Kowalczewski (who earlier had been the liaison officer in Colditz with the Polish underground) at Dössel camp. He announced his safe arrival in Switzerland. The wording he used was considered by the Germans as the report of a junior officer having successfully executed the commands of his senior officer. Colonel Kowalczewski was therefore accused by the camp *Kommandant* of being the leader of the escape organization responsible for the tunnel escape. He was handed over to the Gestapo and murdered in Buchenwald, as were his assistants Pronaszko and Wasilewski.

Jędrzej Giertych was at Dössel when it was liberated by the Americans. He had the opportunity to inspect some German camp dossiers, and found documents revealing that all the captured escapers were handed over to the SS. Another document raised the question of what was to be said to the Red Cross about the executions.

---

* Editors were not able to verify further updates to this information as of publication.

On 19 October there was a heavy air raid on Halle. Hundreds were killed and thousands injured. Electricity for Colditz was cut off for twenty-four hours. This was the closest evidence of bombing activity so far in the Castle. The morning roll-call on the 20th was postponed for an hour. When it took place, Eggers says: "It was just like old times—shouts, whistles, demonstrations, indiscipline." At 11 a.m. Eggers was summoned to the *Kommandant*'s office and shown a telegram sent from the camp at Lamsdorf: "Please collect Lt. Davies-Scourfield from here, he states he is from IVC." Prawitt asked, "Do we have this man at our camp?" Eggers replied, "Yes, I know him well, he wears a black mustache." "Then go and fetch him." Eggers went to the yard and there accosted Colonel Broomhall, the SBO. "Please send for Lieutenant Scourfield, I wish to speak to him." The SBO went off to the British quarters and on return said, "I regret that the lieutenant is no longer in the Castle." To which Eggers replied, "I regret to say that we have him." The *Kommandant* was furious—Davies-Scourfield had claimed at Lamsdorf to have left Colditz three weeks previously: "How is this possible? You and Hauptmann Püpcke show that the roll-calls are correct; do you keep a check or not? Here are your reports, four times a day you are supposed to count them. I will punish you for sending in false reports. At least sixty roll-calls have taken place and no one has noticed that a POW is missing. How is this possible?"

Eggers came to the conclusion that Grismond Davies-Scourfield had got out by concealing himself in a large basket of waste-paper removed by the orderlies. This method had been used successfully on 7 October by Orr-Ewing, who unfortunately was soon recaught. But this did not account to Eggers' satisfaction for the *Appells*. Had the roll-call been fudged since 30 September? The mystery was only solved five months later!

Eggers was sent to a camp for a course of training in propaganda during three days in November. This was at Zossen not far out of Berlin. He learned that a special camp for British POWs under propaganda instruction had been set up near Berlin: No. 30 at Genshagen. More of this later.

In November, two British orderlies escaped from a working party—Corporal Green and Private Fleet. They walked all night to Leipzig and took a train to Kottbus. They had no papers and were caught on the train.

An instance occurred early in December illustrating the gulf that was widening between the *Wehrmacht* and the German Gestapo and SS. A search-party of eighteen men in SS uniform led by the Criminal Commissioner, Herr Bauer, of Dresden, arrived in Colditz Castle for a mass search. They found little. It turned out that none other than Feldwebel Gephard had been bribed and had hidden the POWs' documents and money.

Another truce was agreed, lasting from Christmas Eve to 2 January 1944, though the Colditz garrison were hardly relaxed by an air-raid on Leipzig on Christmas Eve. Padre Platt, writing during this period, regretted the departure of the foreigners, and had this to say about the new British contingent:

> The coming of the Eichstatt boys marked the end of the British family life such as had been its characteristic from the beginning, with one exception. Hitherto newcomers were received into the family and absorbed by it at once. But the Eichstatters came in large numbers from a large camp, were put in separate quarters, fed and lived separately, and the colonel they brought with them at once succeeded to SBO-ship. They have retained the atmosphere of a large camp and, with the exception of a few of their number, have remained in small friendship circles complete in themselves and almost exclusive, hence they are described almost certainly unjustly as cliques.

The year 1944 got off to a good start. On 19 January a soldier saw a rope being pulled quickly back into a window over the terrace. Nothing was found in the room in question, but Eggers found wire-cutters, a hole in the barbed wire on top of the outer wall and a short length hanging down from the outside. He sent men in pursuit:

> I then ordered a special roll-call—the most memorable of my career. Very slowly the prisoners, scarcely 300, assembled. There was no order and I had to send soldiers through the quarters to find the prisoners hidden there. When they were all assembled I began to count, then someone put out the main light by means of a catapult. It would take a long time to repair and it was getting too late for the roll-call to be taken in the yard. I decided to order the prisoners into the empty rooms left by the Dutch. The walk upstairs to these rooms took at least half an hour. Col. Tod, the present S.B.O. who had taken over from Tubby Broomhall on his arrival on the 18th of November 1943 [from Spangenburg], was amongst the last ones up the stairs, pretending that he was finding difficulty in getting up them. I was by this time getting fed up and I ordered the guards to hurry the remainder by pushing them with their rifle butts. The Colonel naturally protested over this. Soon I had them altogether in the four big rooms. A large room was set aside to receive those that I had accounted for. I could not do this in alphabetical order so I did this by way of the

> identity cards we had. I knew nearly all of them by name. Suddenly the lights went out. Someone had caused a short circuit. My guards sat themselves on the boxes of identity cards, otherwise they would soon disappear. The emergency lanterns were sent for and slowly we managed to sort them out. After all the hours that had passed I still was not sure if two or three were missing. Sinclair, I knew for certain, was amongst them. The code word "Mousetrap" went out and the guard company was sent immediately to their search stations but found nothing.

Mike Sinclair had been planning this escape since September 1943, to take place on the terrace where Don Thom had jumped down. For four months, Mike, Dick and Lulu Lawton watched the changing of the guard in this area, looking for a short blind interval at dusk, before the perimeter searchlights were switched on and when the guards were not at their points of vantage. The watchers established two things. First, that there was a blind spot of sixty seconds between the time when the pagoda sentry left his post at dusk and was replaced and the first turret sentry gained his position. Second that in mid-January would come a time when the searchlights (which were governed by the time of the year) were switched on just after a regular guard change. In mid-January therefore the sixty seconds coincided with the maximum possible darkness.

Mike chose as his partner in this attempt Flight-Lieutenant Jack Best, who had been a ghost since April 1943 (see Chapter 15) and whose morale was as a result getting pretty low. Their escape kit ready, as well as ninety feet of home-made rope, the bars of a window in the British quarters, thirty feet above the terrace, were cut. Stooges were arranged.

For the launching ramp they would use a table. One after the other the escapers were to be shot out through the window, holding on to the rope. Reaching the terrace in this spectacular fashion they would have to make another jump down to the orchard. A thirty-yard sprint would take them to the perimeter fence, where they would have to cut a hole. Then a second length of rope would help them down the fifty-foot cliff down which Don Thom had hurtled.

At dusk on 19 January, at a signal from their stooges, the beginning of the sixty seconds was marked by the propulsion of the two men through the window. Just as they were dropping down the second thirty-foot descent, having crossed the terrace, the guardhouse door opened and a German NCO walked out slowly across the terrace, straight for the rope. Not until the escapers had released the rope at the bottom of their second drop could their colleagues whisk it back up again. It whistled past the NCO, not a yard from him. Startled, he drew his revolver. But Sinclair and Best were shinning down the cliff in no time at all. They had to cut through more barbed wire at the bottom.

An announcement was made the next morning, or the morning after that (the date is uncertain), as to who had escaped; there were two, Sinclair and Barnes!

They were both caught a few days later at Rheine on the Dutch border. They were brought back to Colditz. Sinclair was well known in Colditz, but Barnes? The new security officer from October 1943 to February 1944, Dr. Horn, was careless enough not to examine the new Barnes.

Months later it was discovered how it was that the *Unteroffizier* had opened the guardhouse door and walked out on to the terrace just as Mike and Jack dropped over the parapet. Jack, climbing over the balustrading, had accidentally pressed an alarm-bell button which had summoned the German to the very spot where the escape was taking place!

On 18 January, the gate had opened to let in six new arrivals, officers of the British Army: Captain Pierre de Vomécourt (Peter) and Lieutenants Antoine du Puy (Tony), Noël Burdeyron, Jacques Huart (Jack Fincken, now Jack Mackay), George Abbott and Claud Redding. These six were different. They were not "escapers" but had escaped a worse fate. They had spent some eighteen months, ten of them in solitary, at the notorious French prison, Frèsnes, in the hands of the Gestapo.

Peter, born in 1906 into a Lorraine family, in which the principles and demands of patriotism were deeply ingrained, was the youngest of three brothers, all of whom had strong views about continuing the fight against Hitler's Germany. Peter, in 1939, was Franco-British liaison officer with the 7th Regiment of the Cameronians, a Highland Regiment. On 17 June 1940, French liaison officers with the BEF were ordered by the French High Command to leave their regiments and go to Bordeaux. He was then at Cherbourg, where the British were evacuating. Over the radio came the announcement by Pétain that he had asked for an armistice. Peter embarked on the last boat with his regiment, and arrived in England on 18 June.

Soon he learned that there was still resilience amongst the French population—stunned as they were. Two very young Frenchmen in July 1940 cut the telephone wires in the Nantes region; they were caught and shot. Peter was deeply moved on hearing this. He began to think in terms of organized sabotage. In London he contacted General de Gaulle's *Deuxième Bureau*, and also the British SOE (Special Operations Executive). The latter organization, realizing his potential, trained him and parachuted him back into France, near Châteauroux in the Midi on the night of 11/12 May 1941.

In December 1941, needing a radio link with London in order to arrange his return to England, he was introduced to Mathilde Carré—known as "Victoire" to SOE, and as "La Chatte" to German counter-intelligence. Unbeknown to Peter, she had been arrested by the Germans and had agreed to work for them. Although she later confessed her treachery to him, and although he did return to England for about a month, the Germans had penetrated his (and related) organizations so thoroughly that he and seventeen of his associates were arrested in April 1942. Then followed their spell in Frèsnes Prison. In October 1943 they were split into two groups; those holding a commission in the British Army would be sent to a "potential hostage" camp; the others, recruited in France, would go to Lübeck.

On 25 January there was another major search of the premises! The searchers were the same as those who had turned up previously. This time they wore the uniform of the SS. A few British fat lamps, "Rex" Harrison's liquor still and pieces of altered uniforms were all they found; a meager haul. There was, however, no personal "body" search.

A Canadian officer from the famous Dieppe raid, Lieutenant "Bill" Millar RCE disappeared on 28 January. He was never heard of again. Eggers reported that a jacket that "could have been his" was found on the road some miles from the Castle.

He escaped, by night, from the prisoners' kitchen by being hoisted up very high to reach a semi-circular window, which flapped open inwards and was not barred on the outside. He might have needed some rope on the outside but that could have been withdrawn. It is likely that there was an air-raid alarm, which would have placed the window in semi-darkness. How he escaped from the outer courtyard is not known, but a lorry used to park there sometimes. Inquiries elicited from the Canadian High Commissioner in London that his name was on the Canadian war memorial at Bayeux, which would indicate he had made a home-run and gone to Normandy. However, still more recent information from *The History of the Corps of Royal Canadian Engineers 1936–1946* and a covering letter from the Directorate of History indicates that he was recaptured in civilian clothes "during the summer of 1944, near *Stalag* 344, Lamsdorf." He was held there in solitary confinement for a few days. Then he was moved to an unknown destination. The record concludes "that Lieut. Millar had died on or about 14 July 1944."

Leo de Hartog (ex-Colditz), the Dutch author of a book entitled *Officieren achter Prikkeldraad 1940–1945*, has written:

> On 4th March, 1944, Himmler ordered the so-called "*Aktion Kugel*." At the end of 1943 and in the beginning of 1944 so many "kriegies" [POWs] escaped that the Germans decided to execute all POW officers and NCOs who were captured after an escape. They were all sent to the Mauthausen concentration camp (west of Vienna). Thousands of POWs (all nations) were cruelly killed there. . . . It is almost certain that Bill Millar was one of the victims of that horrible camp.

By the end of January 1944 with escapes continuing in mid-winter, the *Kommandant* was jittery about the *Prominenten* escaping. On Friday, 28 January, when the *Prominenten* were about to sit down to supper, they were ordered to go to their rooms and be locked up for the night. They refused, and a few minutes later Püpcke turned an armed guard out and escorted them away in the middle of supper. Platt commented:

> The *Kommandant* is evidently very afraid lest one of them should escape. The special walks they used to get, in lieu of official exercise, when they were guarded by tommy-guns, have been stopped these two months. The poor fellows get no proper exercise and are now locked up each night at seven o'clock.

Jacques Prot was killed this night in the Battle of Monte Cassino in Italy.

18

Ashes and Snow

Spring 1944

FEBRUARY 1944 OPENED with a gallant escape attempt on the 3rd by "Scruffy" Orr-Ewing. Eggers reporting:

> A few French orderlies still remained in the camp after the departure of the main body of French prisoners to Lübeck the previous summer. Mixed parties of British and French orderlies used to go out for exercise outside the Castle, under guard. . . . [Gephard's] successor in Colditz was not so familiar with the faces of the other ranks in his care, and . . . Lieut. Orr-Ewing took the place of one of the Frenchmen. He got away from the walk and away into the woods. The only sentry with the party chased him as far as the river Freiberger Mulde, having left his rifle behind so that he could run faster. Orr-Ewing felt that he could not stop simply because of a river, waded into the water and swam across. The guard funked the swim, but yelled to a railway worker on the other side who caught the escaper when he reached the far bank.

In the same month Eggers was appointed to replace the departed Major Horn as security officer, after the *Kommandant* had insisted that he could accept no responsibility for security if the replacement were a newcomer to Colditz. "It was for me a fateful step, but I did not think so at the time."

At that period of the winter it was very cold. There was deep snow everywhere, though the weather was good. It was just right for the bombers. Heavy raids went on all the time, on Leipzig, on Halle and all around Colditz.

It was some time before the prisoners realized that Eggers was now security officer. He had been one of the duty officers for so long that he was a familiar figure in the camp. As he alone on the staff spoke English, he was more often than most inside the camp during searches and checks, and for the purpose of negotiations.

Eggers arranged a search of the rooms occupied by the three *Prominenten.* Lieutenant Alexander and Giles Romilly shared one room, while Captain the Earl of Hopetoun lived in a second. During the search of Hopetoun's room, a hammer disappeared from a German tool kit. But Hopetoun found out about it, and pointed out that this hammer was the one he always borrowed on parole for stage work. He was one of the theatrical producers in the camp. Hopetoun got the hammer back and saved Eggers a very red face.

Douw van der Krap and "Bear" Kruiminck had escaped from Stanisław, their new camp, on a bitter November night and joined the Polish underground in Warsaw. One day in February 1944 Douw and an Australian escaped POW named Chisholm were walking by the Vistula when a sentry, posted by a bridge, demanded their papers. While he was examining Douw's, Chisholm, without warning, sprang at the sentry, knocking him over the parapet and through the ice into the river. Douw and Chisholm ran, but next day heard that the Germans had found the sentry dead with Douw's papers lying nearby.

The Polish underground advised Bear and Chisholm to leave Warsaw immediately. Equipped with false papers, they set out for Paris and arrived their safely in May. Douw went into hiding and was given protection by the Polish branch of the Dutch Philips concern and eventually returned to Holland with the Dutch members of its staff to escape the Warsaw uprising. There he made his way to Arnhem, where he joined the local underground movement.

Leap Year's Day, 29 February, was used as an excuse for a party. According to Platt's diary:

> Many officers did not go to bed—some were recumbent in unusual places; the no-drunks who did go to bed—unless they were 2a.m. people themselves in a state of intoxication—could not get to sleep. Drunken dancing on the wooden floors of the upper stories of the *Kellerhaus* sounded like thunder. Several parties are still in full swing, and will continue tonight.
>
> Notice on the Medical Inspection room door: "If any British officer thinks he feels worse than the M.O.s, will he please visit them in their room."

On 5 March, Lieutenant Ralph Holroyd, an Australian who arrived at Colditz in May 1942, received a visit from his mother, a German national. Since his capture in 1941 she had pestered the OKW for permission to visit him. Eventually she wrote to Hitler and obtained his approval. They had tea together in the German officers' mess, Eggers discreetly in attendance in the far corner of the room.

There was a new arrival on 8 March. His name was Purdy. The Camp Roll laconically records Sub-Lieutenant E. W. Purdy: "Arrived Colditz 8.3.44. Removed by request of SBO on 11.3.44." In the middle of 1943, after three years as a POW, Purdy contrived to have himself sent to a propaganda camp, Genshagen in Berlin. On arrival in Colditz he claimed that he had absconded and gone to live with a German girl who had been his sister's best friend before the war. Her flat was destroyed by a bomb and in trying to obtain official evacuee papers he ran into the Gestapo on 5 March.

During the evening of his arrival he was examined by two British security officers, and one or two discrepancies in his statement were pointed out, and he was invited to tell the truth. He tried again, but was interrupted and told what would happen to a stool-pigeon in *Oflag* IVC. His composure was completely shaken. The second invitation to tell the truth elicited the following. He had pre-war acquaintance with William Joyce (Lord Haw Haw), and perhaps through his influence was taken to the propaganda camp. After coming to terms with the Germans he allowed himself to be used on the German radio for propaganda broadcasts to England and America. He tried to double-cross the Germans by introducing bits of his own while speaking to England. He was given an identity card and ration cards and permitted to live with a German woman. He admitted he was a rat, but when asked if he would work for the Germans again if offered an attractive reward by them he replied: "I'm afraid I would do it again. I want to get back to my woman in Berlin."

Purdy was removed from the presence of British officers on the representation of the SBO on 10 March. The following dialogue, as reported by Padre Platt, seems to have taken place between the SBO and the *Kommandant*:

> SBO: Purdy must be removed from the presence of British officers. He is a stool-pigeon.
>
> *Kommandant*: He was sent here by the *OKW* and that is enough for me. I will not have him moved.
>
> SBO: I cannot answer for his safety.
>
> *Kommandant*'s adjutant: But Purdy will be safe, will he not?

Kommandant intervening: I don't care whether he is or not. He is an enemy officer.

SBO: Well, I'm sure I don't care. Having worked for the Germans he is no longer a British officer, but you have been warned of what may happen; and it's your affair now.

Eventually, Purdy was taken to a cell in the *Kommandantur* area. By order of the *Kommandant*, on 15 March, a Red Cross food parcel was taken from the British store for Purdy, who was still in the Castle.

The Germans began a very quiet and successful search on 16 March at 4 p.m. On the second floor they walked straight to what they were looking for—a hide—and found it. It produced one of the richest hauls ever discovered by the Germans in IVC. By 4:45 everything was removed, including a liquor still and typewriter parts.

On the morning of the 17th the Germans found a tunnel leading from the first floor. They went straight to the tunnel lid and tapped with hammers and scrutinized it by aid of torches, but the camouflage held good. They knew, however, the actual direction that the tunnel had taken, for, the next morning, a Goon arrived at the foot of the staircase with a workman who drove a hole two feet deep into the wall, and entered the tunnel six feet from the proper entrance. Work had been suspended, so no one was caught.

Purdy was never proven to have been responsible for these losses. The Germans knew something was going on, but so did Purdy. The entrance to the tunnel was on the first floor and Purdy—very inopportunely—passed along the first floor within a few hours of being in the camp, at a moment when the lid was off.

Eggers quotes Douglas Bader as shouting, "Pay the fellow who gave the hole away with your own food parcels and not with ours!" and remarks that Bader was mistaken in attributing the discovery to the stool-pigeon. But his own version is not altogether convincing. For example, having stated that he decided to allow the prisoners to carry on with a tunnel (which he knew they must be digging somewhere) until such time as they came within range of the German microphones, he at once says "However, I . . . began to carry out a search," a search which led to the hide and the tunnel. Why did he not wait?

The fact that stands out is that he knew that Purdy was "blown" and therefore of no further use to him. If then he could show tangible results from information given by Purdy, he could send him away with a good mark and a pat on the back to carry out his work for Germany elsewhere. The case against

Purdy is not proven, but Eggers' evidence is equivocal. He admits that the OKW sent Purdy (to whom he gives the pseudonym "Grey") to Colditz to act as an informer, but claims that all he betrayed was a method of getting letters past the German censor—which indicated the use of a corrupt guard. He correctly points out that Purdy was recognized by Captain Julius Green of the Army Dental Corps, who had known him at his previous camp and learned of his treachery.

In the months before he was transferred to *Stalag* 111D, Berlin, in June 1944, he was supplied with one Red Cross parcel a week. During that time, he was apparently seen in the outer courtyard on 20 April to salute the Nazi flag and to salute a German *Unteroffizier*.

After the war, back in England, Purdy was arrested and charged with high treason. He was prosecuted on three counts; and on the two counts arising out of his broadcasting and the preparation of leaflets for a propaganda branch of the SS he was found guilty, but on the third indictment, arising out of his activities in Colditz, he was found not guilty. He was sentenced to death, and returned to Wandsworth jail, where William Joyce was awaiting his execution. Although Purdy's appeal was rejected, he was reprieved but with a life sentence. He was released in 1954.

Mike Moran, who knew Purdy from Marlag days, has the following to say about him (Purdy spelled his name "Purdie" for the Colditz Camp Roll):

> The Germans had assessed the "vulnerability" of Navy and Merchant Service prisoners. They knew where to find the weak links. Certainly not amongst R.N. officers; not amongst R.N.R. officers, and indeed not amongst R.N.V.R. officers who were assessed as "Gentlemen." The "weak links" were to be found amongst junior R.N.V.R. officers who had been mobilised with their ships, but who had had no naval training. They had been given the rank of temporary Sub Lieutenant R.N.V.R. Purdie was one of these.
>
> Rebecca West refers to Purdie as being uneducated. This, I feel sure, was the key to his behaviour as a prisoner. R.N. and R.N.R. officers were professional seamen, with mutual respect and often with similar backgrounds. R.N.V.R. (ex King Alfred) officers had obtained their commissions because they had "officer-like qualities." There was, therefore, a common factor in terms of education or professionalism, and (I can think of no better phrase) "social behaviour." Purdie had none of these attributes.

Padre Platt has an entry in his diary for 23 March:

> A new arrival was turned into the *Hof* during the course of the morning. He is Rudi Reichoffen, an Alsatian who claims to have been taken prisoner at Nettuno and to be an *aspirant* in de Gaulle's army. He is neither!

Neither Eggers nor any other known source mentions this man again. He remains a mystery.

On 26 March Bush Parker and Mike Harvey made an escape attempt, dropping by rope from a *Saalhaus* window down to a causeway and picking a lock to gain access to an air-raid shelter. They were seen by a sentry, who fired, missed, and ran to the alarm bell. Bush and Mike dashed into the shelter. Its door was made of wooden slats, so Bush was able to put his hand through and relock it, removing his key; when a posse of Goons arrived, it never occurred to them that the escapers might be in the locked-up shelter. But the shelter had no second exit, the vital premise of their escape plan. They had to give themselves up.

Now the fun started. Mike Harvey was a ghost, whom the Germans believed had escaped in April 1943 with Jack Best. But the ghosts had doubles, and Mike's was Lieutenant D. E. Bartlett—they looked quite alike. As soon as Mike was caught he posed as Bartlett and Bartlett went into hiding.

But Eggers was suspicious of the captured Bartlett, and found that his face did not quite fit the photograph in his file: he kept this Bartlett and released Bush:

> As I was still suspicious, I sent the Riot Squad to fetch out Lieut. Bartlett. They came out with an officer they said they knew as Bartlett. But he said his name was Champ. This second officer, Champ, looked far more like the Bartlett in the photo than the so-called Bartlett I had in front of me, and looked from one to the other and back again to the photograph of Bartlett, that I had in my hand.
>
> Again I sent the Riot Squad back into the camp, this time with orders to fetch out the officer whom they knew as Champ. They came out with "Champ" and I asked him at once, "Who are you?" and he replied, "Champ!"
>
> Immediately the first "Champ" (who had been brought out as Bartlett) called out to the second "Champ," "Haven't you been warned?"

> It was getting difficult to keep track of all three identities and officers, but it was now plain to me that the third man really was Champ and the second man was really Bartlett. The question now was who was the first prisoner, the one I had caught with "Bush" Parker?

Eventually the *Feldwebel* in charge of the cells was able to pronounce that he remembered "Bartlett" from a period in solitary and that he was not Bartlett but Harvey. Eggers then persuaded Mike to confess by pointing out that in a few days his file would be returned from the OKW in Berlin (to where it had been sent after his apparently successful escape in April 1943) and he would then be unmasked by comparison of fingerprints. Eggers says he was "staggered" by the reflection that Mike had been concealed in the camp all that time.

But now he had another headache. Where was Best, who had "escaped" at the same time as Harvey?

> Again I sent the Riot Squad into the yard after showing them Best's photograph. "Get this officer," I said. "Go in at about 5 o'clock when it's quiet and they're all having their tea. That's when you'll find him." Two of them went in, and there was Best leaning up against the wall. "Come with us, Herr Leutnant Best," they said. "The game is up."
>
> These two officers had actually been in the camp for one week under twelve months, living at first in total concealment, somewhere we never discovered, and later living in the quarters more or less as they liked, as we let them slip further out of our minds as "gone away." When necessary they had stood in to fill up gaps in the ranks on parade, on behalf of officers who had escaped unknown to us, as in the case of Lieut. Davies-Scourfield three months previously, as I now realised. For the rest of this time they had lived a normal life in the camp except that they did not turn up on parade.

Eggers now knew that the Lieutenant Barnes who had been recaptured with Mike Sinclair in January was actually Jack Best. At first the OKW in Berlin would not believe this story of the ghosts. They insisted that after their escape in April 1943 the two officers had returned to Colditz at their own convenience. The *Kommandant* thought this a very poor joke: "Is this place a damned hotel, where people come and go as they wish?" But before long an OKW detective officer who came to visit Colditz agreed with Eggers' explanation.

Mike and Jack were sentenced to twenty-eight days' solitary for escaping and a further month because "they have hidden intentionally since 5.4.43 until they were found again in *Oflag* IVC intending to prepare an escape, so that they had to be reported as having escaped to the superior authorities, and because they were absent from one thousand, three hundred and twenty-six *Appells*, including three Gestapo *Appells*.

On the same day that Bush Parker and Mike Harvey tried to escape from the German air-raid shelter, Bill Fowler, back in England and promoted to squadron leader, was killed during dive-bombing trials designed to find a weapon against German tanks for the forthcoming Allied invasion of Europe.

19

A Vision of Freedom

Summer and Autumn 1944

CAPTAIN THE EARL OF HOPETOUN, Lothian and Border Horse, was one of the three star theatrical producers of Colditz. He produced *Gaslight* by Patrick Hamilton in October 1944, which played to overflowing houses in the Colditz theater, and later he wrote a play which received quite an ovation.

While on the subject of theatrical productions, which became an important part of camp life in 1944, it is worth recording the versatility of Dick Howe, who found, in conditions of semi-starvation, the energy and the time to carry through major theatrical productions, run the escape nerve-center and control the wireless news service of the camp. Dick produced *George and Margaret*, which had run in England before the war, in June 1944, and *Jupiter Laughs* by A. J. Cronin in November of that year.

The third outstanding producer, and the peer of the trio, was Teddy Barton. He produced *Pygmalion* in February 1943, *Rope* in January 1944, *Duke in Darkness* in March 1944 and *Blithe Spirit* in April 1944, with Hector Christie of the Gordon Highlanders acting superbly the part of Madam Acarti. Padre Platt had the following to say: "The play is completely amoral as all Coward's stuff is, but it is light and amusing and the production and acting were extremely good. Wild applause from a very delighted audience."

Other leading lady parts were excellently performed by Alan Cheetham, a lieutenant of the Fleet Air Arm. In May 1944, the theater was closed by way of reprisal for an offense against the Germans; in June Teddy produced *The Man who Came to Dinner. Hay Fever* and *Tonight at 8:30* followed and several Noël

Coward compositions occupied the theater until the end of 1944, when productions ceased.

The scenery for the theater was painted, mostly by the master hands of John Watton and Roger Marchand, on newspaper glued to wooden frames. Dresses were manufactured out of crêpe paper. There was plenty of Leichner make-up provided by the German YMCA. A carpenter's tool kit was accepted, on parole, but the prisoners soon dispensed with it, preferring to use illicitly manufactured tools, equally good.

Hugo Ironside was invariably stage manager. The electricians were: Lieutenant Trevor Beet (Navigator, HM submarine *Seal*), and later Lulu Lawton, who performed wonders in lighting effects. And the litany would not be complete without mentioning the manufacture of stage props, such as a highly polished concert grand piano for *George and Margaret*, and an ugly-looking brass-festooned coffin for *The Man who Came to Dinner*, made from old Red Cross boxes.

The superior productions of 1944 were a far cry from the early days when a handful of British gathered together in their quarters on Christmas Day 1940 to hear Padre Platt sing "Any old iron, any old iron, any any any old iron!"

The possibility of a general reprisal on the camp theater was always uppermost in the minds of the theater organizers. Until the curtain rose on the opening night, nobody could ever be sure a production would take place; there was so much clandestine activity in progress that might be unearthed at any moment, and the closing of the theater was always among the first acts of retribution carried out by the Germans.

Indeed, no "privilege" lasted long. Two games of rugby took place on the Colditz village green in the winter of 1943–1944. On two occasions in the summer of 1944, a batch of prisoners were escorted down to the river for a bathe. On one occasion a party of officers went to the cinema in the village. These outings constituted "privileges." They were all parole jobs, that is to say prisoners had to sign a promise not to make an attempt to escape during the excursions.

Suspicion was mutual over "privileges." On the one hand, the Germans thought that frequent repetition would ultimately prove to the advantage of prospecting escapers. On the other, to the POWs, parole savored of the thin end of the blackmail wedge, and the Colditz inmates were nothing if not diehard. The number of prisoners willing to sign parole passes always dwindled remarkably after the first outing.

Douglas Bader indulged in a different kind of parole. He demanded parole on the ground that he could not exercise properly in the Castle precincts owing to his physical disability—namely, that of having both legs missing. The very ludicrousness of a legless man demanding parole walks is reminiscent of the defiance of this great airman.

During the summer and autumn of 1944 he had his way. He gave his parole—promising not to make any attempt to escape or even to make preparations to this end. What he did not promise to eschew was the continuation, outside the camp, of the cold-war campaign which he relentlessly carried on against the Germans inside the camp. He would continue to break German morale by every means in his power.

So insisting that he had to be accompanied on his walks, in case his tin legs gave trouble on the hills, he usually obtained permission for Dick Howe or another to go with him. Together they would load themselves with Red Cross food. At first lone farms were visited, then the attack approached the fringes of the town of Colditz itself. The enemy fell like ninepins for the subtle, tempting baits. German morale in the countryside bent under the attack.

As early as the autumn of 1941, Harry Elliott had studiously learned the symptoms of duodenal ulcers, and had applied carefully the lessons he learned. He complained of pains. He lost weight. He had warning prior to being weighed, so he started off with bags, full of sand, hanging down inside his pajama trouser legs, supported at his waist. Thereafter he lost weight regularly by off-loading a few pounds of sand at a time. He painted the skin round his eyes with a mixture of carbon and yellow ochre so regularly that it became ingrained and would not come off with washing. Harrowing pains and the loss of two stone in weight succeeded in sending him to hospital at Elsterhorst in February 1942. Here he found two stalwart Indian doctors captured in Cyrenaica in 1941 who "fixed" blood in his various medical samples. All was ready for a break-out with his French confederate, Lieutenant Lejeune, when the night before the "off," the latter's civilian clothing was found.

The Germans were nothing if not radical and, knowing the Colditz reputation, they acted judiciously. The whole Colditz contingent at Elsterhorst was returned, lock, stock and barrel, under heavy guard by the 4:30 a.m. train the next morning, to their natural home.

Harry lay low for a while, then attempted to convince with a chronic jaundice. By 1943, his back began to trouble him—the result of a fall when he was trying to escape in France, after his capture in 1940. Arthritis set in and showed on X-ray plates, but Harry had cooked his goose as far as hospitalization was concerned. Nobody would take any notice of his serious and troubling complaint. He was becoming a cripple.

"If the Goons won't swallow it one way, they'll jolly well have to swallow it another way," thought Harry. He decided to start up his duodenal ulcer again. This time he had to travel far to make the grade. Already as thin as a rake, he had to lose two more (sand) stone. After several successive weighings he ran out of sand and still the Jerries would not transfer him. His face was the color of an ash heap at dawn, but the German doctors were unsympathetic. Harry decided he had to starve. He ate nothing for a week, could scarcely stand upright and the Germans gave in. He returned to Elsterhorst hospital.

There were several English doctors working in the hospital, including a radiologist, whom Harry made his particular confidant. The result was some really juicy ulcers on an X-ray plate which had his name attached to it. All this time Harry was suffering the real pangs of arthritis, which was turning him into a crippled "old man of the sea."

Harry's ulcers flared up and died down in the traditional manner of the really worst type, and the X-ray plates showed the legitimate and pitiless arthritis mingling with cleverly transposed and awe-inspiring ulcers in such a picture of blended medical misery that expert opinion considered he was at last ripe to appear before the Mixed Medical Commission. Harry was returned to Colditz as an incurable case with not long to live and a ticket of recommendation for interview by the Commission.

The Mixed Medical Commission was a body formalized by the Geneva Convention for the examination of sick and wounded prisoners of war with a view to their repatriation. It was composed of medical officers, one of the belligerent power (Germany) and two nationals (Swiss) of the Protecting Power of the other belligerent. The Mixed Medical Commission at intervals toured around Germany. Doctor von Erlach was the best known of the Swiss delegates. Although the war had been going on for over four years, the Commission had never been allowed to put its nose inside the gates of Colditz.

Now, in May 1944, the miracle happened and Colonel Tod was informed of the forthcoming visit of the Commission to the *Sonderlager* of Germany. Germany was surely losing the war!

Harry realized it was all or nothing. The commission was due the next day, 6 May. He and another officer, Lieutenant C. L. "Kit" Silverwood-Cope, who had thrombosis in one leg, spent the night walking up and down the circular staircase leading to their quarters—a matter of eighty-eight steps—at twenty-minute intervals. They were still alive when the sun rose and they took to their beds in the sick ward as bona-fide stretcher cases.

Unfortunately, this was not the last ditch. The Gestapo had the final word. Silverwood-Cope had been loose, too long for the Gestapo's liking, in Poland after an escape, and knew much that they would like to know. They had already submitted him to torture in a Warsaw prison without success, when he had been in their hands for seventy days. He had a red flag opposite his name (that is, he was *Deutschfeindlich*). It was almost certain they would not let him go.

The other cases submitted to the Commission for examination included Major Miles Reid, an MC of the First World War; Lieutenant "Skipper" Barnett; and Errol Flynn. Dan Hallifax was a special case—already passed. In addition, there were three French de Gaullist officers. De Gaullists, captured fighting in various parts of Europe, were now arriving in Colditz, replenishing the French fire which had added much to the spirit of the prison through the earlier years. There were twenty-nine names in all.

The camp as a whole was resigned to the rejection of the case for Silverwood-Cope. But when, at the last minute, the OKW, through the instigation of the Gestapo, began quibbling over the repatriation of others, including the Frenchmen, they came up against trouble.

The names of those permitted by the Gestapo to be examined by the Commission for repatriation were announced at the mid-day *Appell* on 5 May. Six names out of the twenty-nine were omitted. The SBO stated categorically that either all twenty-nine would appear or none. A special roll-call sounded on Saturday the 6th at 9:15 a.m. and the officers paraded. After the count had been checked by Hauptmann Eggers, Püpcke called once more for the twenty-three to step forward. Nobody moved.

Eggers, speaking in English, addressed Colonel Tod. "Parade the walking cases in front at once, *Herr Oberst*. Stretcher cases will be inspected later."

The tall, gray-haired Royal Scots Fusilier, standing alone in front of his men, replied coldly: "*Herr Hauptmann*, this action of the German High Command is despicable. It is dishonest, unjust and cowardly. The twenty-nine men must be allowed to go forward for examination. I will no longer hold myself responsible for the actions of my officers. The parade from this moment is yours. Take it!" And with that he turned about, marched back to the ranks behind him, turned again, and stood at attention, at the right of the line.

Eggers, speaking in English, started to harangue the parade: "British officers, you will remain on parade until those ordered for examination by . . ." His further words were lost as, with one accord, the parade broke up in disorder and men stamped around the courtyard, drowning his voice with the shuffling of boots and the clatter of wooden clogs on the cobbles.

This was mutiny. Püpcke hurried to the gate and spoke through the grille. Within seconds the Riot Squad entered the courtyard. The two German officers, surrounded by their men with fixed bayonets and followed by three NCOs with revolvers drawn, forged into the crowd before them to identify and seize the men approved for interview, take them out of the courtyard by force, bang the gates behind them and leave the prisoners to nurse their wounded feelings in impotence.

The German officers and their NCO snoops peered, now to the left, now to the right, into the sullen faces around them. The mêlée in the courtyard continued unceasingly. The Swiss members of the Commission were in the *Kommandantur* waiting for the proposed repatriates. They became impatient and demanded to be allowed to see the Senior British Officer. The courtyard was by now in an uproar with jeering, booing, catcalls and singing competing for the maximum volume of sound. The Swiss could hear the riot in progress. The *Kommandant* was spotted from a window giving orders outside the gate. He dared not enter. Püpcke left the courtyard for several minutes, then returned. He sought out Colonel Tod and spoke to him. The SBO was conducted out to meet the Commission at 10:30 a.m.

He apologized for his part in the delay and explained how the *Kommandant*'s list forbade the presence of six officers by order of the OKW. This amazed the Commission and they demanded an explanation. The *Kommandant* and the German member of the Commission then telephoned to Berlin. The deadlock was broken—Berlin gave way.

At 11:45 a.m. the Commission began its work.

Silverwood-Cope surprisingly was passed; also Harry Elliott and nine others. Julius Green was passed but later the OKW categorically refused to let him go because he too was *Deutschfeindlich*! The three de Gaullists were passed. They were of the six initially forbidden to appear. Duggie Bader was not passed. He was also one of the six. Errol Flynn was passed.

The German capitulation was complete and Allied solidarity, aided by the Swiss Commission outside, had won a memorable victory. The Germans' arrogance of 1941 and 1942 was changing and, from this day in May 1944 onwards, the prisoners in Colditz began to feel solid ground once more beneath their feet.

The episode was an important turning-point. The prisoners knew that Hitler and his minions intended to use them as hostages in the hour of defeat. Here was a gleam of hope.

Padre Platt commented in his diary:

> Now it was really like old times, the guard in position and at the ready, and prisoners shouting and singing, and whistling. "If only Priem were here!" was the lament of the old lags! This kind of party was right up his street . . . he would have had musketry loosed off in all direction; but not a shot was fired!

Eggers has some light to throw on this episode:

> Security approval was required for the applicants and the O.K.W. right away ruled out the De Gaullists on our list. They also objected to Wing Commander Douglas Bader, on the grounds that his leg amputations dated from a pre-war accident and were not war wounds. They also objected to Captain Green, the dentist from Lamsdorf, possibly because he had been responsible for spoiling my plan to plant Lieut. "Grey" in the camp as a "stooge." They also objected to the presence on the list of Flight-Lieutenant Hallifax, an officer who had been very badly burnt when shot down during a raid over Berlin.

The case of Dan Hallifax RAF is exceptional and should be recorded.

A fighter pilot, Dan was shot down on 15 May 1942. His aircraft was on fire, as was his oxygen mask. The result—Dan's hair was burnt off, as were his ears. The rest of his face was a mess. As one got to know him the injuries vanished. He was Dan Hallifax—a wonderful, charming man.

From the moment he was shot down his mind was full of just one thing—to get back to England as soon as possible, to the skin-grafting magicians. He was acutely troubled by the belief that the longer it was delayed, the more difficult it would be to rebuild his face and hands.

Efforts to get repatriated achieved nothing, so the only hope for Dan was to get home under his own steam—which got him into Colditz on 14 November 1943.

As soon as he arrived in Colditz he made another bid for repatriation which went through the SBO and the normal channels. He had been passed for repatriation long before he arrived in Colditz under Article 69 of the Geneva Convention as far back as 6 June 1942. The Germans replied that under Article 53 they were entitled to keep him a prisoner for an alleged "criminal offense." But Dan had never been charged with an offense. Even Eggers knew nothing of this "offense." Colonel Tod wrote to the OKW. In the meantime,

Dan missed the repatriation contingent which left Germany on or about 18 May.

The SBO received a reply from the OKW on 12 June, now saying he was not held under Article 53 but "retained on security grounds." The SBO promptly wrote a letter of the case history with all the relevant facts to the Protecting Power, asking them to inform His Majesty's Government, and to the Mixed Medical Commission. Dan Hallifax eventually left Colditz for repatriation on 7 January 1945.

On Whit Sunday, 28 May, Colditz saw and heard the biggest air-raid so far, in the afternoon. Air-raid sirens—no less than ten blasts—at 2:10 p.m. signified planes approaching nearby. Leipzig was attacked and the hot air blast from huge detonations was felt at the Castle windows. When formations of bombers, returning after unloading their bombs, escorted by fighters, for the first time ever passed directly over the Castle, the reaction of the prisoners was uncontrollable. They howled and cheered and danced as no football crowd has ever done. Not an enemy plane seemed to be in sight. The Leipzig anti-aircraft guns had disabled one plane. Four men were seen to bail out. "Straggler" planes came and went, quite low, and were given a tremendous cheer. Far to the west, several planes were seen to crash, whether fighters or bombers, enemy or Allied, could not be discerned.

Later, one of the four unlucky ones who had bailed out was seen approaching the *Schloss* under guard. He was given a rousing cheer. And after he had passed out of sight under the western wall going towards the entrance, the prisoners rushed into the *Saalhaus* hoping to see him if he was brought into the *Kommandantur*. His flying boots and Mae West jacket were spotted in the *Kommandantur* yard but not he. Then an ambulance arrived, evidently with the other three—one of whom at least was thought to be wounded as he made no attempt to keep his parachute from swaying as he came down.

If ever dull monotony was shattered, it was that day! British air supremacy had passed out of the realm of newspaper reports into mass formations of bombers, with an umbrella of fighters, sailing into sight as unmolested as though they were flying over England.

On 4 June after services and the normal mid-day *Appell*, a special King's Birthday parade was held. The officers conducted themselves with military precision and the SBO led three rousing cheers for HM King George VI.

Purdy was seen leaving the Castle under escort two days later, just as rumors floated into the POWs of an Allied invasion. (It indeed began on the 6th.)

In June 1944, shortly after D-Day, two visitors came to Colditz, in the uniforms of the British Free Corps—John Amery's collaboration corps. The initials BFC were on the arm-bands they wore. They said to the Germans they wanted a chance to talk to the prisoners, with a view to getting some of them to join up in the BFC. It was hardly the moment to expect the British to begin active collaboration with the enemy!

While the *Kommandant* would not take the risk of any trouble that might arise from escorting these two "recruiting officers" around the Castle, their leaflets were distributed among the POW mail. These leaflets stated that no action was intended hostile to the British Crown. The war was condemned as the work of Jews and international finance, and it was declared to be a betrayal of the British Empire. The pamphlet ended with an appeal for an Anglo- German alliance.

The prisoners at first burnt all the pamphlets and then, on second thoughts, demanded more as souvenirs. The visitors by then had gone and there were no more of the leaflets left. The SBO protested about the insertion of the pamphlets in the British mail and received an apology from the *Kommandant* stating it was "the error of an underling."

The underling, however, was none other than Eggers!

On Thursday, 8 June, Doc. Henderson, returning from duty at Lamsdorf, reported the first news of the great tunnel escape at *Stalag Luft* III, Sagan. As an indirect result of this escape, Eggers travelled to Sagan to study the security arrangements there. What he found was a German Guard Company of 250 men guarding 7,000 British and American Air Force personnel—i.e. one guard per twenty-eight prisoners. The comparable figure for Colditz was about one for one! There were about 200 POWs in Colditz in May 1944.

On 16 June, the guard under the archway halfway out of the Castle heard a noise beneath his feet. At this spot there was a manhole cover. There was another one further up the approach yard towards the guardroom and a third just outside the courtyard gate. All were in a stretch of about fifty yards of cobbles. The guard gave a shout and out came the Riot Squad and the security officer. "Up with all three drain covers" was the order.

The German Staff Paymaster Heinze, who was born in about 1888, a true Saxon, was wont to strut the cobbles of Colditz complete with boots and spurs, long cloak and sword! He loved to play a warrior-type of the days of the Kaiser and he loved to hunt the British. He came from Dresden. He had lost two sons at the front. As the manhole covers came off, he happened to pass by and looking down one, he spied the English "curs." He spat at them, called them "stinking swine" and passed on. They were indeed "stinking." The SBO obtained an apology later.

Three tunnellers, Dick Lorraine, Bos'n Crisp and Dominic Bruce, were taken out of the last manhole. There was an immediate *Sonderappell.* After this *Appell,* an effort was made to save as much of the tunnel as possible within the POW courtyard. Three men, Bob Barnes, Alan Cocksedge and Rex Baxter, went down the shaft from the entrance in the ex-Polish long-room. There was a vertical shaft in the thickness of the three-yard-thick wall down to the canteen. From this a connection was made to the drain under the canteen. Unfortunately the *Sonderappell* had given the Germans time to work their way up the tunnel (the drains) and they met the three Britishers at the bottom of the shaft. The whole length of this shaft and sewer tunnel was over a hundred yards.

The news of the attempt on Hitler's life came through on 21 July. It altered little as far as the prisoners were concerned. It affected the Germans seriously. Eggers reports that they started wondering: "How would the Armed Forces as a whole come out of this plot formed within their ranks?"

> The Officer *Korps* got its answer very shortly. Up to now the Hitler salute had been given by German officers only when entering or leaving their mess, or as a form of unofficial salute when not wearing their caps. From now on it was to be used officially between ourselves and also as between officers and prisoners. The *Wehrmacht* salute was replaced by the raised arm salute of the *Partei.*
>
> We had to put up with a great deal of ridicule in the yard for the next day or two after this order was propagated, but in the end things quietened down and the Nazi salute came to be taken as something in no way out of the ordinary. . . .
>
> When we [non-*Partei* soldiers] felt safe, with the *Partei* men outside the room, some of us did discuss the point—what to do if and when, and as, the end came. Although with all of us the unspoken hope was "may the Americans get here before the Russians," there were differing reactions even to this possibility.
>
> One said, "I'll shoot myself and my family. But before that I'll go into the yard and finish off a few of the prisoners first." [That was no doubt Paymaster Heinze.]
>
> Another said, "You can do what you like with your family, they're your affair, but the prisoners are the responsibility of all of us, and what one may do may be avenged upon the whole lot of us here."

As a matter of fact, when the order about giving the Hitler salute came through to Colditz, Hauptmann Püpcke visited the SBO privately to explain to him (apologetically) why he would have to use the salute. The SBO called a meeting and explained the situation. Hence normality and courteous reception of Püpcke the next morning at *Appell*.

On 27 July, Harry Elliott, Skipper Barnett and Louis Estève departed from Colditz on their repatriation journey at 4 a.m. Charles Hutt left at the same time on 4 August. On 8 August, a large white painted notice was nailed to the *Kellerhaus* wall in the courtyard with large black lettering proclaiming "Camp Order No 21: POWs escaping will be shot at." Several officers took pleasure in informing Mike Sinclair of the new order! An ironic warning as well as a cynical joke!

On 23 August three counter-intelligence officers of the American Army arrived in Colditz. The senior of them, Colonel Florimund Duke of the American Signal Corps, had parachuted over Hungary with the other two officers on a secret mission code-named "Sparrow" to try and prevent Admiral Horthy (Regent of Hungary) from joining forces with Hitler's Germany. The other two were Captain Guy T. Nunn, US Infantry, and Captain Alfred Suarez of the US Army Engineers. Mission Sparrow originated in the OSS headquarters of Allen W. Dulles in Berne.

The three officers had been dropped in Hungary not far from the Yugoslav border on the night of 15 March 1944. Duke was forty-nine years old. By making this parachute jump, his first ever, he became the second oldest American paratrooper in the Second World War. Hitler pre-empted the scheme by summoning Admiral Horthy to meet him at Klessheim on the 17th. Germany then invaded Hungary, and Duke and his team were captured. They took the opportunity just in time of giving a very large sum in Louis d'Or into the safe-keeping of Major Kiraly, a Hungarian officer.

These Americans suffered months of abominable treatment at the hands of their captors and would have been put to death in obedience to Hitler's secret order (as the Musketoon commandos had been) had their existence not been uncovered by the Swiss Protecting Power.

With them, because he had been discovered by the Swiss at the same time, was an "American" major, Kiril Sabadosh. His captors could not understand why a man in American uniform could not speak his own language. They assumed he was a spy and handed him over to the Gestapo. In fact Sabadosh was Yugoslav. He had volunteered to serve in a Yugoslav bomber squadron which was sent to train in the United States. He was shot down during a bombing raid on his own native city of Belgrade.

Duke had an extraordinary story about his imprisonment in the *Landesgericht* prison in Vienna. In the yard was a bloodstained guillotine. Every cell was a solitary cell. It was an up-to-date prison in that every cell had a flushing lavatory. No private telephone system was provided for the condemned men, but by emptying the lavatory bowl air-lock—a nauseating job—and preventing the bowl from reflushing, an internal telephone system was provided by speaking tube—the lavatory piping. Duke had to put his head into the bowl, along which, with the foul odors, came the sound of voices. He had a last conversation in broken languages with the man in the cell below, who was guillotined the next day. His last words were: "Avenge us!"

By this secret telephone Duke heard of the Normandy Invasion on 6 June long before the news ever became public.

To the Americans, after months in solitary, having a whole castle to roam around seemed for a while like freedom. Suarez found out quickly that they did not need any more wireless experts in Colditz, but he also found out that Kiril Sabadosh was the chess champion of Yugoslavia. Suarez vowed to himself he would beat him and, after many days and games, he did. Now that he was the undefeated chess champion of Yugoslavia, he announced he would not play any more, and he didn't.

Nunn played chess for a while. Then he started to learn Czech from Flight-Lieutenant Cenek Chaloupka RAF.

Duke took to the bridge table. For the first time in his life, he now had a fine handlebar mustache. He had started it long before Colditz to give himself something to think about during the endless solitary hours. Captain Eggers made a point about it.

"Have you always worn a mustache?" he asked.

"Hell, no! I never had time until I became a prisoner-of-war."

"Yes," sighed Eggers, "and it will be the first thing that comes off if you escape."

In dealing with the *Kommandant* the Americans were represented at first by the British Senior Officer. Seeing advantages in separate recognition, Duke went to see Tod. "We have no complaint," Duke explained. "But if the Americans are recognized, we'll be two against one." The SBO was all for it. But the *Kommandant* at first would not see why four Americans should have the same kind of recognition as 200 British. Duke argued, "The Americans fight beside the British, not under them. We are not under British command as POWs. If you deny us separate representation, then you violate the Geneva Convention." He won his point.

Duke had fought in the US Air Force in the First World War. He could not be kept away from the hazards of the Second. He was a handsome, quiet man with a consoling personality. In civilian life he was the advertising manager of the magazine *Time*.

Suarez—known as "Al"—was of Spanish descent. He loved adventure; he had volunteered and fought against the insurgent forces of General Franco during the Spanish Civil War in the 1930s. A gay daredevil with a great sense of humor.

Brigadier Edmund Davies arrived with seven other British officers at the same time as the Americans; they were likewise beneficiaries of Swiss vigilance. Davies had been parachuted into Albania and wounded in an inter-partisan affray in the spring of 1944. One of his team, Major J. H. C. Chesshire RE, had also been wounded. They went to a hospital in Tirana, capital of Albania. Chesshire moved soon. Davies remained for two successive operations and was then moved to Belgrade where he met Captain Victor Vercoe of the Royal Fusiliers, who had been parachuted into Yugoslavia to join Brigadier Armstrong's mission to Mihailovitch. Both of them were moved to Banica concentration camp under Gestapo control. There already was Lieutenant J. Potochnik, a Yugoslav, a wireless operator attached to the Royal Navy, and Captain H. Hawksworth RE.

They moved on to Vienna and then to Mauthausen, where by an amazing twist of fate, the *Kommandant*, Zeireis, instead of disposing of them in the normal way (the gas chamber) returned them to Vienna to a prison under *Wehrmacht* control. From here they were moved to Kaisersteinbruck and thence to Colditz.

One of the first remarks made by Brigadier Davies when he had settled down in Colditz was "You ought to build a glider here!"

On 22 August Padre Platt records that "Bets were laid on the fall of Paris." (Paris fell on the 25th.) On 1 September he wrote:

> If the best of the German soldiers in this camp are able to interpret the situation from their newspaper, and know how near the collapse of their nation's dream is, they deserve congratulation on the level demeanour they maintain, and the calm exterior they present.

Ronnie Littledale, commanding the 2nd Battalion, the King's Royal Rifle Corps, was killed on 1 September in Normandy, his jeep blown up by a land mine.

Bombers flew over the Castle again on 11 September, and Platt inferred from the resulting column of black, belching smoke that the Leuna petrol refinery was once more the target.

A week later, Cyril Lewthwaite attempted to escape on the park walk using a blanket "so adorned," according to Platt, "with dirt and dead grass and leaves (the latter stitched to it) as to represent a heap of rubbish when he fell down and drew the blanket over him." Unfortunately one of the guards spotted him. Platt concludes:

> One of the interesting aspects of the event was that when discovered, there was none of the accustomed abuse or threatening to shoot, and Franz Josef was there!

As the autumn days of 1944 shortened and the second front in France settled down, the prisoners of Colditz gritted their teeth once more to stand another winter behind the bars, hoping for relief in the spring. The prisoner contingent now numbered 254 officers, about twenty-five other ranks and two civilians, of whom about 200 were British, the remainder French de Gaullists and a sprinkling of every other Allied nationality. An air of sadness and depression spread over the camp; the eternal optimists had little enthusiasm left for the victory that was always "next month" and "just around the corner!" They were nearly played out.

A double fence of barbed wire about eight feet high penned in the POWs during their one hour's exercise allowed in the park. About six feet inside this fence, there was another low fence of barbed wire which ran the whole way around the compound. There was a notice in the compound to the effect that anyone crossing over this inner fence would be shot by the guards without warning.

Mike Sinclair had made by this time eight unsuccessful escape attempts. He now decided to try again. His indomitable spirit could not be tamed. He would finish the war in harness, pulling his weight as an officer on active service.

This time he planned a lone and dangerous break. Surprise was the essence of it. He would repeat the escape of Pierre Mairesse Lebrun who, in 1941, had been catapulted over the barbed-wire fence in the park. Mike planned the break alone so that no other man could be blamed if a hand or foot slipped or the timing went wrong.

On 25 September Mike went down to the recreation ground and walked the well-trodden path around the perimeter inside the wire with Grismond Davies-Scourfield. In half an hour the guards had settled down. At the most vulnerable point in the wire, Mike stopped suddenly, turned and shook hands with Scourfield. "Good- bye, Grismond," he said quietly. "It's going to be now or never." He was ashen-pale.

In the next instant he was at the wire, climbing desperately, climbing quickly, spreadeagled in mid-air. To those nearby, his progress seemed painfully slow, yet it was fast for a man mounting those treacherous barbed strands. He had reached the top and was balanced astride the swaying wires when the Germans first saw him. They began shouting: "*Halt! Halt!*" and again, "*Halt oder ich schiesse!* (Halt or I shoot!)" came echoing down the line of sentries.

He took no notice. Freeing himself from the top strands he jumped down to the ground and stumbled at the nine-foot drop. He picked himself up as the first shot rang out. There were shouts again of "*Halt!*" and then a fourth time "*Halt! Halt!*" He was running. The hill was against him. He was not travelling fast. He dodged once, then twice, as two more shots rang out, and he ran straight for the outer wall. But the Germans had his range by now and a volley of shots spattered around him. He dodged again. He could still have turned and raised his hands. He was nearing the wall but he was tiring. Another volley echoed among the trees of the park and he fell to his knees and a gasp of horror rose from the men watching behind the wire. Then, slowly, he crumpled forward amongst the autumn leaves.

He lay still as the sentries rushed forward, swooping on their prey. He did not move when they reached him. A sentry, bending down, turned him over while another quickly opened his shirt and felt with his hand over the heart. He was dead. He had made a home-run.

About twenty shots had been fired at Sinclair as he ran to where, 150 yards away, a stream ran through a grid under a bridge formed by the park wall. Hugh Dickie and the German doctor both examined him and they concurred that a bullet had struck him in the right elbow and glanced off into his heart.

There was little remonstrance by the prisoners over the shooting. There had been fair warning. Sinclair had been shot whilst escaping.

Seven months later, the Castle was relieved and Mike would have been free—alive. That freedom would not have been of his own making, nor to his own liking. He had reached that stage in the humiliating mental revulsion of a prisoner of noble stature when, to desist from trying and to await freedom at the hands of others, would seal his own failure, scar his heart and sear his soul. His duty would have remained unfulfilled.

On 28 September Mike Sinclair was buried in the local cemetery. The burial party was not allowed to have more than ten people in it, and it was thought right that the eight members of his regiment, the King's Royal Rifle Corps, in the camp should all be part of it. Colonel Tod was there as SBO and Padre Heard officiated.

Hauptmann Püpcke and a party of nine German soldiers were present throughout the service in the cemetery chapel and the graveside committal. There were no military honors, but a Union Jack had been provided by the Germans, and a large wreath was already in the chapel.

At 1:30 p.m. a memorial service was held in the *Schloss* chapel, which the *Kommandant* had agreed to open for the occasion. "Abide with me" and "For all the saints" were the hymns chosen by Mike's closest friend, Grismond Davies-Scourfield.

After the war, the Commonwealth War Graves Commission moved Mike Sinclair to the Military Cemetery at Charlottenberg, West Berlin, in the British sector. His grave is numbered 10.L.14 and the inscription on the tombstone reads:

> SINCLAIR Lieut. Albert Michael 75265 D.S.O. 2nd Battalion, Royal Rifle Corps. 25th September, 1944. Age 26. Son of Colonel Thomas Charles Sinclair of Winchester. His brother John Henry Lund Sinclair also died in Service.

I remember talking to Mike late one night. He had recently come out of solitary and we were discussing plans. Mike was weary. He sighed: "How many more times before the wheel changes? I have to go on!"

"We must carry on, Mike. We have to." I had to go on for the sake of my sanity: if I stopped I would go mad. For Mike it was different. For him it was dedication to a duty that he had shouldered, consciously, when he became a professional soldier. His honor was as important to him as his life. A soldier must fight until he is the last man; he must be prepared to die fighting.

Today such a death as Mike's may be regarded as a historical finale, yet the fact that his action can be written down, and read and admired by many, of all ages, carries significance. Deep within the nature of the growing youth lies an instinctive urge to prove himself, and in the aging man an instinctive, self-conscious curiosity to know whether he *has* proved himself. Men must study themselves by studying others and accept or reject what that study reveals, imitate or turn away from what it implies. Human nature being what it is, the scales are weighted on the side of acceptance and imitation by the young and that way, unfortunately for the cynics, lies the hope that honor and chivalry will never die. Because of that, Mike's challenge was worthwhile.

Pierre Mairesse Lebrun says:

> The conception of courage in war is straightforward. A soldier is under orders to act. The action necessitates the demonstration of courage.

> A prisoner-of-war is in an individual situation. He is confronted by the options: to attempt to escape, to risk the consequences, or to do nothing. Each man is thereby confronted by a challenge in his own character. Has he the courage to act or has he not? The decision is his, nobody else's. Uniquely, men who become prisoners-of-war have the opportunity to face this challenge.

Pierre believes it is impossible to estimate the potential for courage in any individual. Sometimes the most unlikely people exhibit the greatest courage, and some of them are astonished at their own undreamt-of resources.

20

They Mingled in the Fray

Autumn and Winter 1944–1945

THE LAST DAYS OF SEPTEMBER 1944 were fateful days for Colditz and ex-Colditz men. The Poles were to suffer great loss. General Bór Komorowski gave up the battle and ended the holocaust that had destroyed Warsaw. He surrendered on 2 October and started on the journey that led him to Colditz on 5 February 1945. On 27 September a tragedy took place at Dössel, *Oflag* IVB, where the Poles from Colditz had ended up.

Jędrzej Giertych was already in his straw-palliassed board-bed at about 9 p.m. in one of the timber barrack blocks of the Polish officers' compound.

There was a single tremendous explosion. It blew the end of his hut clean out. Ten other blocks were more severely damaged, some totally destroyed. In one barrack practically every Pole was killed outright. If an enemy had specifically sought out the Polish contingent with intent to exterminate them he was definitely on the road to success. But why not two or three bombs simultaneously? That would have completed the job satisfactorily. Nobody could ascertain at the time with any degree of accuracy who had perpetrated this wanton carnage. Rumors carried the day; one was that the Germans had vindictively done it. After all it was known they had taken an old ship full of Polish officers battened in the holds and opened the stopcocks of the hulk in the middle of the Baltic Sea and sunk it.

Dominic Bruce carried out research on this episode. It is established that the main bomber force of the British and US Air Force was not in operation that night. From second tactical Air Force records, their planes were not in the area.

No. 8 Group RAF were operating with forty-six Mosquito aircraft (ref: PRO Air 27W 2089 Ops Record Book 139 Squadron). The following targets were attacked: Kassel (flying times 1914–2350 hours); Aschaffenburg (1851–2254 hours); Heilbron (1933–2340 hours); Karlsruhe (flying times of no significance).

Of these, Kassel is easily the nearest to Dössel—only twenty miles away. That raid was carried out by twelve Mosquitos of 139 (B) Squadron. Their take-off time was 1915–1920 hours; they landed back at 2245–2250 hours—a flying time of about three and a half hours. They would have been over the area at about 2020 hours. Their target was the Kassel marshalling yard. Their bomb-load type was almost certainly the light case 4,000 bomb, known as the "Cookie," designed to demolish buildings and the people in them. Each plane would carry one bomb. The air crews were experienced pathfinders. Weather conditions were bad, with 8/10–10/10 cloud and cloud tops up to 14,000 feet. All machines bombed and returned safely. Bombing results were described as "difficult to observe." One target indicator was seen to drop ten miles short of the Kassel target.

The evidence points as certainly as may be to the unfortunate conclusion that the Dössel bomb was dropped by one of our Mosquitos. It is almost impossible to conceive, in the face of weather conditions and the strength and timing of the Allied bomber forces, that a single German bomber carrying a similar bomb load could have been scheduled to take off at a moment's notice on its mission of vengeance and could have achieved it with such deadly accuracy, with full intent to camouflage its bombing as being that of the Allied forces.

Ninety men were killed by the bomb, and about 500 were wounded seriously. Among the killed were nineteen from Colditz, including Adam Niedenthal.

Andrzej Onyszkiewicz (1899–1981) left Colditz direct for Lübeck in April 1942, and moved to Dössel in 1944. He survived the bomb almost miraculously. He was repairing his military overcoat and held it up in his two hands, spread out, just as the bomb exploded. His hut disintegrated and he sailed out, dragged by his overcoat. His sail dragged him for 150 yards along a loose gravel path. When he recovered consciousness his whole body was impregnated with gravel, and his internal organs suffered gravely. He survived and, after the war, came to London, where he edited the Polish periodical *Czyn Katolocki*.

John Arundell, the 16th and last Lord Arundell of Wardour, one of the POWs who had arrived in Colditz from Warburg in June 1943, was transferred to Elsterhorst, to the tuberculosis wing, in June 1944. He had already been in the Colditz *Revier* (sick-bay) for nearly three months.

On 15 October Colditz inmates learned with profound shock that he had died in Chester, England, during his journey of repatriation from Germany. He had succumbed to the disease. The date of his death was 25 September 1944. (On the same day Michael Sinclair had met his end.) He had been wounded when fighting near Douai in May 1940 and was taken prisoner. The title, created in 1605, died with him and the direct male line of the Arundell family became extinct. The 1st Lord rests in the Parish Church at Tisbury, where the helmet he wore at the battle of Gran and in many other conflicts still adorns the wall of the Chancel; the 2nd Lord, who died fighting for his King in the Civil War and his wife, the heroic defender of Wardour Castle against Cromwell's hordes, lie there too, and the last Lord, as brave as they were, rests nearby.

The position of Lord Arundell of Wardour in Colditz was odd in that he was not designated by the German hierarchy to be a *Prominenter*, although he held the oldest aristocratic title of all of them. This was simply because he had no close relation who was a political or military leader.

In the last days of September the final stages of the Battle of Arnhem were taking place. Colditz was represented in this battle, for Airey Neave was up on the south bank of the Rhine. His story tells, among other things, of an astonishing twist of fate.

> A week after the battle the number and location of paratroops hidden behind the enemy lines across the Rhine became known. The power stations in Nijmegen on the Waal and at Ede on the northern bank of the Rhine were linked by private telephone lines which remained intact while the battle raged. The exchanges were controlled by the Resistance and they gave us the information that in the houses and forests of Ede were hidden nearly 140 men. A rescue operation over the Rhine was planned. It came to be known as Operation Pegasus.

On 12 September, Douw van der Krap had gone to Oosterbeek to train a Dutch Resistance group. On the night of 22 October the first Pegasus group were brought back across the Rhine and Douw was with them. He finally reached Allied occupied territory and was hospitalized in Nijmegen. Here, to his delight, he met Airey Neave again. With Airey's help, he was able to get to England where he arrived by plane a few weeks later.

On 29 September it was announced that German camp *Lagermarks* would cease as currency as from 1 October. A chit system was started up, controlled by Mike Moran. Early in October the SBO, according to Eggers, made the following announcement on parade:

> It is no longer an adventure to get out of this camp. Anyone escaping will get home too late to take part in the war anyway. Furthermore I disapprove

> of kicking a man when he's down. There will be no further demonstrations on parade.

The second statement no doubt refers to Goon-baiting, which was indeed falling out of favor at this time, but one may question the likelihood of both these statements being made at the same parade.

On 14 October there was a new arrival. He had made several escape attempts since his capture on 15 July 1942 in North Africa, and was sent to Colditz as *Deutschfeindlich.* He hated Germans and all things German. He was a solitary man of immense valor, modest to an extreme. His name was Captain Charles Upham VC and Bar, NZEF.

Padre Platt reports the cutting down of rations in his entry for 16 October:

> As from today the bread ration is cut by 200 grammes a week, and the potato ration by 150 grammes a day. These are to be compensated weight for weight by millet or peas, or kohlrabi, or something. If the former two are substituted it will be an acceptable exchange, for (a) the bread is pretty terrible, and (b) we have learned to do rather wonderful things with millet; but if kohlrabi or something is the most frequent exchange it will be most unacceptable, for the man who thought of bastardising turnip and cabbage might have expended his genius on producing something less tasteless and insipid. A better cabbage or a better turnip would have been a worthy accomplishment, but why the worst of both?

Sergeant Suza, a Czech, arrived on 27 October. By this time there were seventeen Czechs in Colditz, officers and other ranks. All were Air Force and all were held on charge of deserting from Czechoslovakia after the German occupation.

On 14 August the Czechs Jack Zafouk and Cenek Chaloupka had been suddenly taken to Prague; they were returned safely on the 31st. In Prague they had been handed over to the Gestapo. Only Checko was interrogated at first, but then, on 10 September, Jack was charged with having served with the forces of an enemy power and with having borne arms against the Reich. The penalty was death. Checko was not charged.

It transpired that fourteen new arrivals in Colditz had also been taken to Prague, subjected to the same maltreatment and charged as Jack was. Alan "Black" Campbell prepared the defense for them all, based on constitutional and international rather than criminal law. The highest military tribune in the country was to try them, but the trial was postponed until after the war and so in fact never took place.

Only recently has it come to light that three more RAF Czech officers (British) who arrived in Colditz in January 1945 had been court-martialed on a similar charge, found guilty and sentenced to death.

Eggers, remarking that the kitchen staff was far too small to have time for cleaning carrots, evokes a pathetic picture in early November:

> The carrots—tiny, dirty carrots and as grubby as all carrots seem to be—were cleaned by a volunteer corps, among which I observed a Brigadier, an American Colonel, a Scots Colonel, a Lieutenant-Commander of the Royal Navy, Officers of field rank, officers below, and a Chaplain, all standing in an irregular circle in gusty drizzle, scraping little carrots with pocket knives until their hands were numb with cold, dirt and wet.

Two new *Prominenten*, expected for a week, arrived on 10 November. They were Captain John, the Master of Elphinstone, of the Black Watch, a nephew of the Queen, and Lieutenant F. Max de Hamel, a nephew of Winston Churchill. On the 11th, Armistice Day, Private Bullard sounded the Last Post at 11 a.m. and Reveille at two minutes past. Padre Platt thought it was a more real memorial than the service of previous years. The next day there was the arrival of two more *Prominenten*: Captain Earl Haig, Scots Greys, son of the late Field Marshal, and Lieutenant Viscount Lascelles, Grenadier Guards.

Peter Tunstall was notified on 18 November that the OKW had not confirmed the sentence of his last court-martial, and had ordered a retrial on 5 January 1945.

Padre Platt commented at the end of November that news of the fall of Strasbourg to the French Army Corps had raised hopes of victory before Christmas almost to the point of certainty. A week later, he describes the meager Colditz diet:

> Since German rations were cut, and Red Cross parcels cut by half, the usual complete evening meal could be placed without violence into a four-ounce Three Nuns tobacco tin. Breakfast consists of two very thin slices of rye bread, not quite 1/4" thick, spread with prima fat and a little preserve on one piece, with a cup of ersatz coffee. Lunch consists of one small potato and two or three tablespoonsful of boiled vegetable. Two slices of bread are cut into seven pieces and a two-ounce tin of cheese divided between them. Once a week (but not infrequently a week is missed) meat is served at the

usual rate of one-and-a-half ounces each. A cup of Red Cross tea rounds off the meal.

On 6 December a fourth American arrived in Colditz Castle from the camp at Schubin—a man in serious trouble. He was Lieutenant-Colonel W. H. Schaefer, 45th Division, US Army. As acting Senior Officer in Schubin he had supported a Lieutenant Schmidt who had stood in the way of a German NCO trying to post a notice entitled "Escaping is no longer a game." (The notice confessed, in effect, that the German military could no longer enforce the Geneva Convention rules about escaping prisoners. Civilians—and other elements—were liable to kill runaways on the spot.) Under German military law, any soldier interfering with a German soldier carrying out his order may be court-martialed and sentenced to death. His new captors put him in solitary confinement in a cell outside the regular POW section to await the court-martial.

Duke got permission to take the Colonel his one meal a day. Lieutenant Alan "Black" Campbell, the British barrister in civilian life, framed his defense, which Duke sent off to the OKW. They also notified the Protecting Power. Having by then some idea of how the war might end, the *Kommandant* took no initiative in the matter.

André Perrin, the tough little Frenchman, who had spent eleven weeks in solitary in Colditz, had gone to Lübeck with the other French in the summer of 1943. He had promised his English friends, among them Bader and Romilly, that he would bring news of them to their relatives in England before the end of the war. He kept his promise.

The Belgian contingent were moved from Lübeck on 9 September 1943. Five Frenchmen exchanged places with five Belgians. Perrin changed places with Thibaut de Massières, and escaped from a train. At the end of 1944 he arrived in London. He wrote: "I meet Madame Romilly and Mrs. Bader."

On 13 December two French officers arrived who had been shot down over the western front only three weeks before: Sous-Lieutenant R. Guillerme and Lieutenant N. Heliot.

A coded message had been sent at the end of November to the UK via MI9 as follows:

> All ranks of the British and Dominion forces at *Oflag* IVC present their humble duty to his Majesty and request that he will graciously accept their Xmas Greetings. Signed W. Tod, Lieut. Colonel.

A gracious reply was received by the same means.

Eggers takes up the story of the German Götterdämmerung:

> Morale among our people was reduced to mere stoicism. Thousands were buried every day under the bombed ruins of their houses. The survivors lived as they might through that dreadful winter. Worst of all was the misery of the endless trek of hundreds of thousands of refugees from East Prussia, Silesia, Pomerania and Transylvania, fleeing before the Soviets.

Life in the Castle, where the guard companies now consisted almost wholly of men between the ages of fifty and sixty-five, reflected the growing disorder outside:

> Conditions at the end of 1944 were getting steadily worse. In *Oflag* IVC, Colditz, we reached the lowest level ever in food supplies for the prisoners. A bare 1,300 calories a day was the best we could scrape up after the New Year. Fuel was nearly gone. We were reduced to allowing officers out in the woods on parole and under guard to collect branches for their own fires. No more parcels came from the International Red Cross because the railway to Switzerland was cut. The prisoners ate up most of their last food stocks at Christmas, and their own internal market prices rose to fantastic heights—cigarettes were £10 per 100, while chocolate and raisins were proportionately high. A pound of flour obtained on the black (German!) market was priced at £10 sterling.

Indeed Padre Platt tells of the sale of a 1938 14h.p. Renault coupé on 7 December for five pounds of chocolate and £10, the car and the sterling being in England.

There was another camp truce from 24 December to 2 January. Eggers describes Lieutenant Chaloupka stark naked running three times round the *Hof* on Christmas Eve, having lost a bet that by then the war would be over.

Colonel Schaefer left under escort for court-martial at Schubin on Christmas Day 1944. He was returned on 29 December under sentence of death. Lieutenant Schmidt, who had obstructed the *Unteroffizier*, was also sentenced to death.

Platt records that the only signs Schaefer gave of discomposure were a slight paleness and a failure to keep his cigarette alight. The following day he lodged an appeal against the sentence, drafted by Black Campbell, but it never appeared to get to its destination. Hitler was the last recourse of appeal. Eggers says that

Hitler himself had been advised of the affair and had himself ordered the death penalty. The Swiss representative visited Schaefer during his last visit to Colditz on 6 February 1945. Schaefer suffered the enormous anxiety of uncertainty.

The New Year opened with the trial of Peter Tunstall at Leipzig on 5 January. Black Campbell had prepared his brief very carefully and ably. It was Pete's seventh trip to Leipzig and he returned with a sentence of five months *Gefängnis* (imprisonment). The original charge was "Insulting a German officer and the state: using the words 'Bloody bastards' of Germans." This was a retrial ordered by the appropriate authority which had refused to confirm the sentence of six weeks passed by the same court on 23 July. He was not allowed the services of Herr Naumann, the lawyer who defended him in the first case, and the counsel he was allowed had later refused the case. It was then conceded that he could take Black Campbell, but when the proceedings were opened Campbell was forbidden to defend Tunstall, or even to sit in court. Hugh Bruce, witness for defense, asked if he might give his evidence on oath, but was told it was not necessary. The German witness gave his evidence and afterwards was asked to give his oath. The summing up of the president of the court pointed out that there was contradiction between the two sides, but since the German soldier's evidence was on oath, and that of the defendant's witness was not, they were entitled to believe the evidence of the former. That is the gist of the story as Padre Platt heard it told by Campbell and Tunstall on their return.

When the war ended, Pete had been court-martialed by the Germans five times. Except for one other POW who was court-martialed twice, nobody else had more than one. When Colditz was liberated Pete had served a total of 415 days' solitary confinement, which is probably more than any other POW of the Germans in the Second World War. When the war ended Pete still had many months of "solitary" outstanding!

There were two more Allied bombing raids on the Leuna oil refinery on 16 and 17 January. Platt estimated that the Leuna must have suffered twenty such raids, and concluded that the plant must have been built underground if it had really withstood such attacks. (His assumption was correct; the plant was partially underground.)

Writing about the 17th, Platt says:

> At 10a.m. we had a red-hot rumour that 500 Red Cross parcels had arrived in Colditz station. Confirmation came at 11a.m. Excitedly, like children, dormitories were a perfect babel of vocal anticipation. During the course of the afternoon Colonel German went to the station to check the number.

At supper time my mess was eating a dish of turnip peelings with two small potatoes each.

On 19 January, four French generals, captured in 1940, were brought in four cars from Königstein: Generals de Boisse, Buisson, Daine and Flavigny. Six out of the seventy French generals at Königstein were expected, but only four arrived. Generals Mesny and Gauthier were due in a day or so. But on 22 January, General Flavigny was told that General Mesny was shot dead while attempting to escape en route from Königstein to Colditz. Mesny was known to have assisted in the escape of his old friend General Giraud. His luggage was brought to the camp and Eggers forwarded it to his widow. General Flavigny at once protested, accusing the Germans of murder. Years later Eggers wrote that Hitler had ordered that a French general should be killed "whilst escaping," in retaliation for the death of the German General von Brodowski, shot while attempting to escape from the citadel of Besançon, which was being used as a POW prison. In 1961 the SS General Panzinger was arrested for carrying out this order on Himmler's behalf, but he committed suicide in prison.

On 23 January, a portable X-ray was brought to the camp, in an effort to see if the general loss of weight sustained by the prisoners was caused by tuberculosis. No trace of TB was found.

Platt reported on the anniversary of Stalingrad (1943) that the Red Army under General Zhukov appeared to be about fifty or sixty miles from Berlin. By February, German refugees from the east were already streaming into Colditz town. Eggers comments: "Groups of refugees from the East pass through Colditz. They are in a terrible state. It is strange that no refugees flee before the American and British armies, only the Red."

21

Firm to Their Mark

Winter 1944–1945

ON MY RETURN to Berne from the Swiss frontier where a "Repatriation" train had arrived from Germany, I was moved to write a letter to the War Office which is probably one of the first, if not the first, voicing serious alarm for the safety and lives of the POWs at Colditz in the proximate future. On 29 January I wrote:

> There is no doubt left in my mind that the Officers (including the *Prominente*) of Colditz and for that matter of other Officer Camps, will be held as hostages. The SS already control Colditz though they do not actually guard it. The war may be over sooner than we expect—but it may go on for some months. The POWs will at a specified moment be moved from Colditz to the centre of the Nazi ring wherever that may be.
>
> I feel that something should be done for them just before they are shifted. This should be the optimum time, because they will be moved only when they have to be moved—i.e. when Germany is beginning to crumble. This will give the POWs a chance for their lives—if they are freed.
>
> As for freeing them I have only the one suggestion—and that for Colditz as I know it. Blow the Garrison Courtyard and the guard house to bits by very low accurate bombing—drop arms in the inner courtyard and give the officers a chance for their lives. I know they will react—simply warn them to be ready—saying the above may happen any time. They will do the rest. I am not a brave man but I know that if I was offered a last

> chance free preferably with a weapon, to becoming a Nazi hostage I would choose the former course any time. The men in Colditz already feel they are going to be hostages.

On 9 February the SBO asked for the second time (the first was in September) for a meeting with the *Kommandant* to discuss the procedure and steps to be taken on the approach of the Americans. The *Kommandant* again replied he had no instructions on the point. Yet Eggers has a note on the subject much earlier, implying that in fact the *Kommandant* had received instructions.

The SBO was not letting the grass grow under his feet in this respect. He had already made moves to enable him to act independently of the *Kommandant* in the event of a collapse in Germany. For the following description of what developed from this initiative I am deeply indebted to Major J. "Jack" Pringle MC. Jack had been imprisoned in Gavi, the Colditz of Italy. He very nearly made Switzerland from Gavi in an escape which involved Lieutenant-Colonel David Stirling as well. By January 1944 he and Stirling were in a prison at Marisch Trubau, only six miles from the border of Czechoslovakia. They both eventually and inevitably arrived in Colditz on 20 August 1944, along with Major D. W. G. Lee.

In December 1944 the SBO decided that the information available to the British was inadequate, and that a proper organization would have to be set up to find out, as quickly as possible, what the German plans were and, having found this out, to make all possible arrangements to safeguard the POW position and anticipate any moves the Germans might make against them.

He decided to call on David Stirling to organize an intelligence system, and he gave him, as his object, (1) to find out the entire local set-up of the German Party, Army, Gestapo and SS, with names and dossiers of the important personalities; and (2) to try to locate some weak spot if the Germans ever decided, in the last days, to liquidate the camp.

Stirling's first step was to take over the camp black-market organization, whereby the prisoners obtained from their guards various commodities in exchange usually for items from Red Cross parcels. Only two officers were now allowed to have dealings with these guards. Stirling could thus control the amount of chocolate and cigarettes given to the guards. At the same time the information gleaned from them, channelled through only two contacts, was much more coherent.

The two agents were Flight-Lieutenant Cenek Chaloupka of No. 615 Czech Squadron RAF and Lieutenant Dick Jones. "Checko" Chaloupka had flown for

Czechoslovakia, for Poland after Munich, for France after September 1939, and for England after the fall of France. He was decorated by all four nations. An adopted godson of Eric Linklater, he was puckish, dynamic, uproarious and explosive. Dick Jones, of the Malta Sea Defense Regiment and General List, came from Cairo and was a member of an Allied secret service organization. Captured twice by the Vichy French in North Africa, he escaped both times, only to be taken prisoner by the Germans in Tunisia in February 1943 while crossing the German lines to join the British. Padre Platt commented in November 1944, "We have at present three Mohammedans: two Pukka Arabs and Dick Jones!" Dick spoke Arabic, French, German and Italian, and very little English.

On his arrival in Colditz in April 1944, after thirteen months in the hands of the Gestapo, Dick regaled his new colleagues with tales of his adventures as a spy. They thought the stories a bit highly colored until Stirling, who knew about Dick from his own period in North Africa, was sent to Colditz and verified them. In fact the use of the black market as a spying organization was Dick's idea. Stirling has said that he often had to ask him to use threats if he did not get answers to his questions from the guards. These threats were of such severity that had they been reported he would have been shot.

This control of the black market was not popular with the other prisoners: 300 hungry officers were strongly tempted to use their own devices to obtain food. This problem was solved to some extent by pooling the food received by Chaloupka and Jones and distributing it in equal portions.

Jack Pringle and Pierre de Vomécourt decided what information was needed and directed what questions should be asked by the two agents. They also planned, in conjunction with Stirling, how such information was to be used in their final objective of reaching German collaborators on the outside.

Jack explains how things developed:

> We had one great piece of luck. Chaloupka, who at one time had been taken to a Prague Gestapo prison for interrogation, had been seen leaving the camp by a girl employed in the office of the local dentist. She had followed him to the station, lost her heart completely to him and waited for every return train from Prague until Chaloupka (much to his and our surprise, I must say) eventually returned. She then begged him to try, under some pretext, to get to the dentist. Chaloupka, an extremely good-looking man, with more than his share of attraction for the girls, had been only too pleased to try to do this, and had, in fact, by virtue of smashing some of his teeth, eventually got to the dentists on three occasions. He had never seen

the girl alone but she had managed to tell him that she would do anything for him, and if ever he needed help to try and contact her through a guard.

Up to now, he had not been nearly confident enough of any guard to trust him with a note of this compromising nature, which might easily have got the girl shot. But once we had organised it so that we had full run of all the available guards without any interference from competitors, Chaloupka discovered one local boy who after various preliminary trial runs, he judged to be trustworthy enough to undertake such a mission. Gradually, starting with the unimportant romantic notes, we brought the notes to the subject of the German war effort, the trend of the war, and the likelihood of the German defeat. We asked her to find out about this (always as if coming direct from Chaloupka but, in fact, now all being written by me and de Vomécourt).

Her answers came back carefully thought out and intelligently written. But we noticed that, although she herself was obviously anti-Nazi, she had fears at the back of her mind the insistence of which could only come from living in the strictest Nazi environment. Gradually, we discovered that her father was a leader of the Nazi Party in the local district and that she had access to information, both gossip and fact, which could be of great use to us in assessing the strength of Nazi authority, at any given moment.

Simultaneously, we were making rapid progress with this young guard who acted as our courier. He was a boy of about twenty-two years of age and his father was one of the richest men in the local village, a man of considerable property and with a good deal of influence among the moderate element in the surrounding country. We started a campaign to show the boy the advantages which would be his if the English won the war, and he had assisted us in the final stages. Eventually, we got him to confide in his father that he was aiding us by acting as courier to the girl. Once his father came into his confidence, we started to submit to the boy a list of questions dealing with local organization, and Gestapo, Army and Party personnel in the locality. From these, we compiled dossiers of each man. In some instances, these were very detailed indeed, and included many interesting facts. For instance, we knew that the mistress of the keenest local Nazi was the wife of the most moderate local industrialist.

The boy also supplied maps of the town, on which Jack and Pierre marked the houses of important local people, garages where cars were kept, petrol stores, food stores and medical stores. This sort of information was needed in case the prisoners had to take over the town completely amidst the chaos of Germany's defeat.

> Our next step was to get the boy to introduce the girl to his father so that we had a little group interested in working together for us; the girl, motivated by her love for Chaloupka and the man and his son, motivated by dislike of the Nazis and desire to safeguard their future. This little combination worked very well together.
>
> From information coming from the three of them, we then started to select an alternative local government to replace the Party and the Gestapo, and one which would realise in the last days of the war that their directive was to come from us in the Castle and that their efforts could be concerted and productive instead of unrelated and without purpose. The process of selection progressed fairly rapidly. By this time the father had confided in other local anti-Nazi elements and we were able, from the dossiers given us by the girl, to check on the veracity of the information given us by the father, concerning identical personalities.

But they were also concerned to find out about the *Kommandantur* organization and to gain access to the files and the switchboard so that they could discover everything relating to the prisoners. After an intricate operation, they obtained the confidence of the office staff and in the end were receiving telephone messages in the camp *before* they were transmitted to the German officers for whom they were intended. The switchboard operator in the town likewise relayed messages concerning the prisoners. It was at this stage that Dick Jones had to utter most of his death threats.

A remarkable breakthrough achieved by the Colditz British Intelligence Unit was an early-warning system by coded signals with a well-informed German source in the town. The code cipher was contained in and deciphered by use of an eight-volume history, breakable only by code-breakers of "Enigma" caliber. The German agent was given an innocent-looking map, of which Jack Pringle had a duplicate. It resembled a map of the Nile Delta, and so it was named. The prisoners had a clear view of one or two streets from their windows. Everything bore a code significance. If the agent walked in the center of the road, past the restaurant, halted at the first telegraph pole on the left for half a minute and returned, he would be signaling "Extreme danger. Come out at all costs." That would be if the Castle was to be blown up, for instance. The agent had contact with the authorities in the village who would be responsible for giving these orders, so the prisoners would be warned of anything that was to be done.

Through the dentist's receptionist (Imgara Vernicker), the prisoners were able to perform another astonishing act, namely the transmission of an anonymous letter in perfect German (by Lance Pope) to the *Gauleiter* of Dresden, the most important and dangerous man in the whole region! It was a strongly worded, threatening letter, intended to put the wind up him, beginning: "Your day of power is passed, now you face death." He was led to suspect strongly that the writer was either the Liberal leader Carl Goerdeler or one of his aides. Since the attempted assassination of Hitler in July 1944 a huge price (1 million marks, dead or alive) had been put on Goerdeler's head. Luckily he had been in hiding before the fateful day.

Lieutenant-Colonel David Stirling DSO has earned his place in war history as the initiator of a new conception of daring and dangerous warfare by which valuable objectives are achieved by a combination of first-class intelligence, speed of communication, speed of decision and speed of action, resulting in success, surprise and in most cases a minimum of casualties. He commanded "L" Detachment in the Desert War, which became eventually the 2nd SAS Regiment. He was in effect the progenitor of the SAS as the world knows it today.

Checko was the only POW in Colditz Castle who could lay claim to have kissed a girl while imprisoned there. It occurred probably at the beginning of his romance with the dentist's receptionist, when he "inadvertently" left his muffler behind after a session at the dentist. She appeared at the guardhouse and persuaded the guard commander to let her deliver the muffler personally. Checko was sent for. Through a small grille in the great oak gates of the prison yard, she passed him the muffler and presented her lips for their reward. Checko was not slow to respond.

The starvation diet on which the prisoners existed had an undeniable effect in dampening down the sexual urges of the natural male. In any case the total absence of contact with women made it easier to blot out their existence from the conscious mind, much as would happen in a monastery.

The German censors sometimes had an insight into the workings, warped and tragically despairing, of the prisoner's mind. Eggers reveals:

> Once an officer posted home a drawing of himself, idealized perhaps, but a good likeness, in perfectly fitting uniform, smiling, well and fit. The paper seemed unusually thick and heavy, so we slit the picture, looking for concealed messages behind it. There was indeed a second sheet. It

> contained a message—a very passionate one—and again a sketch of the writer, not this time in uniform, but in all his (perhaps imagined) Olympic nakedness, the true representation he would wish his sweetheart to see.

Platt reports the arrival on 5 February of General Tadeusz Bór Komorowski and his entourage, and comments:

> General Bor is the most insignificant-looking and the worst clad of any of the officers. It was very pleasing to hear Polish voices again, but they have the typical military precision of the last Poles; there is as much heel clicking as ever.

General Bór Komorowski was the head of that courageous, almost suicidal band of Polish patriots who kept the heart of Poland beating throughout the blackest years of the war. The Warsaw insurrection was the culminating point in the general's underground career. He survived, though war, treachery and murder had threatened to engulf him each day. He possessed hostage value in the eyes of the German leaders, a fact which undoubtedly saved his head.

A man of courage and resource, he won the hearts of all who knew him by his simplicity and cheerful friendliness. He was perhaps a man who had greatness thrust upon him, with the modesty of an aesthete, saintly in his detached outlook upon life. His head was partly bald and reminded one of a tonsured monk. Of slender physique, medium in height but wiry, he had direct, searching, hazel eyes under dark eyebrows. A neatly trimmed mustache, beneath an aquiline nose, set off his sensitive nostrils.

General Bór, indisputably *Prominenter*, was given the cell that Giles Romilly and Michael Alexander had occupied. The British group of seven *Prominenten* was concentrated all together in the cell immediately opposite.

Giles Romilly gives the following impressions:

> When John Elphinstone called he found General Bor seated at a table receiving reports from his officers; he was reading with great concentration and "*Nyet!*"—"*Tak!*" (no—yes) were the only expressions that came from him. John was struck not only by this reducing of speech to an economy that evidently General Bor's officers were accustomed to and understood, but also by a sense of the sharp clarity and quick firmness of judgement that it expressed.

Bór was a great horseman. In 1924 he had ridden for Poland in the Olympic Games in Paris. In 1936 the Olympic Games had been held in Berlin. There he captained the Polish jumping team. His team won the first prize, and Colonel Bór (as he then was) received the prize personally from Hitler.

22

Let the Hawk Fly Wild

Early Spring 1945

PLATT ENTERED A CRYPTIC remark in his diary for 12 February:

> The attics seem to be under repair. Evidently either the 1000 . . . or the 1300 new arrivals . . . are expected. *We do not like the idea of the attics being renovated.* [My italics.]

The explanation is not far to seek, for the British were up to something. In fact they had been up to something in those attics for a long time.

Flight-Lieutenant L. J. E. "Bill" Goldfinch and Lieutenant Anthony Rolt, the motor-racing driver, had been laying down detailed plans for a glider for a long time when Jack Best came out of solitary confinement after the terrace escape in the early spring of 1944. Encouraged by his reputation for tireless patience and his skills as a craftsman, they invited him to join them. Jack agreed.

Dick Howe was approached. He was incredulous at first, but when he learned that the entire contraption would be constructed from wooden bedboards and floorboards, cotton palliasse covers and a large quantity of glue, he began to think the scheme might be feasible. Designed to carry two men, the glider would be launched from the Castle roof, catapulted by the dropping of a concrete-filled bath sixty feet down through the Castle floors (in which suitable holes would first have to be made).

But it was really only possible if the team had a workshop where they could labor undisturbed. Tony Rolt had an ingenious idea. Overnight a dozen men walled off a section of the top attic over the chapel with a series of prefabricated frames under a layer of canvas palliasse covers from the unused dormitories. This was then plastered over using local ingredients—the fine grit from the French tunnel debris—to effect the best camouflage.

The next day the attic was inspected by the Germans in a routine visit. They noticed nothing untoward. The shortening of the room would only really be evident after measurement of the lengths of floors at different levels. In fact the attics were inspected almost every day.

Soon Jack constructed a trapdoor into the workshop from the lower attic on the floor below. Stooge Wardle joined the team. The construction of the glider began in earnest. A workbench had been set up. Electric light was provided. The glue came mostly from Checko's black market. The tools were home-made.

The four members of the glider team knew that only two of them would eventually take off in it. They agreed not to make the selection until the machine was ready, thereby ensuring that all four would continue to put their whole effort into the labor of construction.

Work continued on the components and on the assembly of wings, fuselage, rudder and controls and on the runway saddle-boards, pulleys and ropes through the winter of 1944–1945, guarded by an elaborate stooging system. Construction had started seriously in May 1944. The take-off was scheduled for the spring of 1945. By that time, it was estimated, air-raids over the Berlin and Leipzig areas of Germany would be sufficiently intensified to provide ample black-out cover at night in which to break out the hole in the outside wall of the workshop, set up the launching ramp, assemble the glider and take off without being heard by the sentries below or seen by observers farther afield in the village. By the spring, too, the winter floods on the meadows flanking the far side of the river below the Castle should have subsided. They would provide an excellent landing-ground for the glider, over 300 feet below the launching-ramp and 200 yards away.

The stage had been set for the greatest escape in history. Would the spring of 1945 see its fruition?

In February, as the Allied advance continued, Peter Allan asked Eggers for the first refusal of a small hand truck on which to carry his kit should the camp be moved. Eggers replied, "If the Russians get this far, we shall hand you over to your Allies."

Meanwhile Pierre Mairesse Lebrun was serving on the staff of General de Lattre de Tassigny, whose 1st Army had finally crossed the Rhine:

> At last, with our feet on German soil I felt bold enough to approach General de Lattre with an idea that I had been nursing for a long time. I asked him if he would let me go forward to liberate Colditz.
>
> I assumed that many of my comrades were still imprisoned there. I did not know that the French contingent had been moved to Lübeck. Also I knew of the *Prominenten,* not only the British but a few French as well. I was convinced that they, if not every POW in Colditz, all known as *Deutschfeindlich,* would become hostages to be held as such or massacred in the last resort. I also saw that the war of movement was gaining impetus, that it was nearly over. Whatever I did had to be done quickly.
>
> De Lattre listened to my plea and my reasoning and to my request for two squadrons of tanks with supplies and ammunition for a lightning thrust to Colditz. We had crossed the Rhine south of Strasbourg. I reckoned the distance to be covered was about 600 kilometres in a north-north-easterly direction. There was little German resistance behind the Rhine. Germany was beginning to crumble.

De Lattre approved Pierre's plan. He had, however, to alert the American divisional staffs on his left and take into account the position of the Russians advancing from the east, and this is where the plan was frustrated. Politics, as so often happens, made a hash of what was really a simple military situation and a well-planned expedition. The Russians were thought to be advancing fast. In fact they were not. The diplomatic situation that had evolved from the meeting of Russian and Allied leaders at Yalta in February made appeasement of the Russians a priority. De Lattre could not persuade his allies; neither could he take the responsibility of such an internationally crucial decision entirely upon his own shoulders. The plan had to be scrapped.

In retrospect, it is possible to say that during the first half of March there were no major German units in or near Colditz. The French striking force could have taken the Castle with ease. All the prisoners would have been released alive at least one month earlier than they actually were, and all the *Prominenten* would have been rescued long before they were seized and taken to Bavaria. Some terrible events might have occurred in Colditz during the five weeks before the Americans relieved the Castle. That fate was kind to the inmates does not justify the caution or conceit of weak men who make timid decisions imagining them to be wise.

As it happened, and western intelligence must have known it, the Russians were hundreds of miles to the east of Colditz. It was not until March that 1,500 French POWs arrived in Colditz in the general German retreat before the Russian advance. It is justifiable to ask whether the forces in the west were not influenced by national pride when it came to deciding which Army was to provide the spearhead that should advance furthest and first towards the cast.

The prisoners of Colditz witnessed a very long and very heavy aerial bombardment to the north-east during the whole night of 13/14 February 1945. Dresden lies about thirty miles away to the north-east. What the POWs witnessed was the heaviest, most devastating and appalling air-raid of the whole war. To this day, the Germans hold that more people were killed here than at Hiroshima.

Eggers provides the German side of the story:

> Between February 14th and 16th there were three very heavy air raids, two British raids in one night and an American raid by day, on Dresden—a city which up to this time had been untouched by bombing. The wife of the *Kommandant*, who was a refugee from Silesia, was at the time staying in the city with her baby in the house of our Paymaster. The Paymaster went off to help as best he could and was caught in the second raid and barely got to his home through the fire and destruction. He came back to Colditz and next morning a young paymaster of his staff went to Dresden with a lorry, got through, found the woman and the baby safe and brought them back to the castle.
>
> My clerk asked for leave likewise to go to Dresden to help his family. When he got home he found the house burnt out and his family all dead, along with other unidentifiable bodies in the cellar. He told me that in the old market square in Dresden corpses had been piled up high and burnt with flamethrowers. The inner part of the city was completely destroyed, and to prevent the spread of disease it was barred off even to those who had property and relations there. Some of the approach streets were actually walled up. Many officers of the Army District Command No. 4 in Dresden were killed along with their families in these raids. People in the city were quite demoralized by these massive attacks, even to the point of openly mocking at officers in the street that they should still wear Hitler's uniform.

At Colditz the POWs took this raid as the final sign of victory in the war.

A ten percent cut in the bread ration took effect from 19 February. At 6 p.m. the SBO called a meeting of mess representatives. He said, "The thing is so bad as to be funny. 1,500 French will arrive on Friday; they are on foot from IVB, eighty miles away. All the British, including the Gaullistes and Czechs, will have to accommodate themselves in the *Kellerhaus*, officers on first three floors, orderlies on fourth floor, ex-Belgian quarters. No day/dining-place, have to live entirely in dormitories. A twelve percent cut in rations next week!"

The new French prisoners arrived in fact on the following Monday, the 26th, having marched for eight days from Elsterhorst. Padre Platt describes what he saw the next morning:

> I went across the *Hof* to shave at 7.40a.m. Never saw such a sight. The more ingenious of the French had made themselves trolleys, hand barrows, trucks of every conceivable model [used for transporting their possessions from Elsterhorst]. One truck I saw was very ingeniously sprung on two tennis balls. There were three perambulators. Some of the trucks were as rude structures as one can imagine. Wheels in most cases were hand turned and tyred with tin. We had decided to jettison the kit we could not carry (in the event of a move) but many of these trolley manufacturers appear to have brought all they possessed. . . . Col. Schaefer has been in solitary confinement seven weeks yesterday.

Two exalted visitors, Colonel Baron von Beninghausen and Freiherr von Beschwitz, came to Colditz in March in attempts to persuade General Bór to order the Police Home Army to cease fighting against Germany and instead to fight against Russia alongside the Germans. They got nowhere with the implacable Pole. Less happy was the failure of the prisoners to extract from their visitors any assurances about the fate of the *Prominenten*.

On the 8th, immediately after the 8:00 a.m. *Appell*, the SBO warned Padre Platt to be on duty for the burial of an American at 8:15 a.m. the next day. He had no further particulars. The dead man was Corporal Tom Ray Caldwell. He had contracted double pneumonia on the march to Colditz from Gorlitz, *Stalag* VIIIA. A guard of German soldiers was present at the burial the next day.

On the 20th Platt writes:

> Was called this afternoon to the *Kommandantur* to be interviewed by a German Foreign Office official. He was quite a friendly type, but he gave

no indication of the purposes of his visit. After interviewing the Chaplains he visited the S.B.O. and perhaps, though I have not heard, some of the French— General Flavigny refused to see him.

The following day:

General Flavigny was returned to Königstein today. He was not acceptable as S.F.O. to the Germans. His refusal to see the F.O. official sealed it. Surprisingly he arrived at Königstein safely.

Late in March 1945, the Supreme Headquarters, Allied Expeditionary Force (SHAEF) ordered the creation of an irregular force which was called the Special Allied Airborne Reconnaissance Force (SAARF). It consisted of about sixty men, British, French and Belgian and one Pole (Andy Kowerski-Kennedy), recruited from SOE and experienced as parachutists in enemy territories. Teams were set up and allocated to target POW camps all over Germany.

The unit was divided up into teams of three: an officer and an NCO and a signaler with an easily hidden transmitter set. At exactly the right moment the team would be dropped after dark near its allotted prison camp. Dressed in tattered uniforms they would lie up in the woods, spy out the land, then slip unobserved into POW working-parties and get inside the camp, to contact the Senior British Officer and open radio communications with advancing Allied troops; these would then drop arms and supplies and give air cover while the garrison was overpowered or the *Kommandant* bluffed until Allied troops arrived, in order to foil attempted evacuation to the dreaded "Redoubt"—Hitler's mountain retreat in the southern mountains of Bavaria.

Patrick Leigh Fermor and Henry Coombe-Tennant (Welsh Guards, who had already escaped from Germany) found themselves allotted to *Oflag* IVC, Colditz, each commanding a team. A third team was soon allotted to Colditz under an American. Studies and preparations were completed and they waited daily for the order to go.

Out of the blue Patrick heard that an old friend from the days of the Greek campaign and beyond had arrived back in England from, of all places, Colditz. This was Colonel Miles Reid MC, who had just been repatriated with the group which included Harry Elliot. Hurriedly he got permission to visit Miles.

Miles poured cold water on the whole idea and came, himself, a couple of days later to SAARF headquarters where he had a long private session with the Commandant, a brigadier nicknamed "Crasher," who had earlier commanded a division in the desert. Patrick Leigh Fermor writes, "They both emerged scowling" (from the session). Miles said, "He doesn't know what he's up to. I'll go to Churchill if necessary."

As things turned out, it was too late for Miles to go to Churchill. The date was Friday, 13 April 1945. The Castle was relieved by the Americans on Monday the 16th.

Miles's suggestion was that "A special parachute operation should be launched designed not to fail" to relieve the POWs. Before he left Colditz he had been coached by Colonel Tod to stress to the War Office that any rescue operation planned would have to be absolutely "fail-safe." Anything less would be disastrous. As any "fail-safe" plan would undoubtedly be very expensive indeed, Tod, though not in a position to judge or decide, nevertheless considered that such an operation would, if not should, get the "thumbs down."

Hence when Miles was faced with the plan set out to him by Leigh Fermor, his reaction was understandable. The plan was in the "two men and a boy" category. It might succeed and be worthwhile for dozens of *Stalags* if not some *Oflags*, but it would not succeed at Colditz. The other side of the coin was that Tod had a plan which was maturing, with hopeful indications of a successful outcome. The plan's aim was to save the lives of all the POWs. Miles was aware of this.

The month of March in Colditz Castle passed as a month of incessant daily air-raid bombardment in the distant areas around with planes continuously passing overhead. The *Hof* seethed with crowding humanity through the daylight hours. Food was appallingly scarce—all were on a starvation diet and all lived in slum conditions. There were rumors of German revolts in various parts of the country. There were constant air-raid alarms. No sooner did the all-clear sound than another raid was warned. Still the railway line and main road in and out of Colditz had not been affected. In the chaotic conditions which prevailed in the Castle, reflecting the conditions in the whole of Germany, the Red Cross from Switzerland and Denmark continued their noble work, delivering food supplies. They performed wonders. Trucks of supplies looked like gutted charabancs, hooded over and painted white with large red crosses on the roofs, impossible to mistake from the air.

During the early days of April, the Castle was in turmoil. Large numbers of French officers arrived, bedded down on straw, then some departed. No sooner had they departed than other French officers arrived, some in trucks, some on foot with tons of hand cart luggage. More of them left.

The distribution of Red Cross food started a major rumpus between the British and the French. Colonel German, British Parcels Officer, was motivated to make a written report on the affair for the record. He dictated it to Padre Platt, as recorder of the *Oflag*. Colonel German reported:

> On the 3rd of April British and French Parcels Officers were informed of a consignment of parcels having arrived and were taken into the outer courtyard to check the same, and found a large Swiss lorry (the consignment was from Lübeck, not Geneva, as at first supposed), already unloading.
>
> A civilian, one of the drivers, standing by, replying to a question, said: "Here are 960 parcels for *Oflag* IVC." This released the spring in the French parcels officer, who with tongue, pencil and many diagrams began to explain the whereabouts of 6,012 French POW officers, members of IVD (the two camps have been administered separately though located together in Colditz). In the midst of all this, Monsieur Albert Cockatrix who was in charge of the convoy arrived. He had ten lorries, he said, each holding 960 parcels and driven by British POWs. M. Cockatrix was completely unaware that *Oflag* IVC also accommodated members of *Oflag* IVD. He had received instructions from Berlin that same morning to issue one parcel each to any P.O.W. he came across. (This did not deter him from leaving 9,600 parcels for approximately 6,500 prisoners—the combined strength of IVC and IVD.) We maintained that in view of the fact that we had received no direct consignment of parcels since April 1944, and that the S.B.O. received several letters from the Swiss Red Cross stating that various consignments were on the way to IVC, we were entitled to one load, i.e. 960, and the fact that IVD officers were being lodged in the *Schloss* did not materially effect the position. M. Cockatrix showed neither inclination or disposition to give a ruling. The French Parcels Officer remained adamant, hence an impasse was reached.

After hours of interminable wrangling, the solution was reached: one and a half parcels per prisoner. Padre Platt, discussing the affair, concludes:

> The highlight of gossip in both circles was the interview General Daine sought with the S.B.O., which concluded with the General remarking with some asperity that "the English have always been a nation of shop-keepers." The S.B.O. (who is a Scot) may or may not secretly sympathise

with the point of view, but on this occasion he rose, and opening the door of his room (it was one of the cells opening on to the *Hof*) very politely said . . . "*S'il vous plaît, Monsieur le Général*," at which the astonished General with great dignity rose and took his departure.

The way things were going in the camp can be judged by the following record of "current prices in the Camp" on 5 April.

Cigarettes	£10 per 100
Klim (dried milk)	£13 per 1 lb. tin
Flour	£3 per ½ lb.
Bread	£9 per 2 kg loaf
Coffee	£5 per 2 oz tin
Chocolate	£10 per ¼ lb. bar

Early in April, Dick Howe's wireless communiqués began to speak of General Patton's and General Hodge's armored spearheads, moving fast, driving deep into enemy territory.

23

In Spite of Darkness

April 1945

COLONEL "WILLIE" TOD, the SBO of the camp, came into his own as the man to be relied upon in a crisis. In the closing stages of the war he was recognized as the Senior Officer of the whole camp and represented all nationalities in the routine dealings with the Germans. He watched the mounting tide of chaos around the Castle with cool detachment, and, having the confidence of his own officers, he was able to handle the Germans with skill. He was all that a soldier should be.

Dick Howe always remembered a short conversation he had had with him; it must have occurred in 1943. He had lost his son—killed fighting. The news had come to him, a helpless prisoner in Colditz. Dick had said, sympathetically, after some casual conversation: "I'm sorry, Colonel, about the news you've just had."

Tod replied simply, "It happens to soldiers." There was a moment's pause, then they had continued their discussion.

Almost forgotten, as the tornado of world events swept across the globe and the Allied armies from west and east dashed headlong to meet each other in the heart of the German Reich, the Colditz glider was made ready for flight. Discussion centered around the use to be made of it. Dick had recently been criticized for allowing the building of the glider to proceed. Some Senior Officers objected on the ground that it was completed too late for use, saying that a better estimate of the time required to build it should have been made. They were correct in that the glider was finished too late to be of use for an escape, but they were speaking after the event. Others maintained it was a waste of good time and material from the very beginning. The answer to this was a simple one.

None of the men even remotely connected with its production regretted what they had done. As for others, did it concern them?

Nobody could foresee when the climax and conclusion of the war would occur. If it had not occurred in the spring of 1945, but months, perhaps even a year later, which was by no means impossible, then the glider would undoubtedly have been launched. Those who built it were prepared to fly in it. They were certain it would take off.

Colonel Tod did not criticize. Even if he had wanted to, the discipline of a soldier forbade the criticism of junior officers who had been allowed to build the glider with the help of his own staff and with his own knowledge. On the contrary, Tod foresaw the possibility of a last and desperate use for the glider and issued his instructions accordingly: "The glider is to be held in reserve in strict secrecy until the Castle is liberated, or until you have further prior instructions from myself or my successor in command."

On 6 April, Lieutenant John Winant of the US Army Air Force arrived at the Castle from Meisberg, a camp near Munich. He, being the son of the American ambassador to the UK, was at once included as a *Prominenter.* His plane had been shot down over Munich. A fair-haired young man with steel-blue eyes and a strong, though sensitive character, he had gone to war straight from university.

On 7 April, Padre Platt records:

> The number of French already gone to Zeitin [one of the places to which the French were moved from the East] is about 700. Those who remained in the camp chapel moved (evidently at request of Abbé de Maton, the Senior French Priest), to some of the rooms now vacated. The straw was cleaned from the chapel by willing workers, again at the request of the Abbé de Maton, but we were told there would be no time available for Protestant service.

Then, on 10 April, a highly significant move by the Germans:

> Fountain pens, pocket knives with a spike, leather straps for valises, haversacks, and all the things we were not allowed to have in our possession as P.O.W.s were returned to us this morning after about five years. (4 years 11 months.)

In the early afternoon of the same day a messenger arrived at Colditz from the Wilhelmstrasse, in Berlin, carrying an offer to General Bór Komorowski.

The *Kommandant* conveyed to him the instructions of Hitler, to the effect that he should be freed at once along with his staff, who included General Pełczyński, his Chief of Staff, and General Chrusciel, Commandant of the Warsaw Garrison, on condition that they helped Germany to form an underground army to fight against the Russians. It was the third time the offer had been made (the first was after his surrender in Warsaw), and for the third time the general rejected it.

The SBO had an interview with the *Kommandant* the next day and pointed out that Colditz was becoming a battle zone. He asked the *Kommandant* what his intentions were. The reply was that he was awaiting orders from Himmler.

The sentries around the perimeter remained at their posts. Ominously, in the foreground beneath the Castle, could be seen feverish preparations for the defense of the town. The bridge across the River Mulde was mined, ready for detonating. Tanks and motorized artillery rattled through the streets to positions in the woods around. Houses on the outskirts were taken over by troops and barricaded for defense.

The unreality of it all continued to obsess the minds of men like Dick, who had looked down upon the quiet town without ever noticing a change during four and a half weary years. The scene had become so permanent, so indestructible, that nothing could change it; only in their dreams and reveries had the scene ever altered. When they awoke it was always there, the same as before, unchanged. The dreams of years had never materialized. Could it be different now?

Eggers writes that the German *Generalkommando* (district Army Headquarters) had left Dresden and was now at Glauchau. On 12 April they ordered that the *Prominenten* (seven British, one American, and General Bór and his staff) should be transported by bus to *Oflag* IVA, the generals' camp at Königstein. The transport, two buses, was to be sent on the receipt of the code word *Heidenröslein* (rock rose). The word came through in the early afternoon. The *Kommandant* decided not to act until all the prisoners had been locked up for the night.

Padre Platt's entry for that day reads:

> Armoured trucks, armoured cars, army reconnaissance cars, a few tanks, troop carriers, staff cars, have streamed over the bridge all towards Chemnitz and the South. It had all the appearance of an army in retreat. By 10a.m. we had a rumour of an American Army having reached the Elbe. By midday they were reported to have reached Halle, and by 3p.m. 12 miles from Leipzig. The camp was in a furore of excitement, and every inch of

window space was crowded with leaning, crushing bodies. Artillery has been plainly heard since 1.30.

The announcement of the death of President Roosevelt came over the air.

2nd Lieut. Winant, U.S.A. Air Force, was put under orders to leave at 8.30a.m. tomorrow. This is most unpleasant for it may mean that he is to be held as a hostage. The Brigadier [Edmund Davies] and the S.B.O. have gone out to interview the Kommandant. There was present a representative from the German Foreign Office. Assurances were given to the S.B.O. that the Prominenten would not be moved or held as hostages.

The defence preparations continued around the village more furiously. Slit trenches could be seen everywhere, thrown up, like mushrooms during the night, in the fields on the higher slopes and bordering the woods. Boys and girls of all ages could be seen at work with spades and pickaxes alongside their elders in uniform. The Germans looked as if they were going to make a serious stand in the country around the Castle.

Later that evening, after all doors had been locked, Colonel Tod was called to the *Kommandantur*. He was accompanied by Brigadier Davies and Colonel Duke, with Lance Pope to interpret in case of difficulty. Oberst Prawitt, tall and emaciated, standing beside his desk in the plainly furnished office, looked at the commander of his prisoners. There was no softness in the answering glance. Tod stepped forward over the soft pile carpet and took from Prawitt's hand the letter which he held out. It was a letter from Himmler's headquarters, addressed from Himmler personally, but unsigned. It contained the marching orders for the *Prominenten*. They were to be removed that night to an unknown destination. Two buses would be waiting at the *Kommandantur* entrance at midnight. Oberst Prawitt would be answerable with his life if any of them escaped.

Prawitt claimed that they were being moved for their own safety. Tod protested that sending them out into a battle zone was risking their lives. In any case, he said, everyone knew they were really hostages. Prawitt said that the SS was supplying the guard to protect them. "And who will protect them from the SS?" Tod retorted. He demanded that Prawitt ignore the order. Prawitt refused. He refused too to reveal the *Prominenten*'s destination. Tod said that the *Kommandant* and Eggers would answer to the Allies with their heads if the *Prominenten* were harmed. Eventually Prawitt agreed to send Eggers with the *Prominenten*, with orders to bring back a statement of safe arrival signed by each officer.

Back in the prison, extra guards had already been mounted over the cells of the *Prominenten.*

Colonel Tod was allowed to speak to them. He told their senior, Captain the Master of Elphinstone, of his conversation with the *Kommandant,* and advised him, at all costs, to fight for time, wherever they might find themselves. "The situation is changing hourly and in our favor," he concluded, and then gave them a final word to cheer them, saying, "I've foreseen this eventuality for some time. You will not be deserted. The Swiss Protecting Power Authorities have had specific warning and requests to watch this camp and to follow the movement of any prisoners. They are in close contact with German authorities in Berlin, who are in the know. You will probably be followed by a representative in person, or, if not, your movements will be known in their Legation. You are being carefully watched. Goodbye and good luck to all of you."

Later Colonel Duke returned to Prawitt and insisted that if Lieutenant Winant were not taken off the list of *Prominenten,* he would be hidden in the Castle. The *Kommandant* pointed out that if he did that, the SS would enter the Castle and there would be shooting. Once in they would be glad to use the Castle to defend the town and the river crossing. Duke saw the point and that was that.

At 1:30 a.m. the *Prominenten* were escorted to their buses, Winant with them. As they were driven off, watched from the Castle windows by angry prisoners, Giles Romilly, in the British bus, said suddenly, "I thought you'd all like to know today is Friday the thirteenth."

Later that day, a written message was handed to Colonel Tod, signed by Elphinstone, saying the party had arrived safely at the castle of Königstein on the River Elbe; the same from which General Giraud had escaped to rejoin the Allies earlier in the war. Two of them, he added, Hopetoun and Haig, were seriously ill. They had been ill before they left, as the authorities knew well, and the journey had made their condition worse.

On Saturday the 14th, in the afternoon, the *Prominenten* were moved, under heavy guard as before, from Königstein, through Czechoslovakia, to Klattau on the borders of Bavaria. There they spent the night. Hopetoun and Haig were left behind at Königstein being too ill to move. The German *Kommandant* had to obtain permission from Berlin to leave them. The sound of Allied guns could be heard as the two buses and the armored car left Königstein heading for Hitler's redoubt in the Bavarian mountains.

Sunday morning, in bright spring sunshine, the *Prominenten* were moved again. Now they headed towards Austria. As evening drew on, they arrived at Laufen on the River Salzach that divides Austria from Bavaria. They stopped outside the barracks, once the palace of the archbishops of Salzburg, and also the prison from which I and many others graduated to Colditz. The barracks, which, at the beginning of the war, had been *Oflag* VIIC, was now a civilian internee camp.

Elphinstone as head of the British party refused to disembark. He was suspicious. The camp was not under *Wehrmacht* control, and responsibility for any outrage might be difficult to trace. Where he was, he was definitely under *Wehrmacht* control, facing an Army colonel who would pay with his head under Himmler's orders if his prisoners escaped, and who would also pay with his head under Allied retribution if they disappeared by other means. The German colonel in charge agreed to take them to another camp at Tittmoning, ten miles away, occupied by Dutch officers.

It was nearly dark when they reached Tittmoning. They were marched into the prison, another castle perched on a hill, and in the presence of the German *Kommandant*, were introduced to the senior Dutch officers. Giles Romilly could hardly contain himself. Who should he see in the group standing before them but Vandy, grinning all over his face and with the usual devilish twinkle in his eye. Giles was the only one in the British group who had been a contemporary of Vandy in Colditz. The others had all arrived after his departure.

The *Kommandant* of the camp commended the party to the care of the Dutch officers and left them together in order to organize extra precautions amongst the guards. Himmler's orders were clear: German officers responsible for the prisoners would pay with their lives if any of the prisoners escaped.

As soon as they were by themselves, Giles approached Vandy and the two men shook hands warmly.

"I am zo glad you haf come here. Ve vill look after you," said Vandy. "How strange to meet you again in such circumstances."

"Tell me how you got to this camp," said Romilly, "and then I'll give you all the news from Colditz."

Vandy looked at him. "Come vith me. Virst you must haf a hot coffee and something to eat."

He led Romilly through the echoing corridors, to a mess-room where a meal was in full swing. They sat down together and as Romilly ate hungrily, Vandy went on:

"I was sent here in January because the Germans thought to get rid of me. I vas a damn nuisance, they said. I vas *Deutschfeindlich*. They knew I organized all the Dutch escapes and zo they sent me here where there are only old officers and many sick ones—none to vish to escape. Zo they thought, but again they are wrong, vor I haf now some men here ready to escape!" Vandy chuckled with glee. He was looking older and his face was deeply lined, but his eye had not lost its sparkle. "Remember? Wherever there is an entrance there is an outrance!"

Vandy introduced Giles to the officers in the refectory and they talked for some time. Then he escorted him to a dormitory prepared for the five British and the one American, John Winant. The Polish generals were entertained by another Dutch officers' mess in a different part of the castle and slept in a separate dormitory.

The *Prominenten* stayed at Tittmoning for several days.

On Thursday, 19 April, Vandy had news through the German guards, some of whom were in his pay, that Goebbels and Himmler had been seen in cars, passing through Tittmoning at high speed, in a whirlwind of dust, taking the road to the redoubt built around Hitler's Berchtesgaden. On the same day the *Prominenten* were informed they were to be moved to Laufen. There was little doubt as to the implications of this move. At Laufen, out of the control of the Army, Himmler's thugs would take charge of them.

A secret conference was held at which Vandy produced a plan of campaign. He was nothing if not resourceful, but he was not only resourceful, he was far-sighted. He had a method of escape prepared for two of his own officers which could be used in an emergency such as this. This escape could take place the next day, the 20th. He proposed that three officers, of whom one should be Romilly, who spoke German fluently, and the other two his Dutchmen, should escape by his projected route. But he had not finished. He proposed to wall up the other five (including Winant) in a secret radio room which he had prepared for a clandestine wireless set. They would have food and water for a week, and the Germans would think they had escaped with the three.

The *Prominenten* had only to listen to Vandy for ten minutes. They placed themselves entirely in his hands.

20 April was Hitler's birthday. The escape was planned for the evening. Romilly was equipped along with Lieutenant André Tieleman and a young officer cadet, both of whom had come to Tittmoning by mistake, as they were neither elderly nor decrepit, nor sick, nor dangerous like Vandy.

First of all, the five men were walled into the secret radio room with their food reserves. Then, as the moon rose, Vandy and his assistant for the escape, Captain van den Wall Bake, escorted the three escapers to a doorway in the castle from which, one at a time and with suitable distraction of the sentries by helpers in the castle windows, they were able to make a quick dash into the shadows immediately underneath a pagoda sentry-box inside the prison perimeter and beside an eight-foot wall bounding the castle. On the other side of the wall was a seventy-foot drop to a water meadow. Vandy had the rope. He climbed carefully up the pagoda framework to the top of the wall and secured the rope firmly to a timber strut. The sentry was ten feet above him, on the platform, inside a glass shelter with a verandah around it. Vandy helped Tieleman to mount and then eased him over the edge for the long descent. Dutchmen, in their mess-rooms close by, were playing musical instruments and keeping up a continuous cacophony of laughter, music and singing. Romilly and the Dutch cadet came next. Romilly lay flat on the top of the wall and gripped the rope. As he lifted one leg to drop over, he hit one of the timber stanchions a resounding whack with his boot. The sentry came out of his pagoda and leaned over the balustrade. He saw two men standing on the wall and a third lying along it. He had left his rifle inside the pagoda. He yelled "*Halt!*" and ran to fetch it. In that instant Romilly disappeared over the edge and Vandy whispered to van den Wall Bake, "Quick! Quick! On to the wall." Van den Wall Bake had not been seen in the shadows. The next moment he was lying on the top beside Vandy.

The sentry had rung the alarm bell and now dashed on to the verandah again, aiming his rifle over the side at the three men and shouting, "*Hände hoch! Hände hoch!*" The Dutchmen complied as best they could without going over the edge down the seventy-foot drop. The guard was turned out, arrived at the double and arrested the three men. The sentry reported he had caught them in the act and had spotted them in time, before anyone had escaped.

They were led before the *Kommandant,* who treated them jocosely, in conformity with the state of the war at that moment.

"How silly of you to try to escape now! What is the point? The war is nearly over. You will be home soon. I have told you that General Eisenhower has issued strict orders by wireless that prisoners are to remain in their camps. They run excessive dangers of being killed by moving about alone in the open country at this time. I suppose you just wished more quickly to see your wives and sweethearts?"

The *Kommandant* was elderly, gray-haired and formerly a retired senior ranking Army officer. He was not an arrogant personality.

Vandy replied in German.

"Of course, the *Kommandant* has divined our intentions correctly."

"Very well. The matter is closed. I must, according to regulations, hold an *Appell.* I am sorry, but, please remember, it is you who have caused this trouble and not me."

The whistle blew and the floodlights were switched on. The Dutch officers assembled, and the Polish *Prominenten* assembled. . . . There was a pause as the German officers, with horror-stricken incredulity, surveyed the ranks before them. Hurriedly and nervously the count was taken. Six *Prominenten* and one Dutch officer were missing. A second count was taken. The result was the same. It was reported to the *Kommandant* in his office. The elderly soldier's hair rose from his scalp. He sat up in his chair behind his desk. His junior officers were awaiting orders. He would have to give them. He would be signing his own death warrant. He must stall. It was his only hope. He ordered his officers to search the camp at once and to continue until he issued further orders.

Searching continued for two days in the camp. Nothing was found. The *Kommandant* had to report and give himself up. He was arrested, summarily court-martialed and sentenced to death. The order of execution remained only to be signed by Himmler, as being the head of the organization which, under Hitler's authority, had issued the original commands. (Himmler was not easily accessible—he was already in hiding in the mountains—and in the end, the *Kommandant* escaped execution as his sentence was never confirmed.) In the meantime, the search continued desperately, outside the camp. Thousands of Germans scoured the countryside without avail. The Polish *Prominenten* were removed to Laufen. On the fifth day—perhaps information had leaked out, nobody could tell, they began to search inside the camp again, knocking down walls, removing floors and attacking ceilings. Eventually, they came upon the secret hide and unearthed four British officers and John Winant.

This discovery occurred on Tuesday, 24 April. What followed is best told by the Master of Elphinstone himself in a report which was published in the *Times*:

> Under very heavy escort we were taken to the internee camp at Laufen. Here the German general commanding the Munich area visited the camp, and in the course of an interview finally gave me his word of honour that we should remain there until the end of the war—a promise repeated in the presence of a Swiss Minister from the Swiss Foreign Office by the German *Kommandant* next day. The latter, however, could, or would, give no information as to the reason for our detention apart from all other officer-prisoners, except that it was ordered by Himmler.
>
> All remained quiet until the fall of Munich, and then, with the Americans once more rapidly approaching, the orders were given that we were to move at once—in spite of promises given—into the mountains of the Austrian Tyrol. Two officers, an S.S. colonel and a *Luftwaffe* major, were sent by Obergruppenführer and General S.S. Berger to conduct us. At 6.30a.m. we entered the transport, with the colonel fingering his revolver,

watching us, together with a somewhat sinister looking blonde woman who accompanied him in his car. This was possibly the most trying of all the moves, as the whole scene had a gangster-like atmosphere. We drove through Salzburg, past Berchtesgaden, and finally stopped at a *Stalag* in a remote valley in the Tyrol. We were allowed no contact with the prisoners, who included representatives of most of the Allied nations, but were isolated in the German part of the camp.

The representatives of the Swiss Legation (Protecting Power), with admirable and very reassuring promptitude, followed us and visited the *Kommandant* within a very few hours of our arrival. Later the Swiss Minister and his staff started on the series of interviews and discussions with the leading German Government figures who were in the neighbourhood. This work, which they carried out with such wonderful patience and success, was of the utmost difficulty, as the leaders were scattered in remote mountain hamlets, and all roads were choked with army vehicles and personnel.

Finally, S.S. Obergruppenführer Berger, chief, among other things, of all prisoner-of-war affairs, agreed to hand us over to the Swiss and allow them to conduct us through the lines. He did this on his own responsibility, and warned the Swiss that other elements in the Government would, if they knew, resist his orders and lay hands on us. He therefore sent to the camp a special guard under an S.S. colonel, armed with every type of weapon, to guard us against the "other German elements" during this final night of our captivity.

Berger himself came to visit us and in a long and theatrically declaimed speech reiterated, probably for the last time, many of the well-worn phrases of German propaganda together with several revelations of the complete break-up of the German Government and people. He then informed us that owing to this break-up he felt he was no longer in a position to safeguard us properly and had agreed to hand us over to Swiss protection. On leaving, he turned, theatrical to the end, to the German officers in charge of us and, having given his final commands, said: "Gentlemen, these are probably the last orders I shall give as a high official of the Third German Reich." We were due to leave at eleven next morning. The Swiss Legation attaché who was to accompany us in his car arrived early, but for more than three rather tantalizing hours there was no sign of the German trucks which were to take the party, a fact which caused some anxiety in view of Berger's warnings. At length, however, two other trucks were secured locally, thanks once again to the perseverance of the Swiss attaché, and finally at about 5p.m. we set off, each vehicle draped with the Swiss flag, along the densely packed roads. Accompanying us was an S.S. medical officer as personal representative of General Berger.

At about 11.30p.m. this officer stopped the convoy in a small village in the mountains, saying he had orders from Obergruppenführer Berger to see that we had food and drink in his headquarters here. We entered a house filled with S.S. troops, many of them intoxicated, and were shown into an upstairs room where some food and much drink were laid out. In the middle of the meal the *Obergruppenführer* himself once more made a theatrical entry, played the expansive if somewhat nerve-strained host, and again poured out a flood of propaganda and explanation. After some time he gave an order to an S.S. adjutant, who handed him a scarlet leather case. After yet another speech he turned to me, as senior of the British-American party, and handed me the case, as "proof of his good feelings." Inside was an elaborately ornamented pistol of ivory, brass and enamel, with his own signature engraved across the butt.

After this strange interlude we set off once more. At dawn we passed successfully through the last German post, and shortly afterwards were halted, to our joy and relief, by American tanks. A few hours later we were most kindly and hospitably welcomed by an American Divisional Headquarters at Innsbruck. It would be difficult indeed for our party adequately to express our gratitude to the Swiss Minister and his staff for all that they did to make this release possible.

The Polish *Prominenten* were released in the same convoy. It is interesting to note that Colonel Tod's last cheering words to the *Prominenten* before they left Colditz were not said without avail. The Swiss Minister to Germany was on their trail and caught up with them at Laufen on April 25th.

Romilly and Tieleman managed to reach Munich in three days, after some adventures. On one occasion, they were held for questioning at a police station, but their papers, prepared by Vandy, were found to be in order. The officer in charge received an urgent telephone message while they were standing in his office, concerning the escape of important prisoners from Tittmoning. He hurried them out of the office immediately, saying he had an urgent assignment, and politely wished them a pleasant journey.

In Munich, the two men lived as Germans, quietly and inconspicuously in a cheap hotel, awaiting the American advance. They reported themselves to the

American Army Headquarters as soon as the latter entered the city during the last week of April. Romilly was back in England by 2 May.

General Berger cropped up again. George, Viscount Lascelles, now the Earl of Harewood KG, received through the post in the autumn of 1945 a packet containing photostat copies of documents. In his book *The Tongs and the Bones* Lord Harewood wrote:

> The documents and a letter came from a German lawyer asking me to testify that Obergruppenführer Berger, the German General who had liberated us, had indeed done what he claimed. He too was now ill and in prison, and I was asked to pass on the evidence and get support from my fellow *Prominenten*, Dawyck Haig, John Elphinstone, Charlie Hopetoun, and the rest. It was easy (and truthful) to write what we were asked to write, and my only regret is that I did not have one of the supporting documents photographed before passing it on.
>
> It contained all our names, under the German instruction: "The following Allied POWs are not to be allowed to fall into enemy hands."
>
> What amounted to our death warrant was dated March 1945 and was signed by Hitler.

Vandy had not completed his duty as a soldier and an ally. Not satisfied with having delayed for five days the execution of Himmler's orders, perhaps saving the lives of the *Prominenten* thereby, he risked his life by leaving the camp in the dead of night as soon as the Americans had entered Tittmoning, and contrary to American Army orders. There was a severe curfew in operation. Anyone out in the streets was liable to be shot on sight. He appeared at American Headquarters where he reported the transfer of the *Prominenten*, including John Winant, and was able, moreover, through his own German sources of information to give details as to the route they had taken into the Tyrol from Laufen.

24

A Grand Finale

April 1945

MEANWHILE IN COLDITZ, events were approaching the climax. During Saturday, 14 April, the gunfire from the west slowly moved towards the Castle. The German commanding officer of a depleted infantry regiment (SS) in the town had visited the *Kommandant* on about the 12th. He might be ordered to defend the town and in particular the bridge. He demanded to know what resources there were in the Castle.

The *Kommandant* gave him the figures: 200 men between the ages of fifty and sixty-five, armed partly with German and partly with French rifles, with fifteen rounds of ammunition per head, also ten machine-guns of four different makes and calibers, with 3,000 rounds each. In addition a few hand-grenades.

They discussed the pros and cons of defense. The *Kommandant* set out to persuade the German commander that it would be better to leave the Castle garrison with its arms and ammunition to control the 1,500-odd POWs, who might otherwise break out and create mayhem, if and when an Allied attack might begin on the town.

The commander agreed. He insisted, however, that no white flags were to be raised on the Castle, otherwise he would shoot the place up. Still in search of reinforcements he turned to the *Partei Kreisleiter*, who mustered his *Volkssturm* battalion (people's militia). This had enough rifles for barely one in ten, plus a few bazookas. The *Kreisleiter* set up a barricade for the defense of the town out of a few carts and rolls of barbed wire at the far end of the Mulde bridge, an echo from Napoleonic days.

In March, April and May 1813, Colditz was last the scene of battle. Then the bridge over the River Mulde was the center-piece of the struggle and its survival or destruction was always in doubt, for if the French did not destroy it the Germans might, depending on the ebb and flow of the battle. The Castle had always appeared to stand aloof. The battlements were not manned then by cannon nor were they now manned by any armament bigger than machine-guns—which were pointed inwards! The fact that Colditz was not fortified, then as now, is probably explained by the comparative shallowness of the Mulde at points up- or down-stream, which meant that it could be forded—no doubt with difficulty. Command of the bridge might therefore be said to be important rather than vital.

During the morning of the 14th, *Generalkommando*, Glauchau, late *Generalkommando*, Dresden, phoned through the code letters "ZR" to the *Kommandantur*. This meant "*Zerstörung—Räumung*" ("destroy—evacuate").

Eggers explains the implications:

> All papers were to be burnt, all stores to be distributed or destroyed, our warning systems to be broken up, and so on. Furthermore, we were to evacuate the camp of all prisoners and move off "to the east" using such transport as we still had at our own disposal, namely, one antique motor vehicle, barely working, and two horse-drawn carts.

Eggers, Major Howe (German) and Hauptmann Strauss of the guard company, who had accompanied the two bus-loads of *Prominenten* to Königstein, managed to get back to Colditz by train late on Saturday night. Eggers handed to Colonel Tod the letter which had been demanded, certifying that the *Prominenten* had arrived there safely.

Kommandant Prawitt informed Colonel Tod of his orders to move the POWs eastward. Tod flatly refused to move, saying that armed force would have to be used and there would be casualties. He was backed to the hilt in his refusal by General Daine for the French and by Colonel Duke for the Americans.

The *Kommandant* managed to get back to *Generalkommando* at Glauchau by field telephone. There was a long, heated conversation in which the upshot was: who would take the responsibility if there were casualties? Prawitt knew his Colditz prisoners and Colonel Tad well enough to appreciate Tad's refusal was no idle gesture. The OKW still would not accept responsibility.

There were at least two meetings during the day. Each time the OKW's obstinacy weakened until at last Tod got his way. The Castle would be surrendered at discretion to the advancing Americans. A few marker shells had already been dropped into the town. The OKW insisted that the SBO should take responsibility if there were any casualties as he had refused to move his men. Tod agreed.

Having disposed of the OKW, Tod lost no time in persuading Prawitt it was time to hand over the keys of the Castle. He stressed that both the garrison and the POWs stood to risk far more from the SS in the town than from the Americans advancing. So the keys to the armory and ammunition stores were handed over. All sentries were to remain at their posts and change guard as if normal routine continued. No white flags were to be flown from the Castle until further notice. There was a ticklish situation here. If the Americans shelled the Castle, not knowing who was inside, and while the SS were still in control of the town, the latter if they saw white flags or Allied flags exposed would almost certainly storm into the Castle, precipitating a bloody battle. Prawitt ordered his guards on no account to shoot POWs or American advancing troops.

A surrender document was prepared and signed by the Germans and then by the SBO and Brigadier Davies and Colonel Duke. In exchange for acceptance of responsibility by the Germans for any harm that might come to the *Prominenten* and also for an investigation of the shooting into the British quarters in 1943, the German staff were to be given a safe conduct, i.e. into Allied hands as opposed to being handed over to the Russians.

Colonel Schaefer, Peter Tunstall and others in solitary were immediately released.

By Saturday evening, German guards controlling the *Schützenhaus* melted away of their own accord, thereby freeing some 500 French officers who took the place over, but did not venture outside. The SS were in control of the town and still guarding a little-known concentration camp full of Hungarian Jews, formerly slave labor, in the Cina works.

Eggers says the Castle garrison had no contact with this camp.

Sunday morning, 15 April, grew into a beautiful day. Spring blossom was on the fruit trees in the orchards and the meadows were resplendently green with new spring grass.

Reports of the passage of events during the day vary. Three diaries are available: Eggers' German diary; the diary of an Australian officer, Ralph Holroyd; and Padre Platt's diary. This last diary virtually ceases by Saturday the 14th. Colonel Duke has published his account, but it is dated 1969. I wrote my account in 1952 from reports of British POWs who were there. Colonel Leo W. H. Shaughnessy, commander of the task force of the 9th US Armored Division that took Colditz wrote an account for Eggers' book *Colditz Recaptured* in 1972.

Likewise Hauptmann Hans Püpcke wrote his account for Eggers' book. Thus there are seven differing accounts of the battle!

The battle lasted throughout Sunday and Monday morning. On Sunday morning, Thunderbolt planes appeared, unmolested by anti-aircraft fire. They machine-gunned the railway station, situated to the west just across the River Mulde, below the Castle. They also strafed German artillery, a battery of 88s, which was concealed in the woods and higher terrain of the *Tiergarten* to the cast of the Castle. A large home-made Union Jack had been spread out in the POW courtyard, soon followed by a French Tricolor, and lastly by a Polish flag, which was unfurled and spread out to much saluting and heel-clicking. Someone thought better of this idea later in the day. The flags were replaced by three large letters "POW," made out of bedsheets, presumably the blue and white checkered bedsacks.

There was an ominous, expectant hush in the mid-morning. Tommy Catlow, Royal Navy, noted that it felt like being in the eye of a typhoon just before it burst. A more down-to-earth comment was to the effect that the American boys must have retired for their mid-day spam lunch whilst the German side had retired for their sauerkraut. The only active German defense in the morning had been from the concealed guns in the *Tiergarten* area, firing over the Castle at unseen targets to the west, where American artillery and tanks must have been hidden in the forest of Colditz, beyond and above the village called Hohnbach, in the valley quite close to Colditz. From shortly after noon, American howitzer shells had been falling consistently in the town. Several of them hit the Castle. One German was killed; Bader was knocked off his tin legs; and gaping holes appeared in the walls; POWs were ordered to the ground-floor rooms by the SBO. The village of Hohnbach and the forest with a big expanse of open ground in front were plainly visible from the western windows of the Castle, which were naturally crammed with excited, enthusiastic POWs, until the shelling sent most of them down to the lower windows.

Five or six American Sherman tanks appeared out of the forest, maneuvering. They opened fire on the defenders in machine-gun nests, evidently in Hohnbach, and set fire to the village and then disappeared into the Hohnbach valley. Shelling, apparently from the German 88s—though there were no direct hits—may have persuaded the tanks to seek the valley. Shelling of the town continued, with exchanges from the German guns. Thus the Castle found itself in the middle of the opposing batteries. Several more reckless POWs watched from vantage points on the roofs until shell splinters from both directions sent them scurrying below.

A "signals" room had been set up in the German *Kommandantur* of the Castle. What type of wireless communication existed, whether German (both ways) or British (receiving only), is not clear. However, Holroyd reports that at 2:45 p.m., Colditz was given ten minutes to surrender. The German reply was a defiant "We fight to the last."

At this juncture the Germans (the Home Guard) made an effort to blow up the Colditz bridge. The explosive was reputedly old, and there was not enough of it. When the smoke and debris from the blast subsided, only half the roadway had gone. The bridge was still passable. A dozen SS troopers armed with bazookas clambered down the river bank and tried, unsuccessfully, to finish the job. The POWs had a dress-circle view of the failed operation. Their boos and jeers could be distinctly heard by the SS. Apparently they were too busy otherwise to react by spraying the Castle windows with submachine-gun fire. The town brickworks and a small factory were destroyed.

Evening approached and darkness descended but the battle did not diminish. In fact the American advance was being carried out under cover of darkness from a crossing of the Mulde by a railway bridge at a village called Lastau, over a steep rocky valley formed by the river further south. The Americans were "turning" Colditz. During the night their tanks and mechanized infantry attacked a German strongpoint based on a claypit by the road from Lastau to Colditz. Machine-gun fire with tracers, rifle fire and grenade bursts continued through most of the night.

A large kaolin factory near this strongpoint went up in flames, setting the sky aglow. The Americans continued their tank and infantry advance towards the *Tiergarten* side of Colditz. By dawn of the 16th—Monday—the Germans had retired from the claypit, retreating north-eastwards. All firing stopped except for the American heavy battery shelling the town. One heavy shell landed and exploded at the foot of the Castle wall.

Hauptmann Püpcke reported to the *Kommandant* that the POWs possessed national flags, and that the SBO had suggested, was it not the moment to hoist them? The *Kommandant*, seeing that German resistance appeared to be crumbling, agreed. Probably the greater fear at this moment was that of fire. An incendiary shell entering the POW quarters, on a steep trajectory, could have set the whole Castle alight.

So the Union Jack was hoisted above the *Kellerhaus*—the British quarters—and the French flag above the *Saalhaus*, with tremendous cheering from the POWs. The American heavy battery ceased fire soon after this.

As the morning advanced, American tanks and troops began infiltrating the town, both from the Lastau direction on the near side of the river, and from across the Colditz bridge. The German battery retreated eastwards to avoid being surrounded. Colonel Tod placed armed British officers on guard inside the Castle gates.

The British, according to Holroyd, were regaled at regular intervals by radio news bulletins. The British radio must have been working. Dick Howe and Micky Burn were sending out bulletins to the prisoners about the American attack on Colditz as relayed by the BBC from American advance troops with radio transmitters. Thus the POWs were informed about both sides of the battle. Water and electricity had been cut off for some time, so that the radio electricity supply was provided by the "slave gang on the big wheel" (see my book *The Latter Days*).

Mortar fire was turning the town into burning rubble. Two *Panzerfäuste* (bazookas) were firing at short range on the bridge, trying to hold up the Americans. Then the welcome sound of infantry small arms and machine-gun fire was heard from the *Tiergarten* side. The Americans were closing in.

Tiles and shell fragments littered the prison courtyard.

By evening the town was surrounded, but the enemy had not surrendered.

Colonel Leo Shaughnessy's account of the battle is a clear-cut military report in concise and modest terms. The other reports all come from onlookers. Shaughnessy (from Carolina) was at the point of the spear, determining the battle.

He commanded the 3rd Battalion, the 273rd Infantry, in the 69th Infantry Division, under General Emil F. Reinhardt, part of the 1st US Army. His battalion had crossed the Rhine south of the Remagen bridge by boat, shortly after its capture by the 9th Armored Division on 7 March. Early in April they crossed the Fulda River, north of Kassel. Then his battalion was attached to Combat Command "R," 9th Armored Division, commanded by Colonel Charlie Wesner. A task force was organized by attaching armored infantry, artillery and engineers. The task force was completely mounted on wheels or tanks.

There were several divisions operating abreast, each with five or six such task forces operating ahead, clearing the countryside of pockets of resistance, uncovering refugee groups and Allied POW camps.

Shaughnessy's task force took him on a line between Leipzig and Dresden. They lost a dozen men at Altengroitzsch, then reached the River Mulde at Wilderheim on 14 April. They were attacking Hohnbach on Sunday the 15th, when Shaughnessy received orders from Colonel Wesner to concentrate on Colditz, there to relieve "a large number of prisoners-of-war." He adds, "Further information indicated there were V.I.P.s among them." This was not, however, the main object or mission of the force. The force was part of the drive on Leipzig. Its primary role was to provide right-flank security for the troops attacking Leipzig.

Shaughnessy found himself by the observation post on the west bank of the river when the early artillery rounds were being zeroed in on the most prominent point on the other side. "This was," he writes, "one of the towers of a large and imposing Castle." Soon after several rounds had hit the Castle, "we observed three Allied red, white and blue flags appear at the upper windows of one of the buildings. This was the signal we needed to know that the Castle was where the prisoners of war were being held."

Lieutenant Kenny Dobson was the artillery officer in charge of the battery which first spotted the Allied flags, just as he was about to bombard the Castle with high explosive followed by incendiaries.

Shaughnessy lost three first-rate platoon sergeants already recommended for battlefield promotion, and a number of wounded casualties before he had cleared the west bank of the river up to and around the road bridge by midnight of the 15th.

During that night what remained of the SS garrison departed eastwards, presumably fighting some kind of rearguard action—the cause of the small-arms and machine-gun fire from the *Tiergarten* area.

Soon after dawn American sections could be seen from the Castle proceeding under tank protection along the main street and down sideroads—entering houses as white flags went up. Terrified Germans came out with their hands up. One German, crossing the bridge, apparently did not stop when ordered and was shot instantly.

At about 10 a.m. on the 16th an infantry section (reconnaissance) of four men, advancing warily uphill, arrived at the gate of the Castle, which was immediately opened to them by the British guards, who had been placed there by the SBO. Their leader, Private First Class Alan H. Murphy (Bronze Star Medal) of New York State was the first American to enter Colditz. The other three were: Privates First Class Walter V. Burrows, 60th of Pennsylvania, Robert B. Miller, 60th of Pennsylvania, and Francis A. Griegnas, junior of New Jersey.

In the outer courtyard, all the German officers were paraded and disarmed. Eggers, being an English speaker, represented the German staff. He produced a complete list of POWs held, handing it over to Private Murphy. All the German officers remained on parade while Private Burrows escorted Eggers down the hill to report to his commander, Captain Hotchkiss.

The streets were empty. Here and there an American guarded an important place. On crossing the bridge Eggers saw the poor attempt that had been made to blow it up. On the far side lay three dead men of the *Volkssturm*, one of them only about seventeen years old, lying behind a primitive shelter of barrows and barbed wire. "Even a hundred years ago this would not have stopped anyone," Eggers thought.

> What made them die like this? As we walked I saw what lay in store for our women as one was being dragged along by an American soldier who also had a whisky bottle clutched in his hand; she cried to me, "Help, help." [Eggers' implication that the woman was about to be raped is uncorroborated.] We went into the last house in Colditz town where I saw the Captain in charge of the unit. He was satisfied that no prisoner was injured and told me to return and order everyone to stay there until a staff officer arrived to take the formal surrender. I went back with the Sergeant [*sic*]. People now began to leave their houses, one man came up to the Sergeant and told him where the Nazi *Kreisleiter* lived. The Sergeant told him to go back indoors as he didn't like this type of informer. He told me to inform all the people we saw that it was forbidden to leave their houses. So I returned to the castle.

Colonel Tod had only allowed a few officers to leave the inner courtyard during the Sunday and Monday morning on specific duties or as guards. Now he with other senior officers awaited the arrival of an American officer to take over the Castle.

In the meantime Private Murphy continued up the causeway and ordered the gate sentry (still with his rifle but no ammunition) to open up. As the gate opened, he walked through on the cobbles into a small patch of sunshine. His gaze wandered around the roof tops and high walls with the rows of barred windows and then down again to the yard, where a large number of officers were aimlessly walking around or standing in groups talking. Slowly their eyes turned towards the gate and slowly too they began to appreciate that this was no apparition standing before them. It was a real-live, heavily armed American GI. In the next instant all hell broke loose. Private Murphy was swamped by a milling onslaught of cheering, laughing, sobbing, shouting men.

EPILOGUE

After Colditz

IN APRIL 1949 I ARRIVED in Paris after a three-year stint in Ankara as a First Secretary at the British Embassy. I joined the diplomatic staff of the Organization for European Economic Co-operation—the OEEC centered in Paris.

One day, in the summer of 1950, during a polo tournament in the Bois de Boulogne, on the scoreboard recording the competing teams and the chukkas, I saw the name of P. Mairesse Lebrun. During an interval in play, I went to the players' changing rooms and asked for the whereabouts of Pierre.

He was seated, having removed his boots, and immediately recognized me. He rose and advanced to greet me, walking with the aid of a stick. It was nine years since his departure from Colditz in July 1941. I had to find out what had happened to him.

When Pierre crossed the Pyrenees in December 1942, he fell into the hands of the Spanish guards, was imprisoned in a lice-ridden and overcrowded prison in Pamplona and after a week transferred to a holding camp for illicit fugitives from France at Miranda, then after a period to Lerida with other officers of the regular French Army.

He began training for a long cross-country trek over the Spanish mountains to the south coast and thence to Algeria. Some freedom was allowed the officers in Lerida. Pierre went off mountaineering with another officer and suffered a terrifying skree fall. He was carried to a mountain road by stretcher, by ambulance to Lerida and then to a military hospital in Zaragoza; examined thoroughly at last, the verdict was "spinal fracture." Pierre had never lost consciousness throughout his ordeal.

Pierre remained in plaster right up to his neck for nine months, when he was moved to Madrid. Here he began his recuperation. To lift his head from the pillow caused him to faint. Out of plaster at last he started on the long road of rehabilitation. Before Pierre left the Zaragoza hospital he had enlisted the aid of a carpenter. Together they designed metal and wood braces between the hips and knees, which was where support was primarily needed. He began painfully to learn again how to walk. The strength of an iron will was needed.

After four months in Madrid, he was able to walk short distances with two sticks. He was determined to reach Algiers and he did. In Rabat in December 1943, he encountered Colonel de la Villesy, now commander of an armored division, who asked him to join his command as soon as possible. But first he needed time to recuperate. He went to the hospital Maillot in Algiers. There he came across Franklin Roosevelt's little book in which he extolled the benefits, physical and spiritual, that had accrued to him as a polio victim by swimming daily.

Roosevelt's life story had given him the inspiration. Before reading his book it had not occurred to Pierre that, even with limbs paralyzed, he would be able to swim. That was the first inspiration. The second was given to him by a young woman. He admits that for a long time during his convalescence he suffered extremely from moroseness: the spoiled, self-indulged young man with the world at his feet had suddenly become a cripple. He would literally retire to a corner and brood. His conceit, his manly pride, his *amour propre* preyed on his resistance and fortitude. Then, one day, on the beach, he was approached by a stripling of a girl who had admired Pierre from afar when she was a schoolgirl at Orange.

Hélène transformed his life. She gave Pierre all that was needed to restore his self-respect and his *joie de vivre.* In three months he became a new man—resurrected.

General de Gaulle was astonished when he interviewed Pierre after his three months' convalescence. It was then May 1944. Pierre was now walking upright with the assistance of a normal walking stick. De Gaulle allocated him to the Headquarters Staff of General de Lattre de Tassigny. De Lattre was then in Naples, preparing the amphibious invasion of the South of France.

The French seaborne invasion took place on 15 August 1944—about nine weeks after the Normandy invasion. They landed from American assault craft supported by the American Navy and a few French warships. De Lattre had sent Pierre as his representative on the American flagship of the East Navy Force, USS *Augusta,* where he was accorded uniquely hospitable treatment.

When peace returned, Pierre served for two years in De Gaulle's *Service de Renseignements*—in this case, political and civil intelligence—and also in his

Service d'Ordre. Then he went into private business. Near his heart always was the desire to ride a horse again. He relearned how to mount and ride. On the ground he would always walk with a limp, tire quickly and require the assistance of a stick: seated on horseback with the weight of his body off his legs, he felt himself like a centaur, at one with his horse and tireless. He was totally at home on a polo pony. He could play better than most of his colleagues and better than many men much younger than himself.

Before General Bór Komorowski left Colditz with the other *Prominenten* in April 1945, he and four other generals on his staff composed a memorandum containing details of the Warsaw uprising and, in particular, the Allied intervention—or lack of it; it also apparently contained criticisms of some important Allied personalities. The memorandum was to be transmitted to the British Foreign Office at the earliest opportunity. It was given to Jack Pringle, who successfully concealed it in Colditz and in May or June 1945 delivered it to the Foreign Office for action at the appropriate level.

Recent research has failed to unearth this memorandum. It is known that in the Foreign Office section of the Public Record Office certain files have been withheld until the end of the century—not on grounds of national security, but because they might implicate or embarrass people still living today. I think that a document of this importance should be declassified now. While they are still living those who are implicated would at least have the chance to reply. They cannot defend themselves when they are dead.*

Rear Admiral Josef Unrug was liberated by the American Army in April 1945 and went immediately to London, where the Polish government in exile named him head of the Polish Naval Office. When the war ended he decided not to return to communist Poland. In spite of his age and distinguished career, he accepted a modest job in the French fishing industry and worked in that capacity in Agadir, Morocco, for a number of years. He spent his final years in France in a home for former superior officers of the Polish armed forces, and died there in 1973, aged eighty-nine.

Machiel van den Heuvel ("Vandy") returned to the East Indies when the war was over and was promoted to battalion commander. He played an important part in liberating 800 Chinese in West Java, but on 29 June 1946 he was killed

* Editors were not able to verify further updates to this information as of publication.

in action against Indonesian rebels. He was forty-six. For all his great work as escape officer of the loyal Dutch "Sixty-Eight" he deserves, in my opinion, some national recognition for his heroism and self-sacrifice. I hope the Dutch nation will always remember him.

After leaving Colditz, Jędrzej Giertych was imprisoned in five different camps. He made no less than thirty attempts to escape, in six of which he succeeded in regaining his freedom for a short time. While in captivity he also wrote four novels, which he managed to send to his wife in Poland; unfortunately they were destroyed in the firing of Warsaw. After liberation he went to London, where he rejoined the Navy. In the autumn of 1945 he volunteered to return to Poland as a courier of the Polish government in exile, travelling with a false identity, on a mission to make contact with the Polish underground. In Warsaw he was reunited with his wife and children and in December, once more using false papers, he successfully brought his family to London. After demobilization he had a variety of jobs, finally becoming a schoolteacher. He has written seventeen books on Polish politics and history, and three accounts of his life and adventures. As I write, he still lives in London and is now eighty-one years old.*

Airey Neave won French, American and Dutch awards for valor for his outstanding contribution to the Allied resistance during the war. When it ended he had the unique experience of serving the indictments on the surviving Nazi leaders for the Nuremberg trials. He later entered British politics, becoming a leading figure in the Conservative party during the 1970s and one of Margaret Thatcher's most influential advisers. On 30 March 1979 he was tragically killed by a car bomb as he drove out of the House of Commons' car park. Irish terrorists claimed responsibility for the assassination—the first in the parliamentary precincts since 1812.

Cenek Chaloupka returned to Czechoslovakia after the war and became a flying instructor with the Czech Air Force. Sadly, he was killed in a flying accident in 1946.

Unfortunately there has been little or no contact with the RAF Czechs since 1945 until very recently. One of them, Flight-Lieutenant Josef Bryks, who was shot down on 17 June 1941 and arrived in Colditz on 7 November 1944, returned

* Giertych died in 1992, age eighty-nine.

to Czechoslovakia after the war. After the *coup d'état* in February 1948 he was dismissed from his command at Olomouc on 30 April of that year and was arrested by the Communists the following day. He was tortured, jailed and finally condemned to death. This was later changed to a life sentence, and he was sent to the notorious uranium mines at Jachymov in Bohemia. He died there, allegedly of heart failure.

Soon after the war he was awarded the MBE. He was not even allowed to come to Buckingham Palace to receive it.

Bush Parker, who joined No. 56 Operational Training Unit at Millfield, Northumbria, when the war was over, also lost his life when a plane he was piloting crashed on 29 January 1946. He was twenty-six years old.

After the war Solly Goldman emigrated to the USA. There he built up a retail business in Los Angeles, which was burnt down in the Watts riot of 1965. A bayonet wound in the stomach which he had received during the war never healed properly and in 1972 he died of its long-term effects. His unquenchable humor and spirit will never be forgotten by those who knew him in Colditz.

Florimund Duke has the following tailpiece to add to his Mission Sparrow adventure. A Hungarian officer called at American headquarters in Budapest one day in the summer of 1945. He returned safely the gold *Louis d'Or* entrusted by Duke to Major Kiraly. They were worth $6,000. The officer did not give his name and declined a receipt.

Reinhold Eggers returned to Halle when the war was over. This now lay in the Russian zone of Germany but, as Eggers could prove that he had never joined Hitler's party, he was able to re-enter his former profession of teaching, immediately becoming a headmaster and soon after a lecturer at Halle university. In September 1946, however, he was arrested by the Russians and questioned about Gestapo agents at Colditz. Charged with crimes against humanity, spying and supporting a fascist regime, he was sentenced to ten years' labor, which he served in Sachsenhausen concentration camp and Torgau prison. After his release he retired to live near Lake Constance and there he died in 1974, aged eighty-four.

The American Army relieved Colditz Castle on 16 April 1945. The Russian Army arrived in May and in due course the Americans retired to give Russia possession in accordance with the Yalta agreements.

There is now a commemorative plaque in black marble underneath the archway separating the outer and inner courtyards of the Castle. It reads:

> THIS CASTLE SERVED IN 1933–34 AS AN INTERNMENT CAMP. HERE STARTED FOR MANY INFLEXIBLE ANTIFASCISTS THE PAINFUL JOURNEY THROUGH THE CONCENTRATION CAMPS. THEY FOUGHT SO THAT WE MAY LIVE.

The deafening silence concerning the war years 1939–1945 betrays the cynicism of the Iron Curtain countries towards the free world.

Editor's Note: Pat Reid was awarded the Military Cross in 1943 and the MBE in 1945. His experiences at Colditz served as the basis for a film (1955) as well as a television series (1972 to 1974). He died in 1990 at the age of seventy-nine.

APPENDIX 1

Colditz Prisoners and Staff

THE BRITISH CONTINGENT

	Rank	Regiment	Date of Capture	Arrived Colditz	Left Colditz
Abbott, G. W.	Lieut	General List	13.2.42	8.1.44	
Aitken, A. H.	Captain	NZEF	28.11.41	2.11.43 13.1.44	22.11.43 22.3.44
Alexander, M.	Lieut	DCLI	18.8.42	11.1.43	
Allan, A. M.	Lieut	Cameron Highlanders	10.6.40	7.11.40	
Allen, G. R.	L/Cpl	RUR	4.6.40	16.4.43	11.5.44
Anderson, P. H.	Private	NZEF	26.5.41	18.8.43	3.4.44
Anderson, W. F.	Major	RE	30.5.40	11.7.41	
Archer, L. R.	Sapper	AEF	1.6.41	16.4.43	13.12.44
Armstrong, G. R.	Corporal	Calgary Tank Reg.	19.8.42	18.11.44	
Armstrong, R. B.	Lieut	DLI	27.5.40	10.8.41	
Arundell of Wardour, Lord J.	Captain	Wiltshires	23.5.40	26.6.43	18.4.44 (Repat. 6.9.44)
Ascott, F.	Private	RAMC	25.5.41	18.8.43	3.4.44
Bader, D.	W/Cdr	RAF	9.8.41	16.8.42	
Bampfylde, A. G. H.	Lieut	Rifle Brigade	26.5.40	14.7.43	
Barnes, R. D.	Lieut	RNR	6.7.40	12.11.42	
Barnet, R.	Lieut	RN	20.6.42	12.11.42	26.7.44

	Rank	Regiment	Date of Capture	Arrived Colditz	Left Colditz
Barnett, J. M.	Lieut	RE	22.5.40	4.8.41	26.7.44 (Repat. 6.9.44)
Barrott, T. M.	Lieut	Canadian Black Watch	19.8.42	26.6.43	
Barry, R. R. F. T.	Captain	Ox. & Bucks	28.5.40	7.11.40	
Bartlett, D. E.	Lieut	RTR	29.9.41	23.6.43	
Barton, H. E. E.	Lieut	RASC	20.5.40	2.12.40	
Batelka, K.	W/O	RAF (Czech Squadron)	17.1.42	22.9.44	
Baxter, R. R.	Captain	AEF	26.5.41	23.6.43	
Beattie, D.	Private	Seaforths	21.5.40	3.8.43	
Beaumont, J. W.	Lieut	DLI	26.5.40	30.6.43	
Beet, T. A.	Lieut	RN	5.5.40	12.11.42	
Best, J. W.	F/Lieut	RAF	5.5.41	9.9.42	("Ghost" 5.4.43–28.3.44)
Bissell, J. D.	Lieut	RA	28.5.40	17.6.41	
Bissett, A. J. R.	Lieut	Seaforths	12.6.40	21.6.43	
Bobart, C. H.	Private	East Surreys	3.3.41	18.8.43	3.4.44
Bolding, G.	Lieut	AEF	1.6.41	21.6.43	
Boustead, J. R.	Lieut	Seaforths	12.6.40	19.6.41	
Bown, C. J.	Private	RE	1.6.40	2.6.43	13.12.44
Broomhall, W. M.	Lt/Col	RE	8.6.40	14.7.43	
Brown, C. J.	Sapper	RE		2.6.43	
Brown, F. M.	Private	AEF	30.5.41	27.6.43	12.12.44
Brown, J.	Private	Royal Scots	27.5.40	3.8.43	
Bruce, D.	F/Lieut	RAF	9.6.41	16.3.42	
Bruce, H. G.	Lieut	Royal Marines	5.40	1.9.42	
Bryks, J.	F/Lieut	RAF (Czech Squadron)	17.6.41	7.11.44	
Buck, F.	Private	KOR	25.5.40	16.4.43	26.7.44
Bufka, W. E.	W/O	RAF (Czech Squadron)	24.6.41	10.10.44	
Bull	Lt/Col	RAMC		3.9.42	28.4.43

	Rank	Regiment	Date of Capture	Arrived Colditz	Left Colditz
Bullard, H.	Bandsman	Buffs	15.12.41	18.8.43	
Burda, F.	F/Lieut	RAF (Czech Squadron)	27.2.43	10.9.44	
Burdeyron, N.	Lieut	General List	7.5.42	8.1.44	
Burn, M.	Captain	KRR	28.3.42	9.8.43	
Burton, W. J.	Captain	Yorks & Lancs	1.4.41	21.6.43	
Busina, E.	F/Lieut	RAF (Czech Squadron)	6.2.41	10.9.44	
Campbell, A. R.	Lieut	RA	22.5.40	19.6.41 17.6.43	16.3.43
Campbell, V. D. G.	Major	Cameron Highlanders	12.6.40	26.5.42	
Campbell-Preston, G. P.	Captain	Black Watch	12.6.40	26.6.43	
Catlow, T.N.	Lieut	RN	17.2.42	12.11.42	
Cerney, O.	F/Lieut	RAF (Czech Squadron)	19.7.41	26.10.44	
Chaloupka, C.	F/Lieut	RAF	10.10.41	22.1.43	
Champ, J. W. K.	Lieut	AEF	9.5.41	23.6.43	
Champion, E.	Lieut (E)	RNR	9.6.40	1.9.42	
Champion-Jones, M.	Major	RE	26.5.40	1.8.41 17.6.43	16.3.43
Chandler, R. J.	Private	Sussex	28.10.42	28.11.44	
Cheetham, A.	Lieut (A)	RN	29.9.40	16.4.41	
Chesshire, J. H. C.	Major	RE	8.1.44	30.7.44	
Cholmondeley, A. P.	Major	Glosters	31.5.40	14.7.43	
Christie, H. L.	Captain	Gordon Highlanders	12.6.40	23.6.43	
Cigos, F.	F/Lieut	RAF (Czech Squadron)	6.2.41	22.9.44	
Clark, T.	Private	Seaforths	12.6.40	3.8.43	12.12.44
Cleeve, D. W. A.	Major	RE	26.5.40	1.8.41 17.6.43	16.3.43
Clutton, R. W.	Private	Welch Regt	27.5.41	28.11.44	

	Rank	Regiment	Date of Capture	Arrived Colditz	Left Colditz
Cocksedge, A. R. A.	Lieut	lnniskillings	30.5.40	26.6.43	
Collett, H. B.	Lieut	Yorkshire Hussars	30.5.41	21.6.43	
Colt, R. D.	Lieut	Tyneside Scottish	20.5.40	8.8.41	
Cook, C. D.	Private	Royal West Kents	31.5.40	16.4.43	13.12..44
Cooper, E. H.	Captain	Royal Dental Corps	1.6.41	20.10.43	
Cooper, N. A.	Private	DLI	20.5.40	2.5.43	11.12.44
Courtenay, J. M.	Lieut	KRRG	26.5.40	21.6.43	
Cornwall, J. L.	Sergeant	5th African Artillery	19.1.44	28.11.44	
Coughlin, J. A.	Private	Sussex Regt	28.10.42	28.11.44	
Courtice, G. W. A.	Captain	Royal Marines	5.40	1.9.42	
Cowen, R.	Private	KRRC	1.6.41	4.8.43	
Crawford, A. D.	Captain	AIF	12.4.41	26.6.43	7.1.45
Crawford, J. A.	Lieut	Cameron Highlanders	13.6.40	27.10.42	
Crisp, J.	Bos'n	RN	1.6.41	1.9.42	
Crommelin, A. R.	Sergeant	NZEF	21.5.41	20.1.45	
Crook, E. A.	Corporal	Royal Marines	1.6.41	27.6.43	
Crowther, R.	Private	Welch Regt	28.5.41	28.11.44	
Crump, E.	L/Cpl	Sussex Regt	28.10.42	30.11.44	
Davies, C.	Private	Welch Regt	27.5.41	30.11.44	
Davies, E. F.	Brig.	RUR	13.1.44	23.8.44	
Davies, J.	Lieut (A)	RN	30.6.40	16.4.41	
Davies-Scourfield, E. G. B.	Lieut	60th Rifles	26.5.40	12.3.42	
Davis, H.	Gunner	RA	1.6.41	18.11.44	
Dickinson, J. P.	F/Lieut	RAF	7.11.41	5.5.42	
Dickie, H.	Captain	RAMC	12.6.40	13.8.43	
Dieppe, C. I. C.	Lieut	AIF	30.5.41	21.6.43	
Docherty	Private			11.40	
Dollar, P. W.	Major	4th Hussars	9.5.41	14.1.43	

	Rank	Regiment	Date of Capture	Arrived Colditz	Left Colditz
Donaldson, M. W.	F/Lieut	RAF	10.4.40	16.4.41	
Dorsett, J. W.	Private	Sussex Regt	28.10.42	30.11.44	
Doyle, R. E.	Rifleman	Rifle Brigade	26.5.40	3.8.43	13.12.44
Draffin, D. A.	Captain	RAMC	27.5.40	18.8.43	1.9.44
Drew, G. S.	Lieut	N'hamptonshires	28.5.40	30.6.43	
Dvorak, B.	F/Lieut	RAF (Czech Squadron)	3.6.42	9.1.45	
Van Dyken, J.	F/O	RAF	14.3.45	8.4.45	
Edwards, F. M.	Lieut	Welch Fus	28.5.40	21.6.43	
Elliott, H. A. V.	Captain	Irish Guards	5.40	7.11.40	26.7.44
Elliott, T. H.	Lieut	N'umberland Fus	12.6.40	2.12.40	
Elms-Neale, S. C.	Lieut	RA	28.5.40	30.6.43	
Elphinstone, The Master of, J.	Captain	Black Watch	12.6.40	10.11.44	13.4.45
Elson, C. A.	Lieut	Norfolks	25.5.40	21.6.43	
Elstob, W.	Lieut	RN	3.9.40	1.9.42	
Elwell, C. J. L.	Lieut	RNVR	12.3.42	1.9.42	
Ennis, W.	Sergeant	Irish Guards	19.1.44	28.11.44	
Ewart, W. I. C.	Lieut	RNVR	17.1.42	13.1.43	
Falcon, A.	Sgt/Chef	Giraudist		1.10.43	
Farr, M.	Lieut	DLI	27.5.40	30.6.43	
Fautley, S.	F/O	RAF	23.10.43	14.3.45	8.4.45
Fawcus, J.	Captain	N'umberland Fus	12.6.40	21.6.43	18.4.44 (Repat. 6.9.44)
Fellowes, D.	Lieut	Rifle Brigade	26.5.40	21.6.43	
Ferguson, I.	Surgn Capt	RAMC	28.4.41	8.8.42	28.4.43
Fergusson, J. D.	Lieut	RTR	13.6.40	30.6.43	
Fleet, L.	Private	N'hamptonshires	24.5.40	16.4.43	11.12.44
Flynn, F. D.	F/Lieut	RAF	4.9.40	16.4.41	2.6.44 (Repat. 6.9.44)
Forbes, N.	F/Lieut	RAF	27.5.40	14.5.41	

	Rank	Regiment	Date of Capture	Arrived Colditz	Left Colditz
Fowler, H. N.	F/Lieut	RAF			9.9.42
Freeman, V. P.	Sergeant	NZEF	23.5.41	20.1.45	
Gee, H.	Mr	Civilian	40 23.1.42	12.40 23.1.42	2.41
German, G.	Lt/Col	Leicesters	27.4.40	11.40 17.6.43	21.1.42
Gill, D.	Lieut	Norfolks	25.5.40	8.8.41	12.5.44
Gilliat, M. J.	Captain	KRRC	26.5.40	21.6.43	
Ginn, B. D. S.	Major	REME	13.6.40	20.6.43	
Goldman, S.	Private		40	11.40	21.1.42
Goldfinch, L. J. E.	F/Lieut	RAF	28.4.41	9.9.42	
Gollan	Sergeant			4.7.42	14.7.42
Goodwin, H.	Lieut	AIF	1.6.41	13.1.45	
Gray, P. J.	Corporal	RA	9. 1.44 2	8.11.44	
Greaves, G.	Surgn/Cdr	RN	21.1.41	30.11.44	
Green, J.	Captain	Dental Corps	12.6.40	19.2.44	
Green, R. S.	L/Cpl	RE	29.5.40	16.4.43	11.2.44
Greenwell, G. L.	Corporal	Calgary Tank Regt	19.8.42	18.11.44	
Greenwell, Sir P. M.	Captain	Surrey & Sussex Yeo.	23.5.40	14.7.43	
Hacohen, S.	Lieut	RE	29.4.41	25.8.44	
Hagerty, W. R.	Sergeant	Welch	27.5.42	30.11.44	
Haig, Earl, G. D.	Captain	Scots Greys	20.7.42	12.11.44	13.4.45
Hallifax, N. D.	F/Lieut	RAF	15.5.40	14.11.42	7.1.45
Halpin	Rifleman			9.10.43	29.11.43
De Hamel, F. M.	Lieut	RTR	22.5.40	10.11.44	13.4.45
Hamilton, D. K.	Lieut	RA	25.5.41	26.6.43	
Hamilton, G.	Private	RHA	25.5.41	30.11.44	
Hamilton, H.	Private	RASC	12.6.40	3.8.43	13.12.44
Hamilton-Baillie, J. R. E.	Lieut	RE	12.6.40	21.6.43	
Hammond, W.	ERA	RN	6.7.40	1.9.42	27.10.42

	Rank	Regiment	Date of Capture	Arrived Colditz	Left Colditz
Hannay, E. A.	Lieut	Seaforths	12.6.40	2.7.43	19.7.44
Harbinson, W. J.	Corporal	Welch		30.11.44	
Hargreaves, E. C. S.	Captain	8th KRI Hussars	3.12.43	29.6.44	
Harris, J. J.	Private	Welch	27.5.42	28.11.44	
Harrison, E. G. P.	Lieut	Green Howards	28.4.40	8.8.41	
Harvey, E. M.	Lieut	RN	7.1.40	5.11.42	("Ghost" 5.11.43–28.3.44)
Hawksworth, H.	Captain	RE	2.3.44	23.8.44	
Heap, R. A. F.	Lt/Cdr	RN	22.5.41	12.5.43	
Heard, R.	Captain	Chaplain's Dept	27.5.40	12.12.40	
Heath, J.	Private	Welch	6.6.41	30.11.44	
Henderson, W. R.	Major	RAMC		17.10.43 3.6.44	18.2.44 7.8.44
Hendren	Corporal	RAMC		19.4.42	14.9.42
Henley, H. E.	Private	AIF	1.6.41	3.8.43	
Hermon, K. E.	Captain	DLI	2.6.41	30.6.43	
Hill, G.	F/Lieut	RAF	4.2.41	18.8.43	
Hobling, J. C.	Captain	Chaplain's Dept	5.40	2.12.40	21.1.42
Hoggard, J. W.	Lieut	RNR	4.4.41	1.9.42	
Holroyd, R.	Lieut	AIF	15.4.41	1.5.42	
Hopetoun, Earl of, C.	Captain	Lothian & Border Horse	12.6.40	24.6.43	13.4.45
How, G. M. P.	Captain	RASC	30.5.40	19.6.41	
Howard, M. A.	Lieut	AIF	26.5.41	23.6.40	
Howe, R. H.	Captain	RTR	27.5.40	7.11.40	
Huart, J. T.	Lieut	General List	25.4.42	8.1.44	
Huelin, J. L. R.	Captain	Wiltshires	23.5.40	30.9.44	
Hull, V. A.	Driver	RASC	3.7.40	16.4.43	12.12.44
Hunt, T.	Private	Sussex	28.10.42	30.11.44	
Hunter, D. L.	Lieut	Royal Marines	5.40	1.9.42	
Hutt, C. A.	Captain	RAMC	7.6.41	5.1.44	4.8.44 (Repat. 6.9.44)

	Rank	Regiment	Date of Capture	Arrived Colditz	Left Colditz
Hyde-Thompson, J.	Lieut	DLI	15.5.40	16.4.41	
Ironside, H. C. W.	Lieut	RTR	26.5.40	21.6.43	
James, A. M.	Private	Welch	27.5.41	28.11.44	
Jeffries, I.	Captain	RAC	23.12.43	29.6.44	
Jeffries, V.	Private	AEF	27.4.41	28.5.43	
Johnson, J.	L/Cpl	DLI	1.6.41	27.6.43	12.12.44
Johnson	ERA	RN	5.5.40	1.9.42	27.10.42
Jones, L. A.	Private	RMRE	30.5.40	16.4.43	
Jones, M. G.	Private	Welch	28.5.41	28.11.44	
Jones, R. E.	Lieut	Malta Sea Defence	23.2.43	19.4.44	
Keats, C. R.	S/Lieut	RNVR	17.7.41	1.9.42	3.4.45
Keillar, T. M.	Lieut	RE	23.5.40	1.8.41	
Keenlyside, C. H.	Captain	RWK	22.5.40	21.6.43	
Killey, J.	Private	QRR	25.10.42	28.11.44	
Kimber, T.	Major	RE	9.6.40	1.8.41 17.6.43	16.3.43
Lace, J.	Lieut	DLI	27.5.40	8.8.41 17.6.43	16.3.43
Lascelles, Viscount, G. H. H.	Lieut	Grenadier Guards	19.6.44	12.11.44	13.4.45
Lawton, W. T.	Captain	Duke of Wellington's	12.6.40	8.8.41	
Le Cornu, D. F.	Sapper	RE	1.7.40	16.4.43	12.12.44
Le Grys, L. A.	Rifleman	1st QVR	26.5.40	27.6.43	13.12.44
Lee, D. W. G.	Major	General List	17.11.43	20.8.44	
Lee, J. K. V.	Lieut	Royal Corps Signals	12.6.40	8.8.41	
Leah, R. W.	Captain	Cameron Highlanders	28.5.40	2.6.43	
Lewthwaite, C. D.	Captain	Warwickshires	27.5.40	18.5.41	
Lister	ERA	RN	5.5.40	1.9.42	27.10.42
Littledale, R. B.	Major	KRRC		15.7.42	14.10.42
Lochrane, F. H. J.	Lieut	Seaforths	12.6.40	21.6.43	

	Rank	Regiment	Date of Capture	Arrived Colditz	Left Colditz
Lockett, C. E. S.	Sqdn/Ldr	RAF	15.5.40	8.10.41	
Lockwood, K.	Captain	Queen's RR	21.5.40	7.11.40	
Longley, W. C. O.	Private	RAMC	27.4.41	18.8.43	
Lorraine, R. C.	Major	RE	2.6.41	14.4.44	
Macaskie, I. B.	Lieut	RWK	11.6.40	23.6.43	
Mackenzie, C. D.	Lieut	Seaforths	13.6.40	10.7.41	
Mackenzie	Private		40	12.40	
McCall, A. L.	Lieut	Cameron Highlanders	28.5.40	23.6.43	
McColm, M. L.	Sqdn/Ldr	RAF	27.12.40	8.10.41	
McCulloch, G. S.	Captain	Black Watch	28.5.41	23.10.43	
McDonnell, J. A. G.	Lieut	Norfolks	12.6.40	12.5.44	
McIntosh, L.	Private	Seaforths	12.6.40	16.4.43	13.12.44
McLaren, P.	Lieut	Argyll & Sutherland	5.7.40	21.6.44	
McLean, B.	Private	25th Maori Btn	25.5.41	18.11.44	13.4.45
Marchand, A. R.	Lieut	Fusiliers Mont Royal	19.8.42	28.6.43	
Marshall, H. S.	Private	Sussex	28.10.42	30.11.44	
Martin, S. N.	Lieut	RASC	1.6.41	21.6.43	
Matthews	Major	RAMC		19.4.42	28.7.42
Mazumdar, B. N.	Captain	RAMC	22.8.41		22.2.43
Mellor, J. T. P.	Lieut	Argyll & Sutherland	8.6.40	23.6.43	
Merritt, C. C. I.	Lt/Col	South Saskatchewan	19.8.42	27.6.43	
Middleton, D.	F/Lieut	RAF	5.11.40	16.3.43	
Millar, W. A.	Lieut	R. Canadian Engineers	19.8.42	21.6.43	28.1.44
Miller, N. G.	S/Lieut (E)	RN	4.4.41	1.9.42	
Millett, J. R.	Lieut	AIF	30.5.41	30.6.43	

	Rank	Regiment	Date of Capture	Arrived Colditz	Left Colditz
Milne, R. A.	Major	RE	12.6.40	1.8.41 17.6.43	16.3.43
Milne, T. K.	F/Lieut	RAF	23.4.40	5.11.40	
Mitai, R. M.	Driver	25th Maori Btn	28.5.41	18.11.44	13.4.45
Moir, D. N.	Lieut	RTR	28.5.40	30.6.43	
Moody, R. F.	Captain	NZEF	26.5.41	18.9.43	19.1.45
Moore	Major	RAMC		19.4.42	28.7.42
Moran, J. M.	Paymaster Lieut	RN	17.7.41	1.9.42	
Morgan, R. J.	Lieut	Commandos	17.6.43	19.6.43	
Morison, W. M.	F/Lieut	RAF	6.6.42	18.8.43	
Morrison, B. A.	Corporal	NZEF	28.5.41	20.1.45	
Munn	Private		40	12.40	
Neal, G.	Private	QRR	30.9.42	30.11.44	
Neave, A. M. S.	Lieut	RA	24.5.40	14.5.41	5.1.42
Nicholas, W. J.	Guards-man	Welsh Guards		3.2.43	23.3.43
Novotny, E.	W/O	RAF (Czech Squadron)	16.10.40	10.10.44	
Nugent, D. M.	Rifleman	KRRC	26.5.40	24.6.43	
O'Hara, W. L. B.	Lieut	RTR	21.5.40	19.6.41	
Olver	Captain		40	1.8.41	Died End August 1943
Orr-Ewing, A. L.	Lieut	Argyll & Sutherland	5.6.40	8.7.41	
Owens, W. J.	Gunner	RA	1.6.41	18.11.44	
Paddon, B.	Sqdn/Ldr	RAF	14.5.41	11.6.42	
Pardoe, P.	Lieut	KRRC	26.5.40	21.6.43	
Parker, P. H.	Lieut	KRRC	26.5.40	27.6.43	
Parker, V.	F/Lieut	RAF	15.8.40	5.5.42	
Patterson, C. C.	Private	AIF	28.4.41	16.4.43	2.10.44
Penman, J. R.	Lieut	Argyll & Sutherland	28.5.40	21.6.43	

	Rank	Regiment	Date of Capture	Arrived Colditz	Left Colditz
Perry	Staff/Sgt	RTR		21.6.43	10.9.43
Peters, W.	Private	Welch	27.5.41	28.11.44	
Platt, J. E.	Captain	Chaplain's Dept	30.5.40	2.12.40	
Playoust	Captain	AEFMC		19.4.42	28.7.42
Pope, A. L.	Captain	Royal Fus	28.5.40	14.7.43	
Potochnik, J.	Lieut	British Legation Niss	25.2.44	23.8.44	
Price, I. S.	Lieut	Gordon Highlanders	12.6.40	8.8.41	
Pringle, J.	Major	8th Hussars	28.11.41	20.8.44	
Prochazka, Z.	W/O	RAF (Czech Squadron)	20.10.41	22.9.44	
Pumphrey, J. L.	Lieut	Northumberland Fus	1.6.41	21.6.43	
Purdon, C. W. B.	Lieut	RUR	28.3.42	17.6.43	
Du Puy, J. A.	Lieut	General List	13.5.42	8.1.44	
Ransome, G. F.	Lieut	RASC	24.5.40	27.4.41 17.6.43	16.3.43
Rash, E. D.	Lt/Col	RTR	15.7.43	25.7.43	
Rawson, J.	Lieut	AIF	1.6.41	2.10.43	
Ray, P. M.	Private	AIF	30.10.42	28.11.44	
Redding, C.	Lieut	General List	13.2.42	8.1.44	
Reid, M. B.	Major	GHQ Liaison	26.4.41	22.9.43	7.1.45
Reid, P. R.	Captain	RASC	27.5.40	7.11.40	14.10.42
Riviere, M. V. B.	Lieut	Notts Yeo.	1.6.41	27.6.43	
Robinson, E. L.	Sergeant	Royal Corps Signals	19.1.44	28.11.44	
Rogers, D. J.	Captain	RE	22.5.40 17.6.43	1.8.41	16.3.43
Rolfe, G. M.	Major	Royal Canadian Signals	19.8.42	27.6.43	
Rolt, A.	Lieut	Rifle Brigade	26.5.40	14.7.43	
Romilly, G.	Mr	Civilian	9.4.40	26.10.41	

	Rank	Regiment	Date of Capture	Arrived Colditz	Left Colditz
Van Rood, A.	F/Lieut	RAF	12.4.42	6.10.42	
Ross, A.	Bandsman	Seaforths	11.6.40	16.8.42	
Routledge	Lieut			15.10.41	19.3.43
Roy, J. H.	Lieut	Fusiliers Mont Royal	19.8.42	28.6.43	
Sandbach, C. E.	Lieut	Cheshire	1.6.41	27.6.43	
Scarborough, C. P	Captain	Chaplain's Dept	28.5.40	2.12.43	
Schire, I.	Captain	RAMC	1.6.40	27.10.44	
Scott, M.	Lieut	DLI	5.40	27.6.43	
Scott, W. H.	Lieut	Essex Scottish (Canadian)	19.8.42	21.6.43	
Shenton	Sergeant	Staffordshire Yeo.	2.3.44	28.11.44	
Silverwood-Cope, C. L.	Lieut	RA	28.5.40	3.11.42	
Sinclair, A. M.	Lieut	KRRC	26.5.40	15.1.42	25.9.44
Siska, A.	W/O	RAF (Czech Squadron)	28.12.41	22.9.44	
Skelton, G.	F/Lieut	SAAF	12.5.41	18.8.42	
Smith, J.	Private		40	12.40	
Smith, S. F.	Private	Sussex	28.10.42	30.11.44	
Smith, W. E.	Corporal	Cheshire	29.5.40	27.6.43	
Snook, R. J. E.	Major	RA	28.5.41	14.4.44	
Southgate, W.	L/Cpl	Sussex	28.10.42	30.11.44	
Stallard, T.	Major	DLI	27.5.40	17.6.43	
Stayner, D. J.	Lt/Col	Dorset & 1/8th Lancs Fus	27.5.40	12.7.41	
Steele, D. R.	Sergeant	2nd Commando	28.3.42	1.9.42	9.11.42
Stephens, W. L.	Lt/Cdr	RNVR	28.3.42	3.9.42	14.10.42
Stephenson, G. D.	S/Leader	RAF	2.6.40	1.9.41	
Stevenson, F.	Private	RE	28.5.40	27.6.43	12.12.44
Stevenson, O. S.	Lt/Cdr	Fleet Air Arm	9.10.40	14.5.41	
Stirling, A. D.	Lt/Col	Scots Guards	28.1.43	20.8.44	

	Rank	Regiment	Date of Capture	Arrived Colditz	Left Colditz
Storey, A. E.	Private	Sussex	28.10.42	30.11.44	
Storie-Pugh, P. D.	Lieut	RWK	20.5.40	2.12.40	
Susa, J.	W/O	RAF (Czech Squadron)	20.10.41	27.10.44	
Sutcliff, G. A.	Private	Sussex	28.10.42	30.11.44	
Sutherland, K. H.	Lieut	Black Watch	4.6.40	17.12.42	
Sutherland-Sherriff, G. A.	Lieut	East Yorks	9.6.40	14.7.43	
Thom, D.	F/Lieut	RAF		16.4.41	21.6.43
Thompson, P.	Gunner	RA	1.6.41	18.11.44	
Tod, W.	Lt/Col	Royal Scots Fus	28.5.40	18.11.43	
Tonder, I. P.	F/Lieut	RAF (Czech Squadron)	3.6.42	9.1.45	
Trayhorn, F.	Lieut	RE	25.12.43	29.6.44	
Trojacek, K.	F/Lieut	RAF (Czech Squadron)	25.9.40	9.1.45	
Truhlar, J.	F/Lieut	RAF (Czech Squadron)	9.7.41	22.9.44	
Tunstall, P.	F/Lieut	RAF	28.8.40	16.3.42	
Tweedie, J. A.	Captain	Cameron Highlanders	6.6.40	26.6.43	
Upham, C. H.	Captain (VC and Bar)	NZEF	15.7.42	14.10.44	
Uruba, P.	W/O	RAF (Czech Squadron)	7.2.41	10.9.44	
Vallis, T. H.	Sergeant	NZEF	20.5.41	20.1.45	
Vandelac, A. G.	Captain	Fusiliers Mont Royal	19.8.42	28.6.43	
Vercoe, V.	Captain	Royal Fus	23.3.44	23.8.44	7.1.45
Vesely, E.	F/Lieut	RAF (Czech Squadron)	21.10.41	15.9.44	
Vitou, M.	Lieut	RA	27.5.41	31.7.43	
Vizard, D. J.	L/Cpl	Welch	27.5.41	28.11.44	
De Vomécourt, P.	Captain	General List	25.4.42	8.1.44	

	Rank	Regiment	Date of Capture	Arrived Colditz	Left Colditz
Walker, B. S.	Lieut	DLI	30.5.40	16.6.44	
Walker, D. H.	Captain	Black Watch	12.6.40	26.6.43	
Walker, E. H.	Private	AIF	1.6.41	3.8.43	13.12.44
Wallace	Private		40	40	
Walsh, J.	Brigadier	52 LAR RA	20.5.41	30.11.44	
Ward, E. A.	Gunner	RA	1.6.41	27.6.43	13.12.44
Wardle, G.	Lieut	RN	9.1.40	2.12.40	
Wardle, H. D.	F/Lieut	RAF	20.4.40	5.11.40	14.10.42
Watt, D. N.	Captain	RTR	9.1.44	23.8.44	
Watton, J. F.	Lieut	Border	14.6.40	8.8.41 17.6.43	16.3.43
Welch, P. D. L.	F/Lieut	RAF	1.8.42	18.8.43	
Weldon, F. W. C.	Captain	RHA	12.6.40	2.7.43	
Weld-Forester, C. R.	Lieut	Rifle Brigade	26.5.40	26.6.43	
Wheeler, D. E.	Lieut	RN	7.7.40	1.9.42	
Whittingham, E. A. G.	Private	East Surrey	12.6.40	27.6.43	
Wicker, G. E.	L/Cpl	Welch	27.5.41	30.11.44	
Wilkins, J.	L/Tel	RN	9.1.40	11.40	42
Williams, H. E.	L/Cpl	Welch	26.5.41	30.11.44	
Wilson, J. C.	F/Lieut	RAF	27.1.43	22.1.43	
Winton, P. C.	Lieut	Gordon Highlanders	12.6.40	3.2.43	
Wittet, M. G.	Lieut	Royal Scots	8.6.40	23.6.43	
Wood, A. S. W.	Major	RE	23.5.40	1.8.41 17.6.43	16.3.43 26.4.44
Wood, J. E. R.	Lieut	RCE	19.8.42	26.6.43	
Wotherspoon, J.	Fusilier	Lancs Fus	27.5.40	16.4.43	
Wright, S. C.	Captain	Queen's Royal Lancers	8.6.40	21.6.43	
Wylie, C. St. A.	Captain	RE	29.4.41	1.4.44	
Wylie, K. N.	Major	RE	1.6.41	14.4.44	26.4.44

	Rank	Regiment	Date of Capture	Arrived Colditz	Left Colditz
Wynn, M. V.	Lieut	RNVR	28.3.42	13.1.43	2.1.45 (Repat. 10.1.45)
Young, G.	Lt/Col	RE	1.6.41	15.10.41	
Yule, J. de D.	Captain	Royal Corps Signals	1.5.40	8.8.41 17.6.43	16.3.43
Zafouk, J.	F/Lieut	RAF (Czech Squadron)		17.7.41	19.6.42

THE NORWEGIAN COMMANDOS

All captured 22.9.42; arrived Colditz 7.10.42; left 13.10.42; all shot by Germans 23.10.42

	Rank	Regiment
Abram, C.	Rifleman	Rifle Brigade
Black, G.	Captain	Lorne Scots (Canada) Queen's York Rangers (Canada) South Lancashires
Chudley, W.	L/Sgt	RA
Curtis, E.	Private	RWK
Houghton, J.	Captain	Queen's Own Cameron Highlanders (Liverpool Scottish)
Makeham, R.	Private	London Scottish
Smith, M.	CSM	Coldstream Guards

THE TRAITOR

	Rank	Regiment	Date of Capture	Date Arrived	Left Colditz
Purdy, W.	S/Lieut	RNR	9.6.40	8.3.44	11.3.44 (Left for Berlin 5.6.44)

THE POLISH CONTINGENT

	Rank
Adamowicz, M.	Lt/Commander (Navy)
Augusiak, C.	2/Lieut
Bagiński, M.	Captain
Bankiewicz, E.	Captain
Baran, S.	2/Lieut
Baranowski, W.	Major
* Bartoszewicz, S.	2/Lieut
Baumgart, F.	2/Lieut
Bentkowski, S.	2/Lieut
Bialy, L.	2/Lieut
* Biega, J.	Major
Bigo, J.	Colonel
Bobrzyk, W.	Lieut
Borejsza, J.	Colonel
Bratkowski, J.	Captain
Burian, L.	Captain
Busel, J.	2/Lieut
† Chmiel, M.	2/Lieut
Chmielewski, J.	2/Lieut
Czerwionko, Z.	2/Lieut
Danciewicz, Z.	Lieut
Davidowski, D.	Captain
Dębowski, Z.	2/Lieut
Dec	Major
Deryng, B.	2/Lieut
Dlużniewski, W.	Captain
* Dokurno, K.	Lieut
* Dománski, P.	Lieut
Drozdowski, F.	2/Lieut
Fajerman	Captain
Ficek, Z.	W/O (Navy)
Figura, J.	Lieut
* Flis, R.	Lieut
Gąssowski, W.	2/Lieut (Air Force)
Gebert, S.	2/Lieut
Gajsler	Colonel
Giertych, J.	Lieut (Navy)
Gintel, J.	Major
Gójski, M.	Lieut
Goluchowski	Lieut
Górecki, W.	2/Lieut (Air Force)
Górka, A.	Captain
Groblewski, J.	Lieut
* Grudziński, T.	Lieut
Hauptmann, F.	Captain
Hlebowicz, J.	Lieut
Jablonowski, F.	2/Lieut
Jakubiec, T.	Lieut
Jana, M.	Major
* Janic, K.	Captain
Janota	Lieut
Jasicki, T.	Lieut (Navy)
Jasiński, P.	Lieut
* Jedliczka, K.	Lieut
Just, J.	Lieut
Karpf, A.	Cadet
Kępa, Z.	Lieut
Kiciński, Z.	2/Lieut
Kielar, K.	Lieut

	Rank
Klimowicz, W.	Major
Klukowski, J.	2/Lieut
Konitz	Lieut
Kończak, H.	Lieut
Koreywo, L.	2/Lieut
Korzeniowski, W.	2/Lieut
Kostecki, J.	2/Lieut
† Kowalczewski, B.	Lt/Col
Kożniewski, S.	Captain
Krąkowski	Lieut
* Królikiewicz, S.	2/Lieut
Kroner	Lieut
* Krzyszkowski, Z.	2/Lieut
Krug-Smigla	Lt/Col
Kuhlman, A.	Captain
Kwiatek	Lt/Col
* Łączyński, W.	Major
Ladoś, J.	Captain
Lamek, C.	Captain
* Łempicki, S.	Lieut
Lepicki, W.	Lieut
Lewandowski, J.	Lieut
Lewszecki, J.	Lieut
Ligęza, A.	Captain
Likiernik, T.	Captain
Lipicki, S.	2/Lieut
Lipinski, A.	Lieut
* Losert, E.	Captain
Lukasik, M.	Lieut
Lukaszewski, F.	2/Lieut
* Maj, F.	2/Lieut

	Rank
Majewski, M.	Commander (Navy)
* Maresz, T.	Lieut
Markiewicz, M.	Major
Mikusiński, Z.	2/Lieut
Milczarek, J.	2/Lieut
Mozdyniewicz, M.	Colonel
Najda, A.	2/Lieut
* Napiórkowski, A.	Lieut
Niczko, M.	2/Lieut (Navy)
* Niedenthal, A.	2/Lieut
Nierzwicki, T.	2/Lieut
* Niestrzęba, J.	2/Lieut
* Nyk, K.	W/O (Navy)
Ombach	Lt/Col
Onyszkiewicz, A.	Lieut
† Osiecki, T.	2/Lieut
Osuchowski, M.	Captain
Otwinowski, S.	Lieut
Petecki, L.	Cadet
Pilch, T.	Lieut
Pinkowski	Lieut
Piotrowski, W.	Captain
Piskor, T.	General
* Pluciński, F.	2/Lieut
Pluciennik	Major
Ponewczyński, J.	2/Lieut
Popielarski, M.	2/Lieut
Postrach, J.	Captain-Chaplain
Poznański	Colonel
† Pronaszko, S.	Major

	Rank		Rank
Pszczółkowski, W.	Lieut	† Stokwisz, S.	2/Lieut
Pytkowski, A.	W/O	Suwala, J.	2/Lieut
Radzimiński, J.	2/Lieut	Surmanowicz, M.	Lieut
Rowiński, S.	2/Lieut (Navy)	* Szomański, Z.	Major
Rześniowiecki, J.	Captain	Szubert, E.	Lt/Col
Rubinowicz, J.	2/Lieut	Szuwalow, W.	Lt/Col
Rutkowski, S.	Lt/Col	Teska, L.	Lieut
Rydz, A.	Cadet	Trzaska-Durski, A.	Colonel
Sierkuczewski, S.	Lt/Cdr (Navy)	Trynkowski, W.	Lieut
Siefert	Lieut	Tucki, J.	2/Lieut
Silkowski, M.	Captain	Tyblewski, J.	Major
Skierkowski, R.	Lieut	Ujma, P.	2/Lieut
Slawiński, K.	2/Lieut (Air Force)	Ukleja, J.	Lieut
		Unrug, J.	Admiral
Ślipko, A.	2/Lieut	† Wasilewski	Captain
Smekczyński, Z.	Lieut	Wernic, L.	Major
Smokowski, M.	Captain	Wierzbowski, S.	Captain
Smolarski, W.	Colonel	Wilecki, R.	Lieut
Sobieraj, J.	Lieut	Wojciechowski, A.	Lieut
Solek, M.	Lieut	Wojciechowski, J.	2/Lieut
Soltysik, S.	Captain	Wychodcew, W.	2/Lieut
Stajer, B.	Lieut	Wyderko, K.	Lt/Col
Stasiak, A.	Major	Żebrowski, B.	Captain
Steblik, W.	Major	Żelaźniewicz, W.	Lieut
† Stec, J.	2/Lieut	* Zieliński, E.	2/Lieut
Stein, J.	2/Lieut (Navy)	Zieliński, P.	2/Lieut
Stępniak, J.	2/Lieut	Zimiński, W.	Lieut
Stiller, H.	2/Lieut	Żmudziński, J.	Captain

OTHER RANKS

	Rank		Rank
Baranowski, I.	Corporal	Mach, S.	Private
Dudka	Private	Pitsniak, P.	Sergeant Major
Flak, W.	Private	Przybycien, J.	Private
Judenko, H.	Private	Skorski, F.	Private
Kucharski, W.	Private	Sycz, W.	Private
Leszek, J.	Corporal	Taranowicz, W.	Private
Lewniczek, I.	Gunner	Urbaczewski, H.	Corporal
Lonis, J. Orderly	Medical	Zaczkiewicz, K.	Private
		† Zwijacz, J.	Corporal

* Killed by the bomb dropped on Dössel.

† Murdered in Buchenwald after the escape of 19 and 20 September 1943.

THE POLISH WARSAW CONTINGENT

	Rank		Rank
Bór Komorowski, T.	General	Hermel, L.	Lieut
Chrusciel, A.	General	Chorzewski, Z.	2/Lieut
Kossakowski, T.	General	Wojtowicz, J.	2/Lieut
Sawicki, K.	General	Makarewicz, J.	Corporal
Skroczynski, A.	General	Krynicki, Z.	L/Corporal
Pelczynski, T.	Lt/Gen	Matecki, J.	L/Corporal
Osmecki-Iranek, K.	Colonel	Putowski, L.	L/Corporal
Zdanowicz, T.	Lt/Col	Skrobanski, Z.	L/Corporal
Jankowski, S.	Captain	Wegner, C.	Private
Rubach-Potubinski, Z.	Captain	Woyzbun, P.	Private

THE DUTCH CONTINGENT

	Rank	Regiment
Van Ameijden	Lieut	KNIL
Duijm, H. E. C.		
Andringa, B.	Lieut	KNIL
Bajetto, H. C.	Lieut	KNIL
Beets, T.	Lieut	KNIL
Berlijn, A. P.	Captain	KNIL
Bijvoet, F. J.	Captain	KNIL
Boogh, W. K.	Captain	KNIL
Braun, M.	Lieut	KNIL
Claassen, F. M. F.	Lieut	KNIL
Daams, J. H.	Captain	KNIL
Dames, G. W. T.	Lieut	KNIL
Donkers, H. G.	Lieut	KNIL
Van Doorninck AZN, D. J.	Lieut	KM
Douw van der Krap, C. L. J. F.	Lieut	KM
Drijber, O. L.	Lieut	KNIL
Dufour, A. L. C.	Captain	KNIL
Elders, J. A. J.	Captain	KNIL
Van der Elst, L. R.	Captain	KNIL
Engles, E.	Major	KNIL
Eras, J. S. M.	Captain	KL
Feith, G.	Lieut	KM
Fraser, G. I-J. C.	Lieut	KM
Giebel, C.	Major	KNIL
Geerligs, F. V.	Cadet	KNIL
Grijzen, W. G. T.	Lieut	KNIL
Hageman, J. H.	Cadet	KNIL
Se Hartog, L.	Lieut	KNIL
Van der Heuvel, M.	Captain	KNIL
Hinrichs, L. E.	Lieut	KNIL

	Rank	Regiment
Hogerland, N.	Captain	KL
Van der Hoog, M. C.	Captain	KL
Van Hutten, D. C.	Lieut	KNIL
Kok	Sergeant	KNIL
Kruimink, F. E.	Lieut	KM
De Lange, W.	Stoker	KM
Van Langen, D. R. A.	Major	KNIL
Larive, E. H.	Lieut	KM
Ligtermoet, A. G. L.	Cadet	KNIL
Linck, C.	Cadet	KNIL
Van Lingen, O.	Lieut	KNIL
Luchsinger, K. J.	Captain	KNIL
Luteijn, A. P. T.	Lieut	KNIL
Van Lynden, Baron D. W.	Lieut	KM
Van Lynden, Baron J. J. L.	Lieut	KL
Ter Meulen, F. H.	Captain	KNIL
Mojet, J. J.	Captain	KNIL
Moquette, J. P.	Captain	KNIL
Van Nimwegen, G. A.	Captain	KNIL
Nouwens, A. L.	Captain	KNIL
Pereira, A. J . A.	Captain	KNIL
Pesch, E.	Captain	KNIL
Romswinckel, H. O.	Captain	KM
Romswinckel, W.	Captain	KNIL
Rooseboom, T.	Lt Colonel	KL
Schepers, J. D.	Captain	KL
Van der Schraaf, F. J.	Lieut	KNIL
Von Seydlitz Kurzbach, H. R.	Cadet	KNIL
Smit, J. G.	Lieut	KNIL
Spiering, W.	Lieut	KNIL
Steenhouwer, E.	Captain	KNIL

	Rank	Regiment
Steinmetz, F.	Lieut	KM
Van der Valk Bouwman, W. F.	Lieut	KM
Veenendaal, H. J.	Captain	KNIL
De Vries, L. T. W.	Captain	KNIL
Van Walraven, C. W. J.	Captain	KNIL
Welling, R.	Corporal	KL
Westra, S. H. L.	Lieut	KNIL
Willer, T.	Captain	KNIL
Witjens, C. J.	Lieut	KNIL

KM = Royal Netherlands Navy; KL = Royal Netherlands Army;
KNIL = Royal Netherlands Indies Army

THE FRENCH CONTINGENT

THE GENERALS

Rank	Date of Capture
Flavigny, General de CA	23.6.40
Daine, General de Bde	19.5.40
De Boisse, General de Bde	22.6.40
Buisson, General de Bde	18.6.40
Le Bleu, General	

OFFICERS

	Rank		Rank
Aigouy, É.	Lieut	Blum, R.	Captain
Allignol, J.	Lieut	Bolet, G.	
Almeras, A.		Bollack, R.	
Atroles, R. P.	Lieut	Bonté, M.	Lieut
Aubry, P.		Boudaud, A.	
Audibert, J. F.	Lieut	Boulé, E.	Lieut
Augst		Boscheron, G.	Lieut
Aulard, C.	Lieut	Boucheron, A.	Lieut
Auzon, R.		Bouillez, R.	Lieut
Avril, D.		Boutard, P.	Lieut
Bader, P.	Lieut	Boutellier, R.	Lieut (Navy)
Bardelli, R.	Lieut	Boverat, R.	Lieut
Barras, E.	Captain	Bozon, M.	Lieut
Beaulac, R.	Lieut	Bréjoux, J.	
Bechart, L.	Lieut	Bressanges, R.	
Benychou, J.		Le Brigant	Colonel
Bergmann, O.		Brisac	Lieut
Bertron, J.	Lieut	De Broca, H.	Lieut
Besson-Guyard, M.	Lieut	Brunet, B.	Lieut
Billet, J.	Lieut	Bugault, J. P.	

	Rank		Rank
De Bykowitz, N.	Lieut	Damidaux, J.	Colonel
Cagnard, A.	Lieut	Danielou, H.	
Cahen-Salvador, G.		Darrieux, L.	Captain
Caillaud, J.	Lieut	Darthenay, A.	Lieut
Cals, G.		Daubian-Delisle, E.	Lieut (Navy)
Calve, G.		Decaix, L.	Lieut
Carer, R.		De Cottignies, J.	
Carrion, G.		Dehen, R.	
Carteau, L.		Dehollain, H.	Lieut
Castel, J.		Delarue	Lieut
Cazabat	Commandant	Delas, J.	
Cazamayou, B.	Lieut	Deles, A.	
Cazou, J.		Desbats, E.	Lieut
Charvet, J.	Captain	Desjobert, H.	Lieut
Chastenet, M.	Lieut	Desmarcheliers, Y.	Lieut
Chaudrut, J.		Devernay, R.	
Chotard, A.		Diedler, G.	Lieut
Civet, G.	Lieut	Dreyfus	Captain
Clairfond, A.		Drouillet, L.	
Coelenbier, P.	Lieut	Duquet, E.	Lieut
Collet	Lieut	Durand-Hornus, J.	Lieut
Collin, R.	Lieut	Durant, P.	Aspirant
Collineau, F.		Dussert, P.	
Congar, G.		De L'Escalopier, J.	
Congar, Y.	Captain	Escaravage, H.	
Corcoste-Guy, D.	Lieut	Espitalier, J.	
Coulangeon, R.		Eveno, A.	
Courmes, C.		Fabré, G.	
Cousty, M.		Fahy, M.	Lieut
Couves, F.		Fallon, L.	Lieut
Le Coz, Y.	Lieut	Feron, O.	

	Rank		Rank
Feutron, J.		Guigues, F.	Lieut
Fievet, J.		Guillerme, R.	
De Foresta, C.		Guth, J.	Captain
De Forton, R.	Lieut (Navy)	Hanus, R.	Lieut
Fougère, L.		Henard, J.	
Fourrier, M.		Hirsch, A.	
Franchini, J.	Lieut	Hirsch, M.	
Frat, R.		Houdart, P.	
Fromont	Lieut	Hubert, M.	
De Frondeville, G.	Lieut	Le Jan, J.	
Gallais, A.	Lieut	Jean-Jean, P.	Abbé
Gambero, J.	Lieut	Jorna, L.	
Gardette, P.	Lieut	Jung, A.	Lieut
Du Gardin, P.	Lieut	Jurowski, A.	Lieut
Gauthier, P.	Captain	Klein, C.	Captain
Gautier, S.	Lieut	Koltz, A.	
Gavouyère, M.		Kuhnast, A.	
Genin, M.	Lieut	Laborel, F.	
Gérard, G.	Lieut	Lagneux, J.	Aspirant
Girot, M.	Lieut	Laillat, E.	
Givord, R.	Lieut	Laland, R.	Captain
Gobert, J.		Lalue, R.	Lieut
Godfrin, L.	Lieut	Lamache, P.	
Goubaux, G.	Lieut	Lamaison, H.	
De Goys, A.	Lieut	Lamidey, M.	Lieut
Graftiaux, P.		Lamidieu, P.	Lieut
Des Graviers	Captain	Laporte-Many, R.	
Griselin, M.	Lieut	Lasgnier, R.	
Groquet	Lieut	Launay, J.	
Guenet, M.	Lieut	Lejeune, A.	Lieut
Le Guet, M. (Médecin)	Captain	Lejeune, M.	

	Rank
Le Ray, A.	Lieut
Lévy, P.	Lieut
Lévy, R.	Lieut
Lévy-Ginsburger (Levit), A.	Lieut
Louis, R.	
Lussus, A.	Lieut
Madin, R.	Lieut
Maes, A.	Lieut
Mairesse Lebrun, P.	Lieut
Manet, J.	Lieut
Manheimer, P. D.	Lieut
Marchand, R.	Lieut
Martin, J. L.	Lieut
Mas, J.	
Mascret, R.	
Masse, G.	
Mattei, A.	Lieut
De Fabre de Mazan, G.	
Mermoud, A.	
Merpillat, R.	Lieut
Metzger, E.	
Messin, P.	
Michel, D.	Lieut
Le Mintier de Lehelec, P.	Lieut
Mondon, P.	Lieut
Morvan, L.	
Moura, C.	Lieut
Nalet, R.	Captain
Navelet	Lieut
Nichet, G.	
Odry, P.	Lieut
Olive, N.	
Oriol, A.	
Oustric, G.	
Paillie, J.	Lieut
Pawlak, L.	
Penduff, F.	Lieut
Perilhou, J.	Lieut
Perodeau, A.	Lieut
Perrin, A.	Lieut
Perrin, R.	Lieut
Petit, A.	
Petit, M.	Lieut
Petit-Colin, L.	Lieut
Petitpret, J.	
Philippe, P.	Lieut
Pichegru, H.	
Pingeot, J.	Lieut
Poiret, P.	
Porges, L.	
Portefaix, A.	Lieut
Pradoura, H.	Lieut
Prot, J.	Lieut
Proutenchko, M.	Lieut
Renault, A.	Lieut
Reure, G.	Lieut
Reymond, M.	
Ribière, J.	
Ricaud, L.	
Roesch, B.	
Rondenay, A.	Lieut

	Rank		Rank
Rosenberg, E.		Thoreux, P.	
De Rothschild, E.		Tigner, A.	
De la Rousilhe, S.	Lieut	De Tillière, J.	Captain
Royer, A.		Tomasini, A.	Captain
La Sable, R.		Tournon, A.	Lieut
Sagon, H.	Lieut	Trojani, P.	Lieut
Schaeffer, R.	Lieut	Tual, J.	Lieut
Scolary, E.		Vandaele, J.	
De Segonzac, E.		Veron, J.	
De Seyne		Viale	Lieut
Sezary, C.	Lieut	Viallet, P.	Lieut
Siot, L.		Vidal, A.	
Sternberg, A.		Vidalenc, B.	Lieut
Stoeckel, P.	Captain	Vié-Barosi, V.	Lieut
Tarrade, J.		Vignon, P.	
Tatischeff	Lieut	Vilbert	Lieut
Thibaud, A.	Lieut	Warisse, J.	Lieut
Thibaudin, C.	Lieut	De Warren	Colonel
Thomas, H.	Lieut	Willement, R.	Captain
Thoreau de la Salle, R.		Zafiropoulo, C.	

Other Ranks

Ceratti

Cristaldi

Pulizani

THE FREE FRENCH CONTINGENT

	Rank	Regiment	Date of Capture	Arrived Colditz	Left Colditz
Amiel, A.	Lieut	FFL	27.1.44	5.4.44	
Le Bailley, J.	Captain	FFF	24.8.44	9.9.44	
Berge, G. R. P.	Colonel	FAF	19.6.42	5.1.43	
Borelli, L.	Aspirant	FAF	27.3.43	4.4.43	
Butsch, H.	Captain	État-Major Fr.	15.2.42	5.1.43	
De Cocq, J.	S/Lieut	FFL	8.2.43	5.4.44	
Delafon, F.	Captain	4me RCI	14.11.42	20.1.44	
Ecochard, F.	Lieut	Corps Franc d'Afrique	27.2.43	13.10.43	
El Okbi, M.	Lieut	FFL	27.1.44	5.4.44	
Escoubet, J.	Lieut	69 Reg. Art. du Maroque	19.9.44	29.12.44	
Estève, L.	Lieut	5me CSCF DCRE	18.2.43	13.10.43	26.7.44
Grayer, A.	Lieut	FFL	27.5.44	12.8.44	
Guillaume, R.	S/Lieut	FAF Groupe 2/5	20.11.44	13.12.44	
Heliot, N.	Lieut	FAF Groupe 2/62	17.11.44	13.12.44	
Hulin, R.	Aspirant	FAF	27.3.43	4.4.43	
Idrahala, R.	Captain	1re BIM	11.6.42	27.1.44	
Jacquin, D.	Captain	1re Bn Inf. de Marine	9.3.43	13.10.43	6.5.44
Jeanney	S/Lieut	FFL	18.2.42	12.11.43	6.5.44
Jordan, A.	Captain	FAF	28.1.43	20.2.43	
Khelil, H.	S/Lieut	FFL	19.5.44	12.8.44	
Klein	S/Lieut	FAF	28.1.43	20.2.43	
Labitte, M.	S/Lieut	FFL	19.5.44	12.8.44	
Lahille, E.	Lieut	FFL	19.6.44	12.8.44	
Lassalle-Astis, J.	Captain	FAF	23.3.43	10.12.43	
Leoni, J.	Captain	FFL	27.1.44	5.4.44	
Ledan, J.	Aspirant	FAF	27.3.43	4.4.43	
Micciolli, L.	Major	1re Spahis Algérien	25.1.43	11.8.44	21.8.44
Moglia, M.	Lieut	FFL	16.1.43	12.7.44	

	Rank	Regiment	Date of Capture	Arrived Colditz	Left Colditz
Morvan, A.	S/Lieut	FFL	10.6.42	13.10.43	
Puchois, J.	Colonel	·FFL	11.6.42	26.1.44	
Ratinaud, A.	Lieut	FFL	15.6.44	12.8.44	
Repkin, V.	S/Lieut	Inf.	26.2.43	27.1.44	
Sabot, E.	Aspirant	FAF	27.3.43	4.4.43	
Saunier, G.	S/Lieut	FFL	17.6.44	12.8.44	
Tiné, J. C.	Lieut	1re Spahis Algérien	9.12.42	15.2.44	
Ville, G.	Captain	1re REC	22.1.43	13.10.43	
Other Ranks					
Blomme, N.	Corporal	1re Reg. Parachutistes	17.10.44	5.11.44	
Blondin, J.	Sergeant	Groupe de Chasse 1/7	17.11.44	13.12.44	
Centellas, C.	1re Classe	1re Inf.	25.4.43	11.11.43	
Crepet, J.	1re Classe	CFA	17.3.43	11.11.43	9.1.45
Croxo, C.	2me Classe		23.6.40	19.1.45	
Grabanskas, F.	1re Classe	3me lnf.	22.1.43	11.11.43	15.11.44
Grajan, J.	1re Classe	6me lnf.	16.4.43	2.11.43	
Graziani, J.	2me Classe	66 Art.	16.4.43	2.11.43	9.1.45
Guigner, P.	2me Classe	6me lnf.	16.4.43	2.11.43	9.1.45
Monthus, R.	Sergeant	FAF Groupe de Chasse 4/5	17.11.44	13.12.44	
Moy, G.	Corporal	6me Inf.	9.4.43	2.11.43	
Nedjar, H.	Corporal	CFA	26.2.43	11.11.43	
Paraire, J.	2me Classe	1re Reg. Parachutistes	17.10.44	5.11.44	
Pognon, J. F.	2me Classe	Btn Pacifique	11.6.42	23.6.44	9.1.45
Riboulet, M.	2me Classe	66 Art.	13.4.43	2.11.43	
Saulnier, J. C.	Corporal	3me REI	19.1.43	23.6.44	9.1.45
Tenier, R.			10.6.40	19.1.45	
Tempère, R.	Sergeant Clef	Groupe 2/20 42me BOING	9.9.44	5.11.44	

THE BELGIAN CONTINGENT

	Rank		Rank
Arcq, E.	Lieut	Gille, G.	Lieut
Baudoin, E.	Lieut	Jooris, M.	
Cuvelier		Le Cocq, L.	Lieut
De Fays, M.	Lieut	Leroy, M.	Lieut
D'Hoop, H.		Liegeois, A.	Lieut
De Liedekerke, Baron R.	Commandant	Marlière, L.	Lieut
Denis, H.		Rémy, L.	Lieut
Depage, H.		Renier, R.	Lieut
De Roy, H.	Lieut	Rey, J.	Lieut
Desmet, R.	Colonel	Scheere, J.	Lieut
Destenay, M.		Schmickradt, J.	Aumonier
Devyver, A. A.	Lieut	Thibaut de Maisières, G.	Captain
De Winiwarter, A.	Chevalier	t'Kint, J.-P.	Lieut
Dubois, I.	Lieut	Verkest, J.	Lieut
Dutron, P.		Verleye, A.	Lieut
Duwez		Vinckenbosch, H.	Lieut
Fallon, A.		Wigoureux, A.	Lieut
Flébus	Commandant	Wuyts, J.	

THE AMERICAN CONTINGENT

	Rank	Regiment	Date of Capture	Arrived Colditz	Left Colditz
Duke, F.	Colonel	Signal Corps	16.3.44	23.8.44	
Le Forsonney, J.	Lieut	USAAF	3.11.43	4.8.44	21.8.44
Nunn, G.T.	Captain	Infantry	16.3.44	23.8.44	
Sabadosh, K.	Major	USAAF	24.3.44	23.8.44	
Schaefer, W. H.	Lt/Col	45th Div	14.7.43	6.12.44	
Shannon, M. C.	1/Lieut	USAAF	4.12.44	14.3.45	
Suarez, A. M.	Captain	Corps of Engineers	16.3.44	23.8.44	
Winant, J. G.	Lieut	USAAF	10.10.43	7.4.45	13.4.45

THE YUGOSLAV OFFICER

	Rank
Lucic, R.	Lieut Col

THE GERMAN STAFF

KOMMANDANTS

	Rank	Service
Schmidt	Oberst	1939–31 July 1942
Glaesche	Oberst	1 August 1942–13 February 1943
Prawitt	Oberst	14 February 1943–15 April 1945

SECONDS-IN-COMMAND

	Rank	Service
Menz	Major	1939–August 1941
Von Kirchbach	Oberst	August 1941–February 1942
Kalivius	Oberst	July 1942–February 1943
Amthor	Major	May 1943–February 1945
Howe	Major	February 1945–April 1945

STAFF

	Rank	Service
Eggers, Dr. R.	Hauptmann	Lageroffizier, November 1940–May 1942 and August 1942–February 1944; Security Officer, February 1944–April 1945
Priem, P.	Hauptmann	Lageroffizier 1939–January 1943
Püpcke, H.	Hauptmann	Lageroffizier, March 1941–April 1945
Lange	Hauptmann	Security Officer, 1939–January 1943
Horn, H.	Major	Security Officer, October 1943–February 1944
Kunze	Hauptmann	Adjutant
Müller	Hauptmann	Assistant Adjutant, 1939–March 1945
Auerich	Rittmeister	1939–1941
Lessel	Hauptmann	1939–1941
Kunath	Hauptmann	Law Officer
Heinze	Staff-Paymaster	1939–1945
Lehmann	Leutnant	Pay
Uhlmann	Hauptmann	Oberzahlmeister

	Rank	Service
Rahm, Dr.	Hauptmann	Doctor
Teichert	Hauptmann	In charge of dogs
Thomann	Hauptmann	Guard Commander
Strauss	Hauptmann	Guard Company
Hirschbeck	Leutnant	Guard Company
Winze	Leutnant	
Gephard, "Mussolini"	Stabsfeldwebel	
Rothenberger, "Franz Josef"	Stabsfeldwebel	
Grünert, "Nichtwahr" or "Beau Max"	Feldwebel	
Wünache, "Sonderführer"	Feldwebel	
Bar	Feldwebel	
Starremeyer	Feldwebel	
Reichmann	Feldwebel	Town Cells Warder
Wichnewski	Feldwebel	
Schadlich, "Dixon Hawke," "The Ferret" or "La Fouine"	Unteroffizier	
Mudroch	Unteroffizier	
Pfeifer, H.	Unteroffizier	Interpreter
Schubert	Sonderführer	Interpreter
Pilz, "Big Bum"	Gefreiter	

APPENDIX 2

Escapes

BRITISH ESCAPES

	Date	Method of Escape
SUCCESSFUL		
Lieut. A. M. S. Neave	5.1.42	Under theater stage, dressed as German officer, then out of guardhouse (with Lieut. A. P. T. Luteijn—Dutch).
Sqdn. Leader B. Paddon	11.6.42	Sent for court-martial to Thorn and escaped out of cell.
F./Lieut. H. N. Fowler	9.9.42	From Gephardt's office, dressed as Polish orderly (with Lieut. von Doorninck—Dutch).
Captain P. R. Reid F./Lieut. H. D. Wardle Lt. Cdr. W. B. Stephens Major R. B. Littledale	14.10.42	Through kitchen.
E.R.A. W. Hammond E.R.A. Lister	13.12.42	By transfer to Lamsdorf, to working party in Breslau.
Lieut. W. A. Millar	28.1.44	Through kitchen, then under lorry.
Captain H. A. V. Elliott	26.7.44	Faked ulcer.

	Date	Method of Escape
UNSUCCESSFUL—RECAPTURED		
Lieut. A. M. Allan	8.5.41	In straw palliasse to store in town.
Lieut. J. R. Boustead	4.8.41	(1) On a walk, disguised as a Hitler *Jugend* (with F./Lieut. D. Thom).
		(2) Exchanged with Lieut. F. Jablonowski (Poles being sent to Lübeck).
Lieut. T. M. Barrott	13.7.43	Exchanged with Lieut. Denis (French—being sent to Lübeck).
F./Lieut. D. Bruce	8.9.42	(1) In empty Red Cross packing case to store in town.
		(2) Out of window on north side of Castle, then through wire.
Lieut. J. Beaumont	2.5.44	On park walk—hid under leaves on blanket.
F./Lieut. J. Best	19.1.44	Over terrace (with Lieut. A. M. Sinclair).
F./Lieut. J. P. Dickinson	18.8.42	(1), (2) Over wall of old town jail when on exercise.
	7.3.43	
	28.8.42	(3) Under bread van.
Lieut. G. Davies-Scourfield	30.9.43	In waste-paper box.
F./Lieut. N. Forbes	25.8.42	On court-martial at Leipzig (with Lieut. Lee).
F./Lieut. F. D. Flynn	2.3.42	On way to town jail (with Cadet Linck—Dutch).
Corporal L. Fleet Corporal R. E. Green	3.11.43	On working party.
Lieut. J. Hyde-Thomson	6.1.42	(1) From theater, disguised as German officer (with Lieut. Donkers—Dutch).
	3.9.43	(2) The "Franz Josef" escape.
Lieut. D. K. Hamilton	13.7.43	Exchanged with Lieut. Le Jeune (French departure for Lübeck).
Lieut. M. Kellar	15.7.42	Exchanged with Corporal Hendren and sent to Lamsdorf.
Lieut. J. K. V. Lee	25.8.42	On court-martial at Leipzig (with F./Lieut. Forbes).

	Date	Method of Escape
Captain C. Lewthwaite	31.1.44	(1) On return from park walk.
	18.9.44	(2) From park.
Captain W. T. Lawton	26.8.41	(1) Orderlies' working party in park.
	9.9.42	(2) Through Gephard's office (with Lieut. T. Beets—Dutch).
Lieut. W. A. Millar	11.8.43	Exchanged with Lieut. Stepniac (Polish departure).
Lieut. A. Orr-Ewing	.8.43	(1) As French orderly on exercise.
	7.10.43	(2) In basket of waste paper.
	3.2.44	(3) As an orderly on working party.
F./Lieut. V. Parker	15.7.42	Exchanged with Sergeant Gollan.
Captain L. Pope	3.9.43	The "Franz-Josef" escape.
Lieut. I. S. Price	28.5.42	Exchanged with Lieut. Fleury (French departure).
Lieut. J. Rawson	25.11.43	Exchanged with Captain A. H. Aitken, to Mühlberg.
F./Lieut. A. van Rood	5.4.43	As German officer at start of walk (with Captain Dufour—Dutch).
Lieut. C. E. Sandbach	13.7.43	Exchanged with Lieut. Cazamayou (French departure).
Captain H. A. V. Elliott	26.7.41	Park walk air-raid shelter (with Captain Lados—Pole).
Sqdn./Ldr. B. Paddon	26.4.42	From hospital at Gnäschwitz.
Lieut. A. M. Sinclair	?	(1) On way from Posen to Colditz (twice).
	2.6.42	(2) Treatment in hospital at Leipzig.
	26.11.42	(3) As German soldier through kitchen (with Lieut. Klein—French).
	?.12.42	(4) From Weinsberg, after being recaptured from previous escape (twice).
	3.9.43	(5) As "Franz Josef."
	19.1.44	(6) Over terrace (with F./Lieut. Best).
	25.9.44	(7) The final escape—over the wire in the park.
F./Lieut. D. Thom	4.8.41	(1) On walk, as a *Hitlerjugend* (with Lieut. Boustead).

	Date	Method of Escape
	11.5.43	(2) Vault over wall, west front of Castle.
	14.7.44	(3) From hospital at Schmorkau.
Lieut. G. Wardle	9.9.42	(1) Through park manhole (with Lieut. J. Wojciechowski—Polish).
	22.11.41	(2) Through Gephard's office (with Lieut. Donkers—Dutch).
Mr. G. Romilly	13.7.43	In luggage of departing French.
TENTATIVE ESCAPES		
Lieut. A. M. Allan	31.7.41	(1) Through subaltern's room loo.
	9.8.43	(2) Clothes-store tunnel ("Whitechapel Deep").
Major W. F. Anderson	1.9.41	Through kitchen basement.
Captain R. R. F. T. Barry	29.5.41	(1) Via canteen tunnel.
	26.11.42	(2) As German soldier through German kitchen (with Lieut. Aulard—French).
	19.8.42	(3) Through delousing shed shaft.
	29.8.42	(4) Through cell bars.
F./Lieut. D. Bruce	16.6.44	Through courtyard drains.
Captain R. R. Baxter	16.6.44	Via shaft entrance to sewer.
Lieut. R. Barnes	16.6.44	Via shaft entrance to sewer.
Lieut. A. R. Campbell	9.8.43	Through dothes-store tunnel ("Whitechapel Deep").
Lieut. A. Cheetham	31.7.41	Through subaltern's room loo.
Bo'sun J. Crisp	16.6.44	Through courtyard drains
Lieut. A. R. A. Cocksedge	16.6.44	Via shaft entrance to sewer.
F./Lieut. J. P. Dickinson	9.6.42	Via attic above English quarters.
F./Lieut. D. Donaldson	23.11.41	Over the roof.
Lieut. F. M. Edwards	29.4.44	?
F./Lieut. N. Forbes	29.5.41	(1) Via canteen tunnel.
	1.5.43	(2) Via Revier tunnel.
Captain H. A. V. Elliott	29.5.41	Through canteen tunnel.
F./Lieut. F. D. Flynn	31.7.41	(1) Through subaltern's room loo.
	3.4.42	(2) Through subaltern's room tunnel.

	Date	Method of Escape
Lieut. D. Gill	10.5.42	Through kitchen (with a Polish officer).
Lt./Col. G. German	29.5.41	(1) Via canteen tunnel.
	1.9.41	(2) Via kitchen basement.
Lieut. R. Harrison	9.6.42	Through attic above English quarters.
Lieut. E. M. Harvey	26.3.44	From air-raid shelter.
Captain G. M. Pemberton-How	5.11.42	On Shützenhaus search.
Captain R. H. Howe	29.5.41	(1) Through canteen tunnel.
	9.6.42	(2) Via attic above English quarters.
Lieut. J. Hyde-Thomson	8.5.41	(1) In straw palliase.
	31.7.41	(2) Through subaltern's room loo.
Captain C. Lewthwaite	23.11.41	Via Polish orderlies' quarters.
Captain K. Lockwood	29.5.41	Through canteen tunnel.
Major R. C. Lorraine	16.6.44	Through courtyard sewer.
F./Lieut. D. Middleton	31.7.41	Via subaltern's room loo.
Lieut. D. N. Moir	29.4.44	From English quarters.
Lieut. A. M. S. Neave	28.8.41	(1) As German *Unteroffizier* via main gate.
	23.11.41	(2) Through Polish orderlies' quarters.
Lieut. W. L. B. O'Hara	21.2.42	(1) Via loft and snow tunnel.
	9.6.42	(2) From attic above English quarters.
Lieut. A. Orr-Ewing	21.2.42	Via loft and snow tunnel.
F./Lieut. V. Parker	26.3.44	(1) From air-raid shelter.
	1.5.43	(2) Through Revier tunnel.
Sqdn./Ldr. B. Paddon	1.9.41	Via kitchen basement.
Lieut. J. L. Pumphrey	13.6.44	Through English kitchen.
Captain P. R. Reid	29.5.41	(1) Via canteen tunnel.
	19.8.42	(2) From delousing shed shaft.
	29.8.42	(3) From cell digging.
Captain J. Rogers	23.11.41	Through Polish orderlies' quarters.
Lieut. M. V. B. Riviere	13.6.44	Via English kitchen.
Lieut. P. D. Storie-Pugh	29.5.41	(1) Via canteen tunnel.
	?.9.42	(2) In a loft (with Lieut. Kruimink—Dutch).

	Date	Method of Escape
F./Lieut. D. Thom	23.11.41	Over the roof.
Lieut. G. Wardle	29.5.41	(1) Through canteen tunnel.
	23.11.41	(2) from Polish orderlies' quarters.
F./Lieut. H. Wardle	29.5.41	Via canteen tunnel.
Lieut. D. E. Wheeler	1.5.43	(1) Through Revier tunnel.
	29.4.44	(2) From English quarters.

POLISH ESCAPES

SUCCESSFUL

Lieut. Kroner	20.8.41	From hospital at Königswartha.

UNSUCCESSFUL—RECAPTURED

Lieut. Chmiel Lieut. Surmanowicz	11.5.41	From the courtyard cells.
Lieut. Just	5.4.41	(1) From hospital at Königswartha.
	13.4.41	(2) From archway cell (taken to hospital at Villigen).
	20.5.41	(3) From hospital at Villigen.
	26.4.42	(4) From hospital at Gnäschwitz.
Captain Ladas	26.7.41	On return from park walk, through air-raid shelter (with Captain H. A. V. Elliott).
Lieut. Niestrzęba Lieut. Wychodczew	26.4.42	From hospital at Gnäschwitz.
Lieut. J. Wojciechowski	22.11.41	Via park manhole (with Lieut. G. Wardle).
Lieut. Żelaźniewicz	1.9.42	On park walk.

TENTATIVE—RECAPTURED IN CASTLE

Aspirant A. Karpf	31.7.41	From English subalterns' long room.
Captain Lados Lieut. Mikusiński	29.5.41	Through canteen tunnel.

	Date	Method of Escape
Lieut. Kępa Lieut. Oslecki Lieut. Slipko	6.12.42	Over orderlies' roof.
Lieut. J. Tucki	?.7.42	In Polish orderlies' working party.

DUTCH ESCAPES

SUCCESSFUL

Lieut. E. H. Larive Lieut. P. Steinmetz	16.8.41	Through park manhole.
Major C. Giebel	20.9.41	Through park manhole.
Lieut. O. L. Drijber 2/Lieut. A. P. T. Luteijn	5.1.42	Disguised as German officer, under theater stage and out of guardhouse (with Lieut. A. M. S. Neave).
Lieut. D. J. van Doorninck	9.9.42	Through Gephard's office, disguised as German officer.

UNSUCCESSFUL—RECAPTURED

Captain A. L. C. Dufour Lieut. J. G. Smit	13.8.41	Through park manhole.
Lieut. G. W. T. Dames	15.8.41	Through hole—in wire in park.
Cadet J. H. Hageman Cadet F. V. Geerligs	17.11.41	Disguised as German workmen from courtyard.
Lieut. C. L. J. F. Douw van der Krap	11.12.41	From park.
Lieut. F. E. Krulmink		
Captain E. Steenhouwer Lieut. D. W. Baron van Lynden	15.12.41	Through gate and archway.
Lieut. H. G. Donkers	6.1.42	(1) From theater (with Lieut. Hyde-Thompson).
	9.9.42	(2) Through Gephard's office (with Lieut. G. Wardle).

	Date	Method of Escape
Cadet C. Linck	?.1.42	(1) In empty sack from parcel office.
	2.3.42	(2) On way to town jail (with F./Lieut. Flynn).
Lieut. D. W. Baron van Lynden	?.3.42	Via German guard quarters.
Lieut. T. Beets	9.9.42	Through Gephard's office (with Captain W. T. Lawton).
Lieut. W. F. van der Valk Bouwman	15.12.42	Disguised as German soldier out of main gate during search.
Captain A. L. C. Dufour	5.4.43	Disguised as German officer at start of walk (with F./Lieut. van Rood).

FRENCH ESCAPES

SUCCESSFUL

Lieut. A. Le Ray	11.4.41	On return from park walk.
Lieut. R. Collin	31.5.41	Camouflaged in park shelter.
Lieut. Tatischeff	18.7.41	From Shützenhaus during visit of Russian Orthodox choir.
Lieut. P. Mairesse Lebrun	2.7.41	Over wire and wall in park.
Lieut. A. Boucheron	?.9.41	From hospital, recaptured, then from prison at Düsseldorf.
Lieut. P. Odry Lieut. Navelet	13.10.41	On return journey from hospital.
Lieut. J. Durand-Hornus Lieut. G. de Frondeville Lieut. J. Prot	17.12.41	From visit to town dentist.
Lieut. R. Bouillez	25.6.42	From hospital.
Lieut. A. Darthenay	12.7.43	From hospital.

	Date	Method of Escape
UNSUCCESFUL—RECAPTURED		
Lieut. E. Boulé	15.6.41	On park walk, disguised as woman.
Lieut. A. Mattei Lieut. R. Perrin	28.7.41	As German workmen across German quarters.
Captain M. Le Guet Abbé P. Jean-Jean	20.1.42	On walk.
Lieut. H. Dejobert Lieut. A. Thibaud	20.3.42	In rubbish cart.
Lieut. M. Girot	27.5.42	In place of a French orderly on working party.
Captain C. Kleln	25.11.42	Through German kitchen disguised as German soldier.
Lieut. A. Perrodeau	28.12.42	From courtyard, disguised as Willie Pönert (an electrician).
Lieut. J. Caillaud Lieut. E. Desbats	8.4.43	Over the roof.

BELGIAN ESCAPES

SUCCESSFUL

Lieut. Louis Rémy	26.4.42	From hospital at Gnäschwitz.

TENTATIVE

Lieut. A. A. Devyver	21.7.42	
Lieut. H. Vinckenbosch Lieut. A. Verleye	9.42	

APPENDIX 3

The Code

Sample Letter

Oflag IVC
Germany
Sept. 23rd 1941

Dear Aunt Sally,

I hope you are keeping well. Please write to me soon. Are *the* Smiths keeping *fully* active? *Offer* regards to *Uncle* Tom. *Really* he should *talk* to *Henry*! Sometime in *the* spring *June* will be seen as *the mature* and *lovely* girl *everyone* has expected. *I* wish *Peter* was more *zealous* and *interested* in the *girl*. He *and* she are *the* most *suited* couple in *Petworth* that *I* know of.

Try to *find* some clever *ingenious* way *round* their problem *easily*. Push *and* he'll be *driven* eventually *over* the top *like* John *and* Mary. He *really* must *open* his eyes. *Cliff* and *Kathleen* should really *enjoy* their *times* in Brighton *and* Hove, *and* their little *Albert* loves *it* there too. *Remember* we *came* last year? *Richard* was *away* and I *found* a *toad* sitting on *the* garden *seat*. Just one *single* toad *but* he proved difficult to catch. Eventually I caught him and put him back in the pond out of the very hot sun. Memories! I look forward to more long hot summers like that one when this war is finally over.

Love

Archie

To be decoded using Frequency 23—see date

Spelling on or off—"the" or "and"

End of code sequence—"but"

First List		Final List	
the	(start spelling)		
fully	F		
offer	O		
uncle	U	FOURTH	1
really	R		
talk	T		
Henry	H		
the	(end spelling)		
June		JUNE	2
seen		SEEN	3
the	(start spelling)		
lovely	L		
everyone	E		
I	I		
Peter	P	LEIPZIG	4
Zealous	Z		
interested	I		
girl	G		
and	(end spelling)		
the	(start spelling)		
suited	S		
Petworth	P		
I	I		
try	T	SPITFIRE	5
find	F		
ingenious	I		
round	R		
easily	E		

and	(end spelling)		
driven		DRIVEN	6
over		OVER	7
like		LIKE	8
and	(start spelling)		
really	R		
open	O		
Cliff	C		
Kathleen	K	ROCKET	9
enjoy	E		
times	T		
and	(end spelling)		
and	(start spelling)		
Albert	A		
it	I		
remember	R		
came	C		
Richard	R	AIRCRAFT	10
away	A		
found	F		
toad	T		
the	(end spelling)		
seat		SEAT	11
single		SINGLE	12
but	(end code sequence)		

SINGLE	SEAT	ROCKET	DRIVEN
AIRCRAFT	LIKE	SPITFIRE	SEEN
OVER	LEIPZIG	JUNE	FOURTH

12	11	9	6
10	8	5	3
7	4	2	1

APPENDIX 4

An Exchange of Letters

between the Author and Professor R. V. Jones, Author of *Most Secret War*

London SW1
10 October 1983

Dear Professor

I wonder if you remember me and an exchange of letters which we had a few years ago, when your great book *Most Secret War* came out.

I related to you a story about how, in Colditz Castle as early as the winter of 1940/41, I read a little book about Rocket developments centred on the island of Rugen. . . . Now I come to the other end of the story! I am writing the complete history of Colditz for Macmillan and while doing research for this in the British Museum Library—I thought to look up Rocketry, and lo and behold I found a copy of "the little book" I read in Colditz!

I have had the important section of it photostated and I enclose a set of copies. The book was published by Pitman in 1935. It contains the names of all the great Rocketry scientists from Oberth downwards and also pinpoints the Island of Rugen (Peenemunde) as a Research base and with links in the OKW.

You mention on page 69 of your book: ". . . Peenemunde—the first mention we had ever had of this establishment." I surmise this is about November 1939.

Would you be so kind as to write me, perhaps, a few lines of comment on the above which I might publish, of course with your approval, in my forthcoming book?

With my kind regards,
Yours sincerely,
Pat Reid

* * * * *

Professor R. V. Jones 25 October 1983

Dear Pat

. . . I know exactly how you must have felt in running that exasperatingly elusive book to earth after forty years.

I for one did not know of its existence and such knowledge could have helped to put us more on our toes in 1943. Only after we had done all the intelligence the hard way, in the autumn of 1944 did we discover Willi Ley's *Rockets and Space Travel* which he had published in the 30s, and in which he described the early German rocket programme and the *Verein für Raumschiffahrt*.

One still puzzling aspect of Philp's account is the *Sunday Referee* story of the man-carrying rocket ascent on Rugen in October/November 1933. I know of three German accounts of that period: Willi Ley's (and I enclose a short excerpt from the 1951 edition of his book), Dornberger's, and the *Birth of the Missile* by Klee and Merck, one of whom kept the Peenemunde archives. None of these mentions the Fischers or any trial in Rugen in 1933, which is very surprising. Indeed, according to Ley there was to have been a man-carrying demonstration at Magdeburg in 1933 but it turned out to be much too ambitious. The only details on which Ley and the *Sunday Referee* agree are (1) 1933 and (2) the length of the rocket (25 feet, Ley, and 24 feet, *Sunday Referee*). I think that Ley is likely to be much the more reliable. It looks as though the *Sunday Referee* had picked up some garbled version of the Magdeburg story, but some of the details are convincingly circumstantial and the mention of Rugen is curious. Incidentally I enclose part of Ley's bibliography which refers to Philp's book, but describes it as "unreliable in detail!"

But even though it may have been unreliable in detail, Philp's book (and Ley's, for that matter) could have been valuable in alerting Allied Intelligence to what was going on in Germany, including such features as liquid oxygen, gyroscopic stabilization and radio control. Philp's pages 78–80 (1st entry) and 95–97 (2nd entry) are astonishingly prescient. As he said, "It is almost beyond belief that in England until quite recently very little was officially known about rockets in 1935" and he would have been still more surprised to find how much longer official ignorance was to continue. It is a most telling example of the danger of official insensitivity to new ideas.

How fascinating it is that you had read Philp's book in Colditz, and had remembered it in Berne. I know how maddening it must have been—you begin to wonder whether memory is playing false and whether you had imagined it or dreamed it instead. And then, after 40 years, your memory is vindicated.

With kind regards,
Yours sincerely,
R. V.

PS Perhaps, in fairness to officialdom, it ought to be mentioned that it did not in fact prove sensible, so far as World War II was concerned, to concentrate effort on the development of large rockets, as the Germans did to their disadvantage.

The conclusion of this episode remains an intriguing "if" story:

All the time, throughout those painful years of the war, this "little book" containing its valuable information must have reposed untouched on its shelf in the British Museum Library. How might the knowledge it contained have saved lives and influenced the course of events "if" it had been found.

APPENDIX 5

Prisoners of War

in the Western Theaters of the Second World War

THE "INTERNATIONAL CONVENTION Relative to the Treatment of Prisoners of War" was signed by most nations' plenipotentiaries, including Germany's and Japan's, but excluding Russia's, on 27 July 1929. Sir Horace Rumbold signed for the United Kingdom. It was a development arising out of the Hague Convention of 18 October 1907, concerning the Laws and Customs of War. The United Kingdom and the Commonwealth ratified it on 23 June 1931. Neither Russia nor Japan ratified it. Germany ratified on 21 February 1934. Significantly, Hitler came to power as German Chancellor on 19 August of that year. This presumably accounts for the Nazi claim that they were not bound by it.

As far as prisoners of war were concerned, up to that date there had been few, if any, rules of war to deal with them. The result was that they came off very badly, as the history of wars abundantly illustrates. I have written a book about this: *Prisoners-of-war—the inside story of the POW from the ancient world to Colditz and after* (published in the UK by Hamlyn). Traditionally, it was understood, if not openly taught, that you just did not allow yourself to become a prisoner. You fought to the death. Thus war ministries were not interested in making rules for prisoners when they possessed the stick of "fight to the death or suffer a living death if you are foolish enough to be captured." The "carrot" was the glory and honor of a hero's death. The French guard at Waterloo were offered quarter but refused, and died almost to a man.

Ever since the end of the Second World War, a question has been repeatedly posed: why did officers try to escape and why were they aided in this, whereas other ranks were not aided and did not try to escape?

Prisoners of war in the West were separated at the outset into two categories, and treated with more or less regard to the rules laid down for the conduct and incarceration of POWs by the Geneva Convention.

Officers went to officers' prison camps, and other ranks went to troops' camps. An important difference between the two was that troops were put to work for the enemy. That was permitted and no soldier could later be upbraided for working for the enemy. But an officer's honor would have been deemed to be sullied for life and his allegiance to be in default if he worked for an enemy. Further, it was clearly understood by the signatories of the Convention that an Officer would and should consider it a matter of honor to attempt to regain his liberty and return to his fighting unit—in other words to escape. What followed was inescapable! The Geneva Convention permitted his captor to keep him locked up.

While troops went out daily from their moderately guarded cantonments to work—often unguarded—in factory or field, the officer was lucky to have an hour's exercise in a barbed-wire pen surrounded by sentries before being returned to the closely guarded confinement of his quarters.

This introduction to the major difference in the form of imprisonment between officers and men leads naturally to a diagnosis of the psychology of escape. The first element is the "fear of the unknown." It will hardly be contested that education tends to dispel or reduce the areas of the unknown to a man's mind. The more educated (and that includes here "experienced") a man is, the less are his fears of the unknown. To a prisoner, the vast area of enemy country surrounding him is the "unknown," with all its bogeys and traps, which are emphasized by the enemy to attain nightmare proportions.

Some time ago, on a television program in which other-ranks ex-POWs were questioned, an ex-soldier admitted, "If I had tried to escape, I just wouldn't have known what to do—I'd have been scared stiff at the idea of facing up to a 400-mile journey across enemy territory." This man was expressing openly "fear of the unknown." A more educated man might well have similar fears, but if he expressed them he could be accused of being chicken-hearted.

Two more psychological factors apply. The desire for freedom grows in inverse ratio to the amount of freedom one possesses. When a prisoner can go to work in a field under the open sky and return to his billet physically tired, he is almost a free man already, compared with his officer colleague who is pent up all day behind barbed-wire with no work to exhaust him, and with all the time in the world to consider his loss of freedom and how to regain it.

The other factor is a plain, healthy fear of retribution. Because troops do not have obligations to try to escape from enemy hands, they are considered by the enemy justifiably punishable if they do. The Germans in the Second World War lived up to this, with physical violence and, sometimes, a concentration camp as the end for a recaptured other rank.

As for officers in this context, the Geneva Convention laid down certain acceptable punishments. But, as Second World War history records, if an escaped officer on recapture got into the wrong hands, it could easily be "curtains"—a *klimtin* or *Stufe drei*.

There is no veracity in any conception of privilege being attached to the incarceration of officers in a closely guarded camp. Most officers, had they been given the option, would have opted for incarceration in a troops' prison camp, whereas with other ranks the opposite would certainly not have applied. Many officers, after capture, regretted that they had not torn off their badges of rank and posed as other ranks.

There were often clandestine opportunities, which were naturally seized upon, for other ranks outside their camps to meet and have intercourse with women; this was denied officers permanently behind barbed-wire. Further, sexual frustration became an important incentive to escape in many cases.

Other ranks did try to escape but, as a proportion of the numbers who were POWs, the figure is small; and the percentage of those who succeeded is again small. Those who did succeed were very exceptional men. This is borne out by the stories recounted by Elvel Williams in a well-documented book about other ranks entitled *Arbeits-Kommando* (published by Victor Gollancz).

Assistance by way of escaping aids from the home country became largely a matter of war economics. What had to be weighed up was the proportion and value of success relative to the amount of expenditure in time, money and effort to achieve it. There was no discrimination whatever in equipping Air-Force crews of all ranks with evasion kit. This was efficiently and cheaply accomplished at their home base. But when it came to getting escape kits into POW camps, this was another matter. It was not easy; it was expensive. If not well organized within the camp, losses were such that the game was not worth the candle. Correspondingly, war economics demanded that the more valuable personnel for the war effort should receive priority. This was recognized. Submarine officers were about on a par with "Mosquito" and Reconnaissance (aerial photography) pilots; ERAs of the Royal Navy were about on a par with Flight Sergeants; Army officers and other ranks were a low priority.

However, an escape-minded other-ranker would have little difficulty in obtaining civilian clothing, legitimate currency, a local plan, a map, a railway timetable—all without assistance from the home front. With men like

Regimental Sergeant Major Sherriff at Lamsdorf, encouraging skillful assistance was always available.

The last point is that of leadership, or the absence of it. Other ranks, time and again, have stated how they missed it and needed it. With or without the Geneva Convention, any enemy taking prisoners will segregate officers from the men, for the very purpose of removing leadership. The only solution here is to use deception. The officer, the leader, should rip off his officer's insignia if he can do so, and become another ranker. Then he must organize his men for escape, while probably himself remaining the last to leave. This solution for an officer is to be commended, provided it is taken for commendable reasons. Some Russian officers in the Second World War were known to have gone into battle dressed as their men. But then German troops were known to shoot Russian officers at once—no quarter. The world knows what the Russians did with Polish officers at Katyn.

There is a lesson to be learned from an excellent treatise on the conduct of prisoners of war of many different nationalities in captivity during the Korean War from 1950–1953 entitled *Why They Collaborated* by Eugene Kinkead (published by Longman). In that war, officers, taken prisoner, were at once separated from their men. It transpired that both amongst officers and amongst men there were equally regrettable lapses from loyal or manly behavior under duress. But the redeeming feature that shines out, which transcended entirely the status—whether officer or other rank—of the prisoner, was discipline. Where there was discipline men and officers survived with honor. None exemplified this better than the 229 Turkish POWs. Amongst them, without officers, there was exemplary discipline, which started from a simple human concept: if there was no senior in rank amongst a group, then the oldest automatically became the senior. Obedience to the senior and total commitment to each other within the group, as well as total solidarity of the group vis-à-vis external forces, was their recipe for a successful outcome; and, in the event, so it proved to be.

> It was generally believed that the Chinese feared the Turks to some degree, because they stuck together as a group and resisted as a group. Their discipline and military organisation saw them through as prisoners, with no fatalities and no indoctrination.

Therefore, let an officer who is contemplating the solution that is to be commended ask himself whether he will ultimately contribute to the escape proclivities of his men or to their self-preservation through discipline or to both.

Bibliography

Barker, A. J., *Prisoners of War* (UK edition: *Behind Barbed Wire*) (Universe Books, New York, 1975)

Brickhill, P. C. J., *Reach for the Sky* (William Collins, 1954)

Le Brigant, General, *Les Indomptables* (Editions Berger-Levrault, 1948)

Borrie, J., *Despite Captivity* (William Kimber, 1975)

Brown, J., *In Durance Vile* (Robert Hale, 1981)

Bruce, G. L., *The Warsaw Uprising: 1 August–2 October, 1944* (Rupert Hart-Davis, 1972)

Burn, M., *Yes Farewell* (Jonathan Cape, 1946) and *The Flying Castle* (Rupert Hart-Davis, 1954)

Burt, K., and Leasor, J., *The One That Got Away* (Collins/Michael Joseph, 1956)

Burton, G., *Escape from the Swastika* (Marshall Cavendish, 1975)

Campbell, A., *Colditz Cameo* (Ditchling Press, 1954)

Carre, M., *I was the Cat* (Souvenir Press Ltd., 1960)

Champ, J., and Burgess, C., *Diggers in Colditz* (Allen & Unwin, Australia, 1985)

Chrisp, J., *The Tunnellers of Sandbostel* (Robert Hale, 1959)

Congar, Y., *Leur Résistance: Témoignage d'Yves Congar* (M. Albert Renault, Paris, 1947)

Cowburn, B., *No Cloak, No Dagger* (Jarrolds, 1960)

Datner, S., *Tragedia w Dössel* (Ksiazka i Wiedza, Warsaw, 1970) and *Ucieczki z Niewoli Niemieckiej 1939–45* (Ksiazka i Wiedza, Warsaw, 1966)

Davies, Brigadier, *Illyrian Adventure* (The Bodley Head, 1952)

Duggan, M. (ed.), *Padré in Colditz* (Hodder & Stoughton, 1978)

Duke, F., *Mission Sparrow* (Meredith Press, New York)

Eggers, R., *Colditz: The German Story* (New English Library, 1972)

Eggers, R., *Colditz Recaptured* (Robert Hale, 1973)

Evans, A. J., *Escape and Liberation 1940/45* (Hodder & Stoughton, 1945) and *The Escaping Club* (John Lane/The Bodley Head, 2nd edition)

Ferguson, I., *Doctor at War* (Christopher Johnson, 1955)

Foot, M. R. D., *Resistance* (Eyre Methuen, 1976) and *S. O. E. in France* (Miscellaneous Official Publications, 1966)

Foot, M. R. D., and Langley, J. M., *MI9—Escape and Evasion 1939/45* (The Bodley Head, 1979)

Giertych, J., *Europe w Niemoli* (Biblioteka Polska, London, 1958) and *Wrzesniowcy* (Biblioteka Polska, London, 1957)

Green, J. M., *From Colditz in Code* (Robert Hale, 1971)

Guénet, M., *Le Secret de Colditz* (Editions France Empire, Paris)

Guigues, F., *Colditz 1941–1943* (private publication)

Harewood, Lorn, *The Tongs and the Bones* (Weidenfeld & Nicolson, 1981)

De Hartog, L., *Officieren Achter Prikkeldraad 1940–1945* (Hollandia B. V., Baarn, Holland, 1983)

De Jong, L., *Het Koninkrijk der Nederlanden in de Tweede Wereldoorlog Gravenhage* (Martinus Nijhoff, the Hague, 1969)

Hutton, C., *Official Secret* (Max Parrish, 1960)

Kawalec, W., *Pięcdziesięciu z Dössel* (Ministerstwo Obrony Narodowej, Warsaw, 1963)

Kinkead, E., *Why They Collaborated* (Longman, 1960)

Komorowski, T. B., *The Secret Army* (Victor Gollancz, 1951)

Van der Krap, C. D., *Against the Swastika* (Van Holkema en Warendorf, Bussum, Holland, 1981)

Larive, E. H., *The Man who came in from Colditz* (Robert Hale, 1975)

Le Brun, M., *Deux Fois Evadé de la Fortresse de Colditz* (private publication)

Le Ray, A., *Première à Colditz* (Editions Arthoud, 1980)

Lovell, I. and Baybutt, R., *Camera in Colditz* (Hodder & Stoughton, 1982)

Maloire, A., *Colditz—le Grand Refus* (Le Condor, Vincennes, 1982)

Naumann, H. (ed.), *700 Jahre Stadt Colditz* (Umschlaggestaltung Ehnert, Dresden)

Neave, A., *They Have Their Exits* (Hodder & Stoughton, 1953) and Saturday at MI9 (Hodder & Stoughton, 1959)

Perrin, A., *Evadé de Guerre via Colditz* (La Pensée Universelle, Paris)

Philps, C. G., *Stratosphere and Rocket Flight (Astronautics)* (Pitman, 1935)

Reid, M., *Into Colditz* (Michael Russell, 1983)

Reid, P. R., *The Colditz Story* (Hodder & Stoughton, 1952) and *The Latter Days* (Hodder & Stoughton, 1953)

Romilly, G., and Alexander, M., *The Privileged Nightmare* (Hostages at Colditz) (George Weidenfeld & Nicolson, 1954)

Sandford, K., *The Mark of the Lion* (Popular Library, 1964)

Schofield, S., *Musketoon* (Jonathan Cape, 1964)

Seth, R., *Jackals of the Reich: The Story of the British Free Corps* (New English Library, 1972)

Slawiński, K., *Jeniecki Oboz Specjalny Colditz* (Biblioteka Pamieci Pokolen)

Thibaut de Maisières, G., *Tourisme Clandestin* (L'Office de Publicité, Brussels, 1961)

Warren, C. E. T., and Benson, J., *Will Not We Fear* (Harrap, 1961)

West, R., *The Meaning of Treason* (Macmillan & Co. Ltd., 1949)

Williams, E., *Arbeitskommando* (Victor Gollancz, 1975)

Wood, J. E. R. (ed.), *Detour* (Falcon Press)

De Vomécourt, P., *Who Lived to See the Day* (Hutchinson, 1963)

Zimiński, W., *Colditz—Dössel ou le Refus de la Captivité* (Incepa Faivre, Pontarlien, 1978)

Index